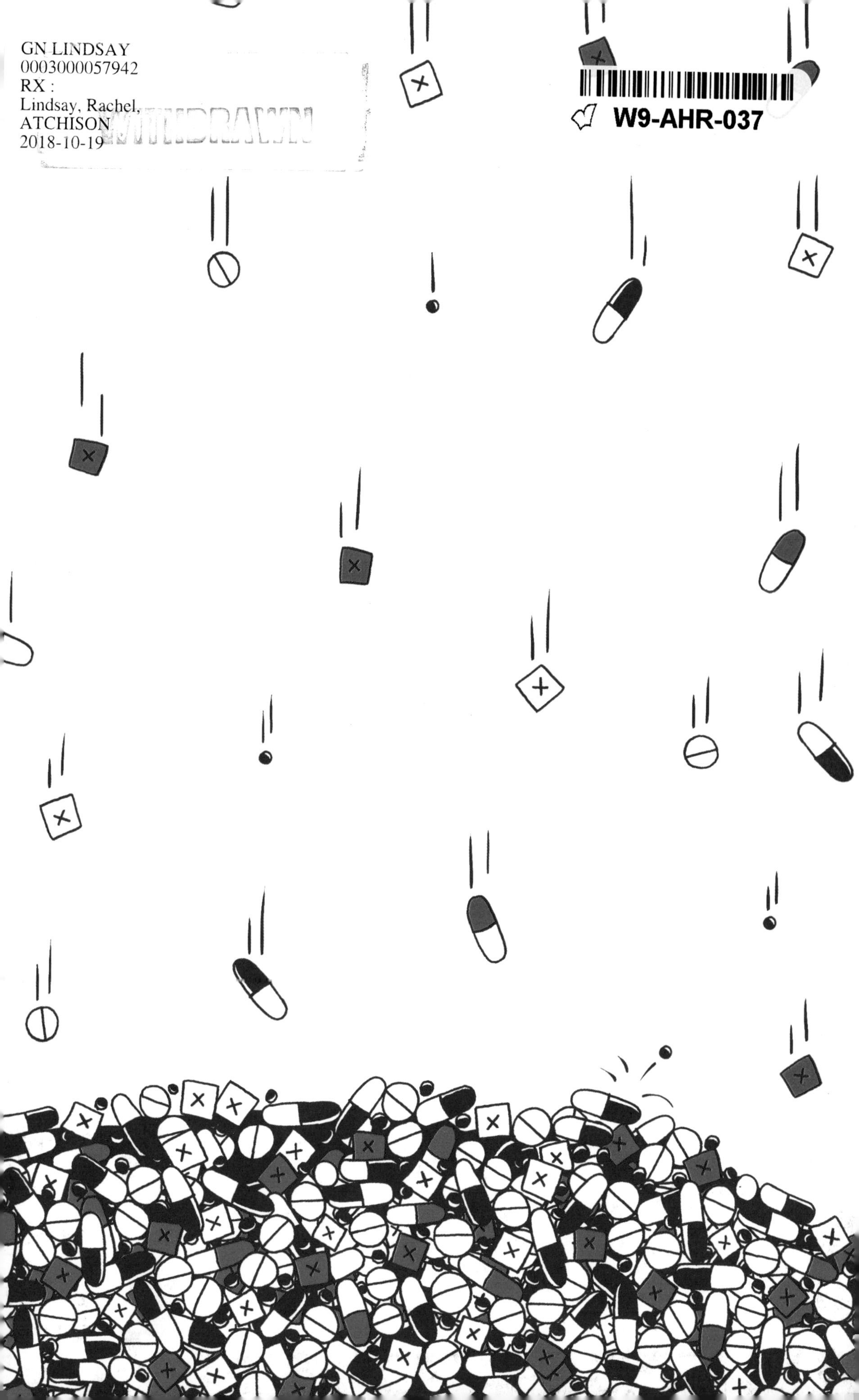

A GRAPHIC MEMOIR

RACHEL LINDSAY

GRAND CENTRAL
PUBLISHING

NEW YORK   BOSTON

This memoir reflects the author's life faithfully rendered to the best of her ability. Some names and identifying details have been changed to protect the privacy of others.

Copyright © 2018 by Rachel Lindsay

Illustrations copyright © 2018 by Rachel Lindsay

Cover design by Rachel Lindsay. Cover copyright © 2018 by Hachette Book Group, Inc.

Hachette Book Group supports the right to free expression and the value of copyright. The purpose of copyright is to encourage writers and artists to produce the creative works that enrich our culture.

The scanning, uploading, and distribution of this book without permission is a theft of the author's intellectual property. If you would like permission to use material from the book (other than for review purposes), please contact permissions@hbgusa.com. Thank you for your support of the author's rights.

Grand Central Publishing
Hachette Book Group
1290 Avenue of the Americas, New York, NY 10104
grandcentralpublishing.com
twitter.com/grandcentralpub

First Edition: September 2018

Grand Central Publishing is a division of Hachette Book Group, Inc. The Grand Central Publishing name and logo is a trademark of Hachette Book Group, Inc.

The publisher is not responsible for websites (or their content) that are not owned by the publisher.

The Hachette Speakers Bureau provides a wide range of authors for speaking events. To find out more, go to www.hachettespeakersbureau.com or call (866) 376-6591.

Library of Congress Control Number: 2018930826

ISBNs: 978-1-4555-9854-0 (paper over board), 978-1-4555-9853-3 (ebook)

Printed in the United States of America

LSC-W

10 9 8 7 6 5 4 3 2 1

FOR BURLINGTON, VERMONT.

"WHAT'S MADNESS BUT NOBILITY OF
SOUL AT ODDS WITH CIRCUMSTANCE?"

— THEODORE ROETHKE

APRIL 13ᵀᴴ, 2011

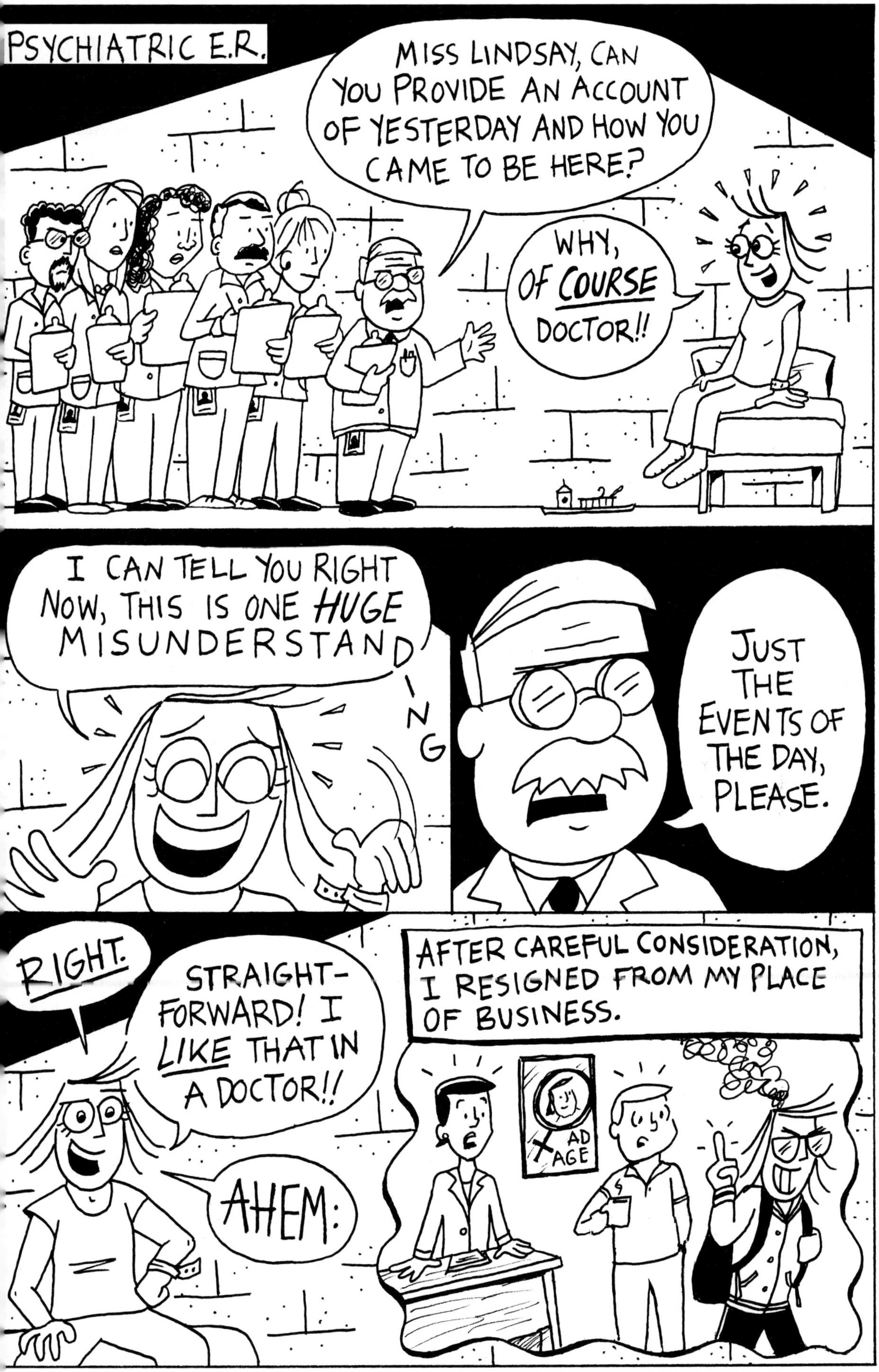
PSYCHIATRIC E.R.
MISS LINDSAY, CAN YOU PROVIDE AN ACCOUNT OF YESTERDAY AND HOW YOU CAME TO BE HERE?
WHY, OF COURSE DOCTOR!!
I CAN TELL YOU RIGHT NOW, THIS IS ONE HUGE MISUNDERSTANDING
JUST THE EVENTS OF THE DAY, PLEASE.
RIGHT.
STRAIGHT-FORWARD! I LIKE THAT IN A DOCTOR!!
AHEM:
AFTER CAREFUL CONSIDERATION, I RESIGNED FROM MY PLACE OF BUSINESS.
AD AGE

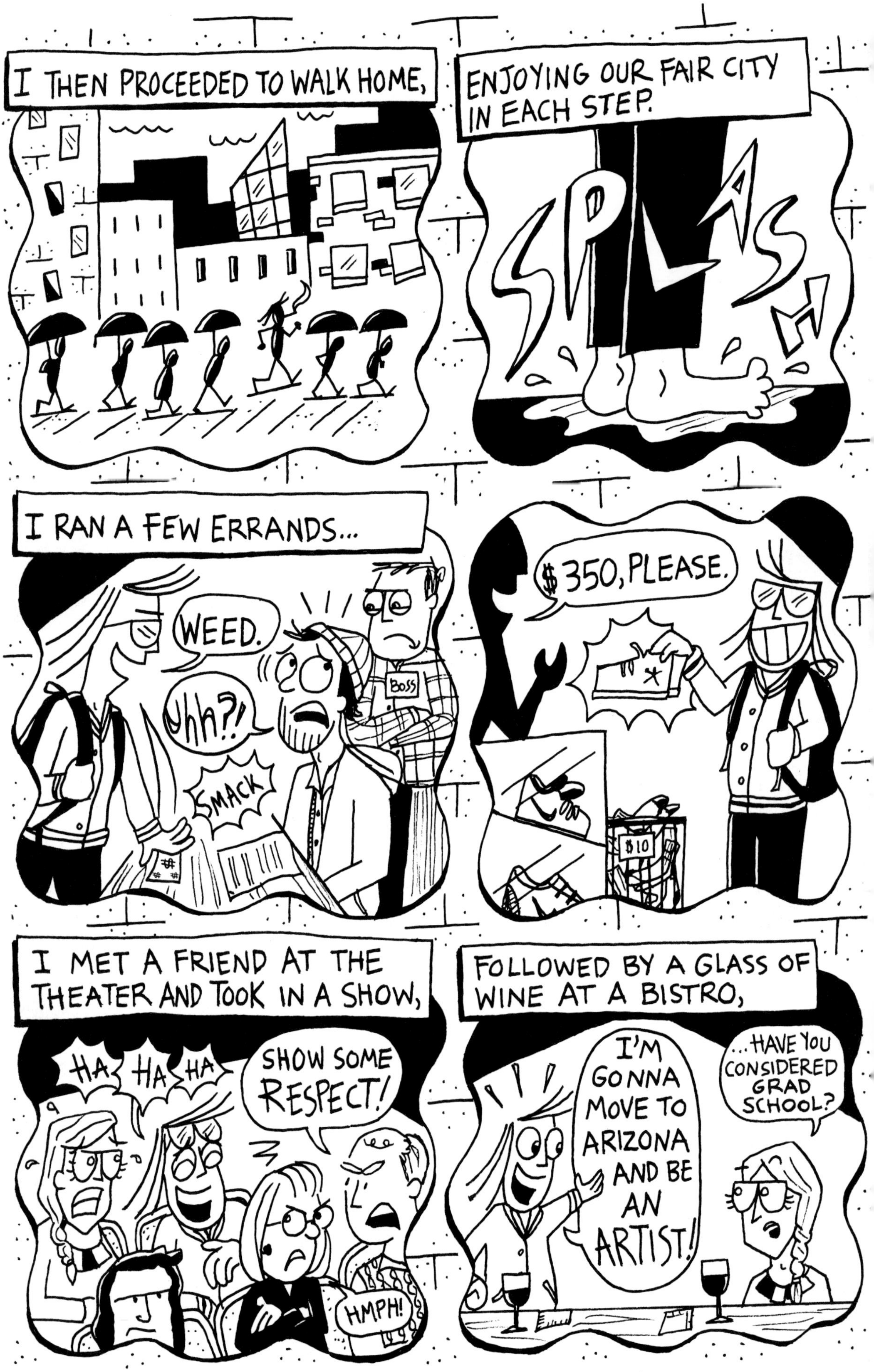
I THEN PROCEEDED TO WALK HOME,
ENJOYING OUR FAIR CITY IN EACH STEP.
SPLASH
I RAN A FEW ERRANDS...
WEED.
UHH?!
SMACK
BOSS
$350, PLEASE.
$10
I MET A FRIEND AT THE THEATER AND TOOK IN A SHOW,
HA HA HA
SHOW SOME RESPECT!
HMPH!
FOLLOWED BY A GLASS OF WINE AT A BISTRO,
I'M GONNA MOVE TO ARIZONA AND BE AN ARTIST!
...HAVE YOU CONSIDERED GRAD SCHOOL?

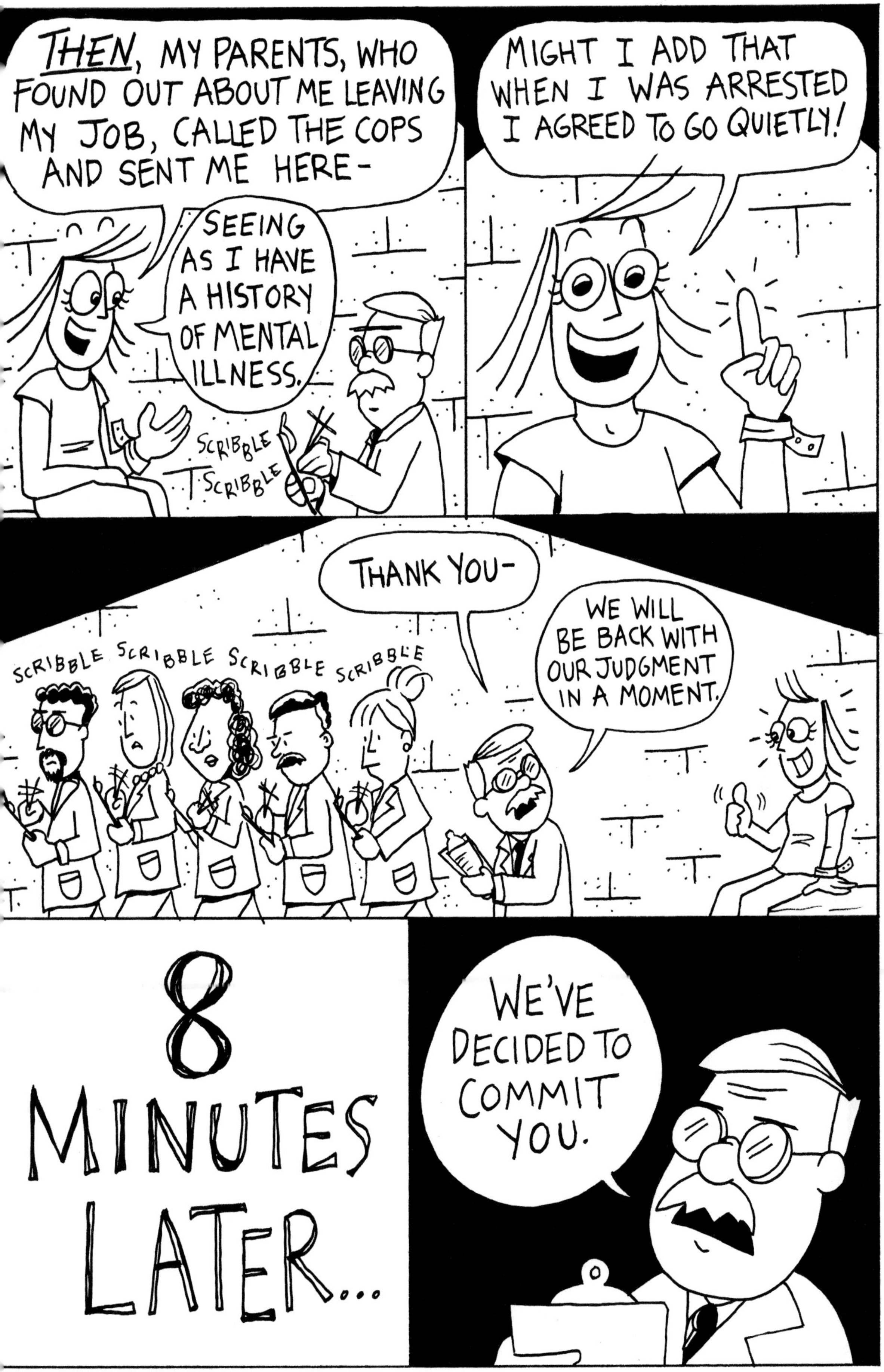
THEN, MY PARENTS, WHO FOUND OUT ABOUT ME LEAVING MY JOB, CALLED THE COPS AND SENT ME HERE-
SEEING AS I HAVE A HISTORY OF MENTAL ILLNESS.
SCRIBBLE
SCRIBBLE
MIGHT I ADD THAT WHEN I WAS ARRESTED I AGREED TO GO QUIETLY!
THANK YOU-
WE WILL BE BACK WITH OUR JUDGMENT IN A MOMENT.
SCRIBBLE SCRIBBLE SCRIBBLE SCRIBBLE
8 MINUTES LATER...
WE'VE DECIDED TO COMMIT YOU.

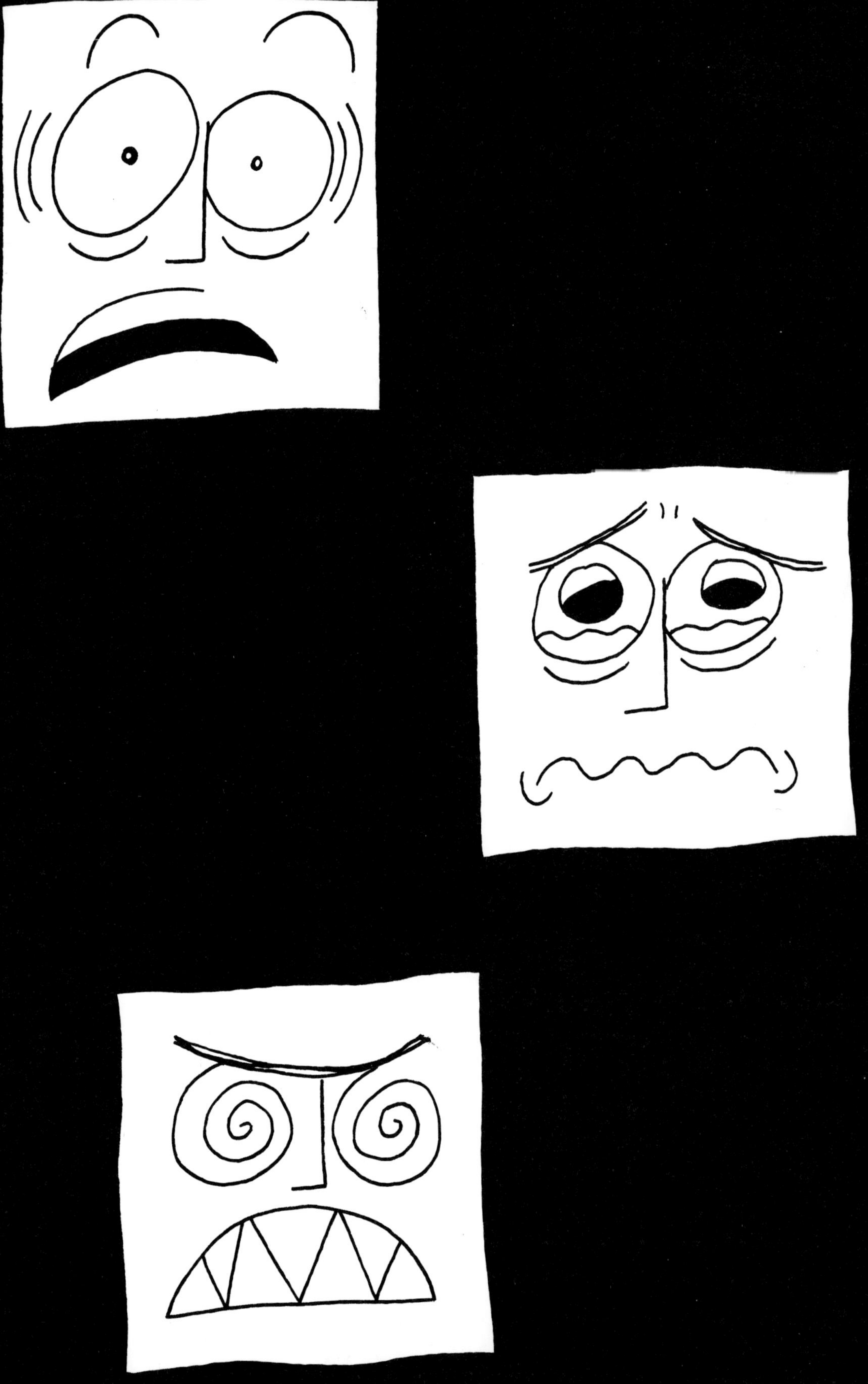

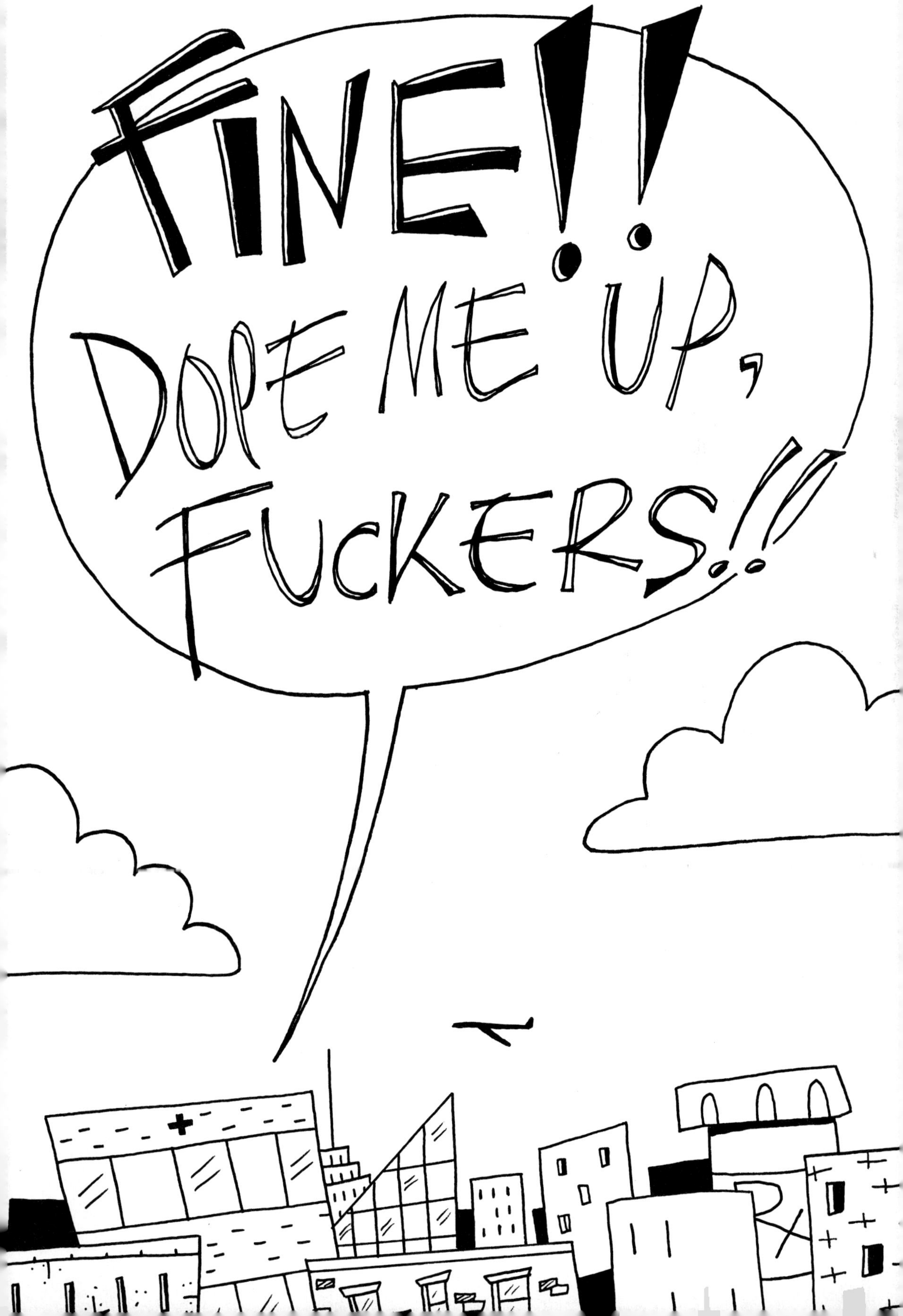
FINE!! DOPE ME UP, FUCKERS!!

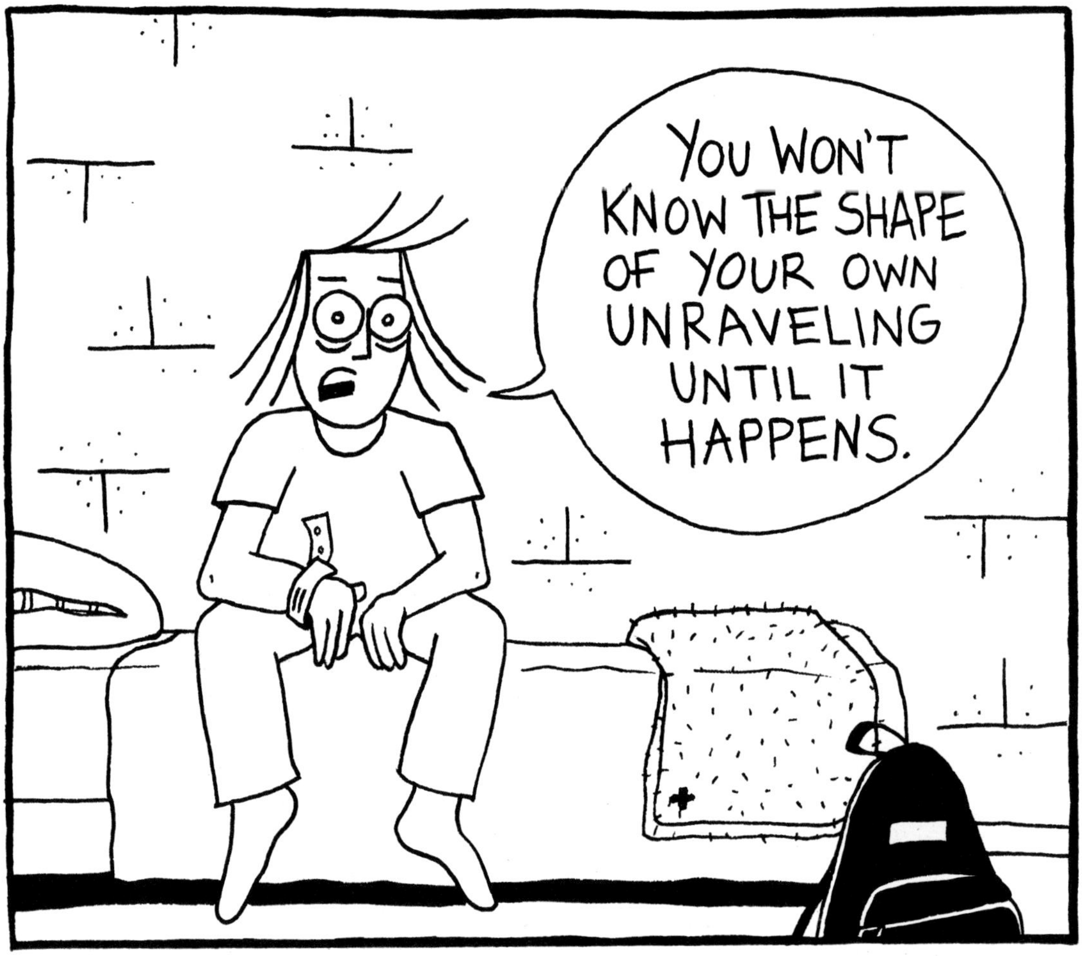
YOU WON'T KNOW THE SHAPE OF YOUR OWN UNRAVELING UNTIL IT HAPPENS.

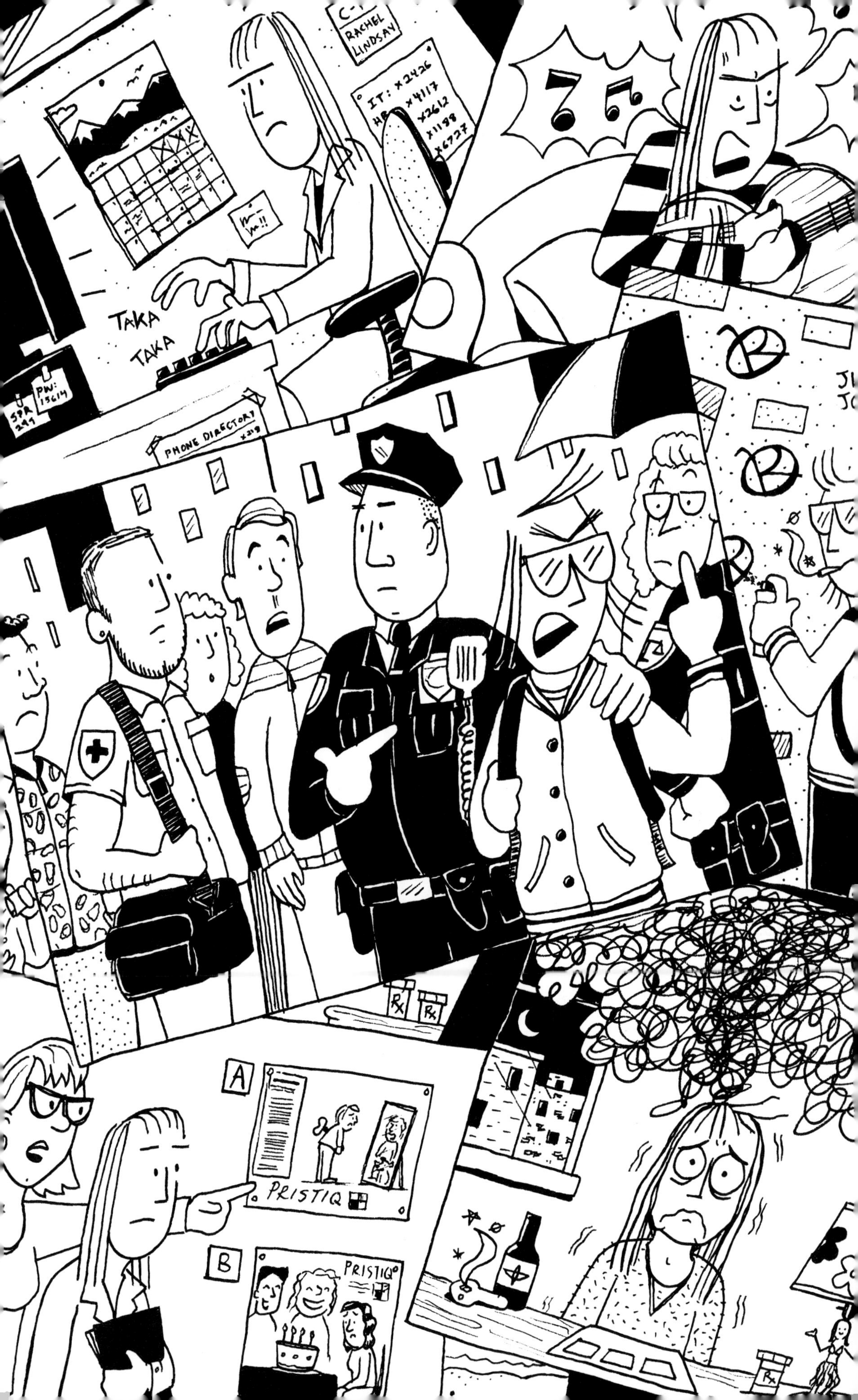
RACHEL LINDSAY
IT: x2426
x4117
x2612
x1198
x6727
TAKA
TAKA
PW: 15614
SPR 291
PHONE DIRECTORY
A
PRISTIQ
B
PRISTIQ

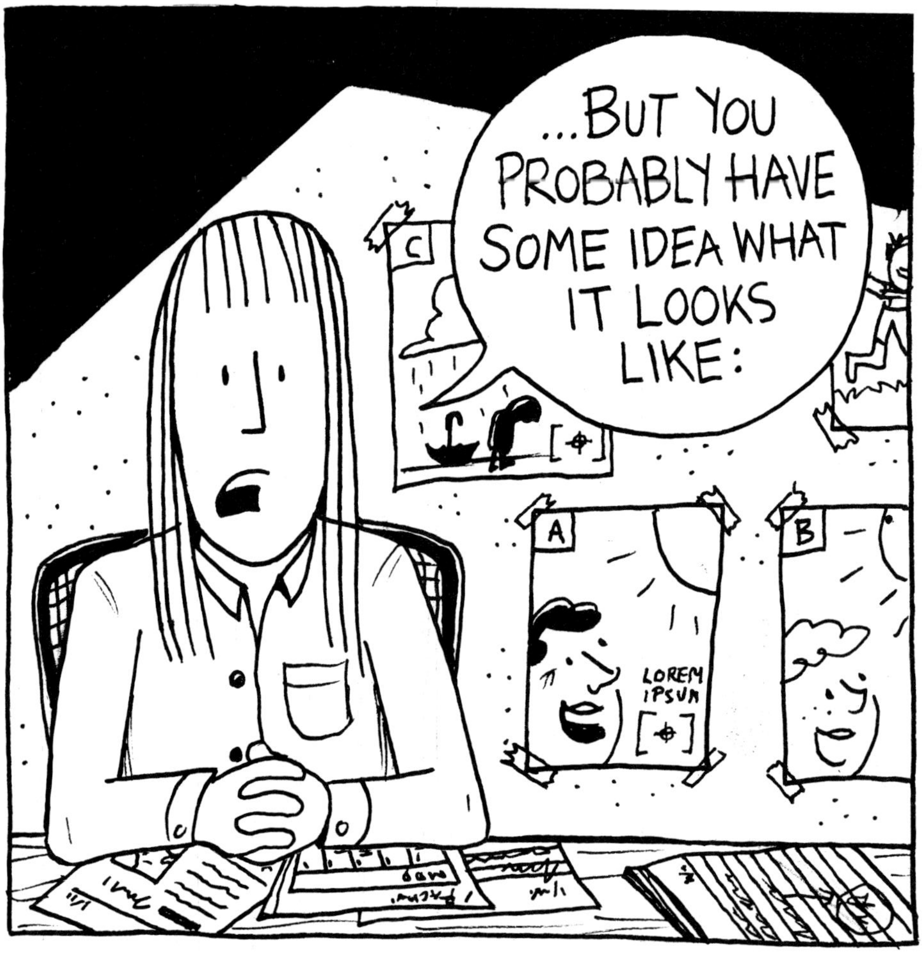
...BUT YOU PROBABLY HAVE SOME IDEA WHAT IT LOOKS LIKE:
C
A
B
LOREM IPSUM

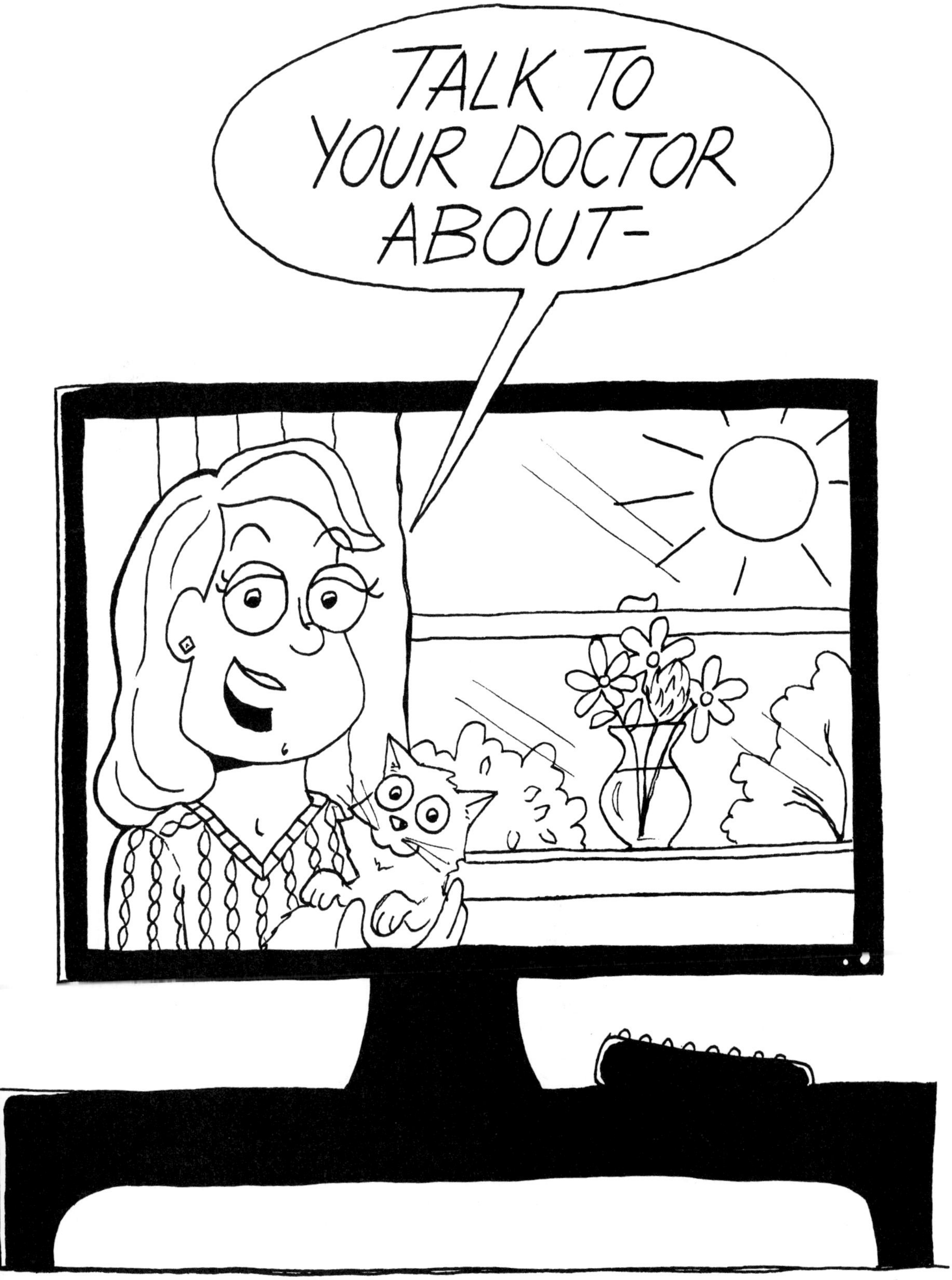
TALK TO YOUR DOCTOR ABOUT-

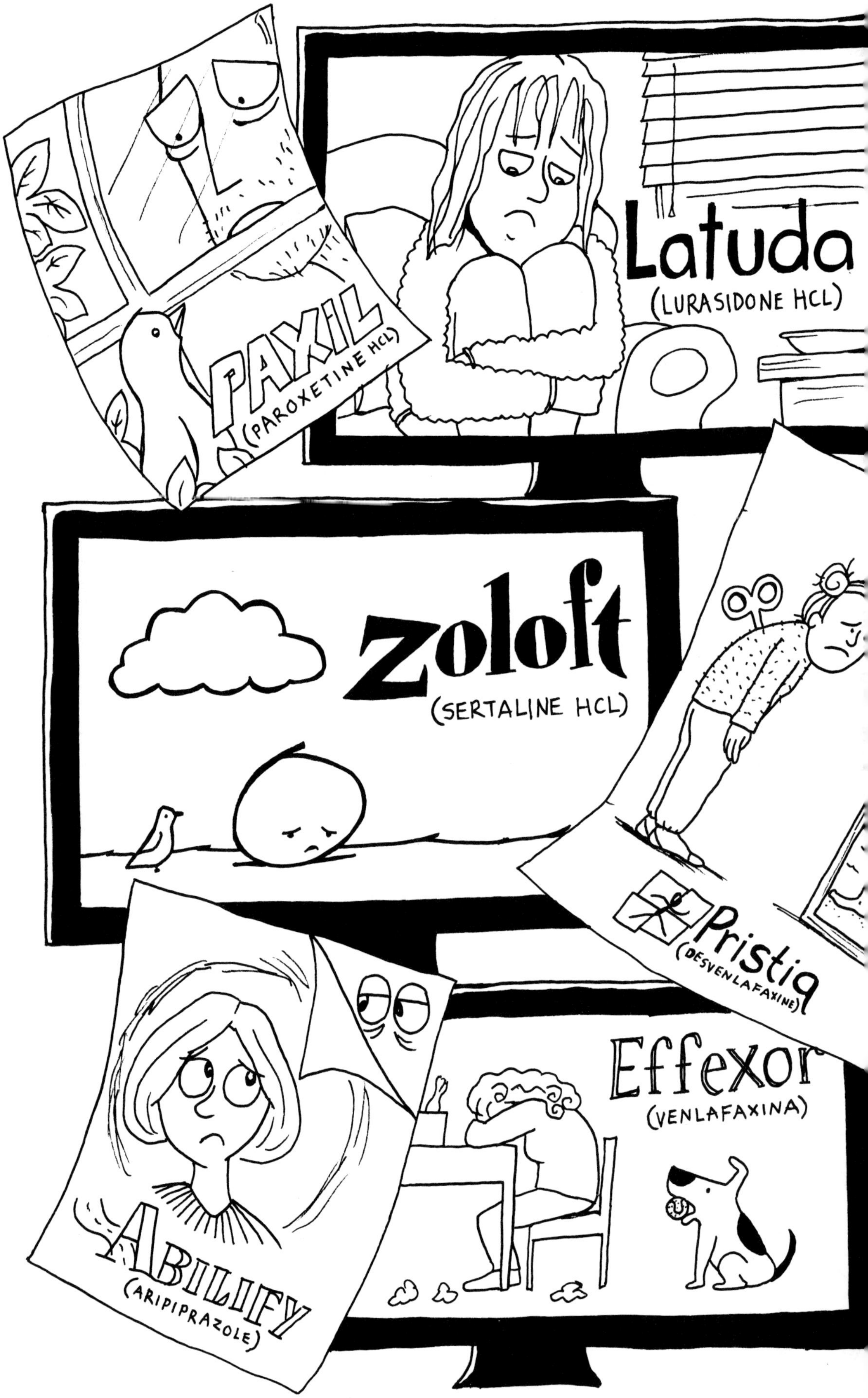

PAXIL
(PAROXETINE HCL)
Latuda
(LURASIDONE HCL)
zoloft
(SERTALINE HCL)
Pristiq
(DESVENLAFAXINE)
Effexor
(VENLAFAXINA)
ABILIFY
(ARIPIPRAZOLE)

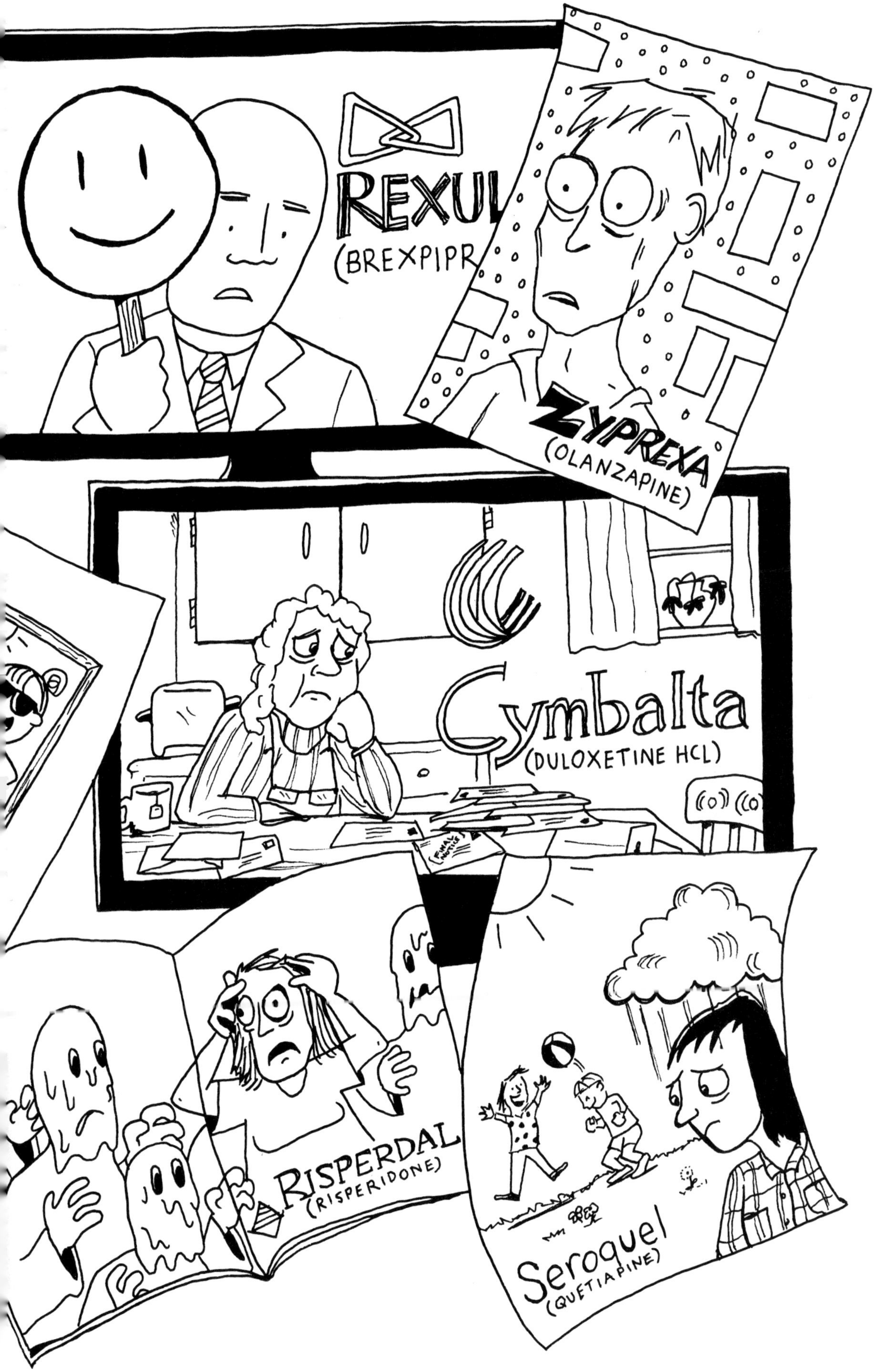

REXUL
(BREXPIPR
ZYPREXA
(OLANZAPINE)
Cymbalta
(DULOXETINE HCL)
RISPERDAL
(RISPERIDONE)
Seroquel
(QUETIAPINE)

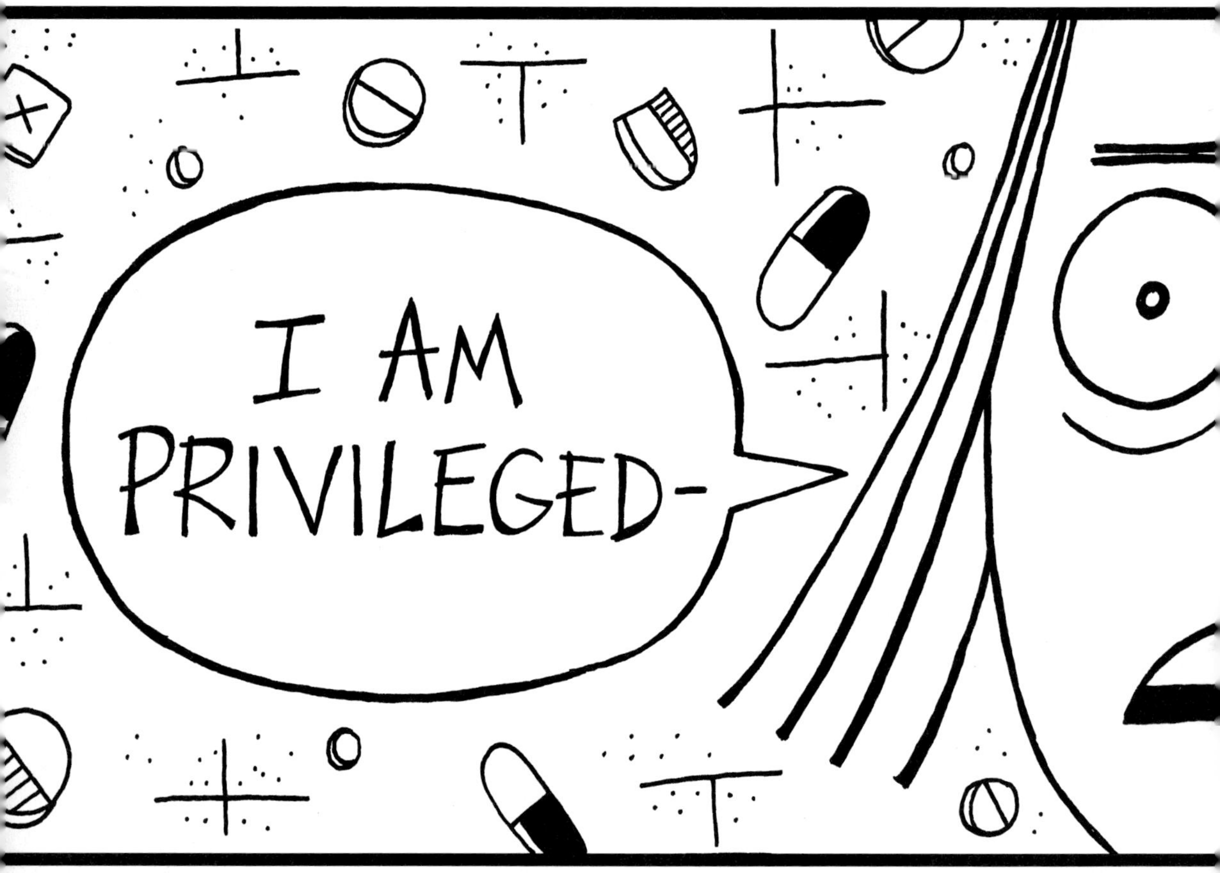
I AM PRIVILEGED-

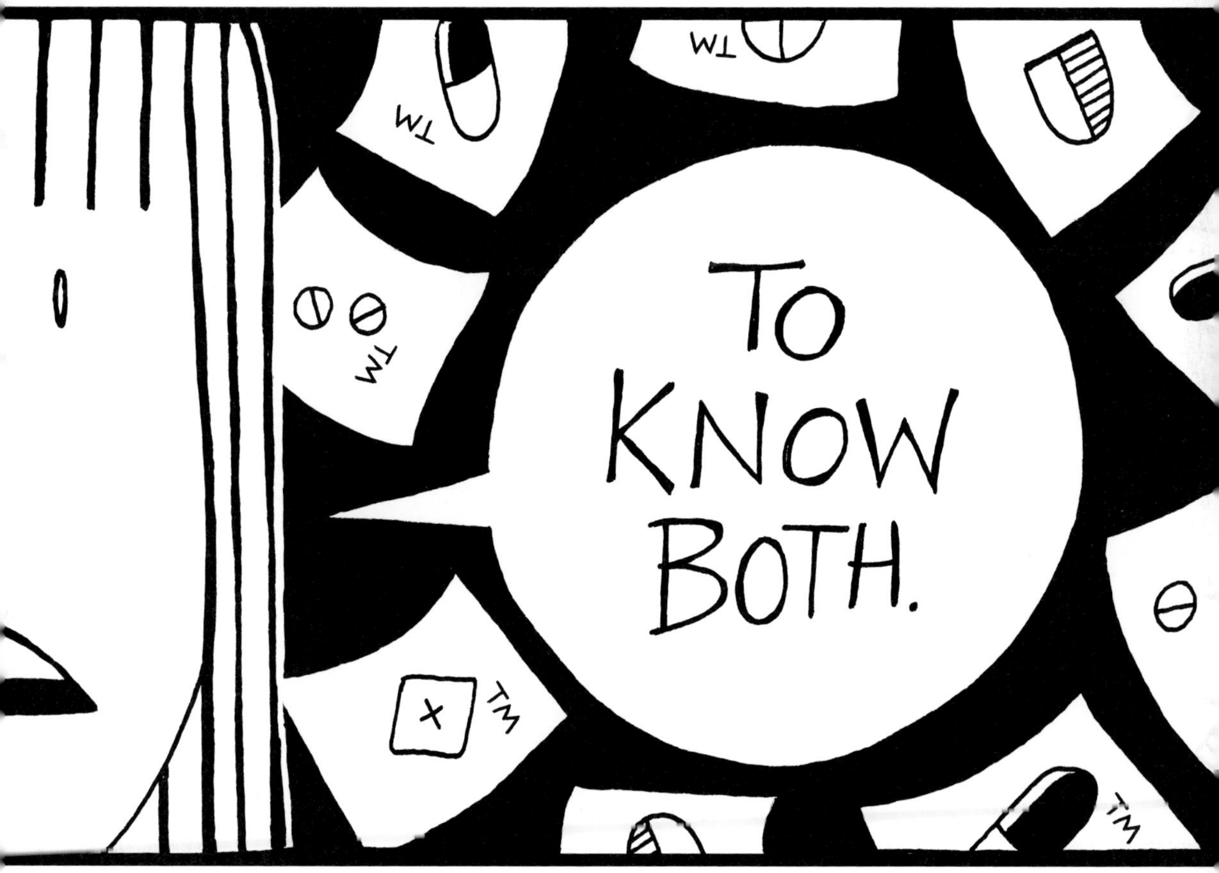
TO KNOW BOTH.

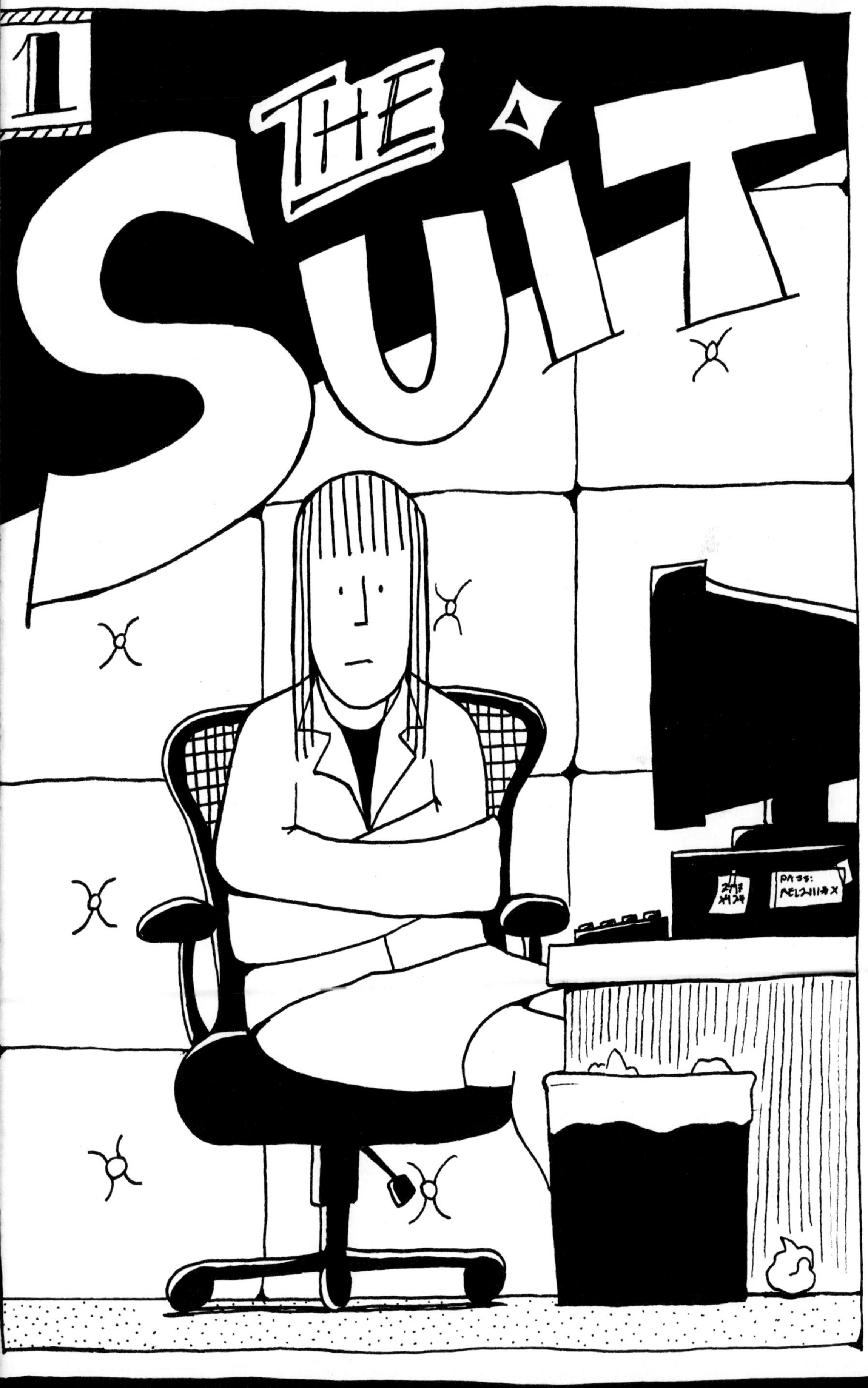
1
THE SUIT

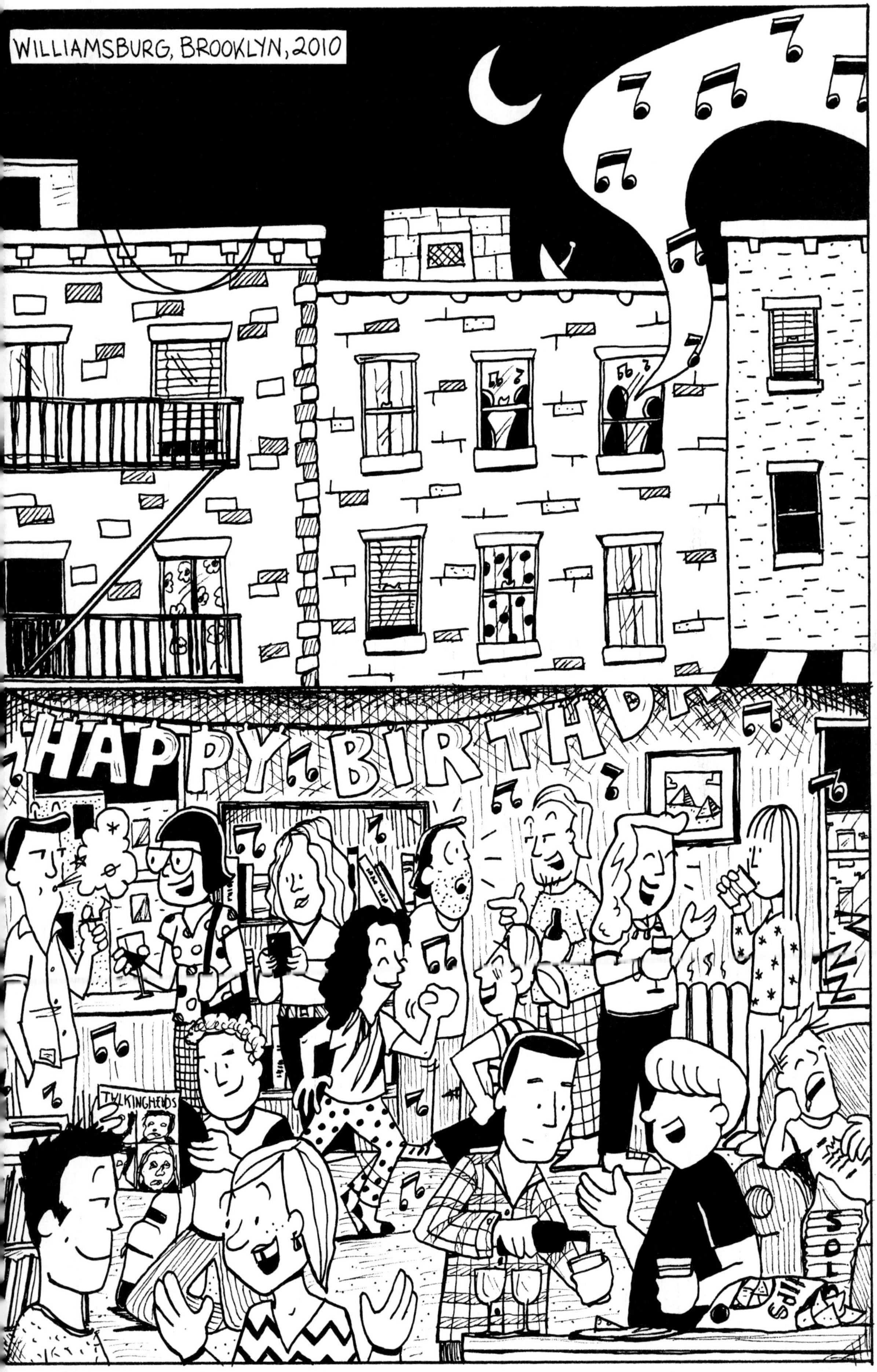
WILLIAMSBURG, BROOKLYN, 2010
HAPPY BIRTHD

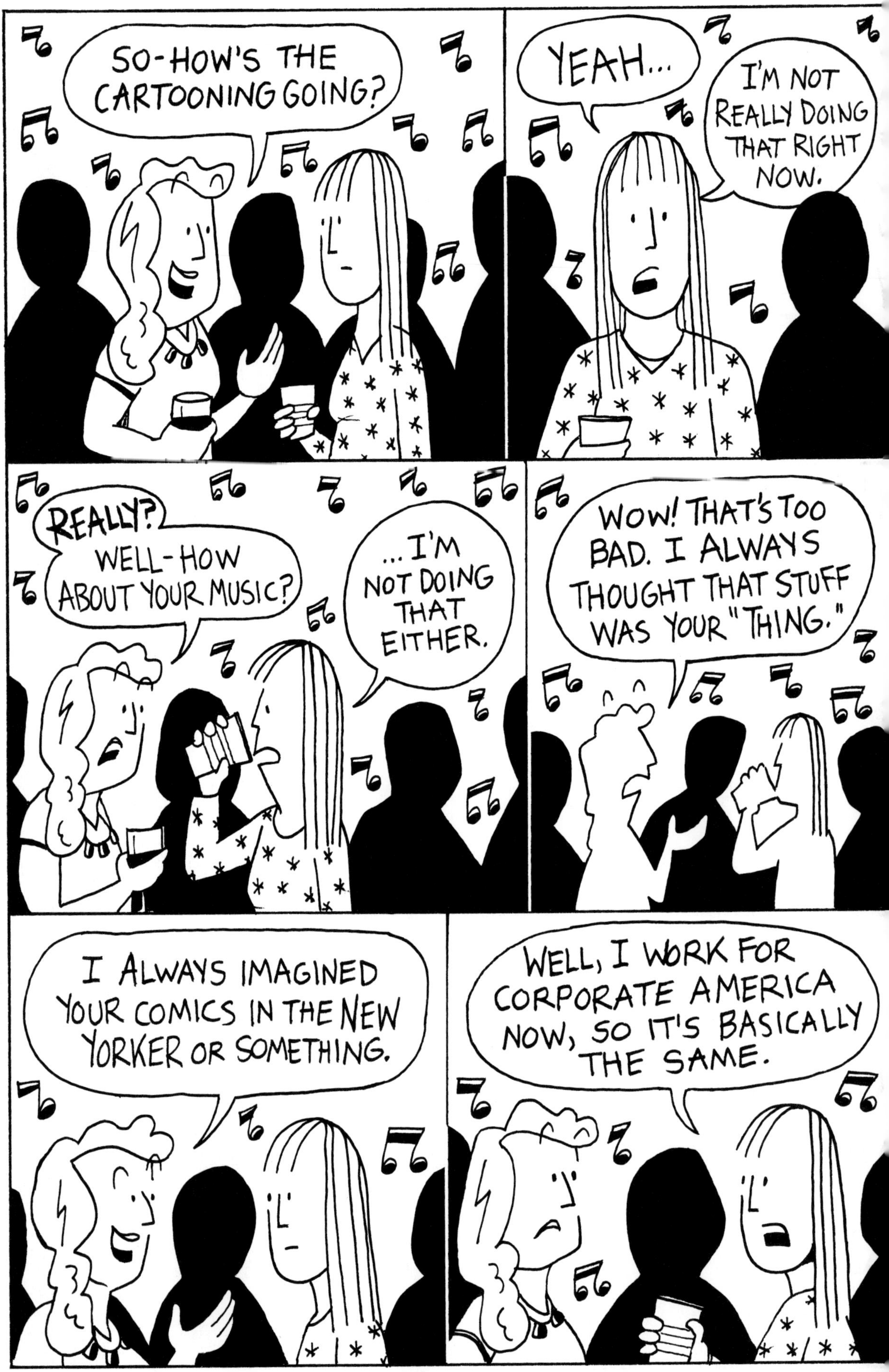
SO-HOW'S THE CARTOONING GOING?
YEAH...
I'M NOT REALLY DOING THAT RIGHT NOW.
REALLY? WELL-HOW ABOUT YOUR MUSIC?
...I'M NOT DOING THAT EITHER.
WOW! THAT'S TOO BAD. I ALWAYS THOUGHT THAT STUFF WAS YOUR "THING."
I ALWAYS IMAGINED YOUR COMICS IN THE NEW YORKER OR SOMETHING.
WELL, I WORK FOR CORPORATE AMERICA NOW, SO IT'S BASICALLY THE SAME.

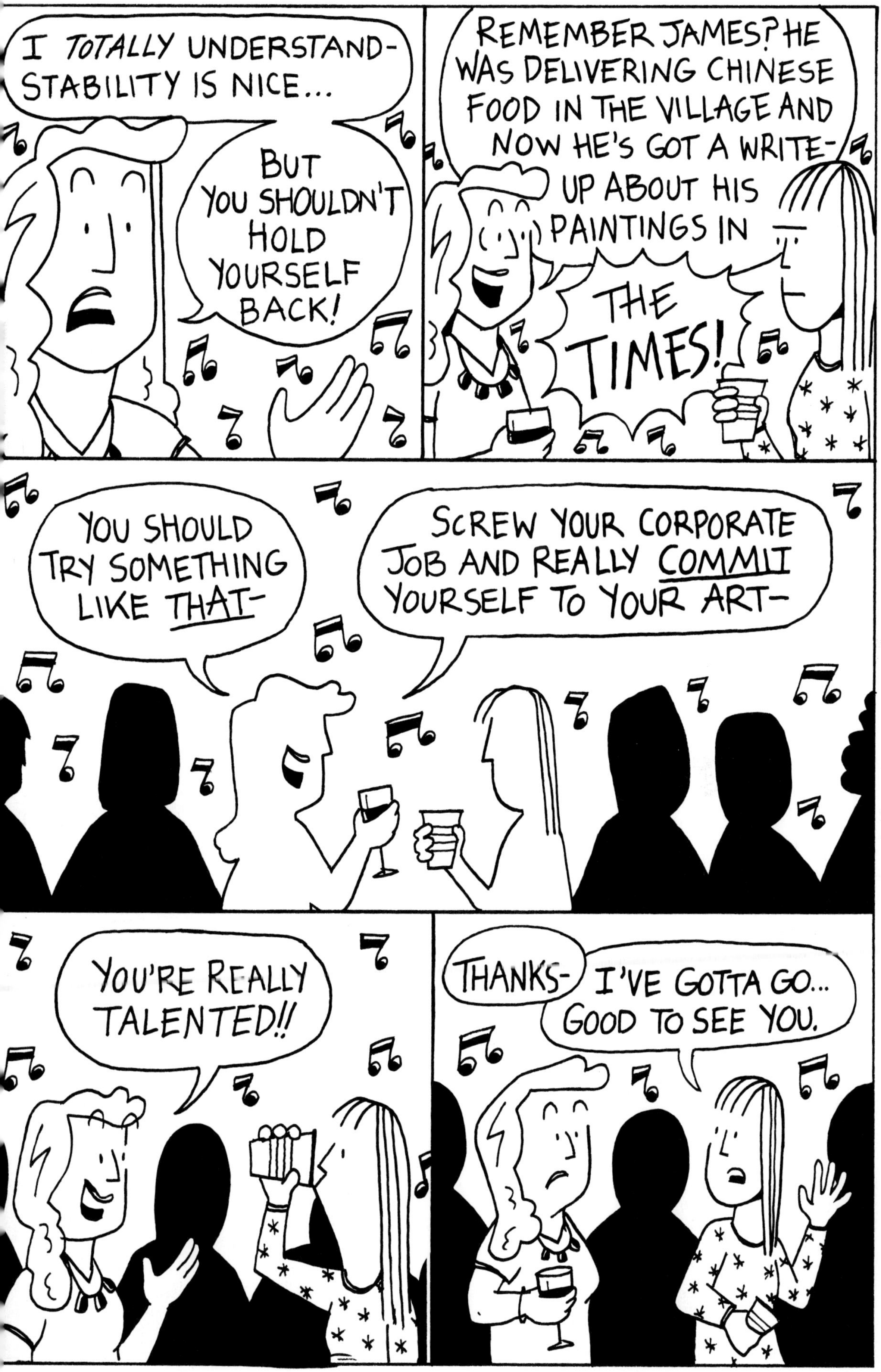
I TOTALLY UNDERSTAND- STABILITY IS NICE...
BUT YOU SHOULDN'T HOLD YOURSELF BACK!
REMEMBER JAMES? HE WAS DELIVERING CHINESE FOOD IN THE VILLAGE AND NOW HE'S GOT A WRITE-UP ABOUT HIS PAINTINGS IN
THE TIMES!
YOU SHOULD TRY SOMETHING LIKE THAT-
SCREW YOUR CORPORATE JOB AND REALLY COMMIT YOURSELF TO YOUR ART-
YOU'RE REALLY TALENTED!!
THANKS-
I'VE GOTTA GO... GOOD TO SEE YOU.

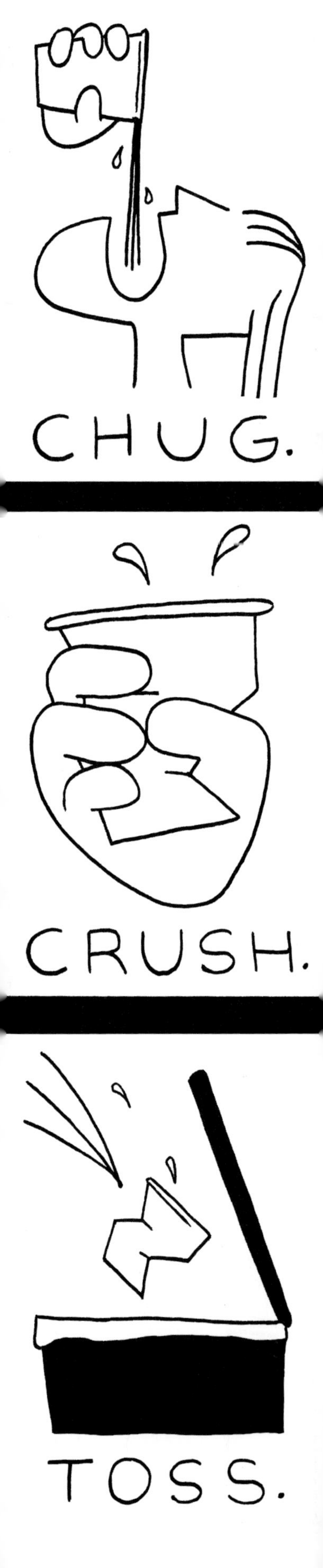
CHUG.
CRUSH.
TOSS.

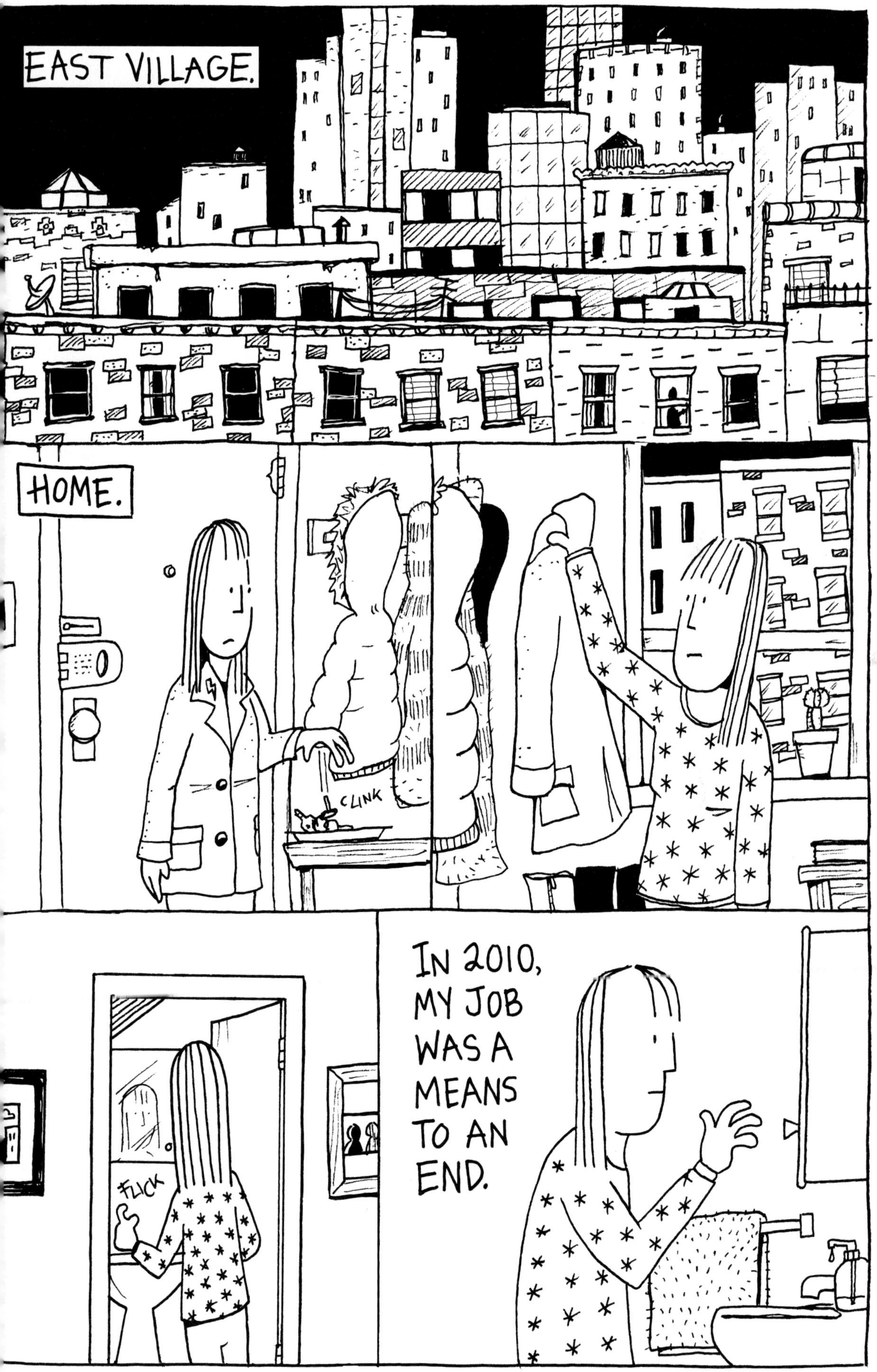
EAST VILLAGE.
HOME.
CLINK
FLICK
IN 2010, MY JOB WAS A MEANS TO AN END.

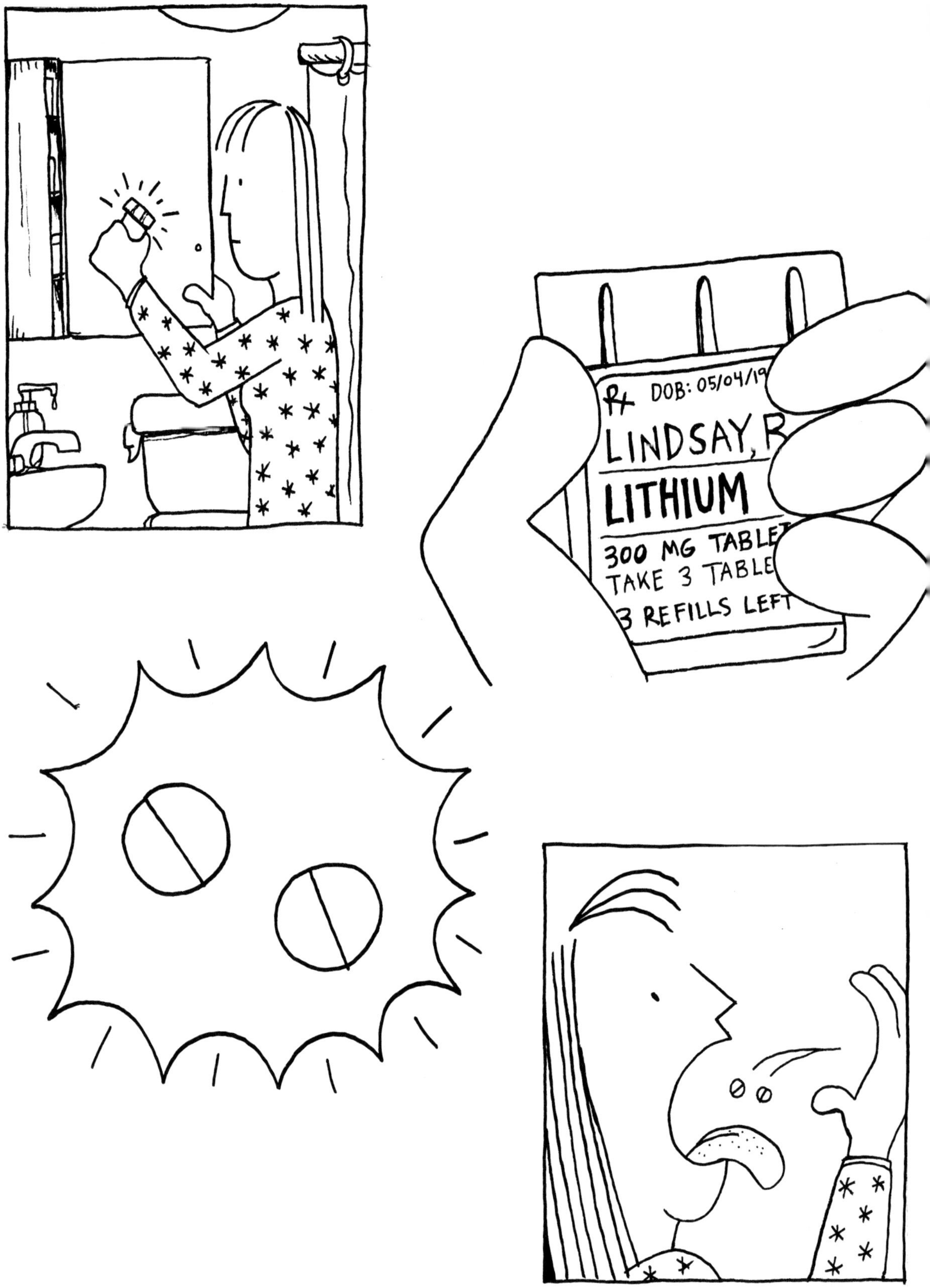
℞ DOB: 05/04/19
LINDSAY, R
LITHIUM
300 MG TABLE
TAKE 3 TABLE
3 REFILLS LEFT

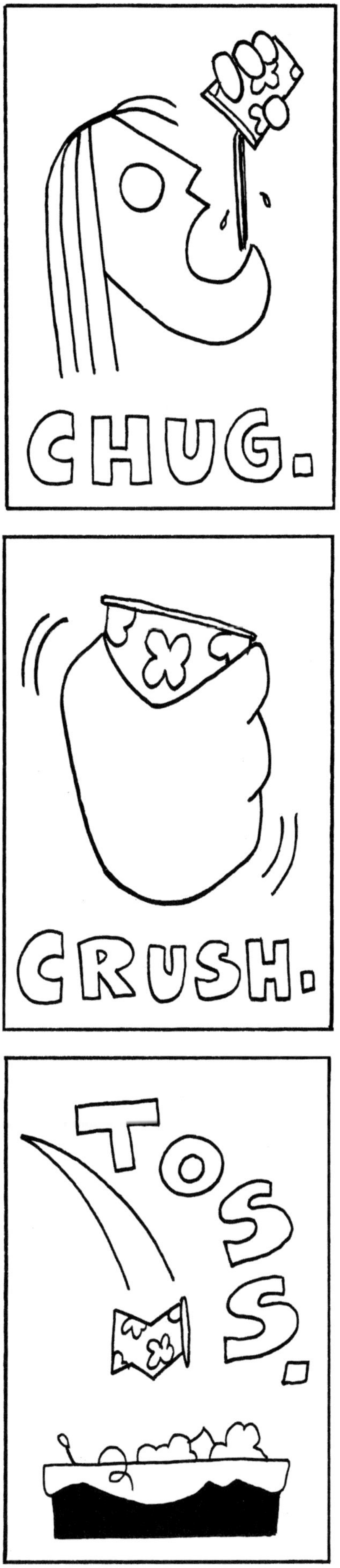
CHUG.
CRUSH.
TOSS.

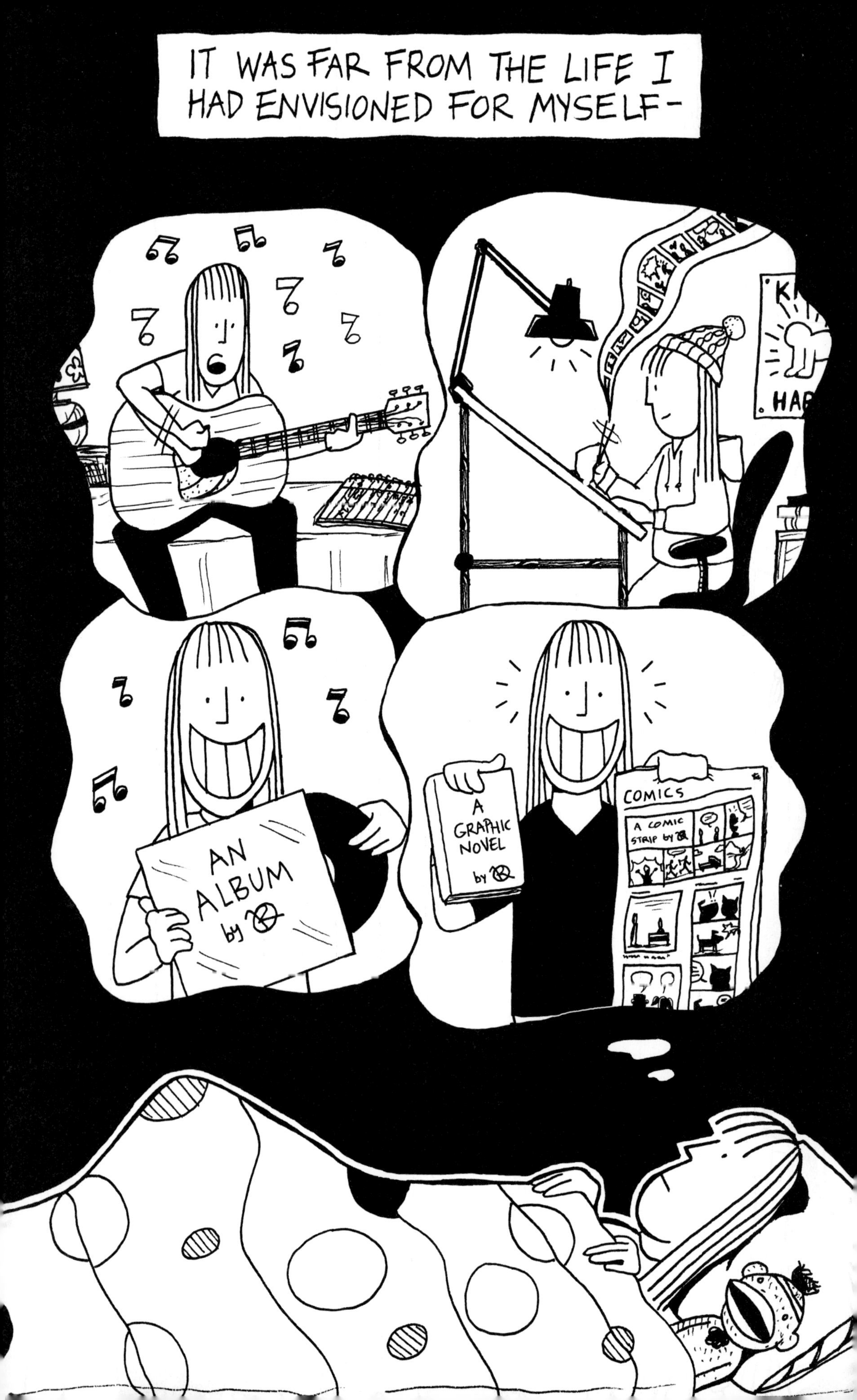
IT WAS FAR FROM THE LIFE I HAD ENVISIONED FOR MYSELF-
AN ALBUM by
A GRAPHIC NOVEL by
COMICS
A COMIC STRIP by

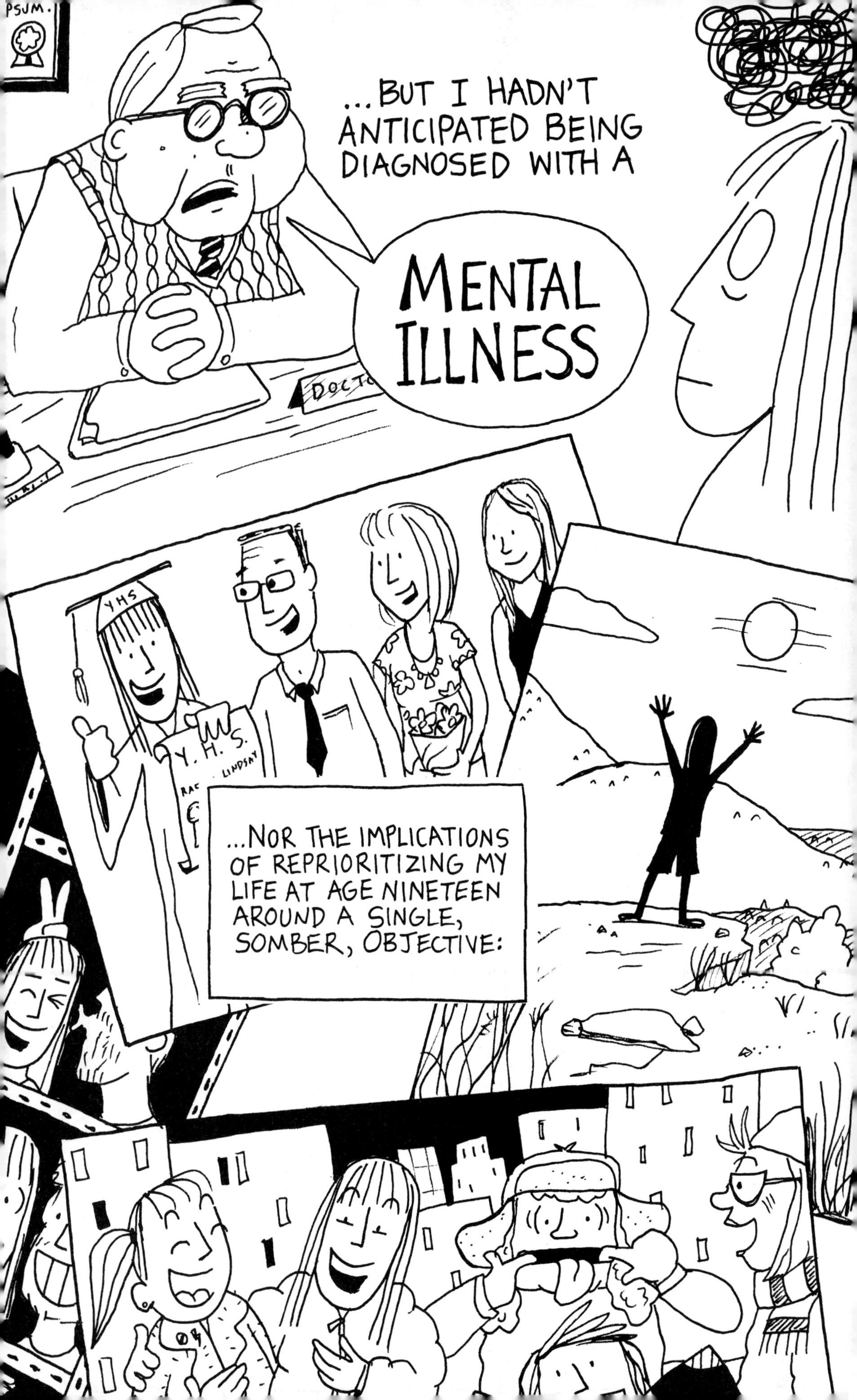
...BUT I HADN'T ANTICIPATED BEING DIAGNOSED WITH A
MENTAL ILLNESS
...NOR THE IMPLICATIONS OF REPRIORITIZING MY LIFE AT AGE NINETEEN AROUND A SINGLE, SOMBER, OBJECTIVE:

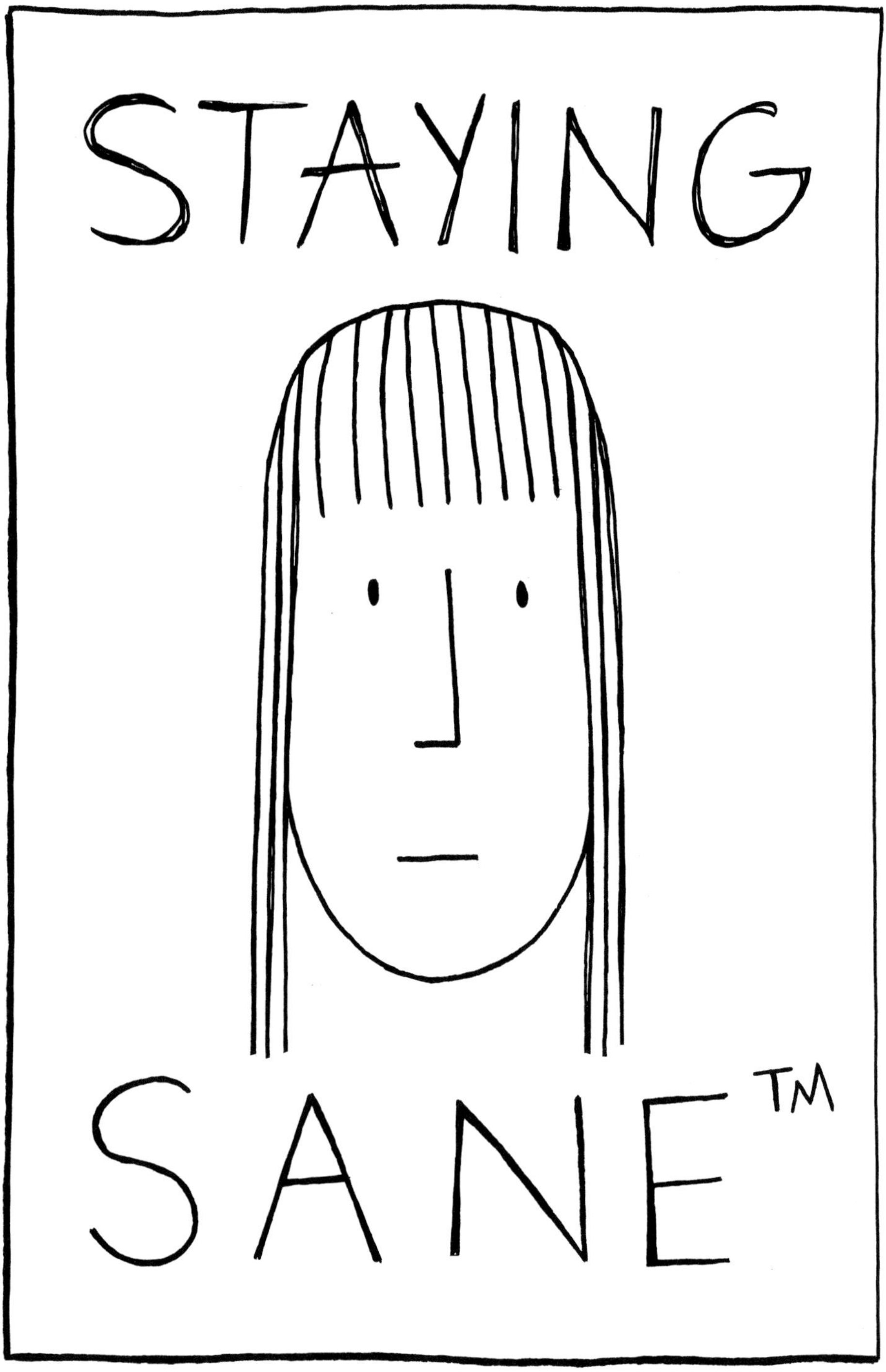
STAYING
SANE™

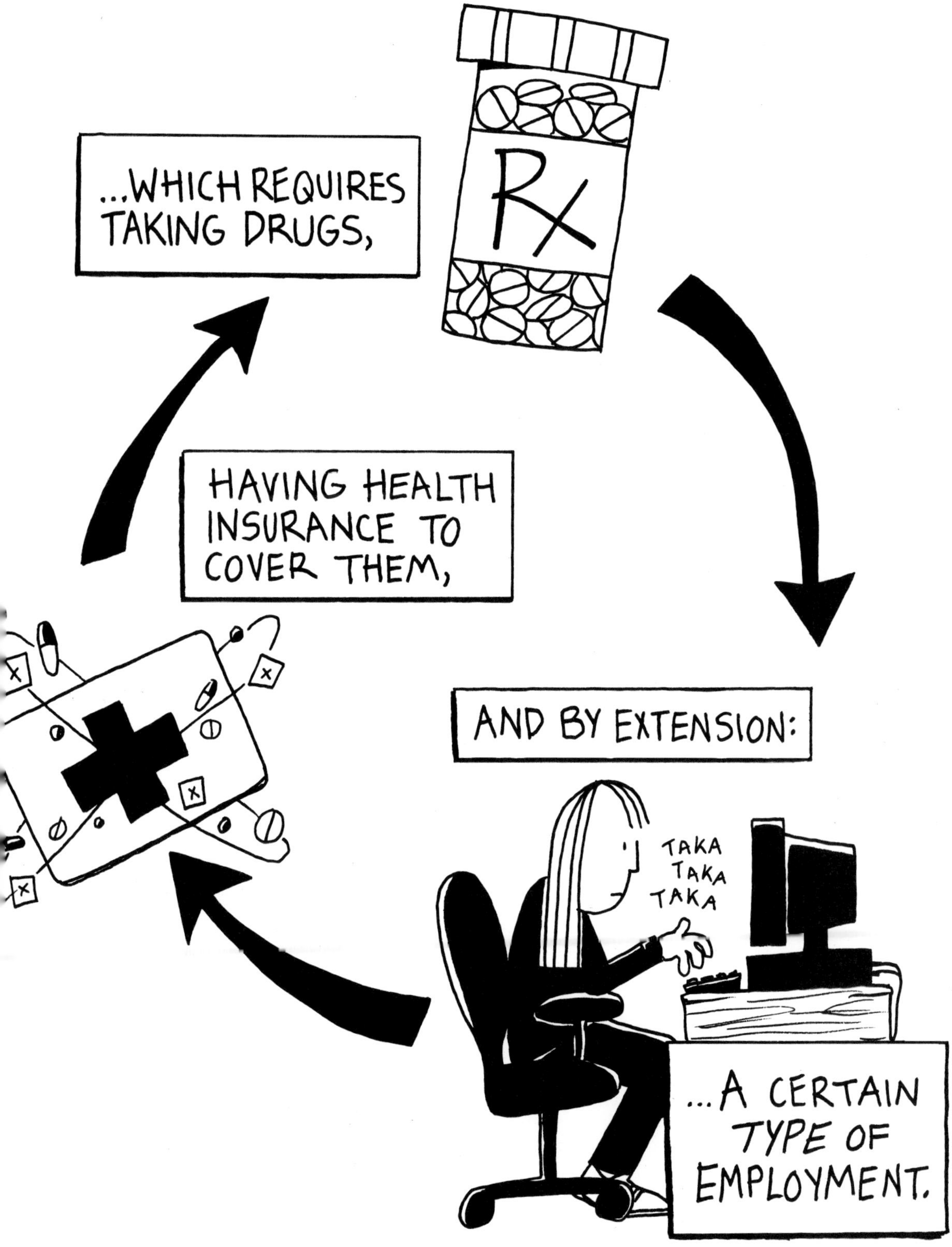

...WHICH REQUIRES TAKING DRUGS,
HAVING HEALTH INSURANCE TO COVER THEM,
AND BY EXTENSION:
TAKA TAKA TAKA
...A CERTAIN *TYPE* OF EMPLOYMENT.

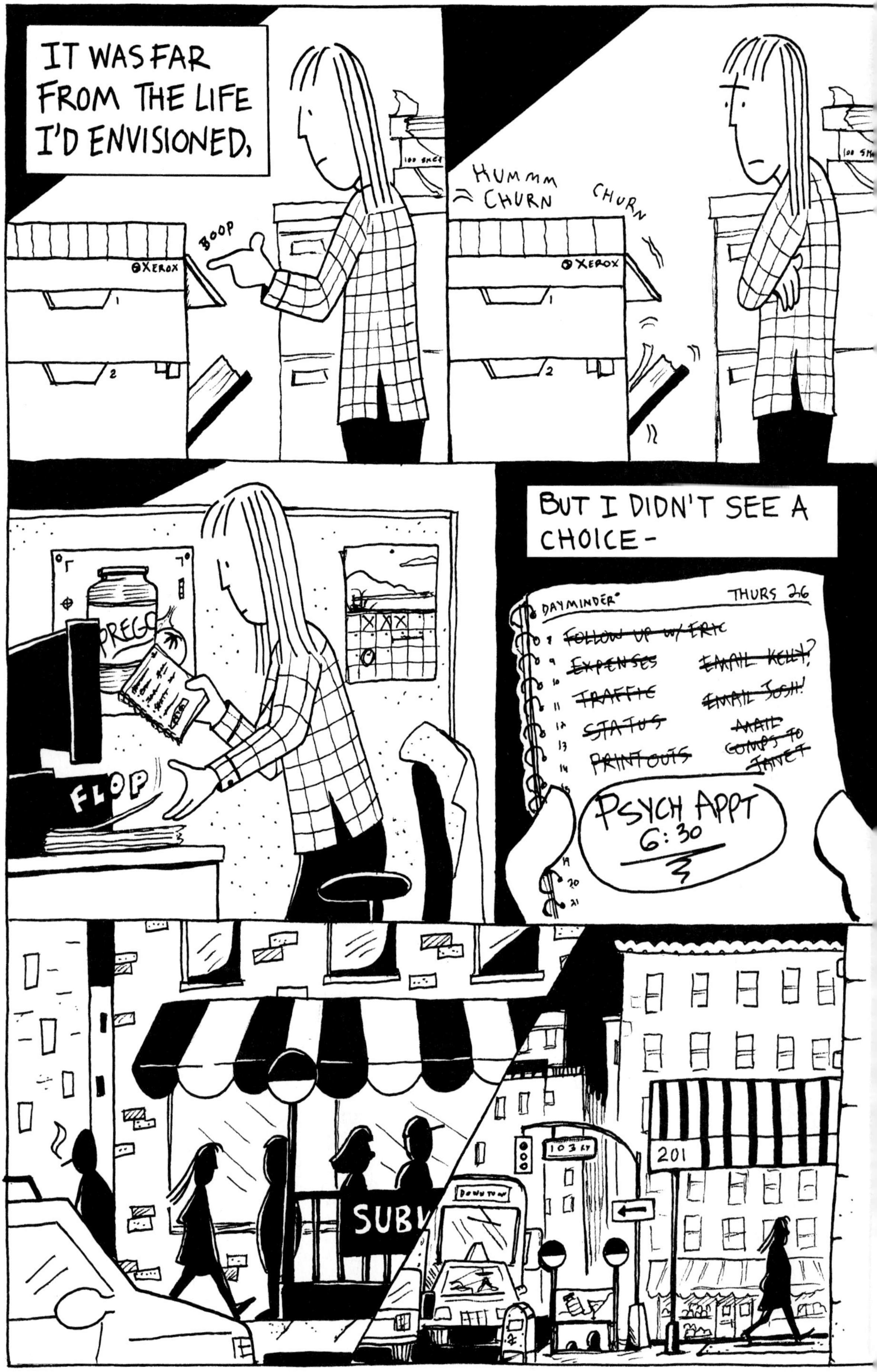
IT WAS FAR FROM THE LIFE I'D ENVISIONED,
XEROX
BOOP
HUMMM CHURN
CHURN
XEROX
PREGO
FLOP
BUT I DIDN'T SEE A CHOICE-
DAYMINDER
THURS 26
FOLLOW UP W/ ERIC
EXPENSES
EMAIL KELLY?
TRAFFIC
EMAIL JOSH!
STATUS
MAIL COMPS TO JANET
PRINTOUTS
PSYCH APPT 6:30
103 RD
201

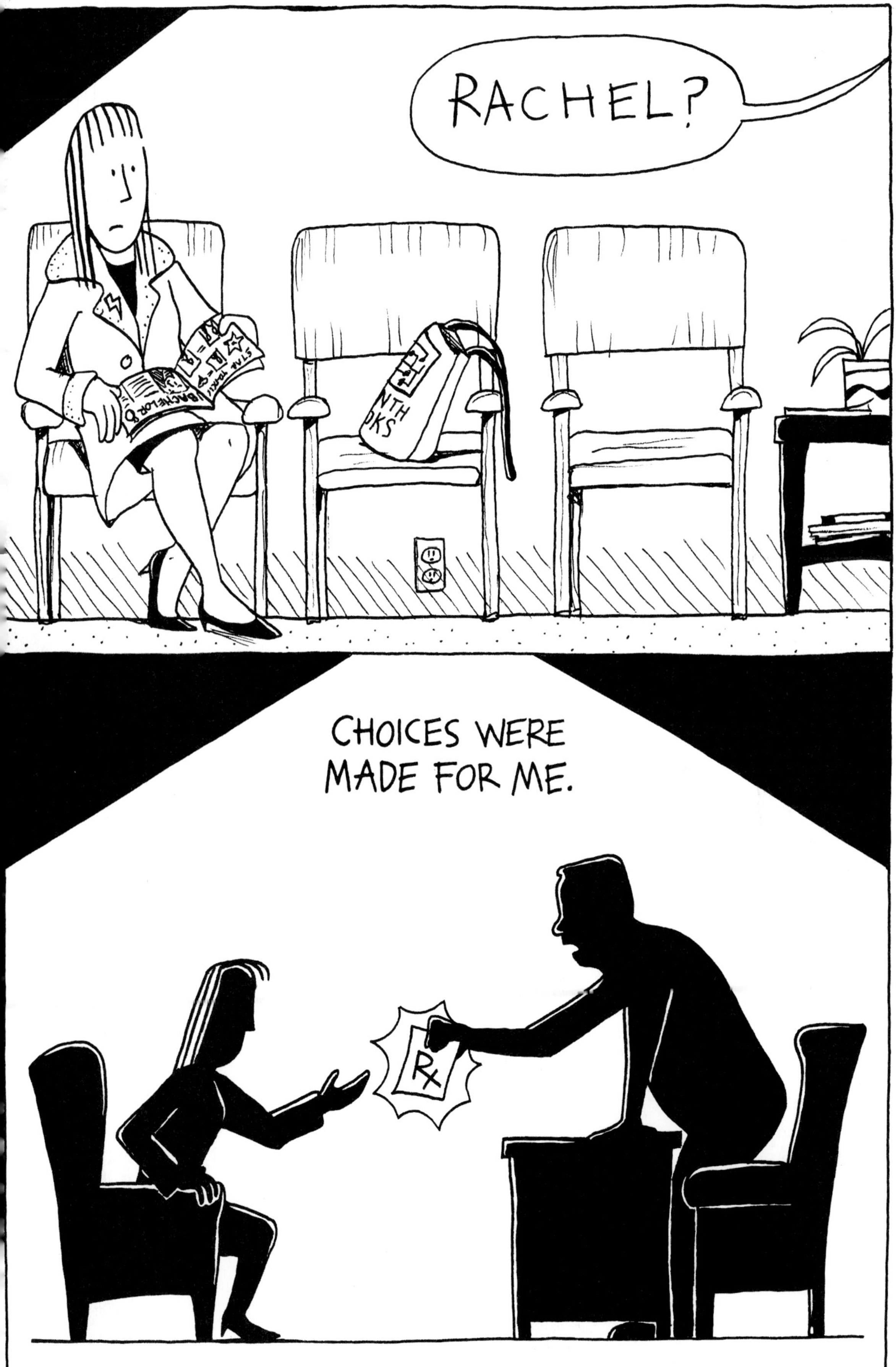
RACHEL?
CHOICES WERE MADE FOR ME.
Rx

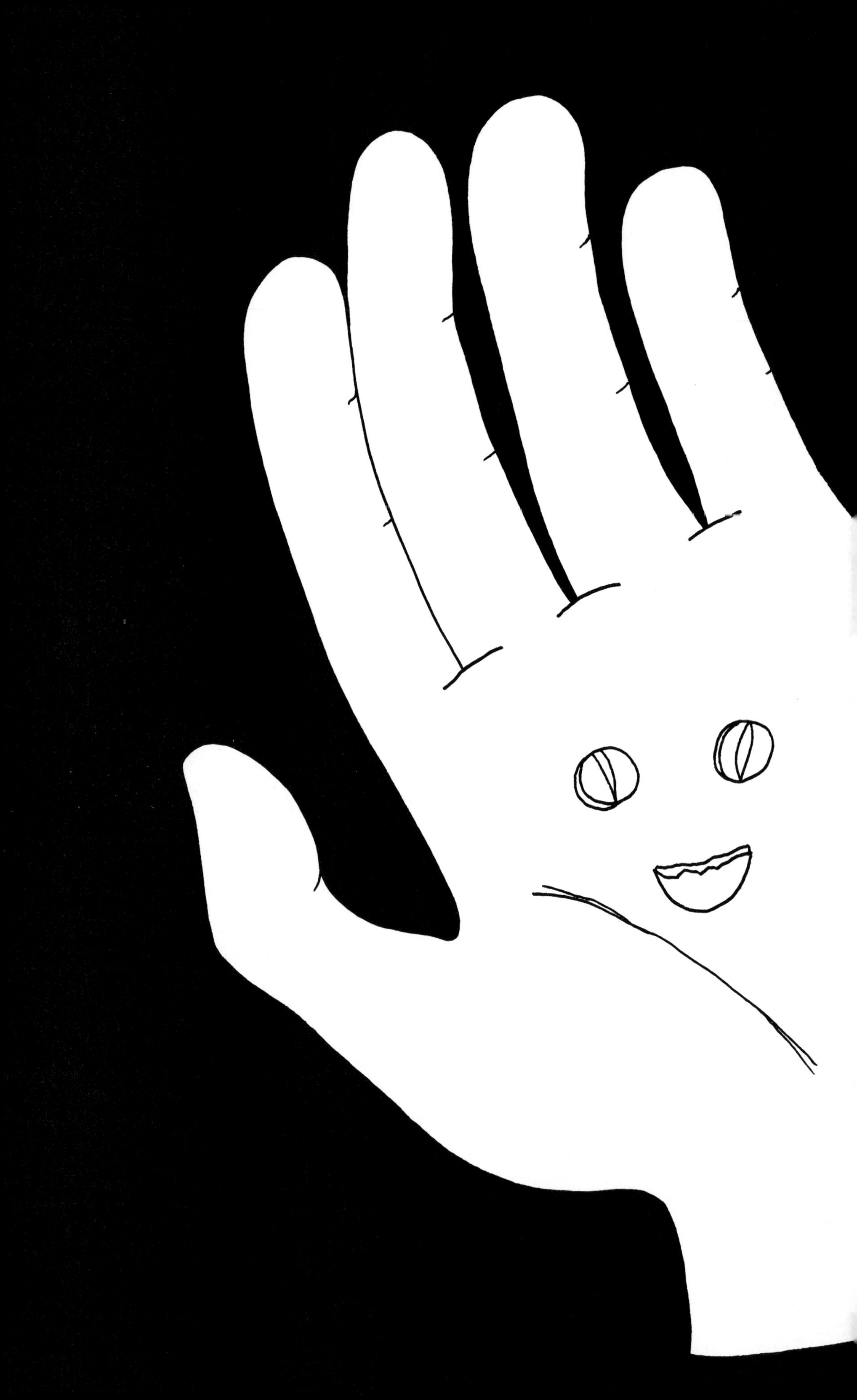

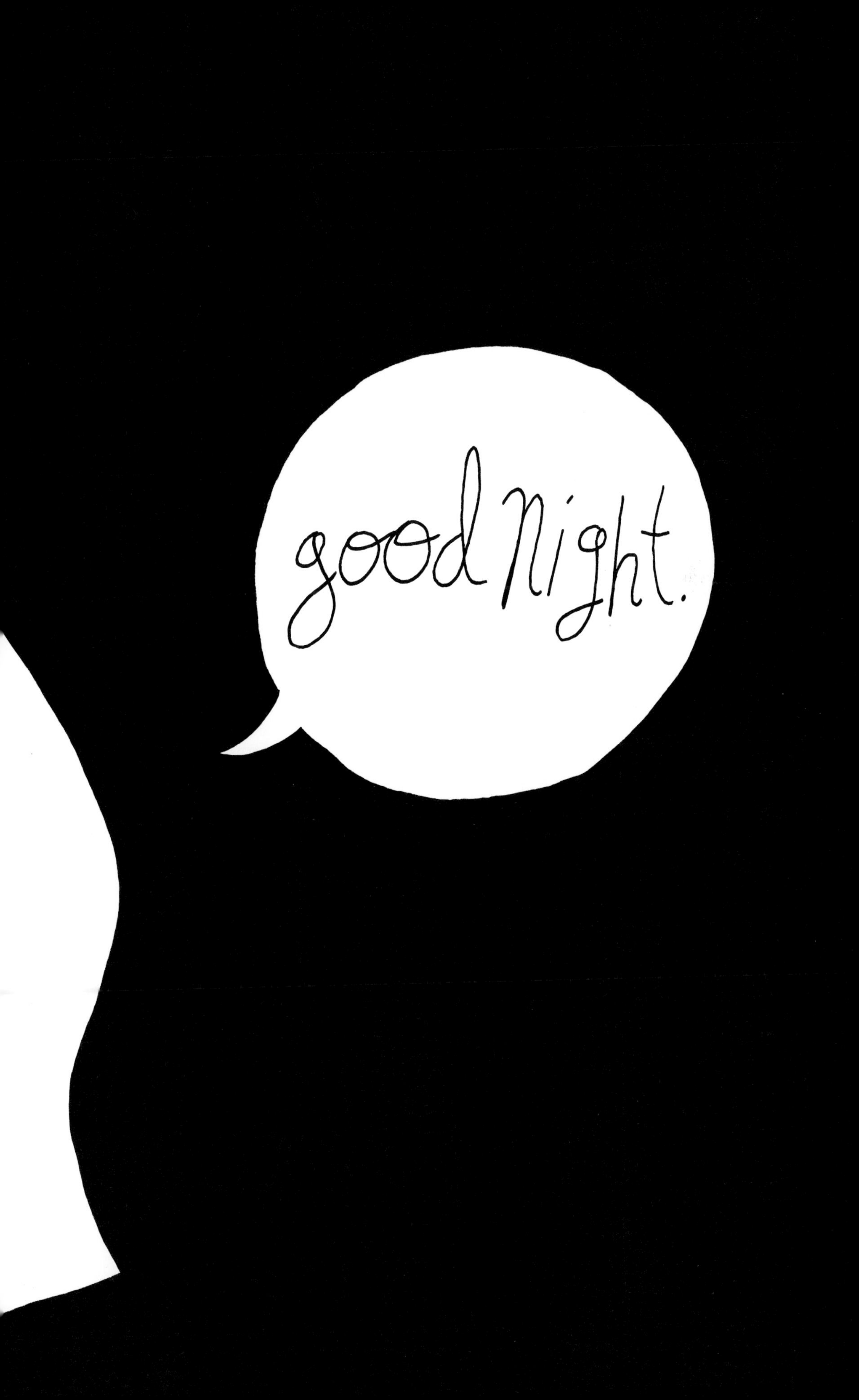
good Night.

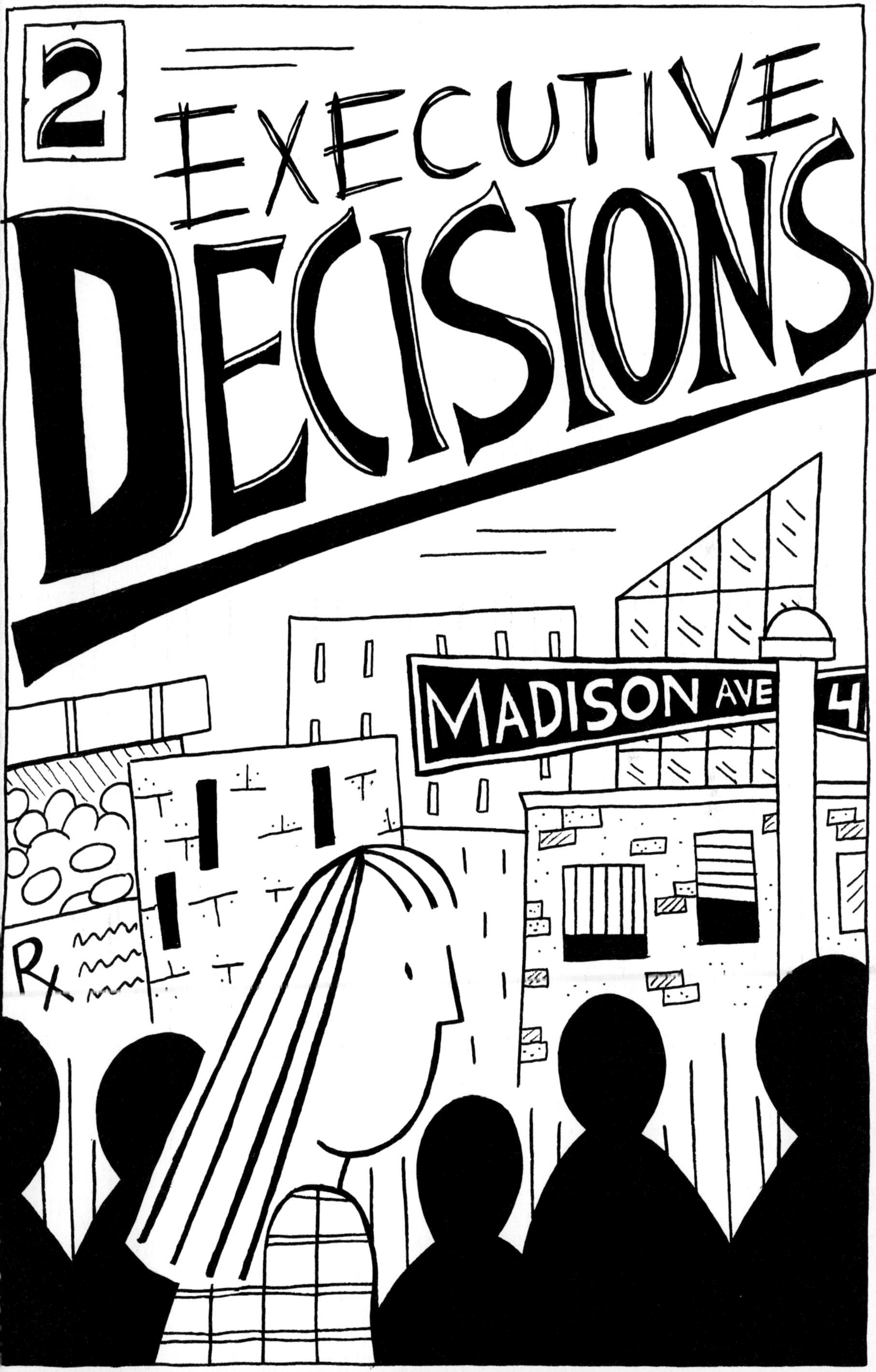
2
EXECUTIVE
DECISIONS
MADISON AVE
4
Rx

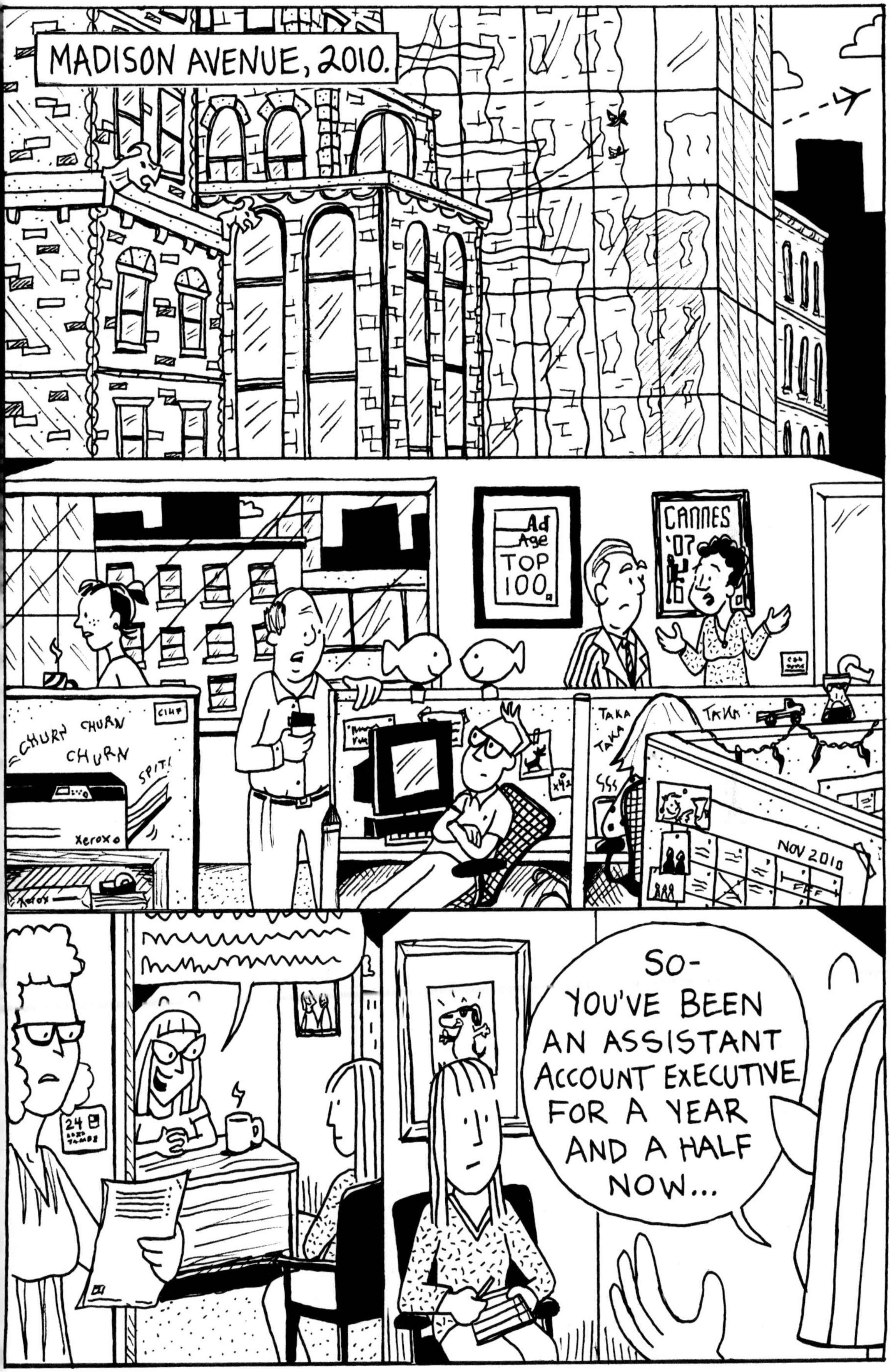
MADISON AVENUE, 2010.
Ad Age TOP 100
CANNES '07
CHURN CHURN CHURN
SPIT!
Xerox
TAKA TAKA TAKA
NOV 2010
SO- YOU'VE BEEN AN ASSISTANT ACCOUNT EXECUTIVE FOR A YEAR AND A HALF NOW...

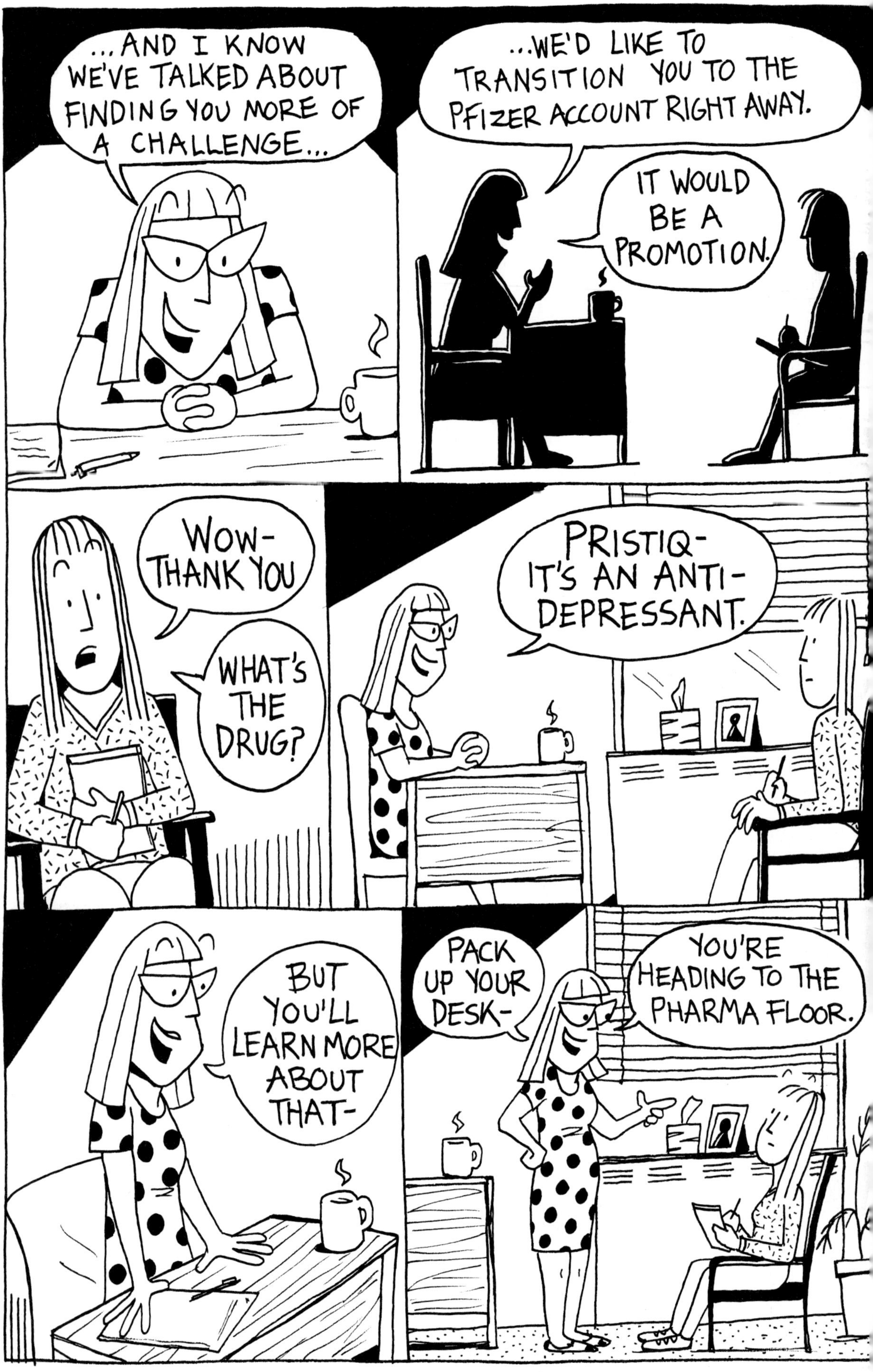
...AND I KNOW WE'VE TALKED ABOUT FINDING YOU MORE OF A CHALLENGE...
...WE'D LIKE TO TRANSITION YOU TO THE PFIZER ACCOUNT RIGHT AWAY.
IT WOULD BE A PROMOTION.
WOW- THANK YOU
WHAT'S THE DRUG?
PRISTIQ- IT'S AN ANTI-DEPRESSANT.
BUT YOU'LL LEARN MORE ABOUT THAT-
PACK UP YOUR DESK-
YOU'RE HEADING TO THE PHARMA FLOOR.

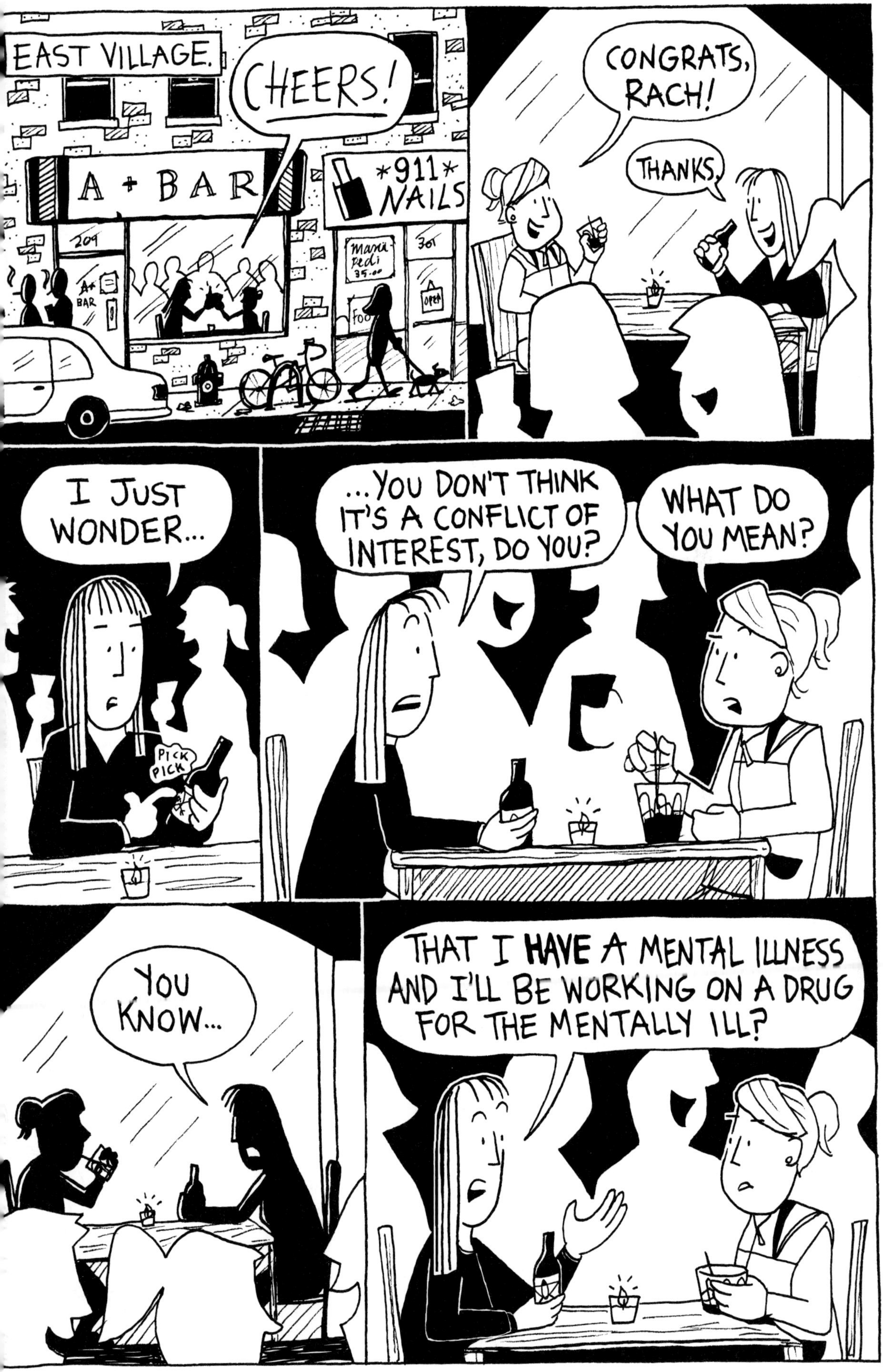
EAST VILLAGE.
CHEERS!
A + BAR
911 NAILS
209
A+ BAR
Mani Pedi 35.00
301
OPEN
CONGRATS, RACH!
THANKS.
I JUST WONDER...
PICK PICK
...YOU DON'T THINK IT'S A CONFLICT OF INTEREST, DO YOU?
WHAT DO YOU MEAN?
YOU KNOW...
THAT I **HAVE** A MENTAL ILLNESS AND I'LL BE WORKING ON A DRUG FOR THE MENTALLY ILL?

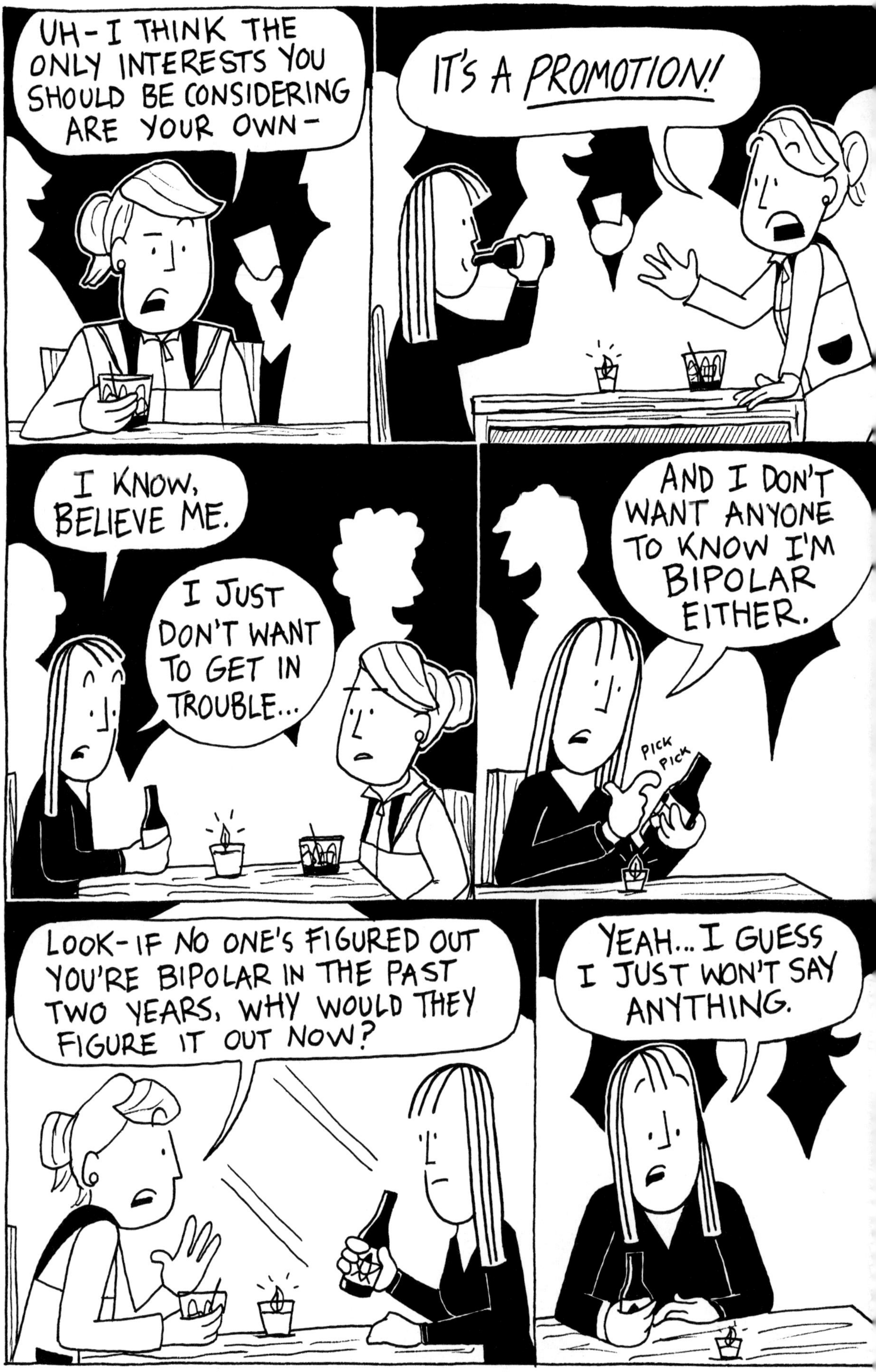
UH-I THINK THE ONLY INTERESTS YOU SHOULD BE CONSIDERING ARE YOUR OWN-
IT'S A PROMOTION!
I KNOW, BELIEVE ME.
I JUST DON'T WANT TO GET IN TROUBLE...
AND I DON'T WANT ANYONE TO KNOW I'M BIPOLAR EITHER.
PICK PICK
LOOK-IF NO ONE'S FIGURED OUT YOU'RE BIPOLAR IN THE PAST TWO YEARS, WHY WOULD THEY FIGURE IT OUT NOW?
YEAH... I GUESS I JUST WON'T SAY ANYTHING.

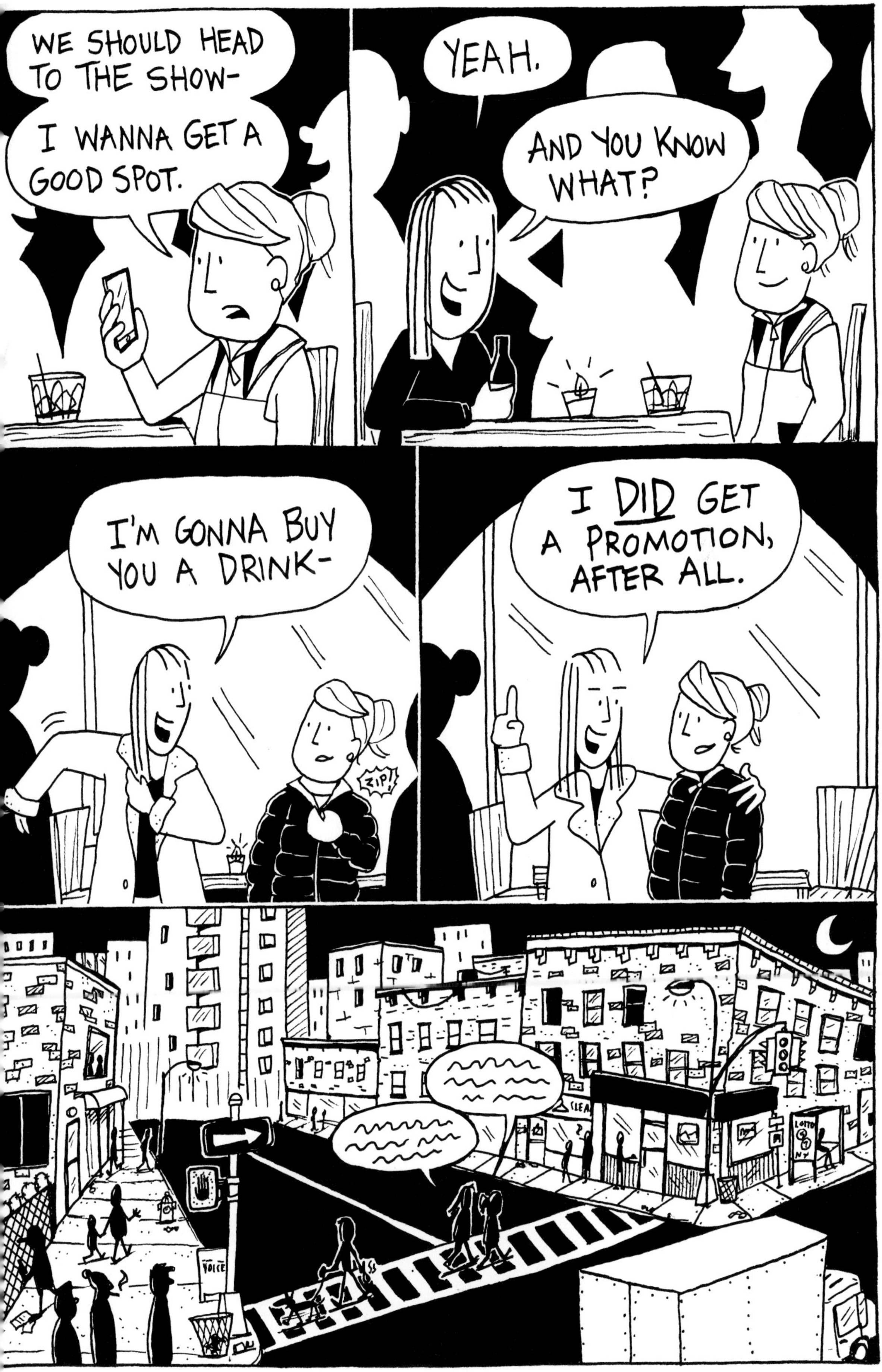
WE SHOULD HEAD TO THE SHOW-
I WANNA GET A GOOD SPOT.
YEAH.
AND YOU KNOW WHAT?
I'M GONNA BUY YOU A DRINK-
ZIP!
I DID GET A PROMOTION, AFTER ALL.
VOICE
LOTTO NY

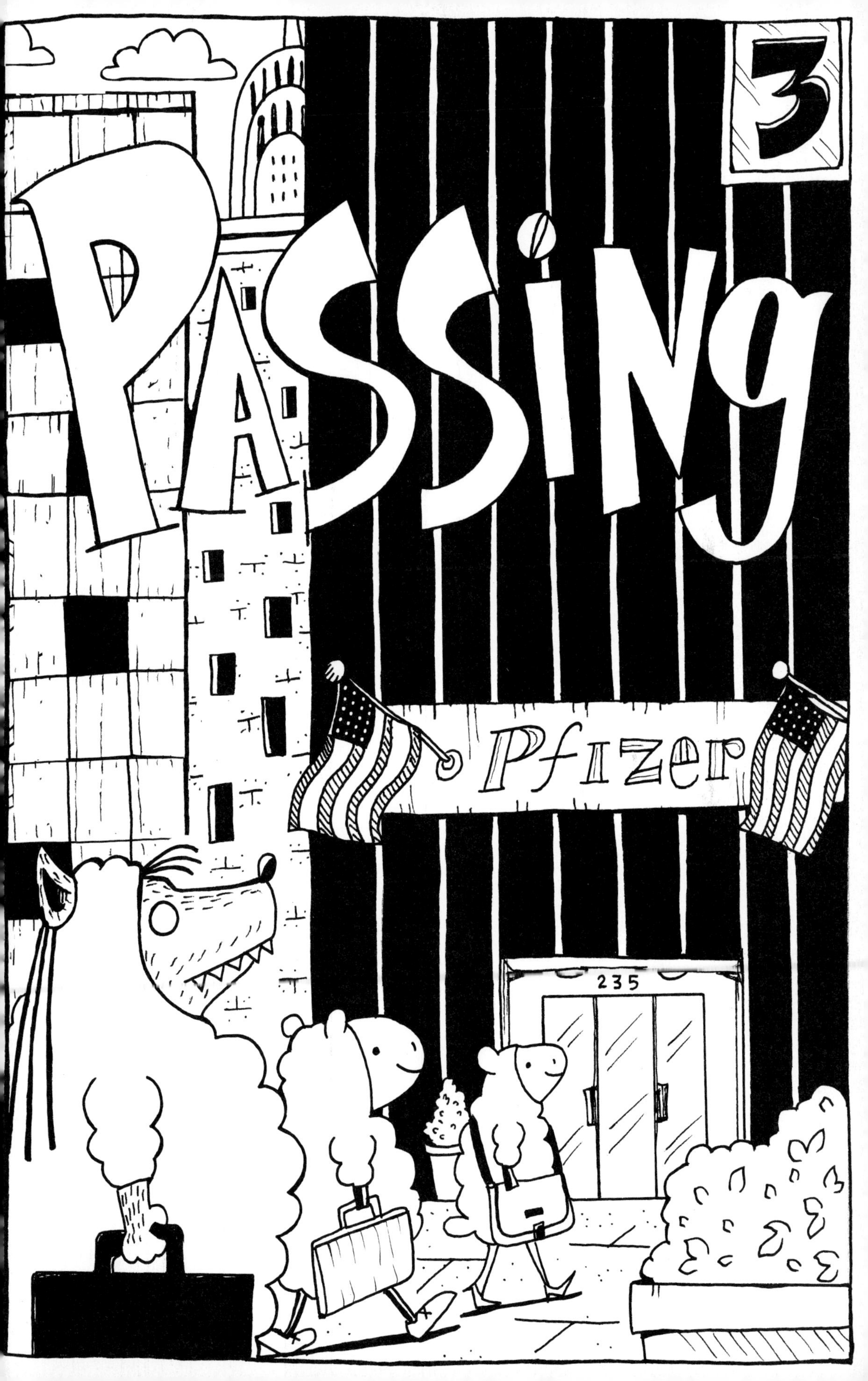
3
PASSING
Pfizer
235

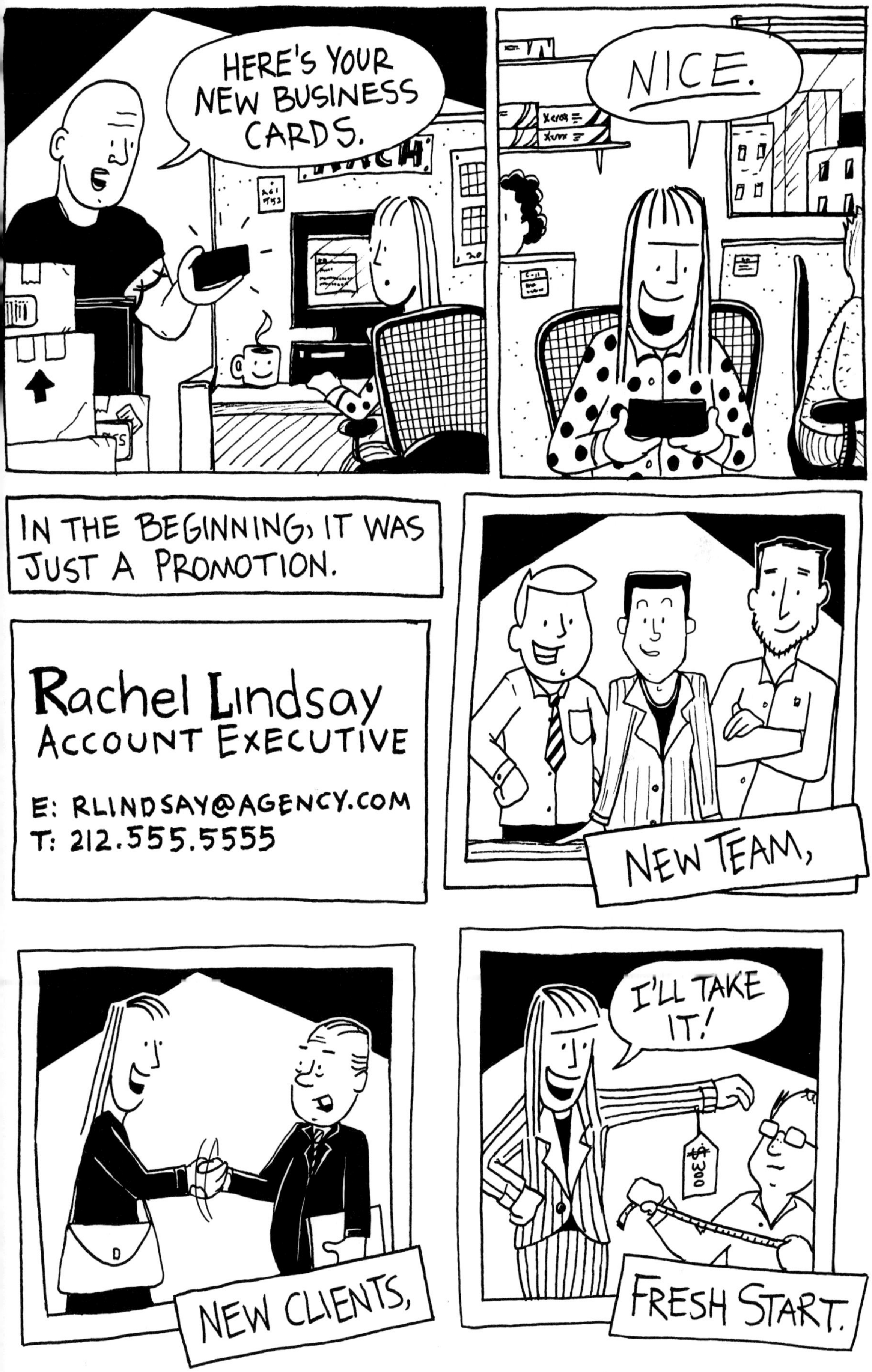
HERE'S YOUR NEW BUSINESS CARDS.
NICE.
IN THE BEGINNING, IT WAS JUST A PROMOTION.
Rachel Lindsay
ACCOUNT EXECUTIVE
E: RLINDSAY@AGENCY.COM
T: 212.555.5555
NEW TEAM,
NEW CLIENTS,
I'LL TAKE IT!
FRESH START.

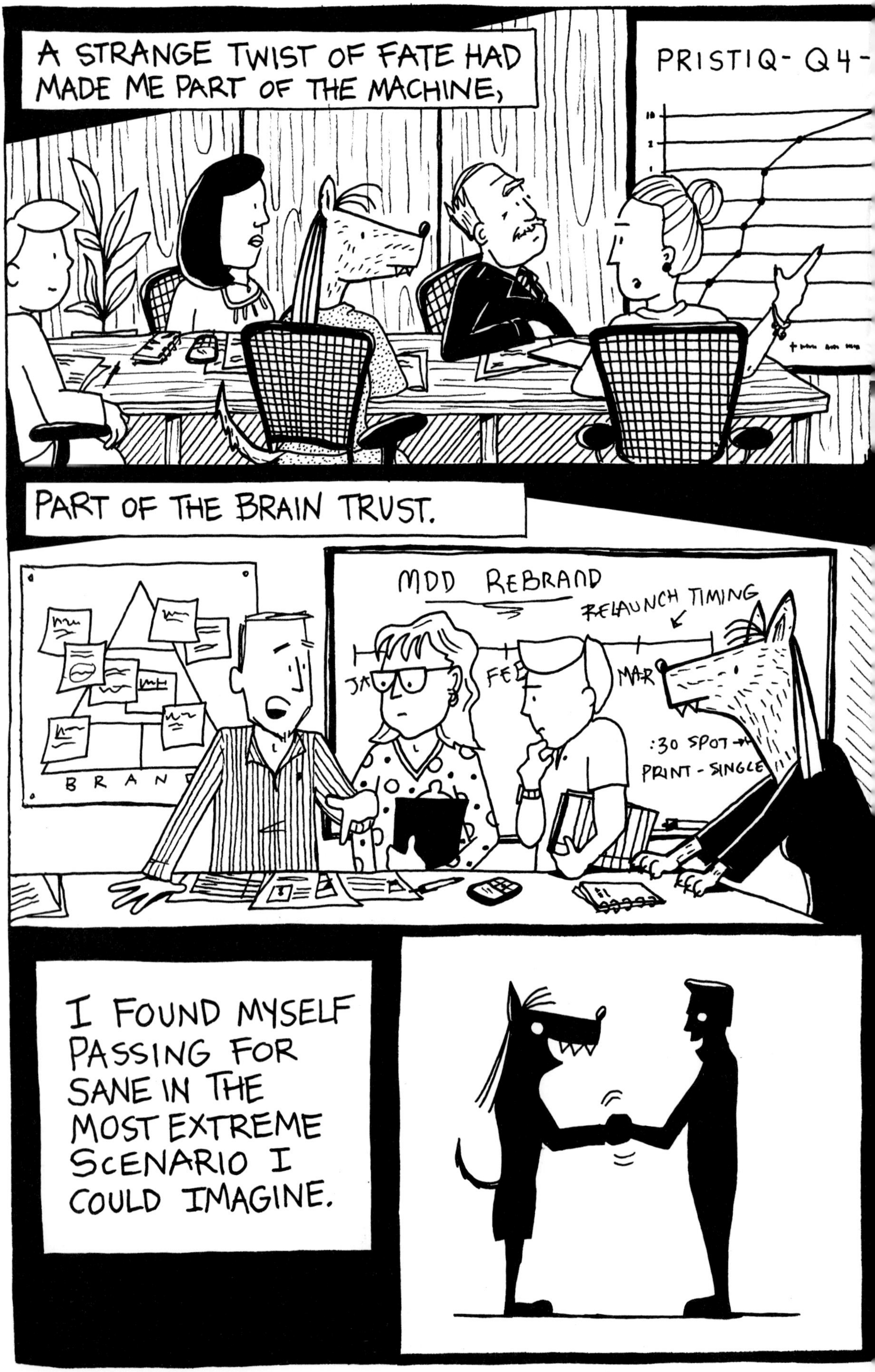
A STRANGE TWIST OF FATE HAD MADE ME PART OF THE MACHINE,
PRISTIQ- Q4-
PART OF THE BRAIN TRUST.
MDD REBRAND
RELAUNCH TIMING
JA
FEB
MAR
:30 SPOT
PRINT - SINGLE
BRAND
I FOUND MYSELF PASSING FOR SANE IN THE MOST EXTREME SCENARIO I COULD IMAGINE.

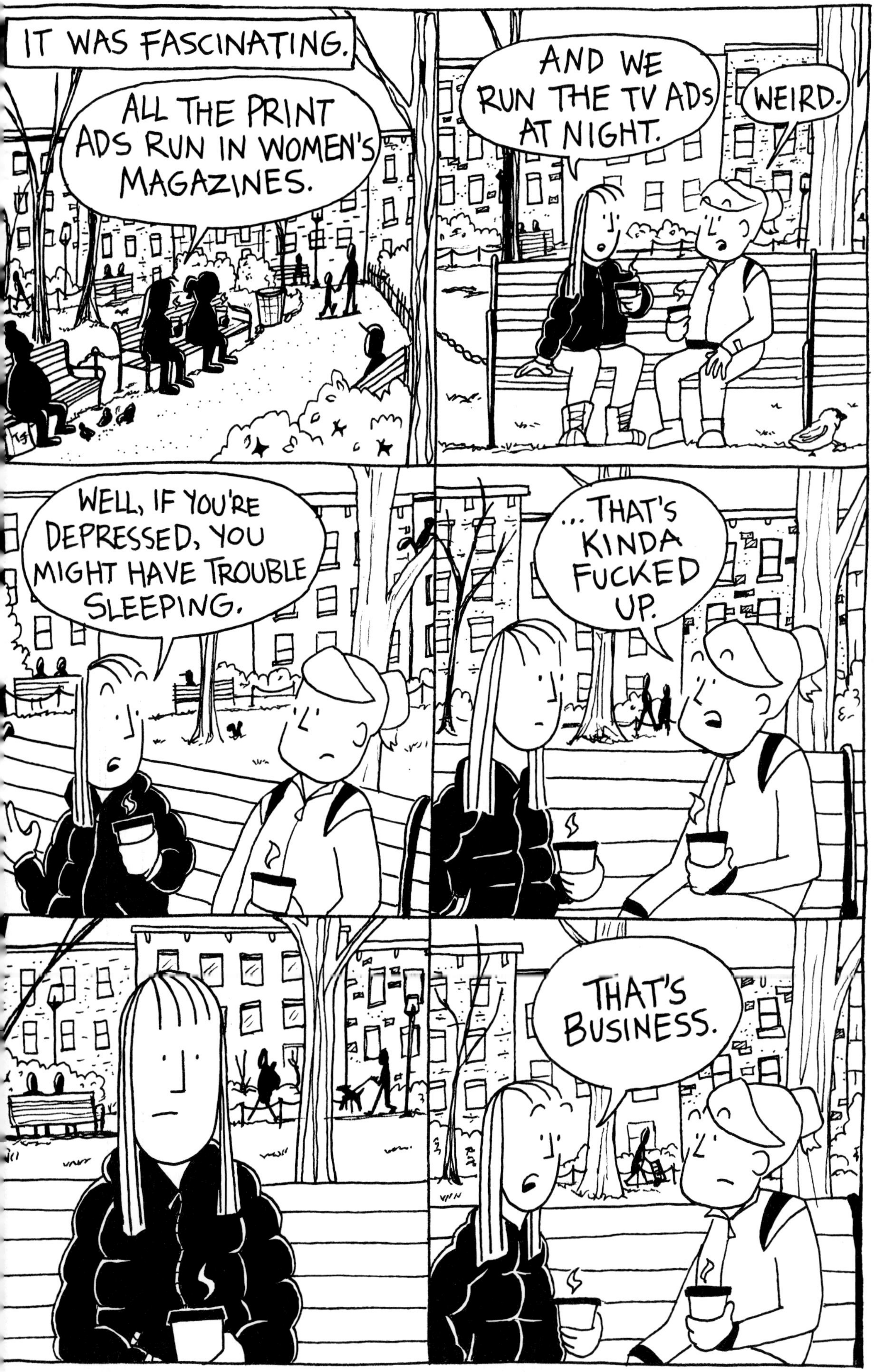
IT WAS FASCINATING.
ALL THE PRINT ADS RUN IN WOMEN'S MAGAZINES.
AND WE RUN THE TV ADS AT NIGHT.
WEIRD.
WELL, IF YOU'RE DEPRESSED, YOU MIGHT HAVE TROUBLE SLEEPING.
...THAT'S KINDA FUCKED UP.
THAT'S BUSINESS.

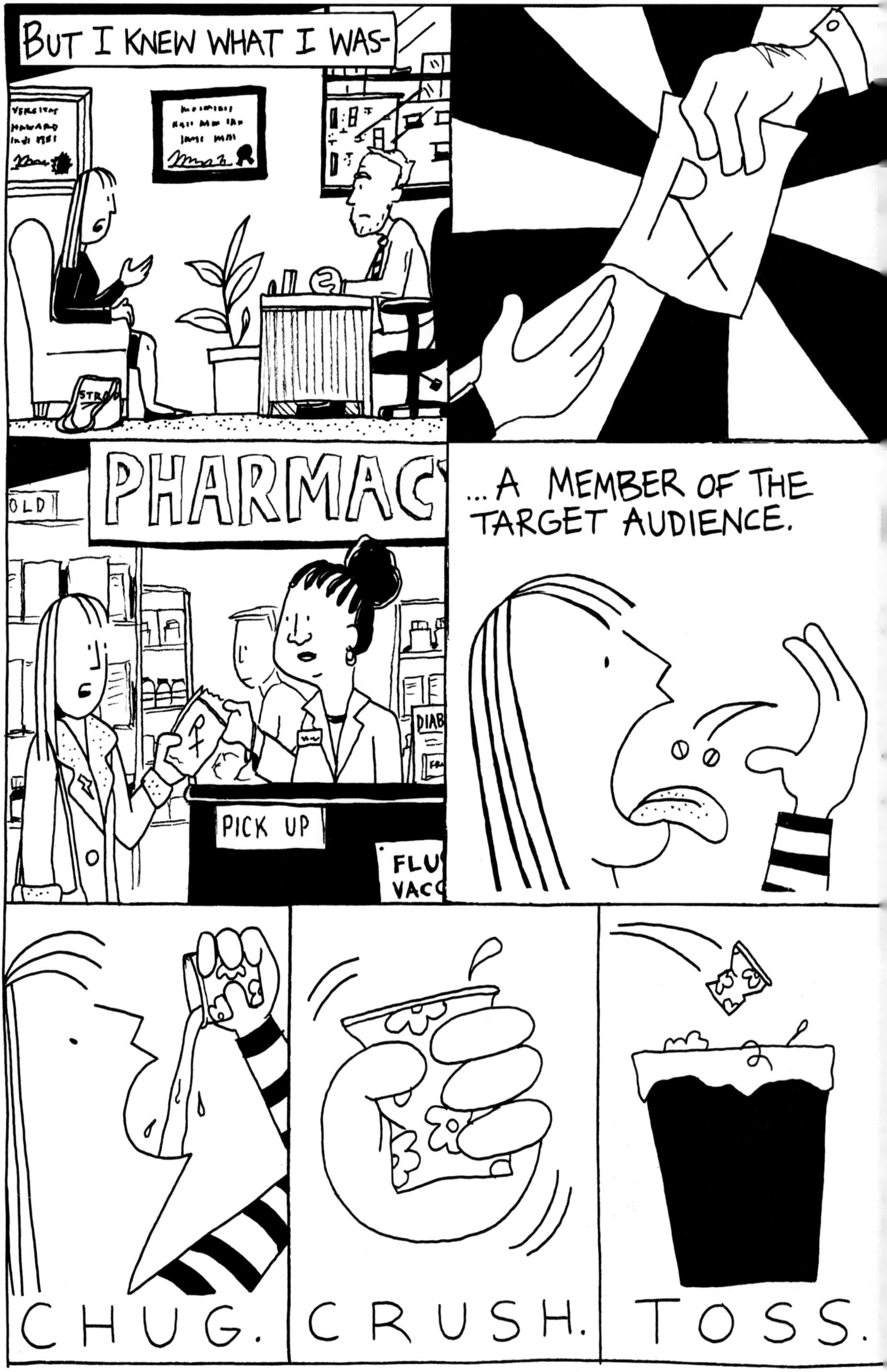

BUT I KNEW WHAT I WAS-
PHARMAC
PICK UP
...A MEMBER OF THE TARGET AUDIENCE.
CHUG.
CRUSH.
TOSS.

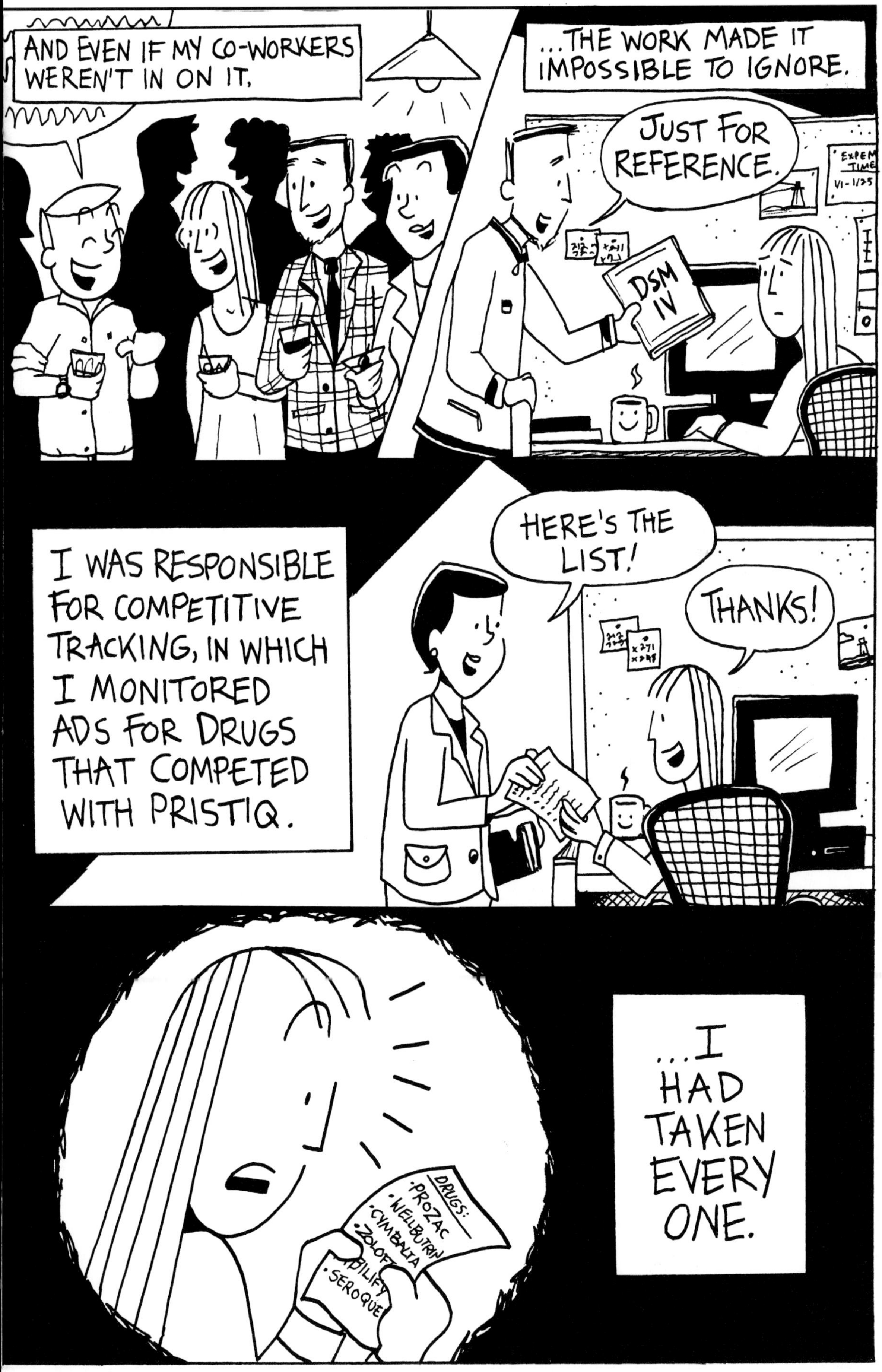
AND EVEN IF MY CO-WORKERS WEREN'T IN ON IT,
...THE WORK MADE IT IMPOSSIBLE TO IGNORE.
JUST FOR REFERENCE.
DSM IV
I WAS RESPONSIBLE FOR COMPETITIVE TRACKING, IN WHICH I MONITORED ADS FOR DRUGS THAT COMPETED WITH PRISTIQ.
HERE'S THE LIST!
THANKS!
DRUGS:
·PROZAC
·WELLBUTRIN
·CYMBALTA
·ZOLOF
BILIFY
·SEROQUE
...I HAD TAKEN EVERY ONE.

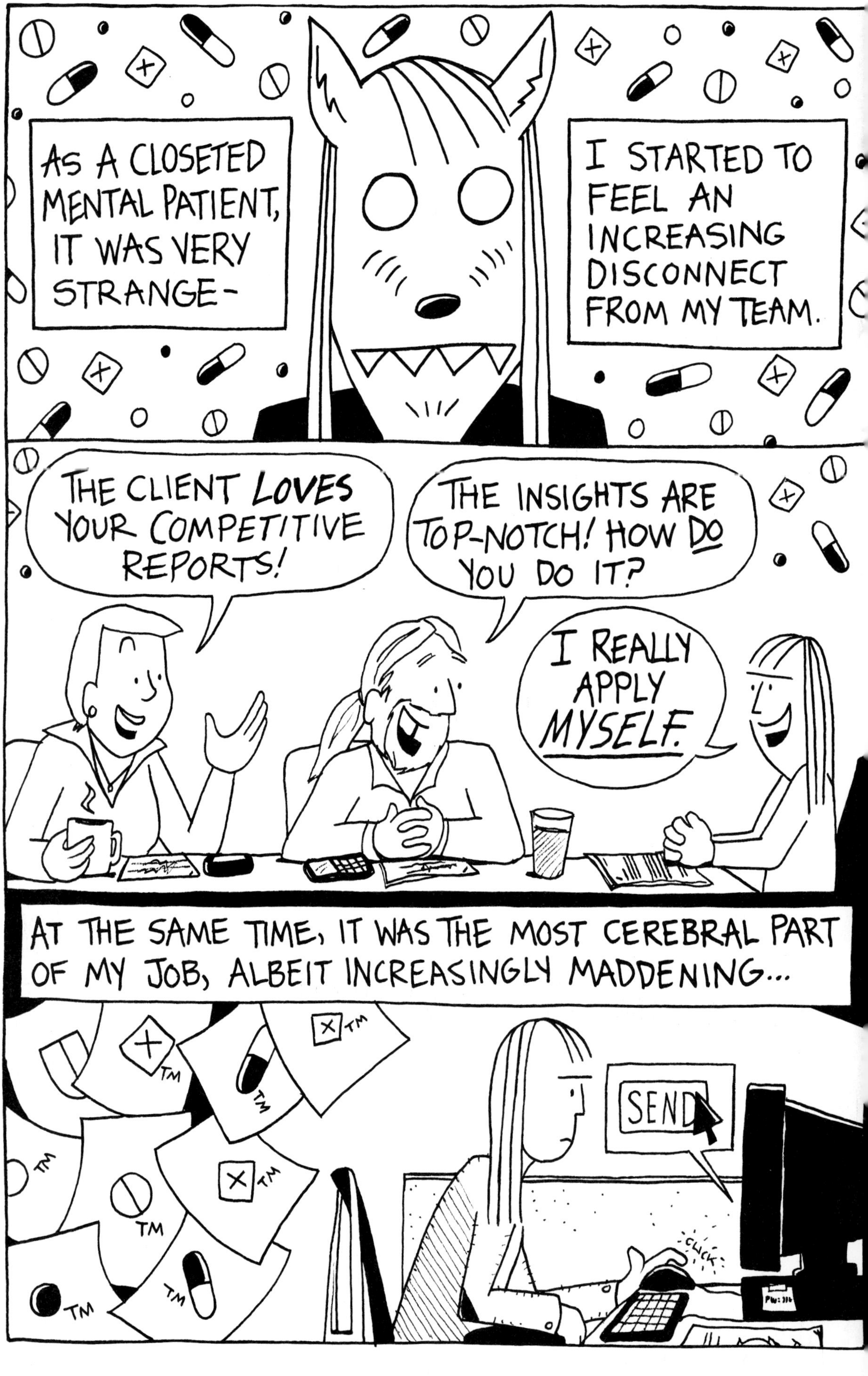
AS A CLOSETED MENTAL PATIENT, IT WAS VERY STRANGE-
I STARTED TO FEEL AN INCREASING DISCONNECT FROM MY TEAM.
THE CLIENT LOVES YOUR COMPETITIVE REPORTS!
THE INSIGHTS ARE TOP-NOTCH! HOW DO YOU DO IT?
I REALLY APPLY MYSELF.
AT THE SAME TIME, IT WAS THE MOST CEREBRAL PART OF MY JOB, ALBEIT INCREASINGLY MADDENING...
TM
SEND
CLICK

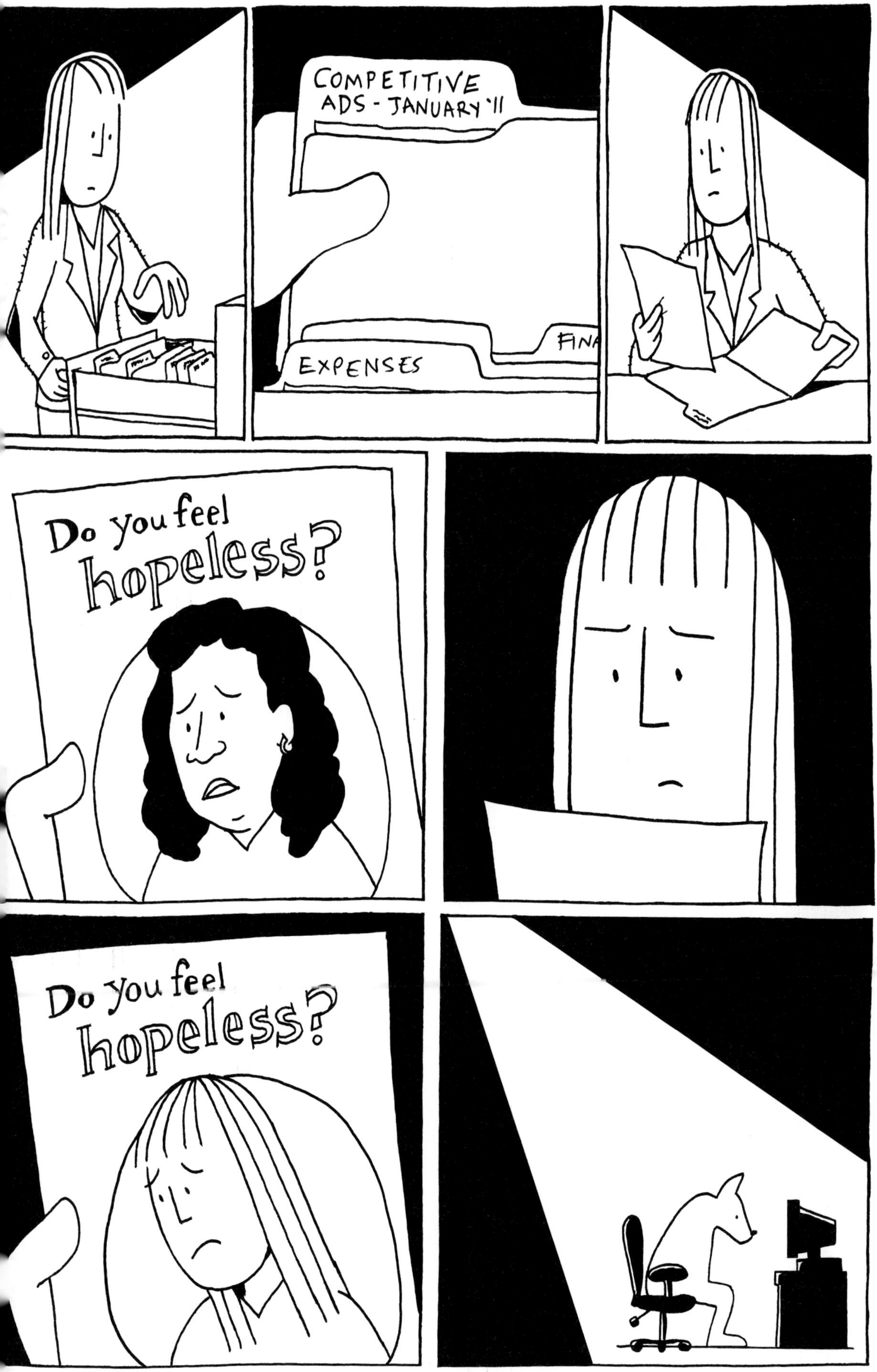
COMPETITIVE ADS - JANUARY '11
EXPENSES
FINA
Do you feel hopeless?
Do you feel hopeless?

CHAPTER FOUR

MIRROR MIRROR

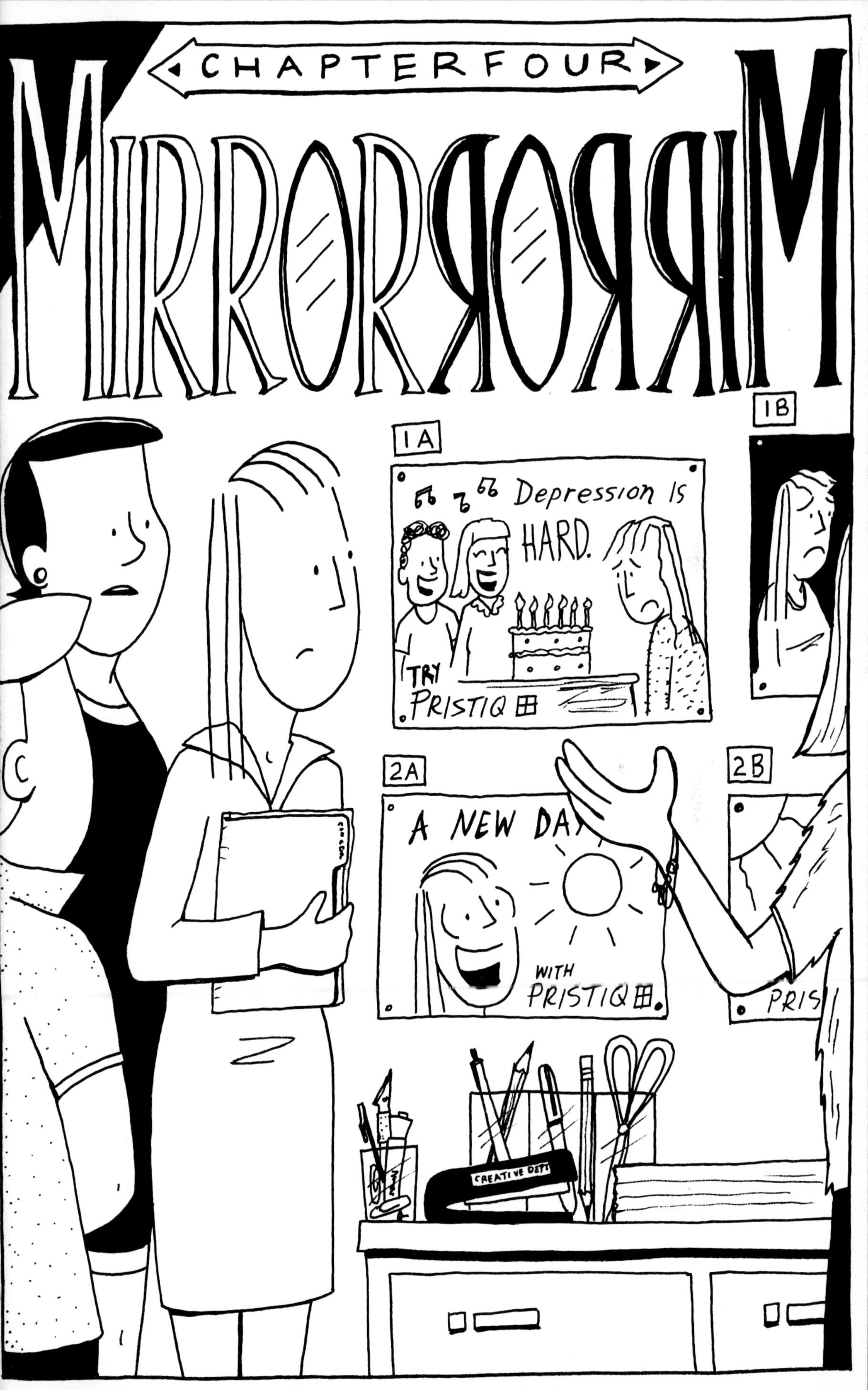

1A
Depression is HARD.
TRY PRISTIQ
1B
2A
A NEW DA
WITH PRISTIQ
2B
PRIS
CREATIVE DEPT

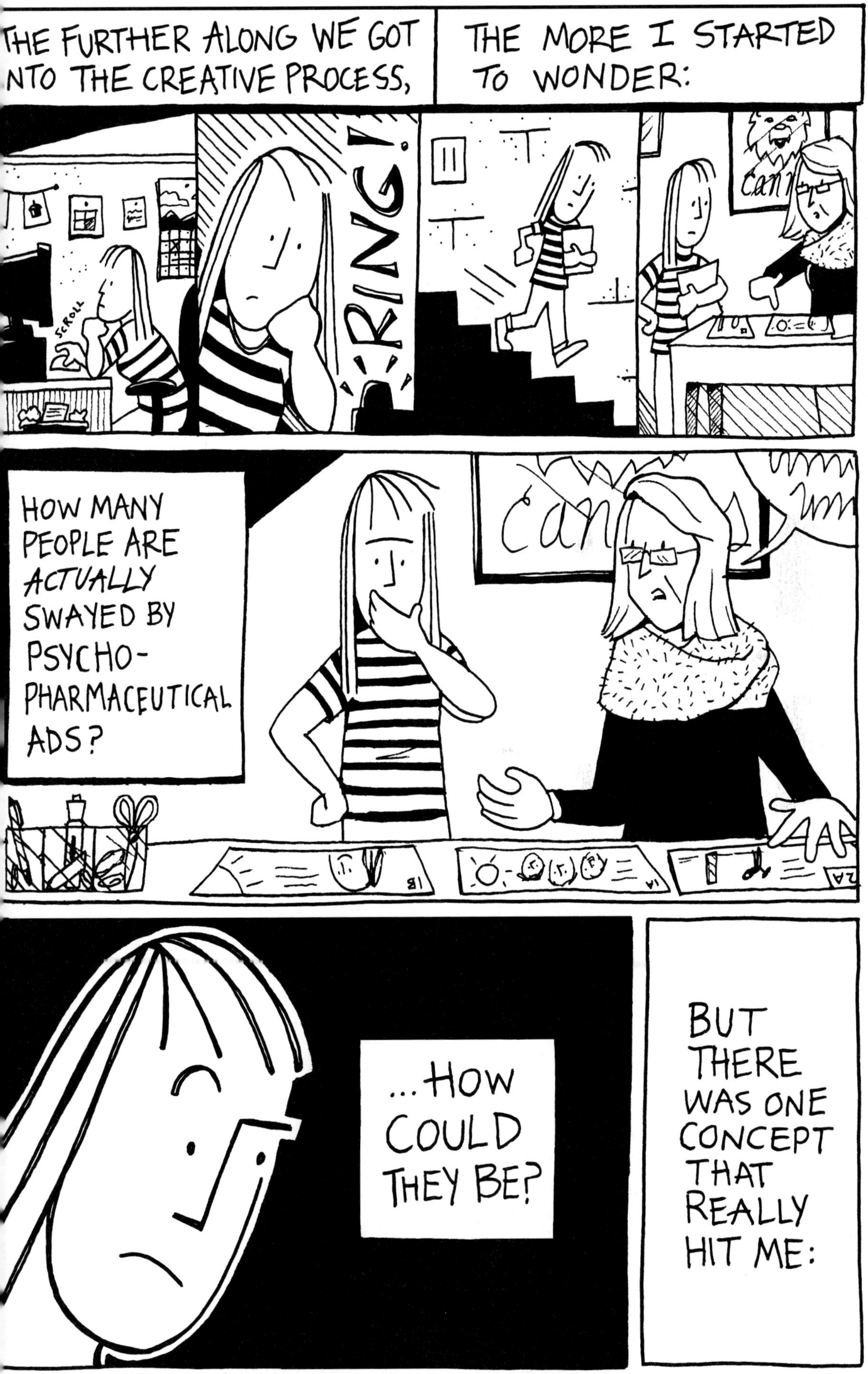
THE FURTHER ALONG WE GOT INTO THE CREATIVE PROCESS,
THE MORE I STARTED TO WONDER:
SCROLL
RING!
HOW MANY PEOPLE ARE *ACTUALLY* SWAYED BY PSYCHO-PHARMACEUTICAL ADS?
...HOW COULD THEY BE?
BUT THERE WAS ONE CONCEPT THAT REALLY HIT ME:

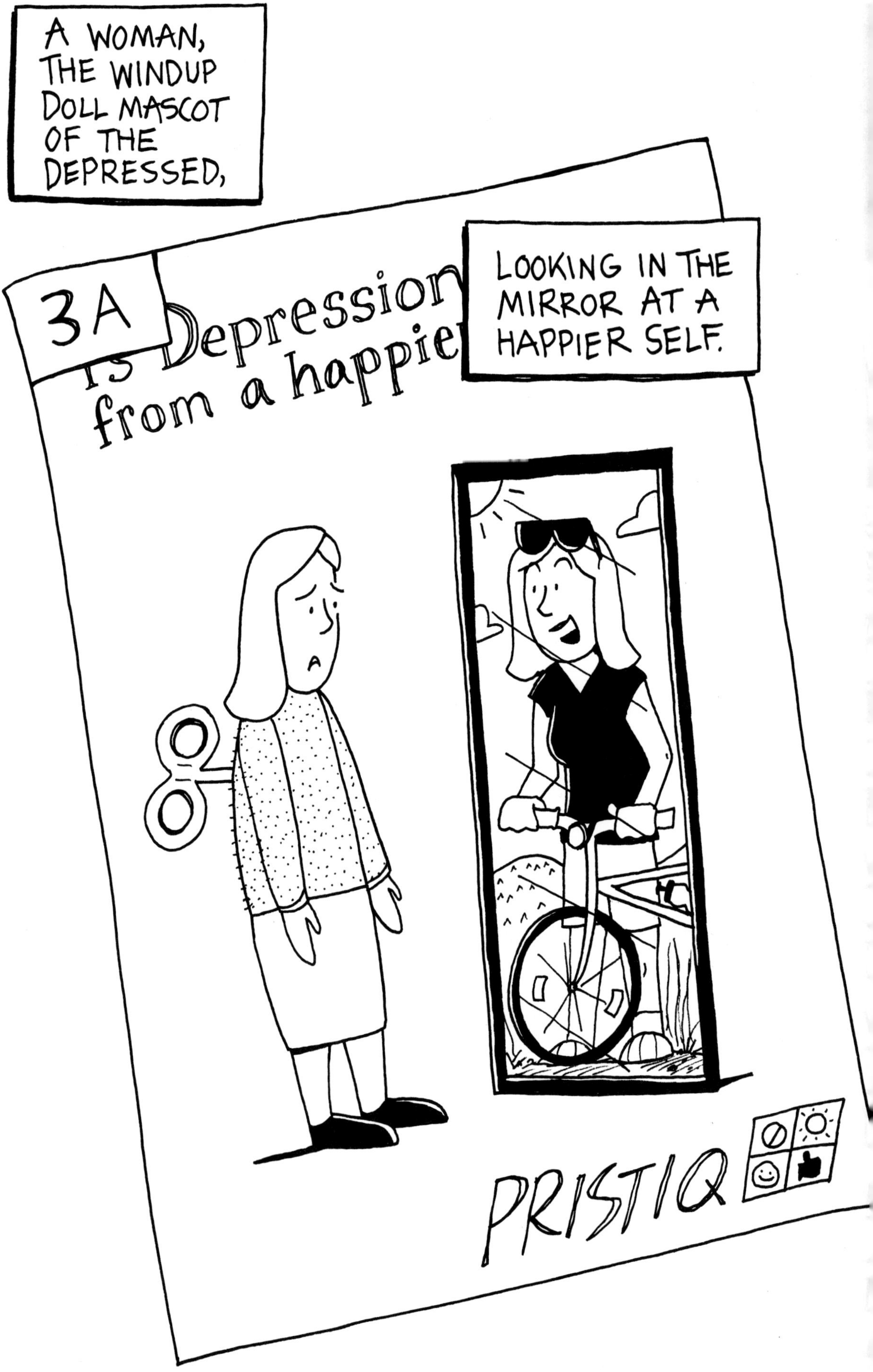
A WOMAN, THE WINDUP DOLL MASCOT OF THE DEPRESSED,
3A
Depression
from a
LOOKING IN THE MIRROR AT A HAPPIER SELF.
PRISTIQ

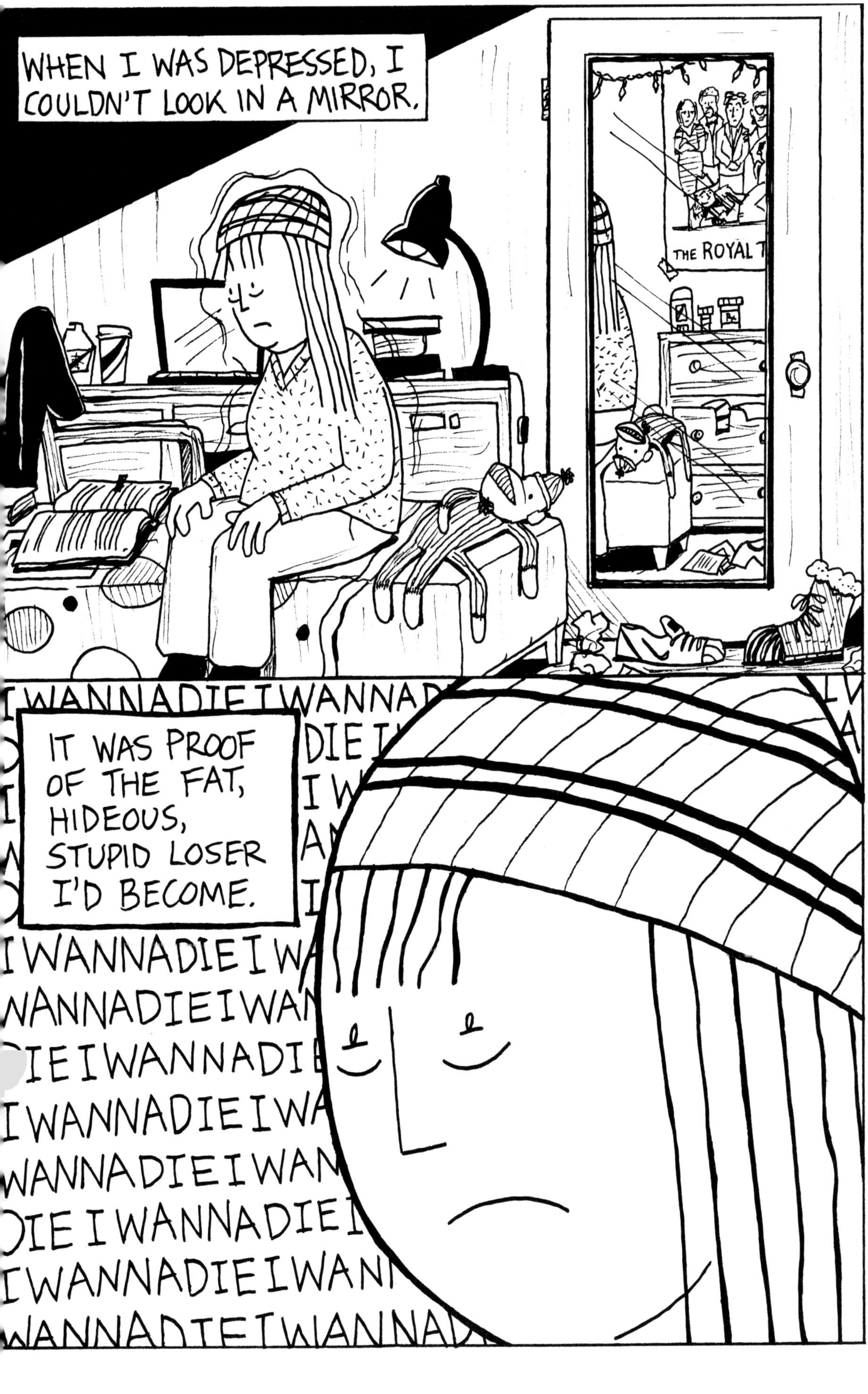
WHEN I WAS DEPRESSED, I COULDN'T LOOK IN A MIRROR.
THE ROYAL T
IT WAS PROOF OF THE FAT, HIDEOUS, STUPID LOSER I'D BECOME.
IWANNADIEIWANNAD
IWANNADIEIWA
WANNADIEIWAN
IEIWANNADIE
IWANNADIEIWA
WANNADIEIWAN
IEIWANNADIEI
IWANNADIEIWAN
WANNADIEIWANNAD

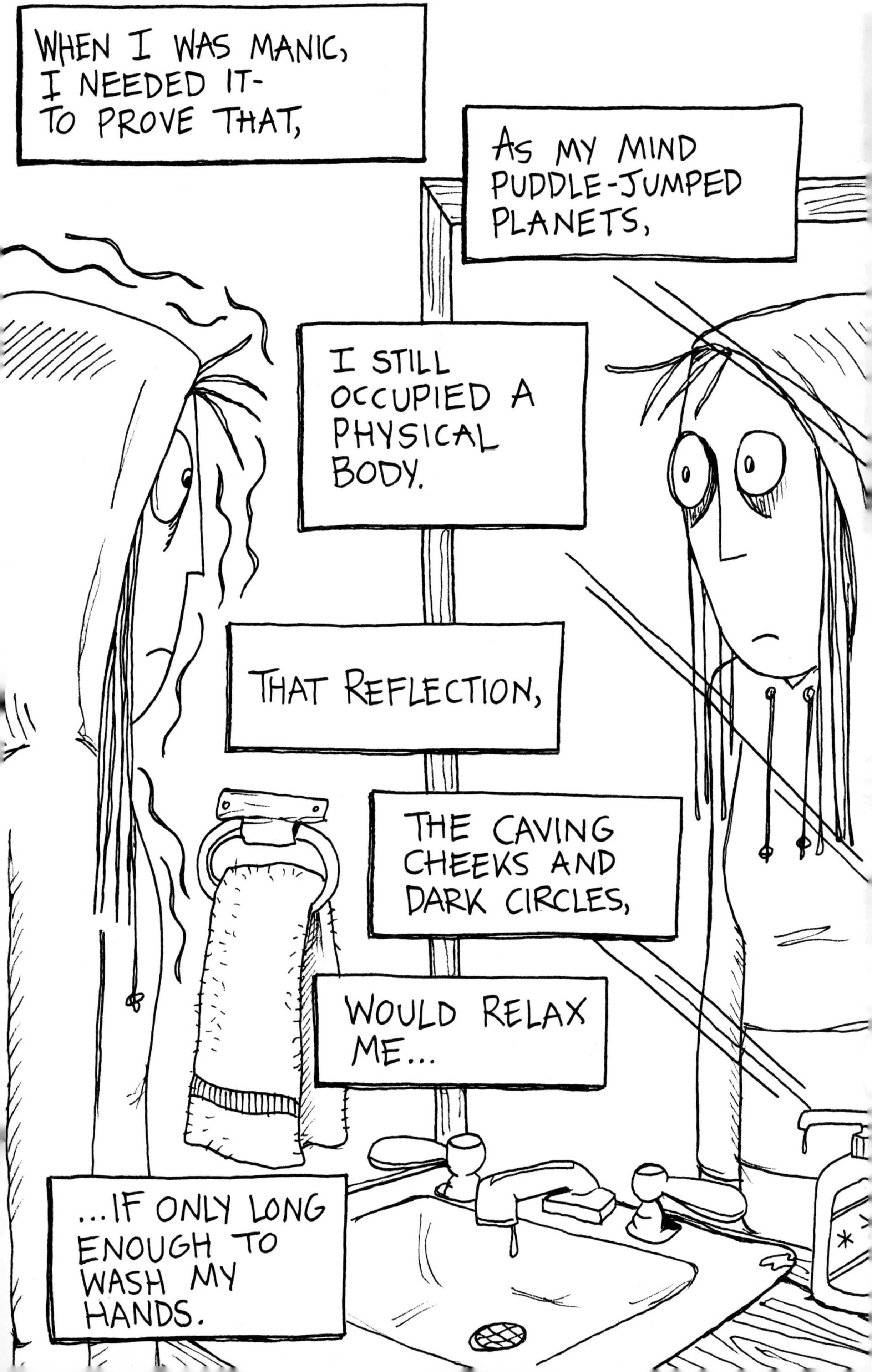
WHEN I WAS MANIC, I NEEDED IT- TO PROVE THAT,
AS MY MIND PUDDLE-JUMPED PLANETS,
I STILL OCCUPIED A PHYSICAL BODY.
THAT REFLECTION,
THE CAVING CHEEKS AND DARK CIRCLES,
WOULD RELAX ME...
...IF ONLY LONG ENOUGH TO WASH MY HANDS.

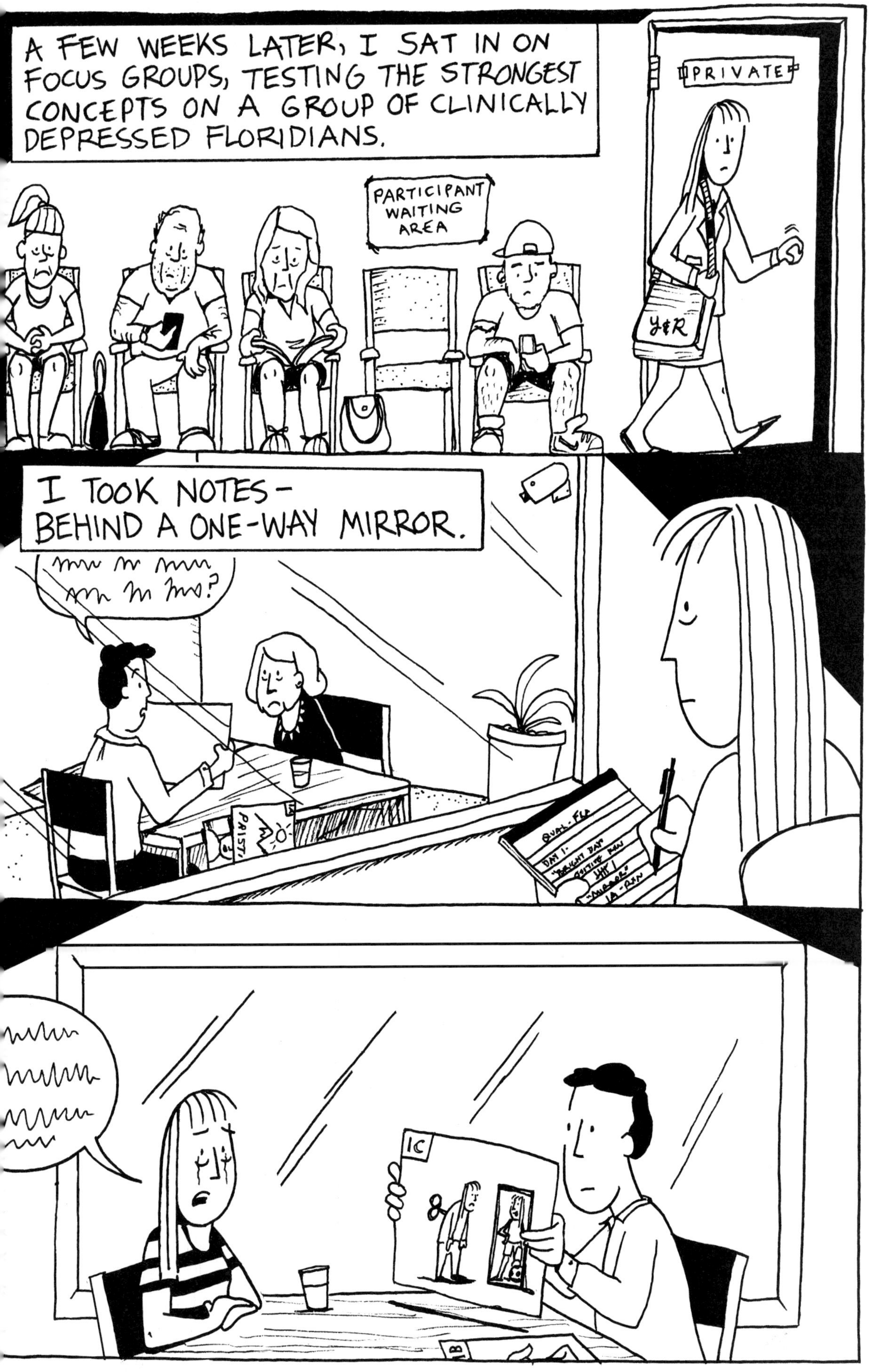
A FEW WEEKS LATER, I SAT IN ON FOCUS GROUPS, TESTING THE STRONGEST CONCEPTS ON A GROUP OF CLINICALLY DEPRESSED FLORIDIANS.
PRIVATE
PARTICIPANT WAITING AREA
Y&R
I TOOK NOTES—BEHIND A ONE-WAY MIRROR.
1C

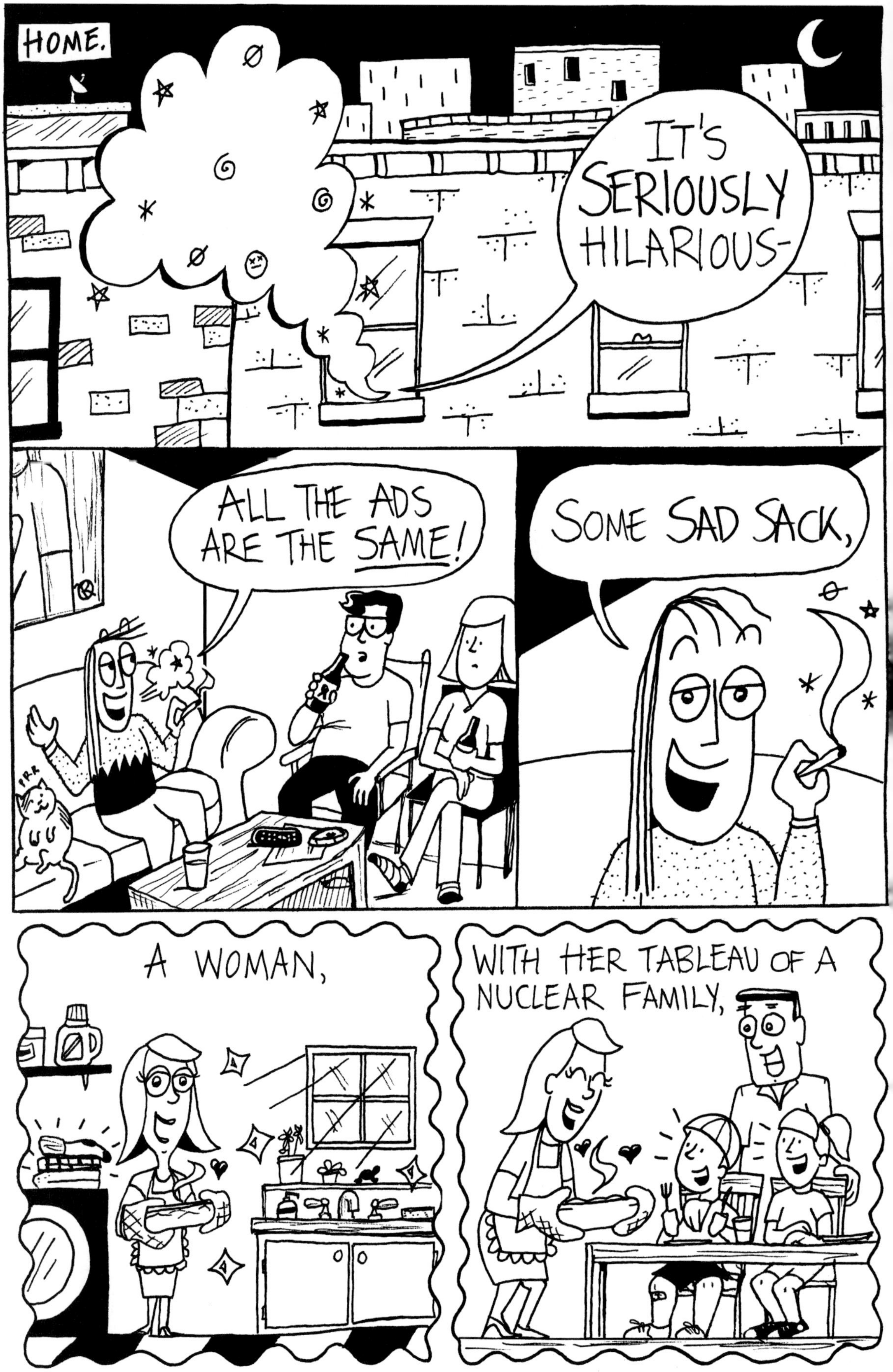
HOME.
IT'S SERIOUSLY HILARIOUS-
ALL THE ADS ARE THE SAME!
SOME SAD SACK,
A WOMAN,
WITH HER TABLEAU OF A NUCLEAR FAMILY,

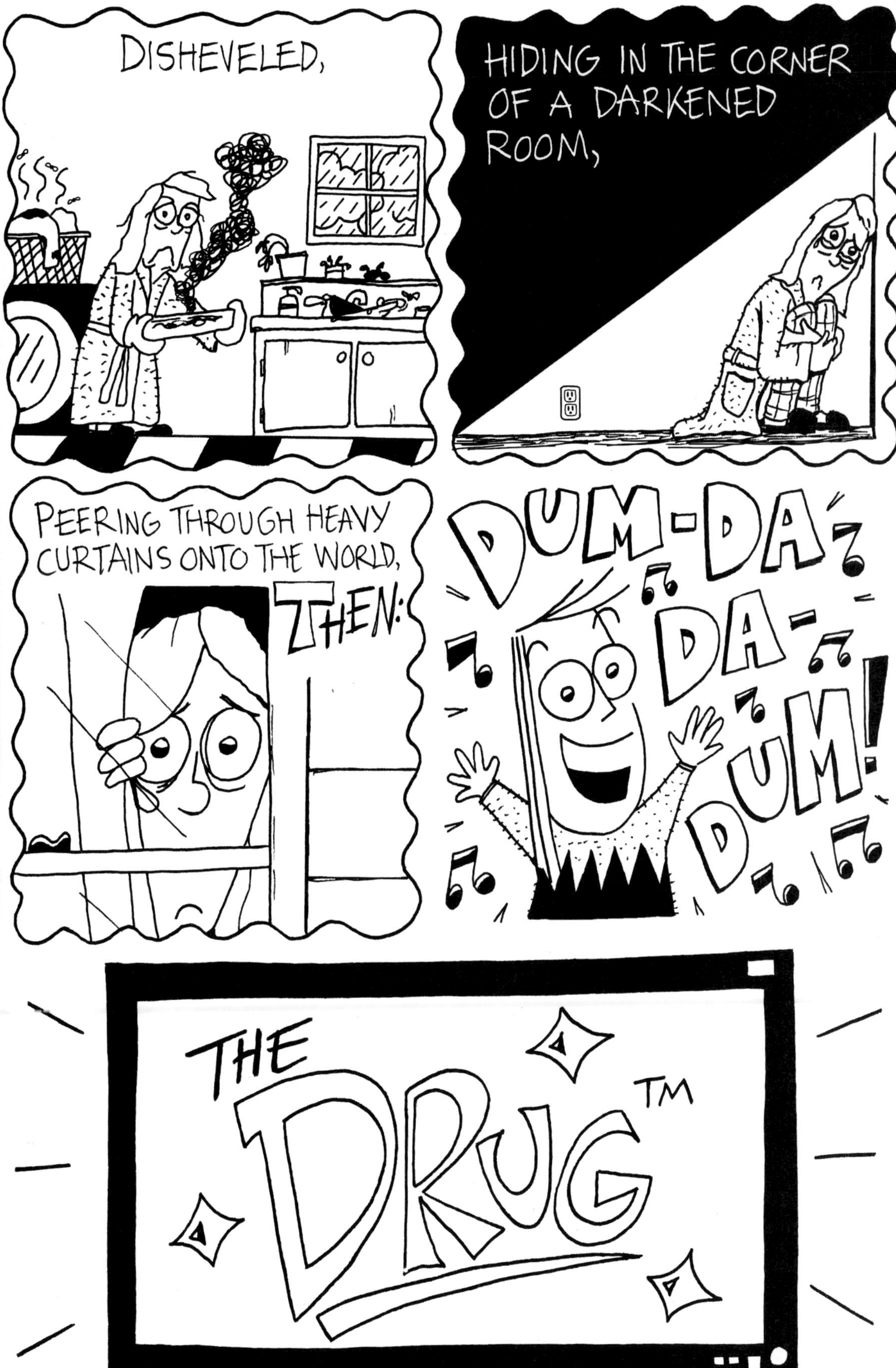
DISHEVELED,
HIDING IN THE CORNER OF A DARKENED ROOM,
PEERING THROUGH HEAVY CURTAINS ONTO THE WORLD,
THEN:
DUM-DA-DA-DUM!
THE DRUG™

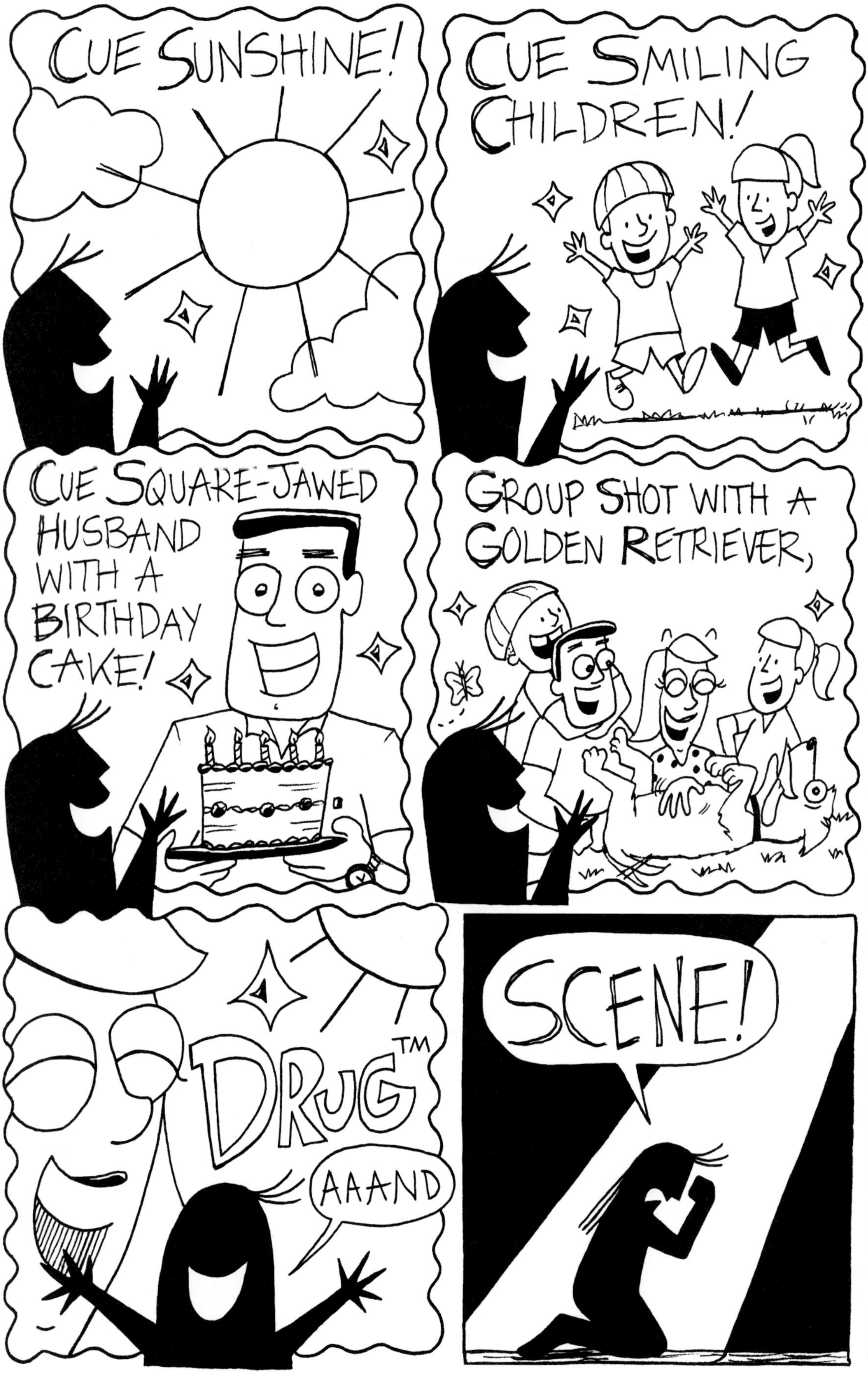
CUE SUNSHINE!
CUE SMILING CHILDREN!
CUE SQUARE-JAWED HUSBAND WITH A BIRTHDAY CAKE!
GROUP SHOT WITH A GOLDEN RETRIEVER,
DRUG™
AAAND
SCENE!

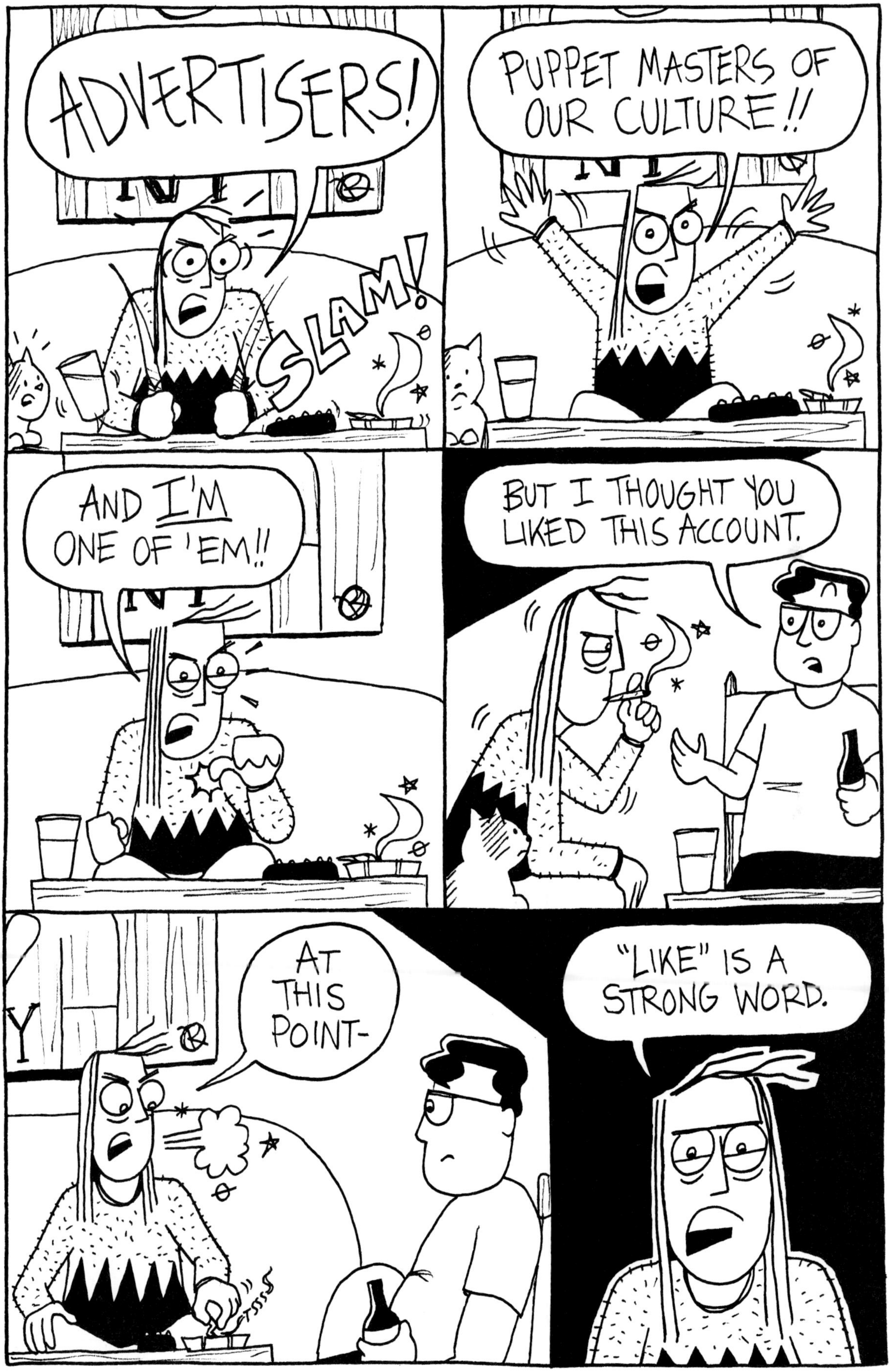
ADVERTISERS!
SLAM!
PUPPET MASTERS OF OUR CULTURE!!
AND I'M ONE OF 'EM!!
BUT I THOUGHT YOU LIKED THIS ACCOUNT.
AT THIS POINT-
"LIKE" IS A STRONG WORD.

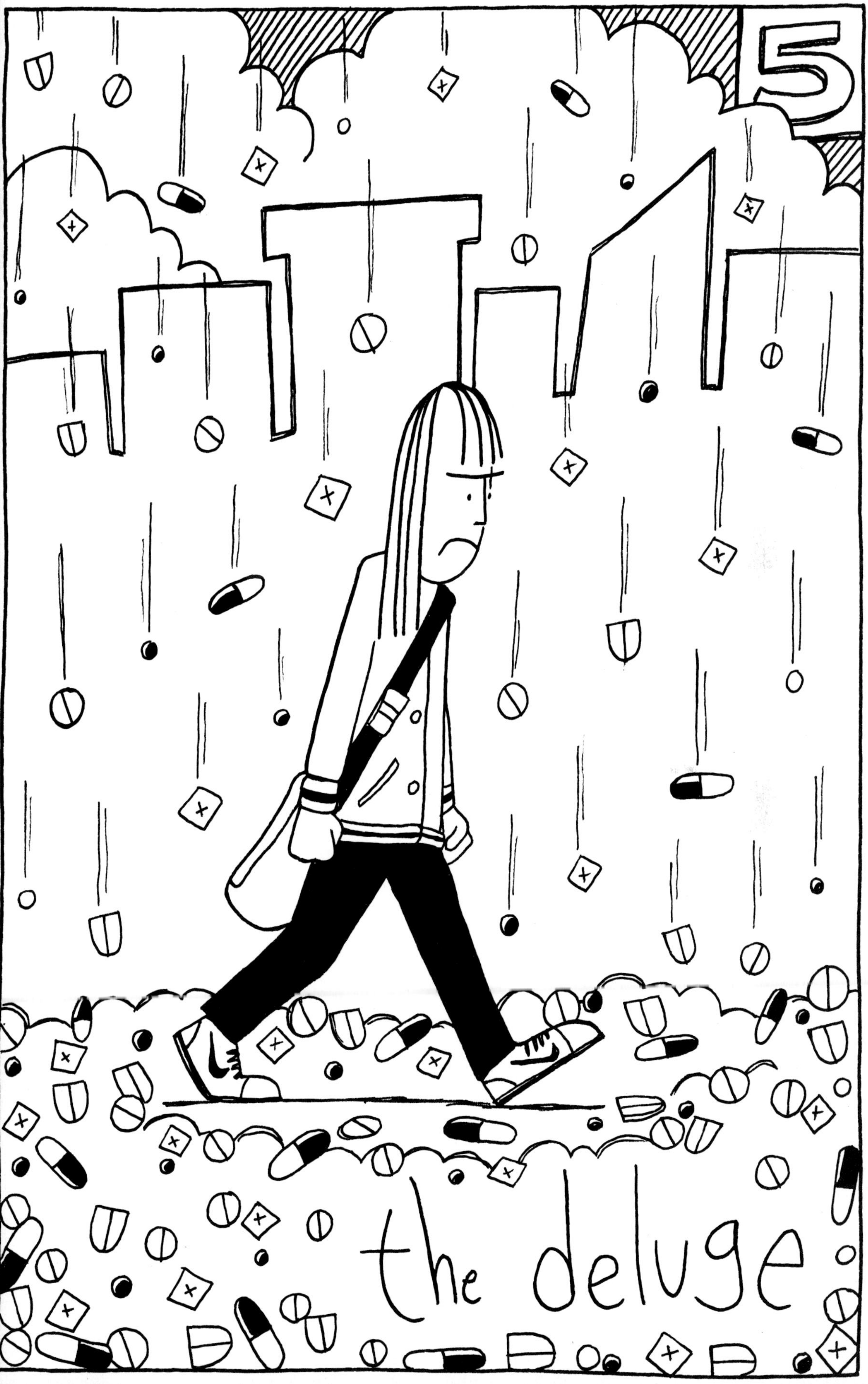
5
the deluge

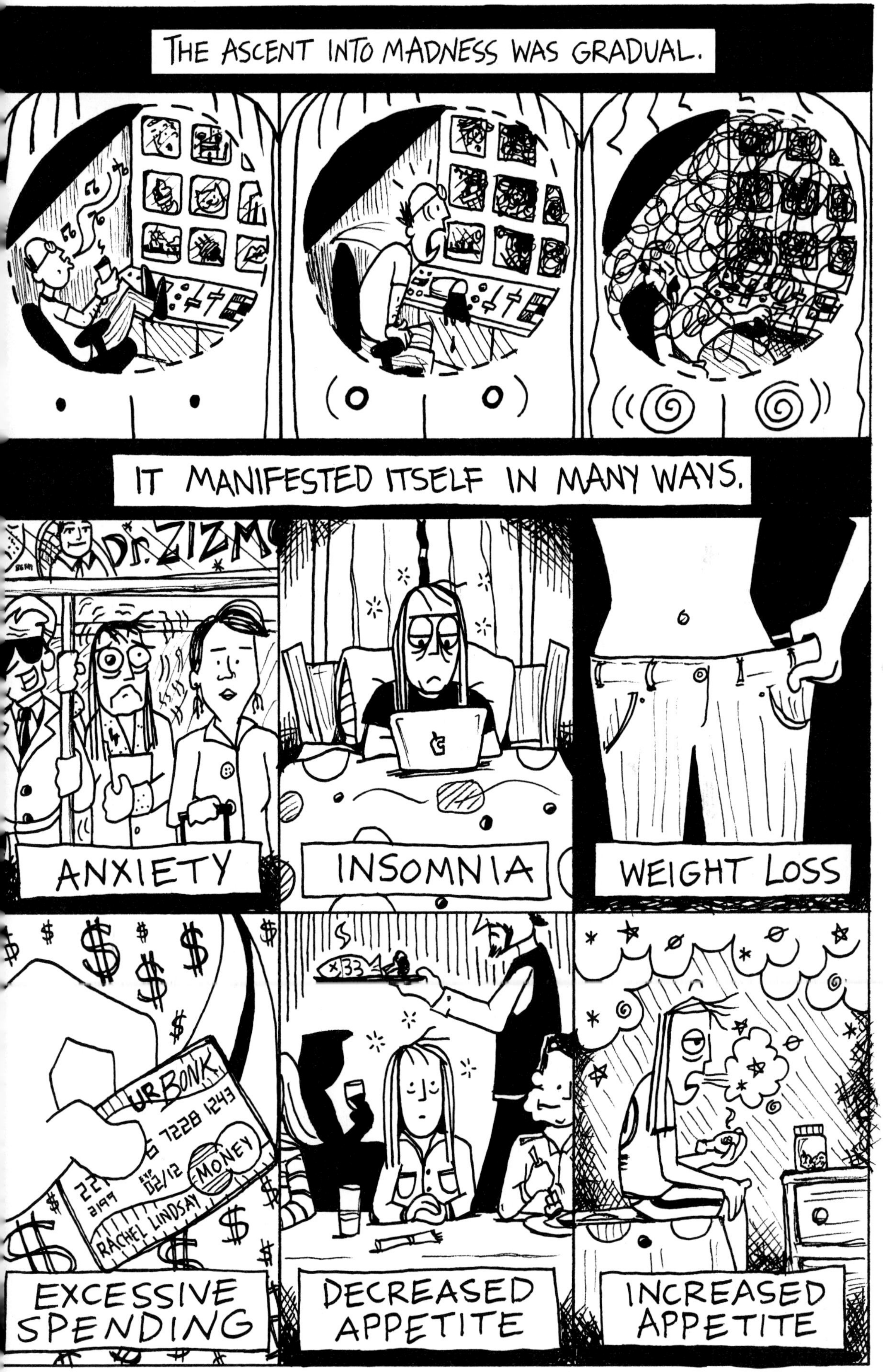
THE ASCENT INTO MADNESS WAS GRADUAL.
IT MANIFESTED ITSELF IN MANY WAYS.
ANXIETY
INSOMNIA
WEIGHT LOSS
URBONK
7228 1243
EXP 02/12
MONEY
RACHEL LINDSAY
EXCESSIVE SPENDING
DECREASED APPETITE
INCREASED APPETITE

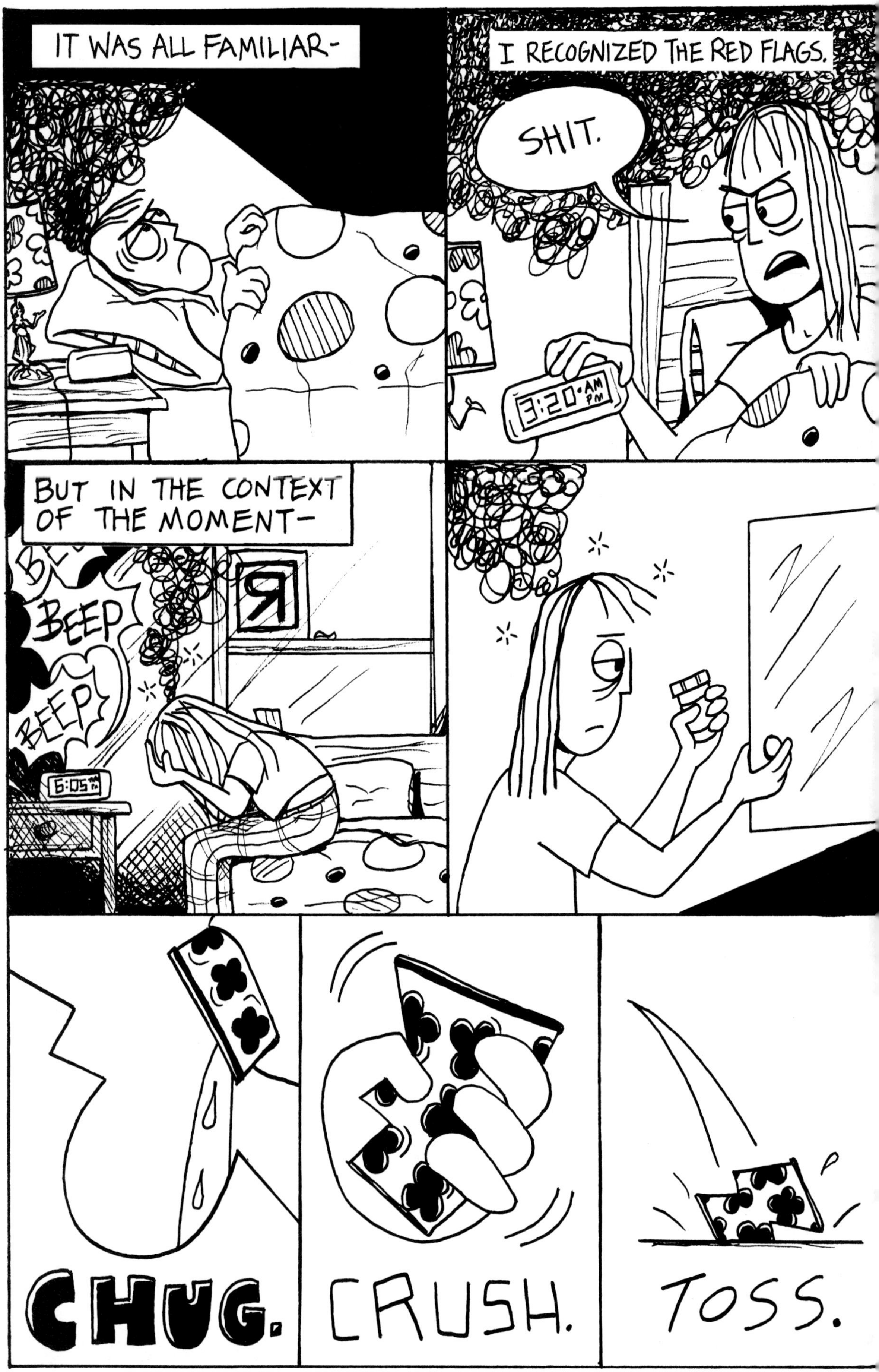
IT WAS ALL FAMILIAR-
I RECOGNIZED THE RED FLAGS.
SHIT.
3:20 AM PM
BUT IN THE CONTEXT OF THE MOMENT-
BEEP
BEEP
6:05
CHUG.
CRUSH.
TOSS.

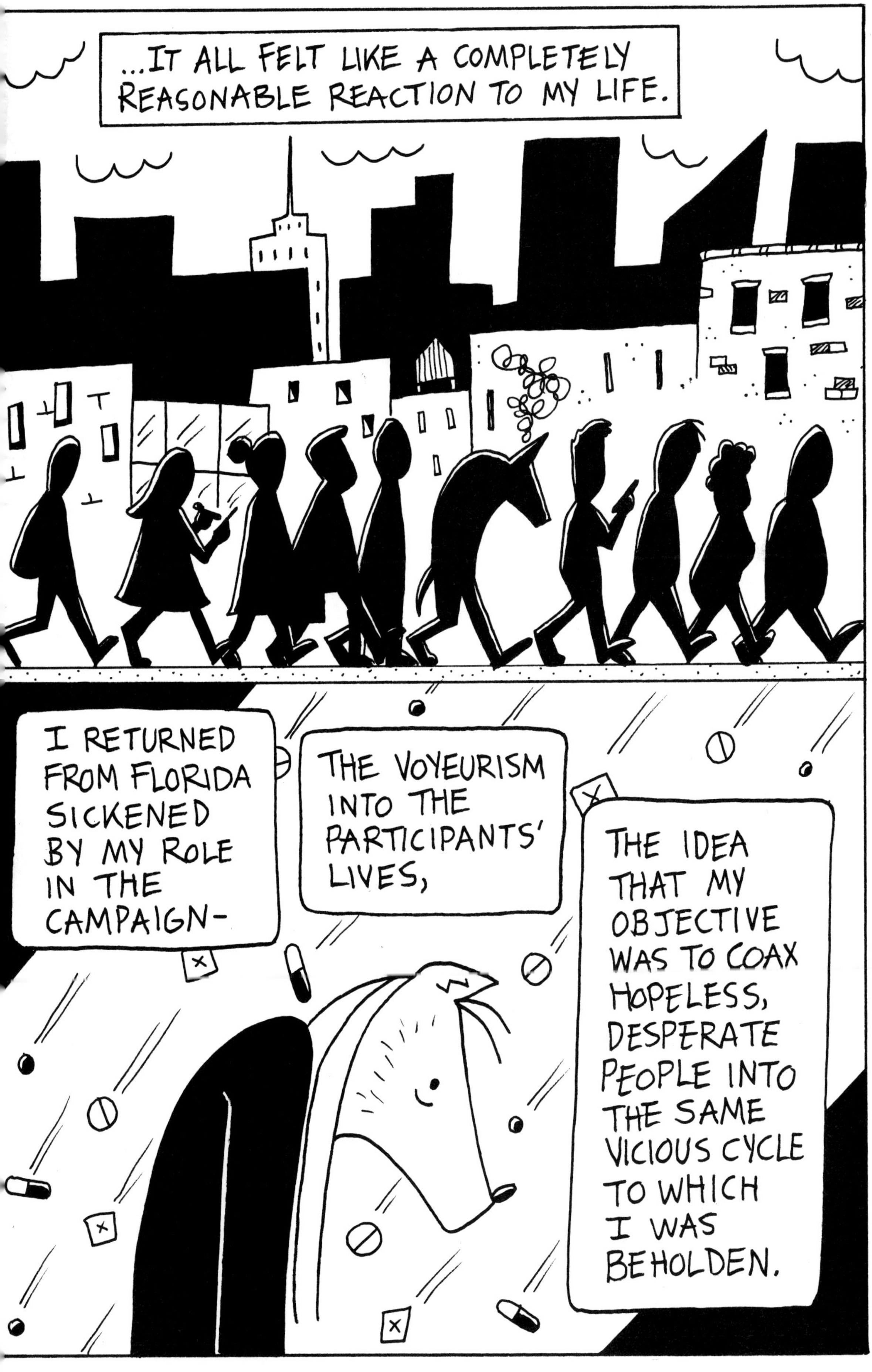
...IT ALL FELT LIKE A COMPLETELY REASONABLE REACTION TO MY LIFE.
I RETURNED FROM FLORIDA SICKENED BY MY ROLE IN THE CAMPAIGN-
THE VOYEURISM INTO THE PARTICIPANTS' LIVES,
THE IDEA THAT MY OBJECTIVE WAS TO COAX HOPELESS, DESPERATE PEOPLE INTO THE SAME VICIOUS CYCLE TO WHICH I WAS BEHOLDEN.

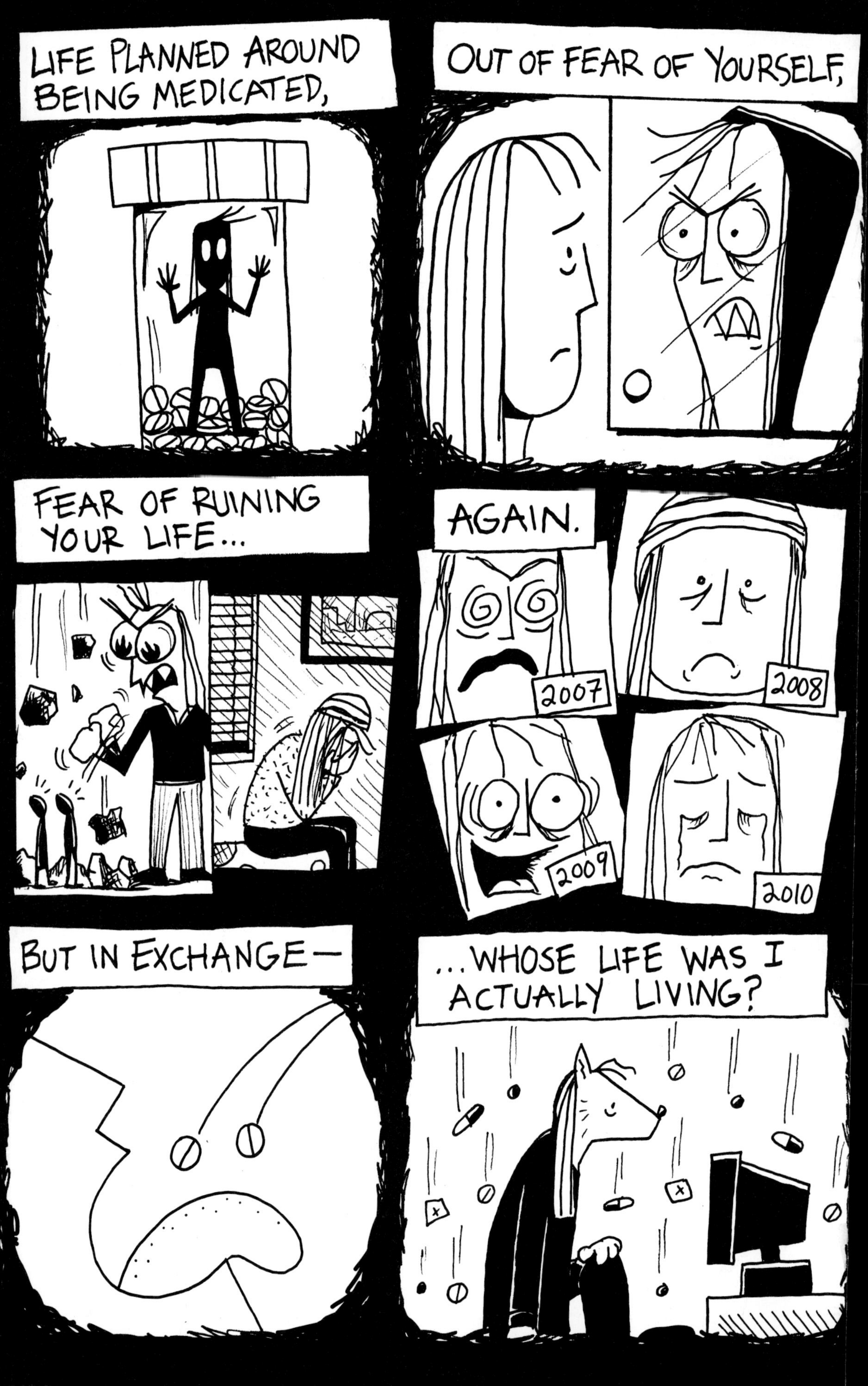
LIFE PLANNED AROUND BEING MEDICATED,
OUT OF FEAR OF YOURSELF,
FEAR OF RUINING YOUR LIFE...
AGAIN.
2007
2008
2009
2010
BUT IN EXCHANGE—
...WHOSE LIFE WAS I ACTUALLY LIVING?

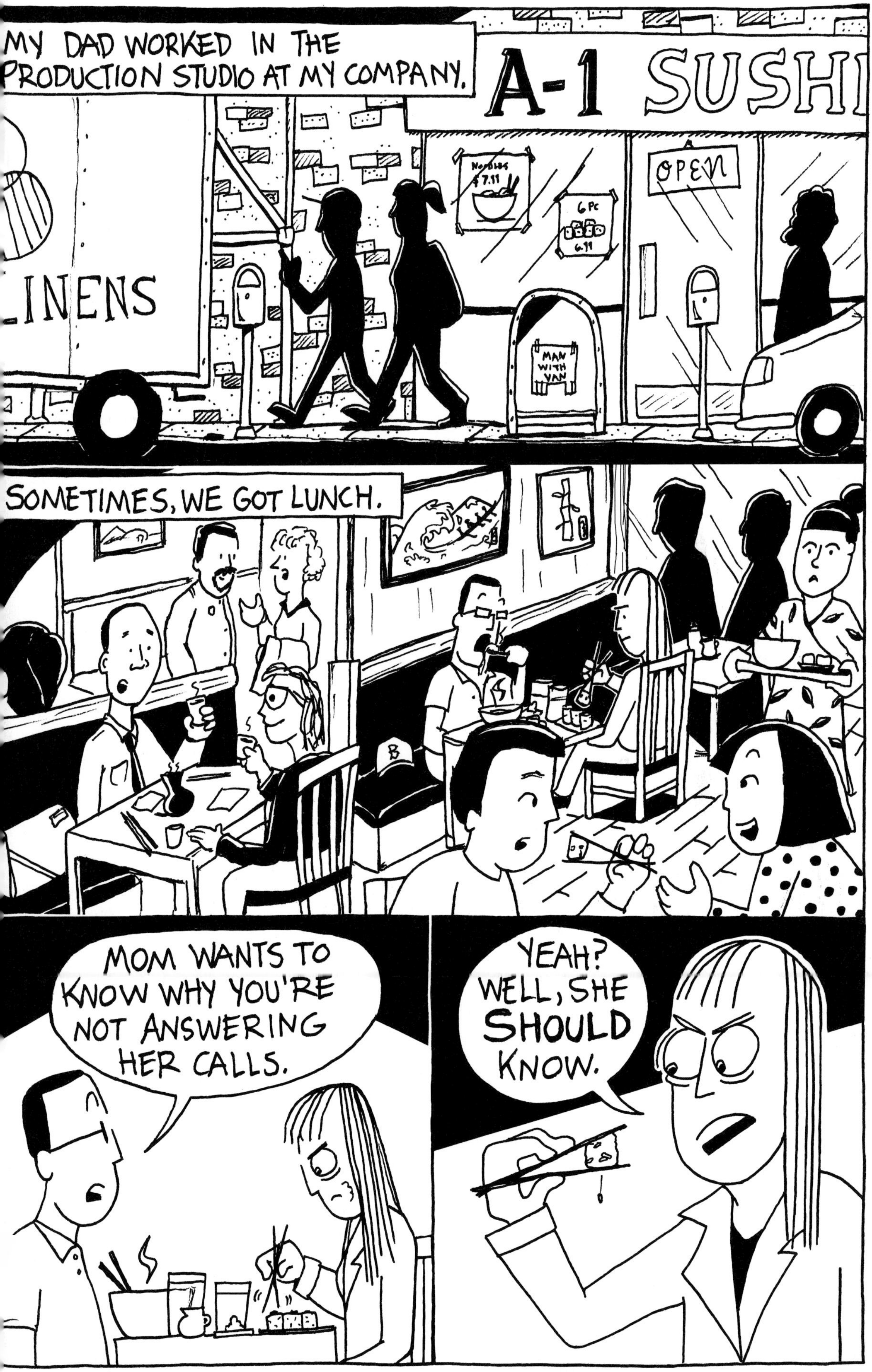
MY DAD WORKED IN THE PRODUCTION STUDIO AT MY COMPANY.
A-1 SUSHI
OPEN
LINENS
MAN WITH VAN
SOMETIMES, WE GOT LUNCH.
MOM WANTS TO KNOW WHY YOU'RE NOT ANSWERING HER CALLS.
YEAH? WELL, SHE SHOULD KNOW.

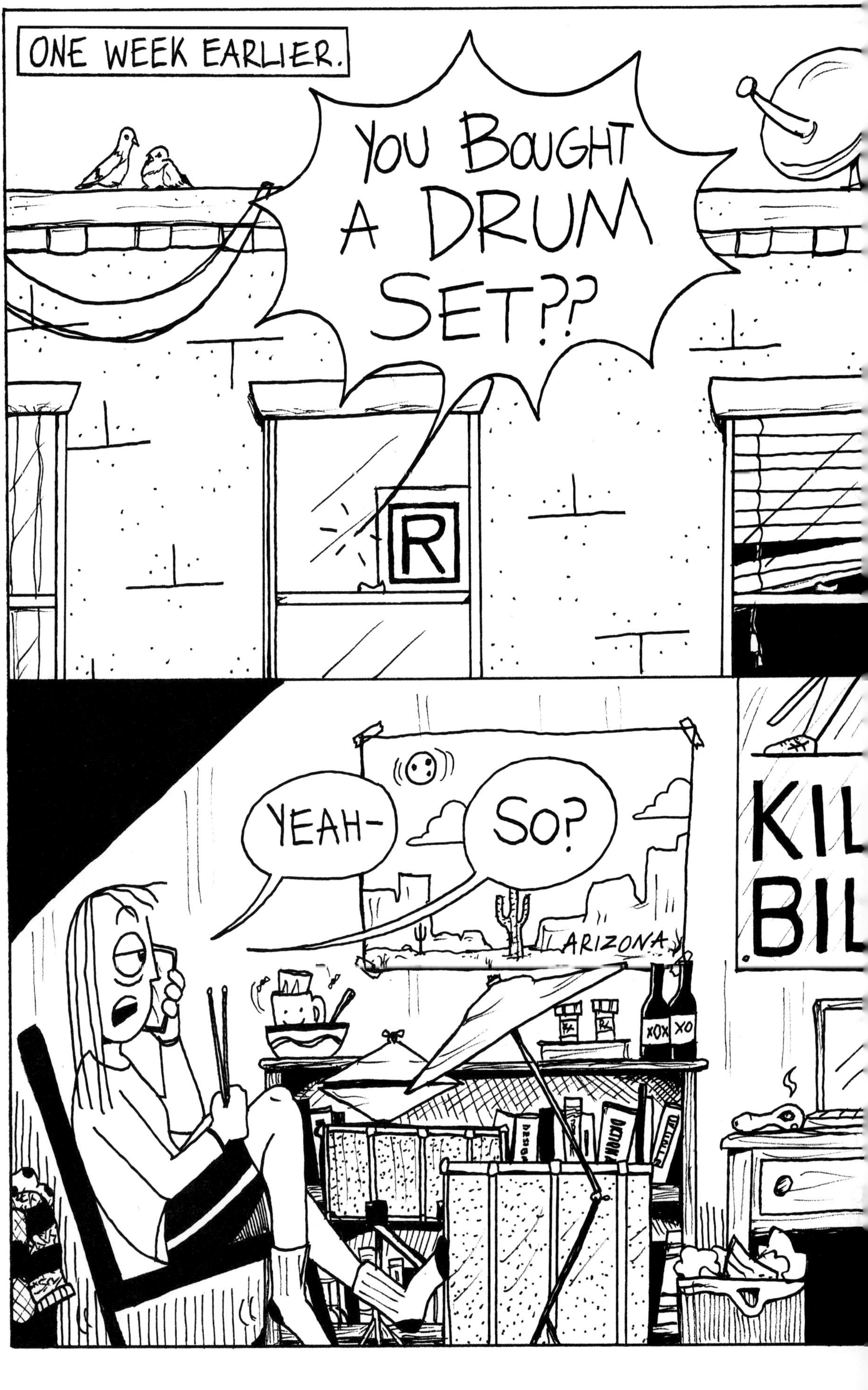
ONE WEEK EARLIER.
YOU BOUGHT A DRUM SET??
R
YEAH-
SO?
ARIZONA

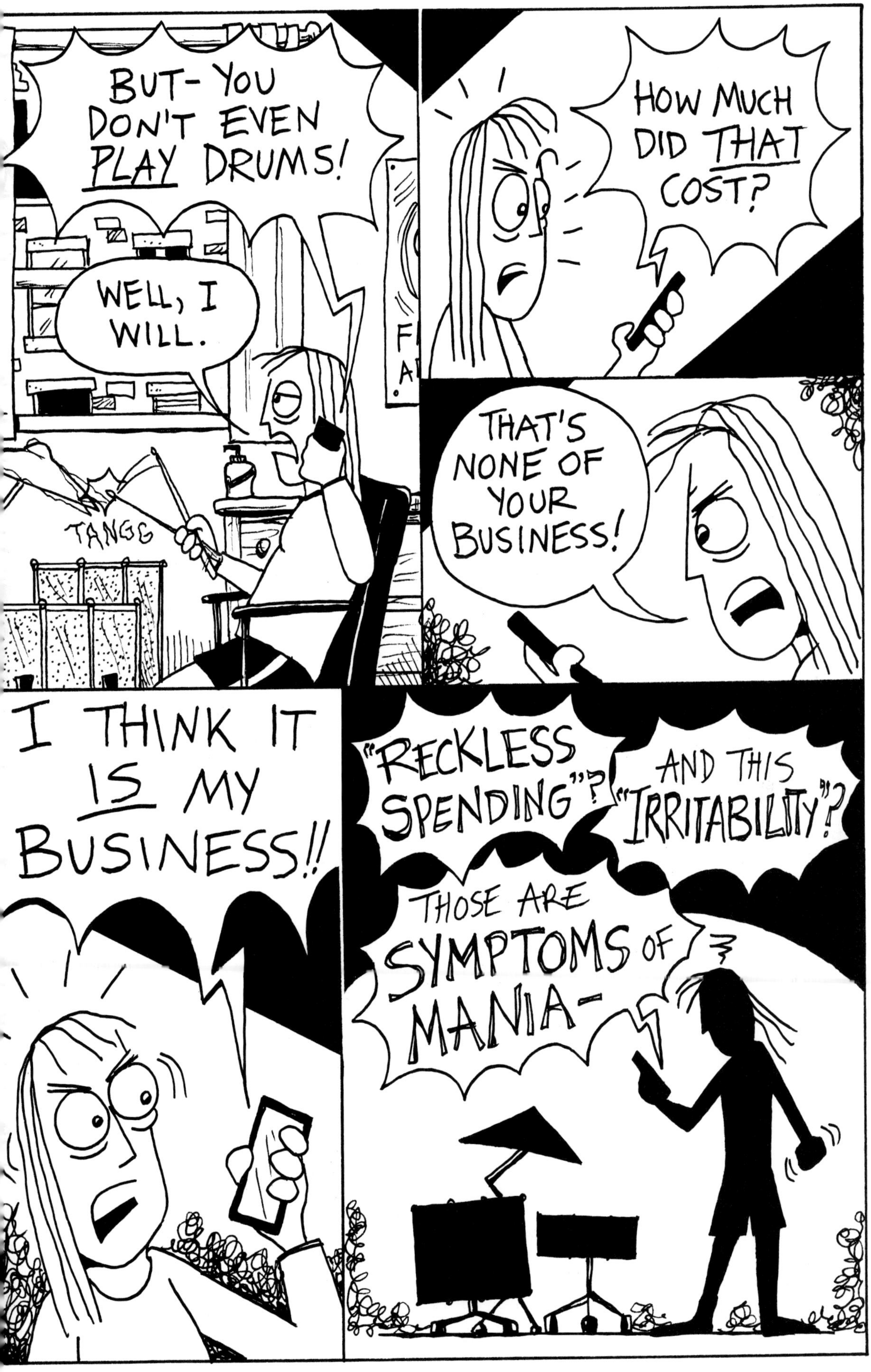
BUT- YOU DON'T EVEN PLAY DRUMS!
WELL, I WILL.
TANGG
HOW MUCH DID THAT COST?
THAT'S NONE OF YOUR BUSINESS!
I THINK IT IS MY BUSINESS!!
"RECKLESS SPENDING"?
AND THIS "IRRITABILITY"?
THOSE ARE SYMPTOMS OF MANIA-

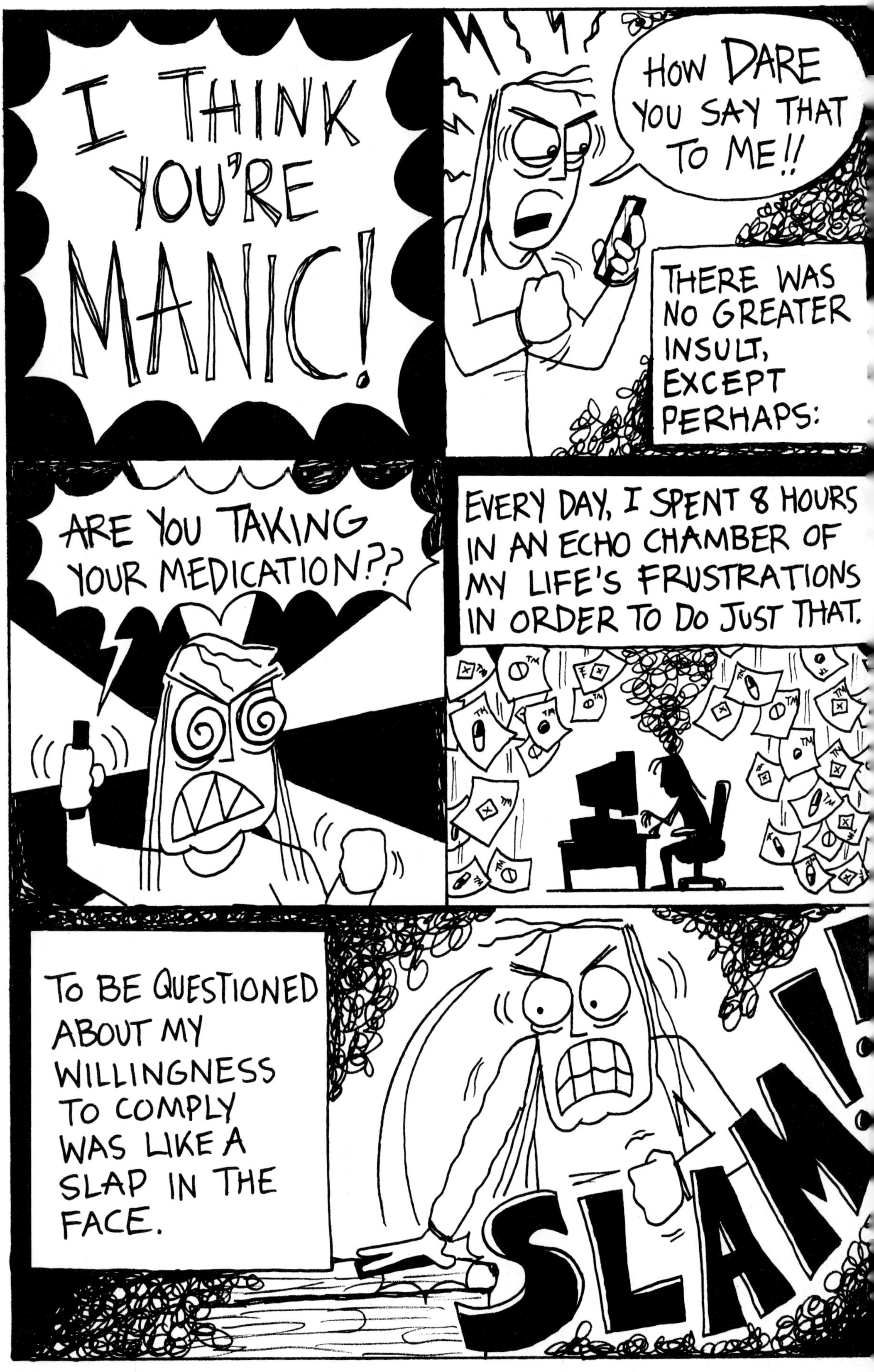
I THINK YOU'RE MANIC!
HOW DARE YOU SAY THAT TO ME!!
THERE WAS NO GREATER INSULT, EXCEPT PERHAPS:
ARE YOU TAKING YOUR MEDICATION??
EVERY DAY, I SPENT 8 HOURS IN AN ECHO CHAMBER OF MY LIFE'S FRUSTRATIONS IN ORDER TO DO JUST THAT.
TO BE QUESTIONED ABOUT MY WILLINGNESS TO COMPLY WAS LIKE A SLAP IN THE FACE.
SLAM!!

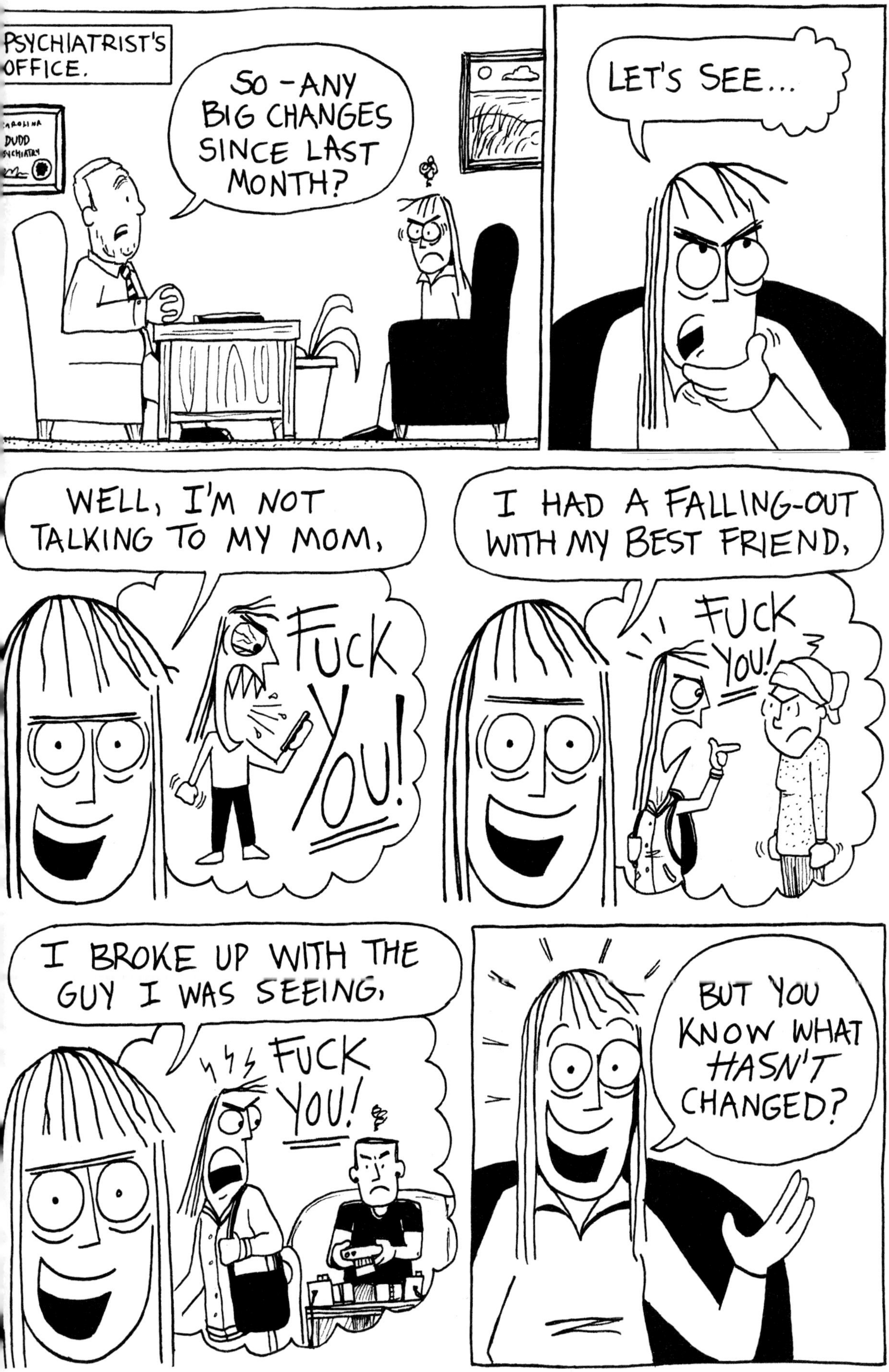
PSYCHIATRIST'S OFFICE.
SO - ANY BIG CHANGES SINCE LAST MONTH?
LET'S SEE...
WELL, I'M NOT TALKING TO MY MOM,
FUCK YOU!
I HAD A FALLING-OUT WITH MY BEST FRIEND,
FUCK YOU!
I BROKE UP WITH THE GUY I WAS SEEING,
FUCK YOU!
BUT YOU KNOW WHAT *HASN'T* CHANGED?

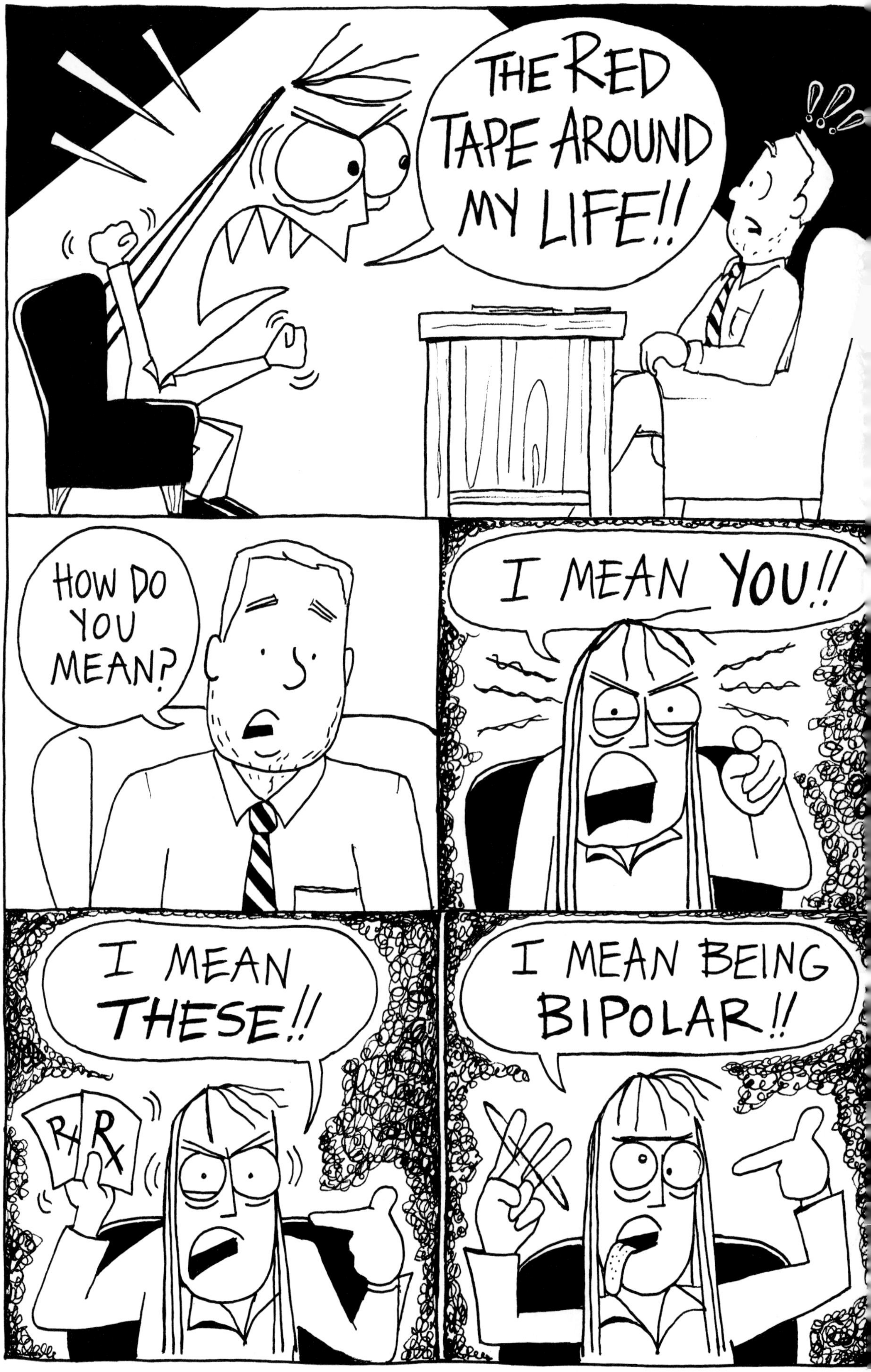
THE RED TAPE AROUND MY LIFE!!
HOW DO YOU MEAN?
I MEAN YOU!!
I MEAN THESE!!
I MEAN BEING BIPOLAR!!

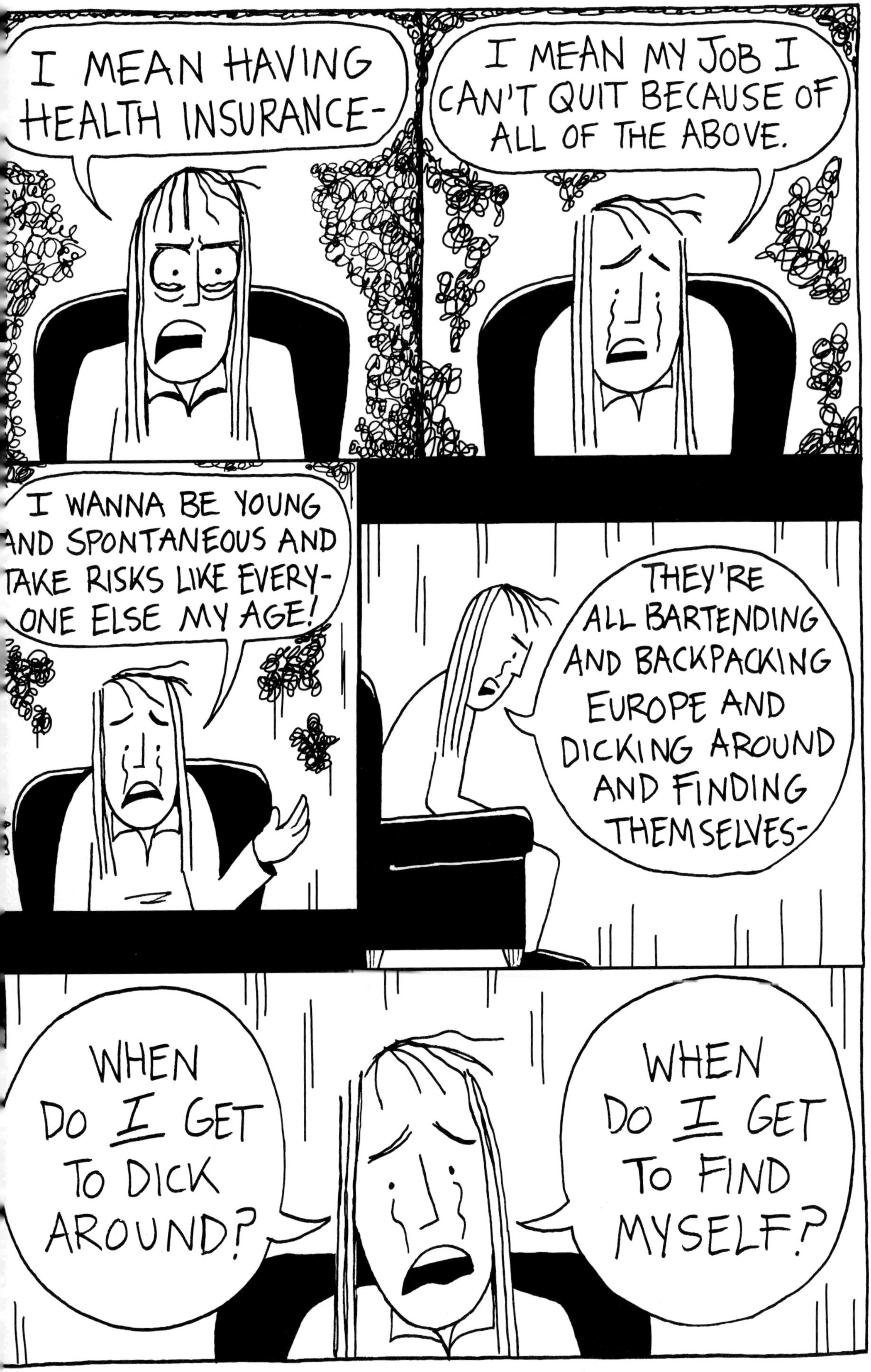
I MEAN HAVING HEALTH INSURANCE-
I MEAN MY JOB I CAN'T QUIT BECAUSE OF ALL OF THE ABOVE.
I WANNA BE YOUNG AND SPONTANEOUS AND TAKE RISKS LIKE EVERY-ONE ELSE MY AGE!
THEY'RE ALL BARTENDING AND BACKPACKING EUROPE AND DICKING AROUND AND FINDING THEMSELVES-
WHEN DO I GET TO DICK AROUND?
WHEN DO I GET TO FIND MYSELF?

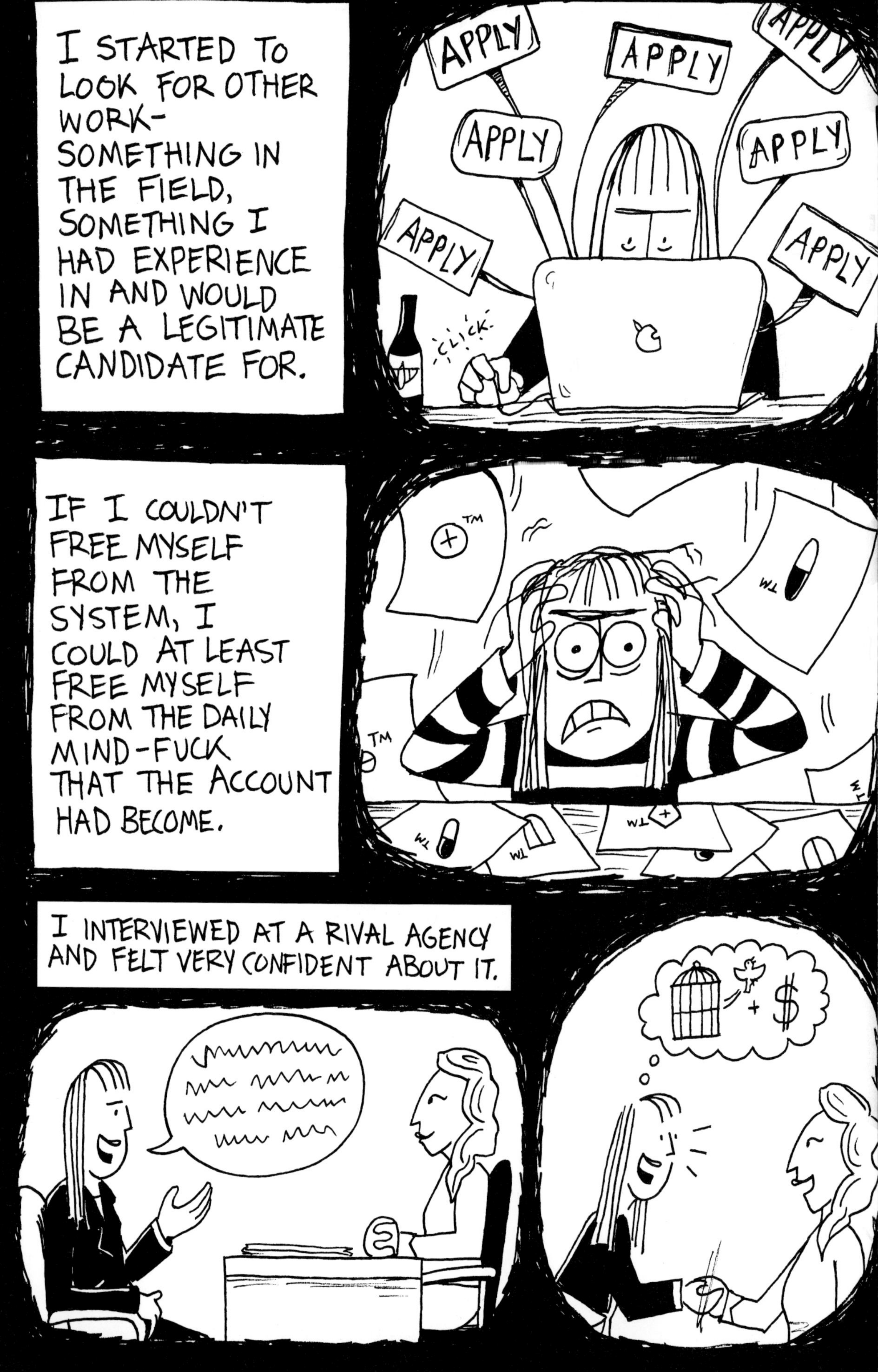

I STARTED TO LOOK FOR OTHER WORK- SOMETHING IN THE FIELD, SOMETHING I HAD EXPERIENCE IN AND WOULD BE A LEGITIMATE CANDIDATE FOR.
APPLY
APPLY
APPLY
APPLY
APPLY
APPLY
APPLY
CLICK
IF I COULDN'T FREE MYSELF FROM THE SYSTEM, I COULD AT LEAST FREE MYSELF FROM THE DAILY MIND-FUCK THAT THE ACCOUNT HAD BECOME.
TM
TM
I INTERVIEWED AT A RIVAL AGENCY AND FELT VERY CONFIDENT ABOUT IT.

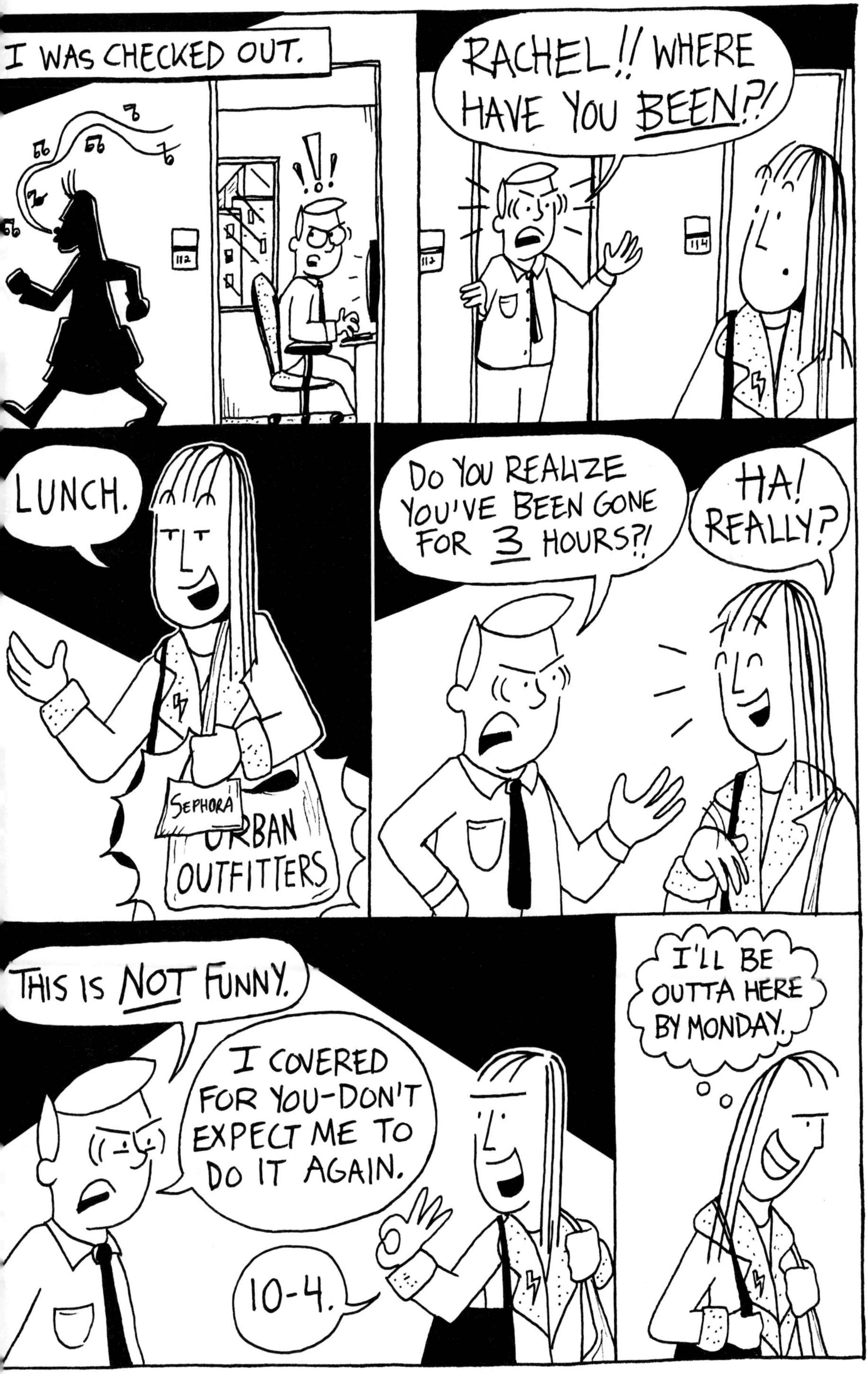
I WAS CHECKED OUT.
!!
112
RACHEL!! WHERE HAVE YOU BEEN?!
112
114
LUNCH.
SEPHORA
URBAN OUTFITTERS
DO YOU REALIZE YOU'VE BEEN GONE FOR 3 HOURS?!
HA! REALLY?
THIS IS NOT FUNNY.
I COVERED FOR YOU-DON'T EXPECT ME TO DO IT AGAIN.
10-4.
I'LL BE OUTTA HERE BY MONDAY.

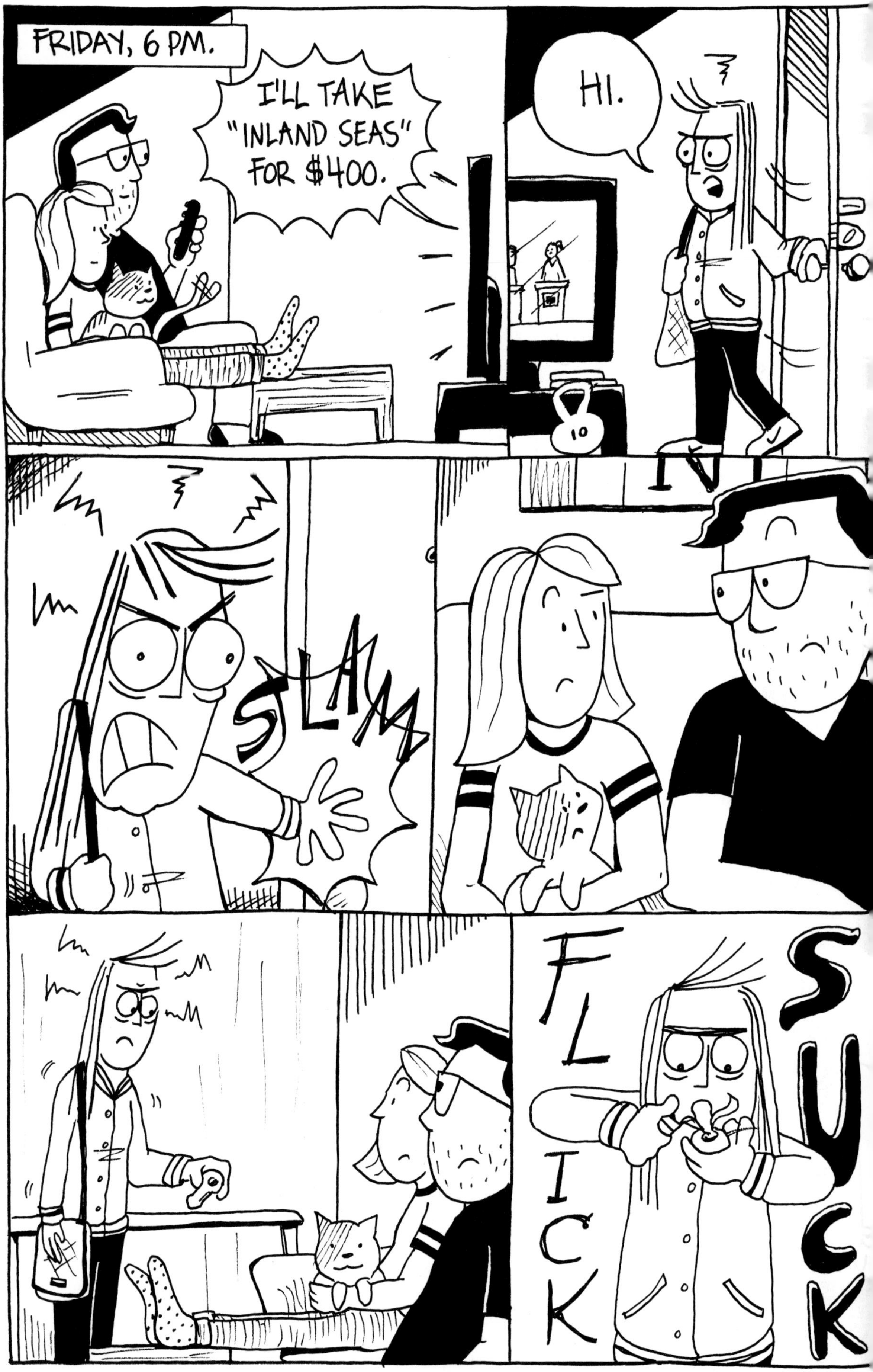
FRIDAY, 6 PM.
I'LL TAKE "INLAND SEAS" FOR $400.
HI.
SLAM
FLICK
SUCK

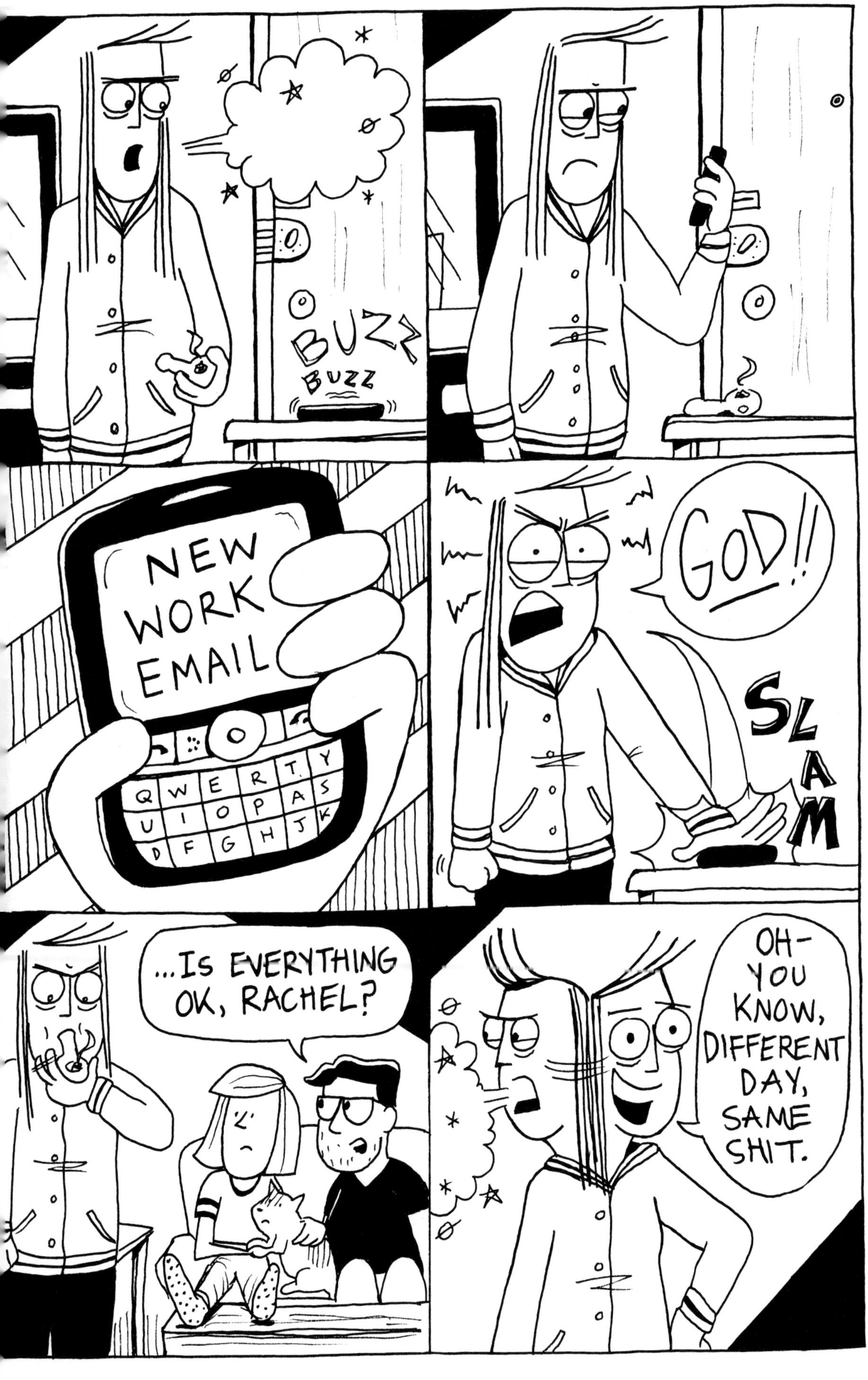
BUZZ
BUZZ
NEW WORK EMAIL
GOD!!
SLAM
...IS EVERYTHING OK, RACHEL?
OH- YOU KNOW, DIFFERENT DAY, SAME SHIT.

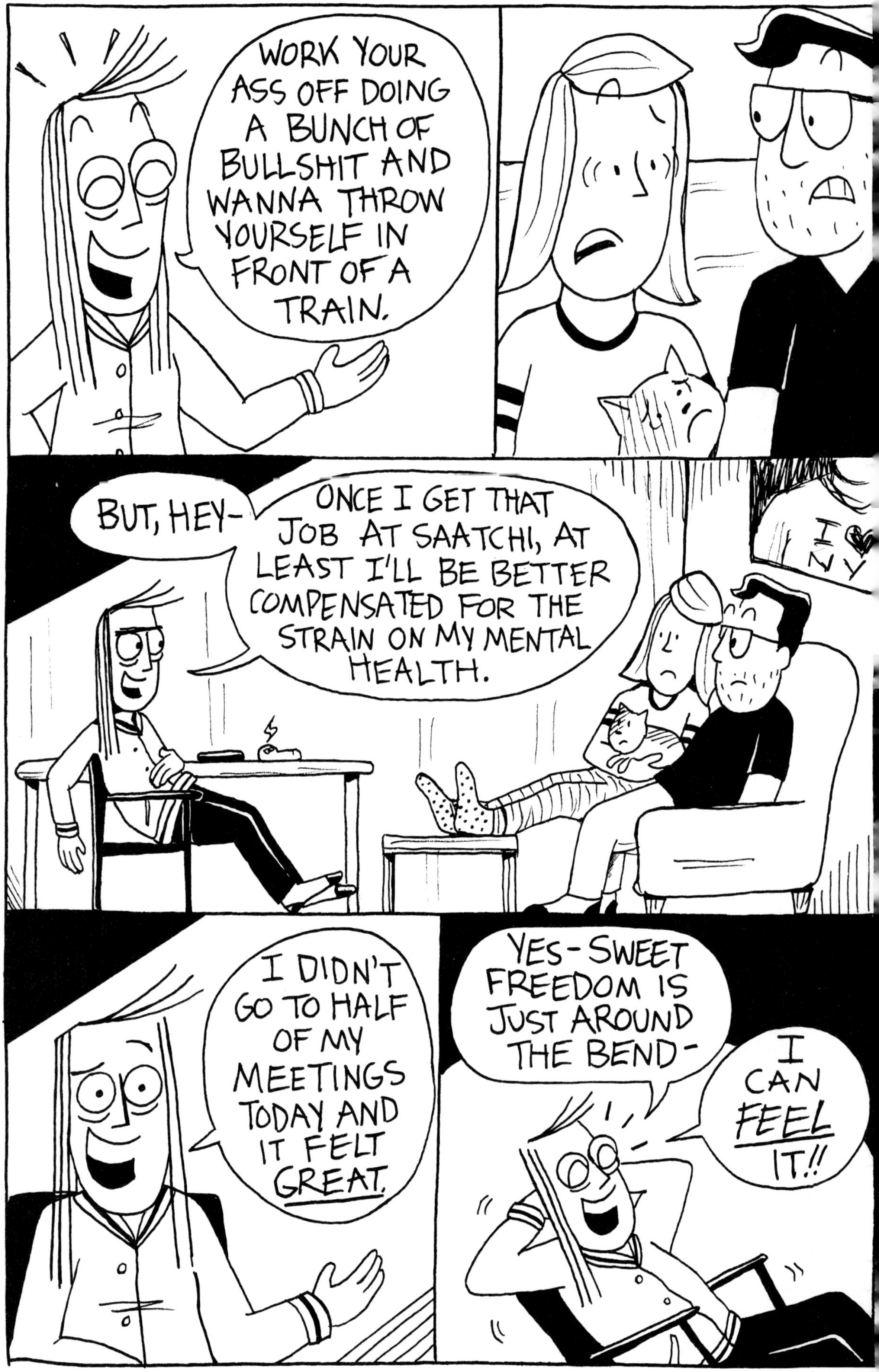
WORK YOUR ASS OFF DOING A BUNCH OF BULLSHIT AND WANNA THROW YOURSELF IN FRONT OF A TRAIN.
BUT, HEY-
ONCE I GET THAT JOB AT SAATCHI, AT LEAST I'LL BE BETTER COMPENSATED FOR THE STRAIN ON MY MENTAL HEALTH.
I ♥ NY
I DIDN'T GO TO HALF OF MY MEETINGS TODAY AND IT FELT GREAT.
YES- SWEET FREEDOM IS JUST AROUND THE BEND-
I CAN FEEL IT!!

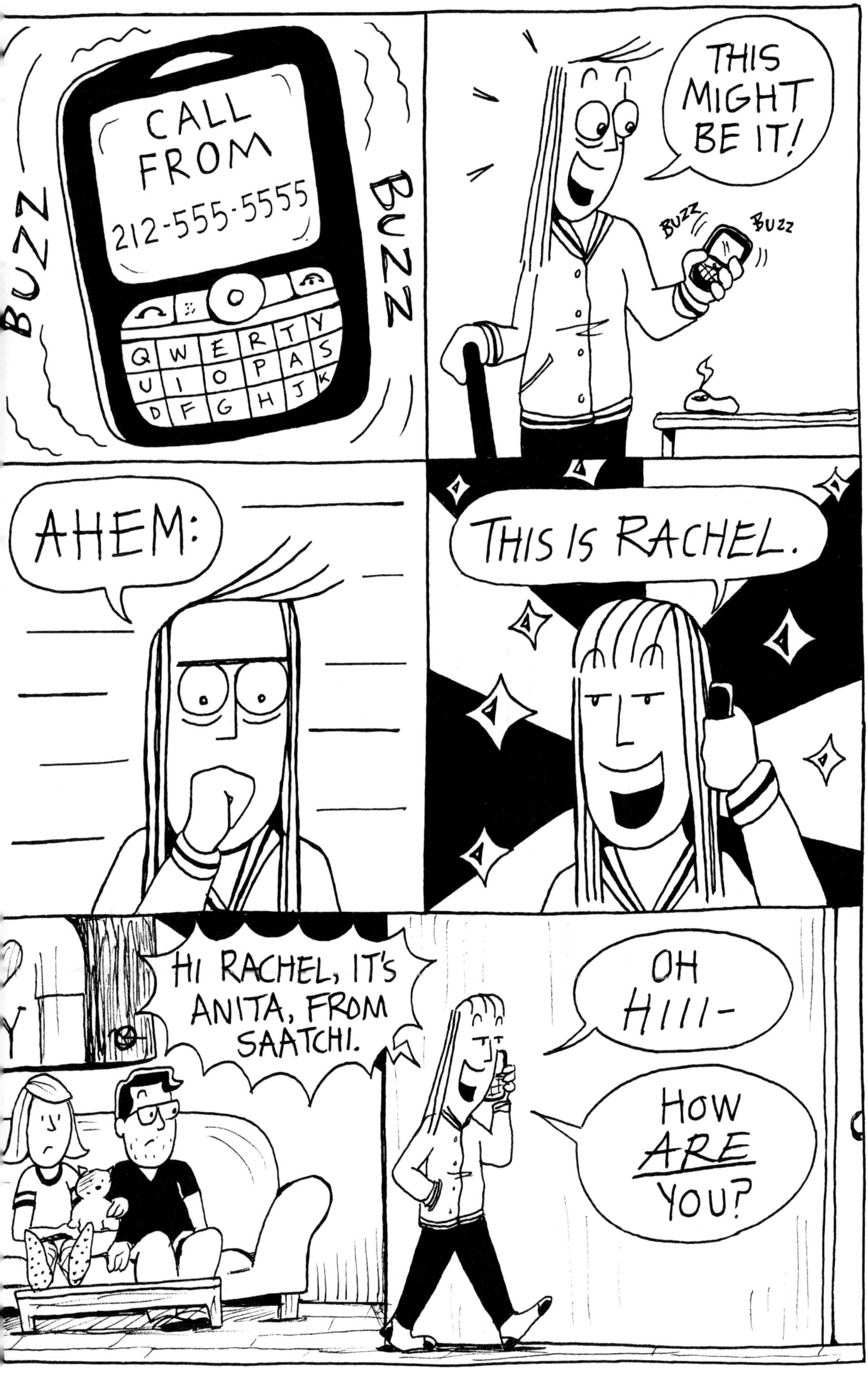
BUZZ
CALL FROM 212-555-5555
BUZZ
QWERTY
UIOPAS
DFGHJK
THIS MIGHT BE IT!
BUZZ
BUZZ
AHEM:
THIS IS RACHEL.
HI RACHEL, IT'S ANITA, FROM SAATCHI.
OH HIII-
HOW ARE YOU?

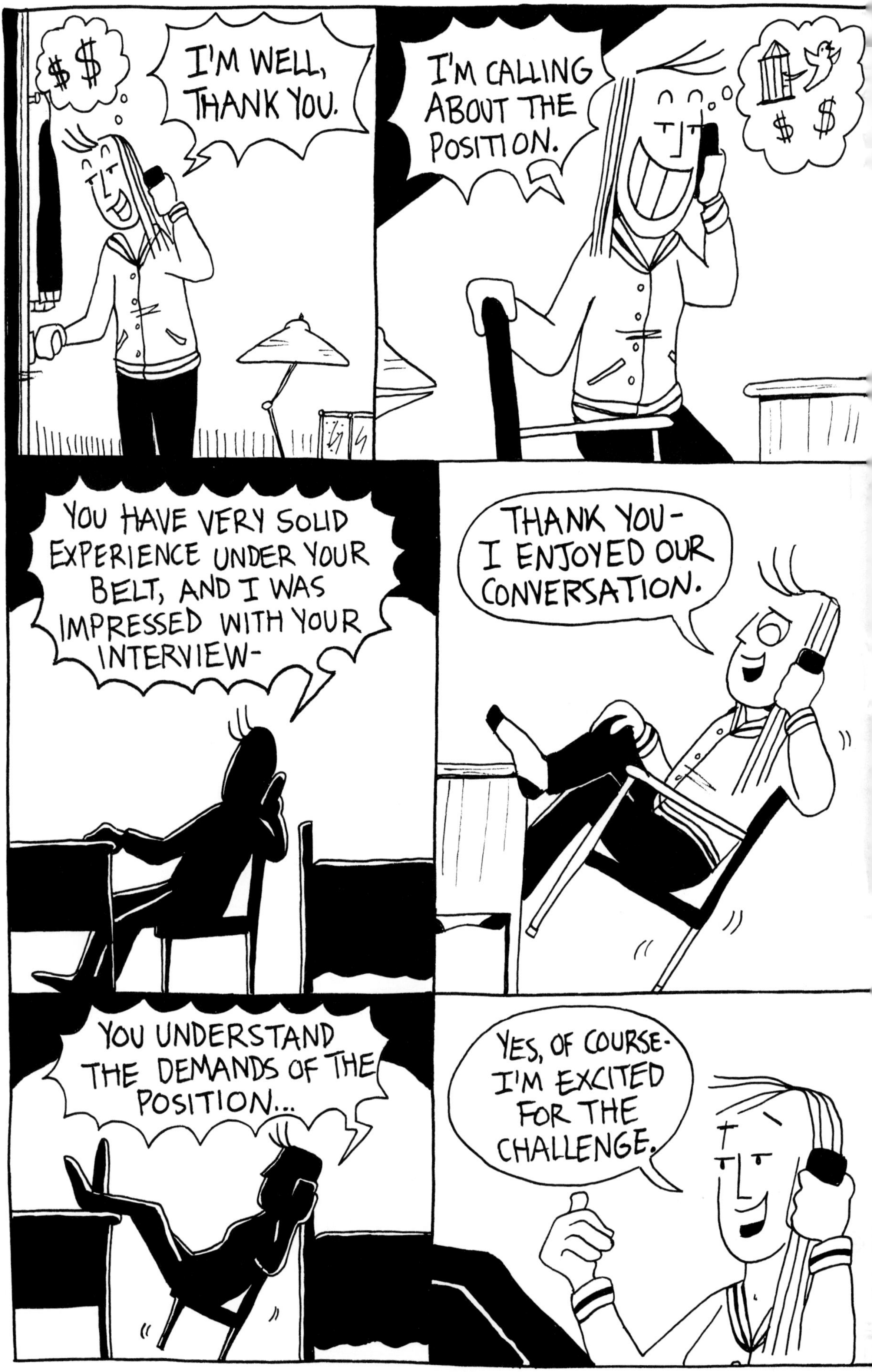
$ $
I'M WELL, THANK YOU.
I'M CALLING ABOUT THE POSITION.
$ $
YOU HAVE VERY SOLID EXPERIENCE UNDER YOUR BELT, AND I WAS IMPRESSED WITH YOUR INTERVIEW-
THANK YOU- I ENJOYED OUR CONVERSATION.
YOU UNDERSTAND THE DEMANDS OF THE POSITION...
YES, OF COURSE- I'M EXCITED FOR THE CHALLENGE.

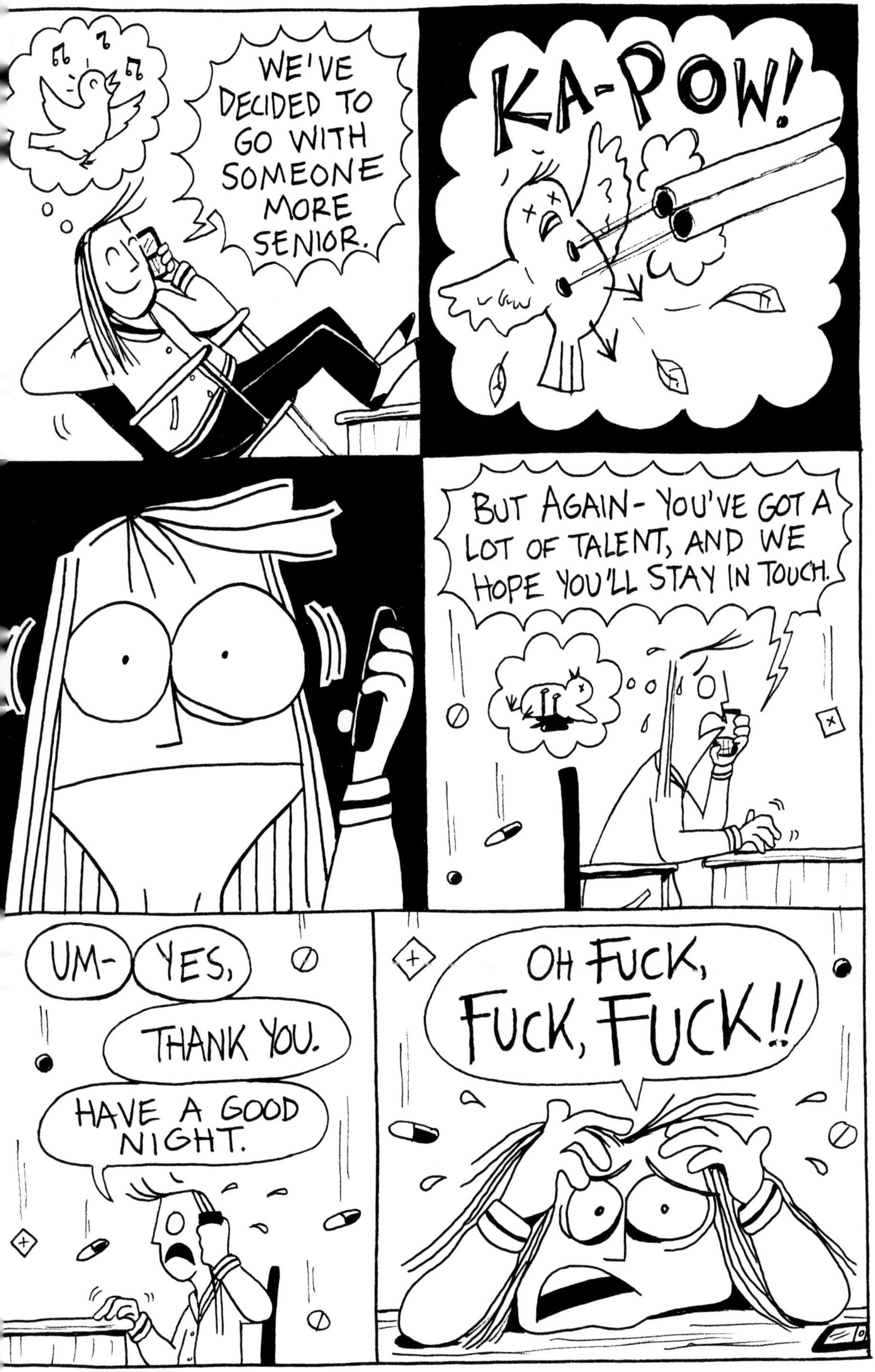
WE'VE DECIDED TO GO WITH SOMEONE MORE SENIOR.
KA-POW!
BUT AGAIN- YOU'VE GOT A LOT OF TALENT, AND WE HOPE YOU'LL STAY IN TOUCH.
UM-
YES,
THANK YOU.
HAVE A GOOD NIGHT.
OH FUCK, FUCK, FUCK!!

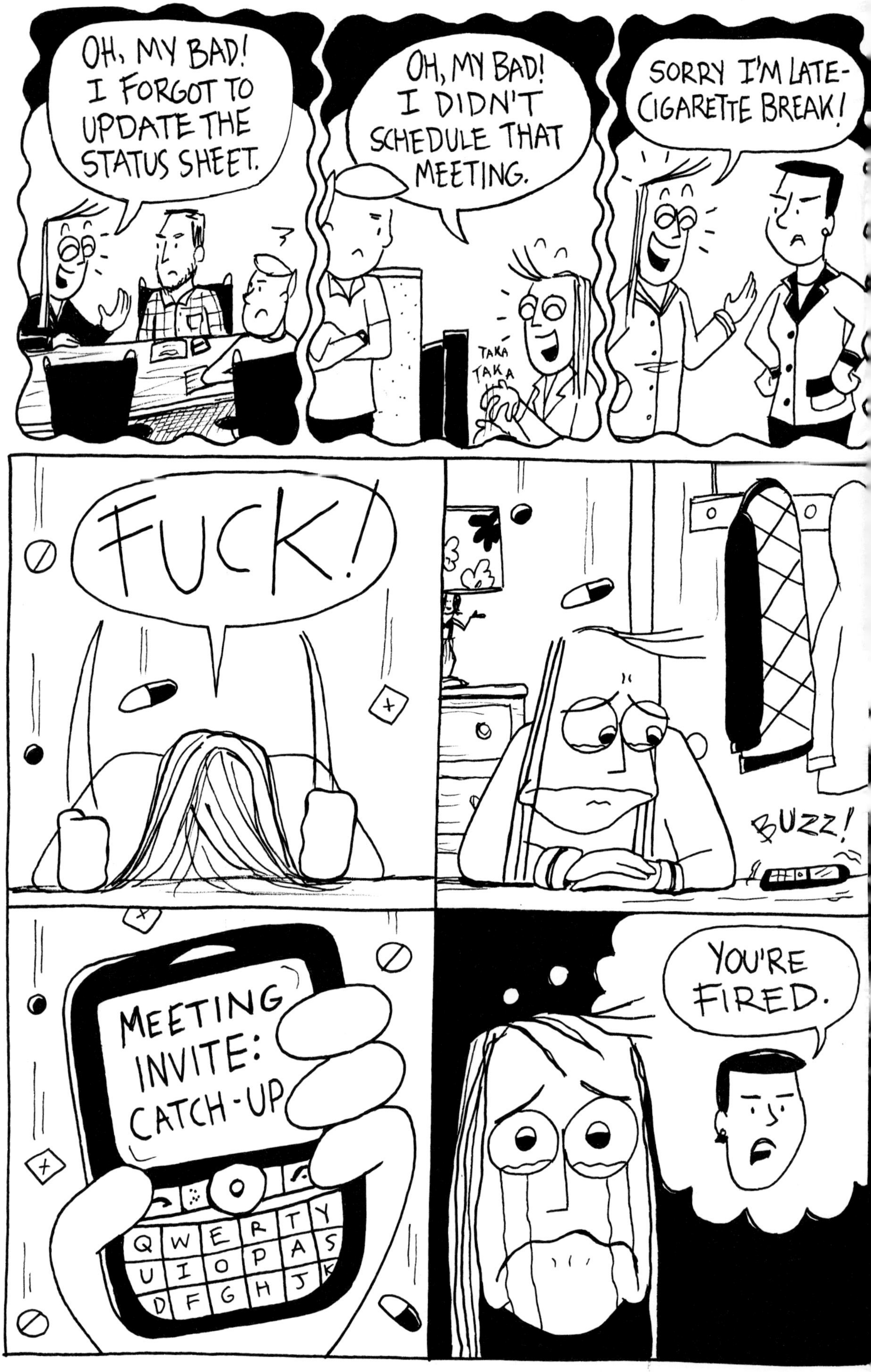
OH, MY BAD! I FORGOT TO UPDATE THE STATUS SHEET.
OH, MY BAD! I DIDN'T SCHEDULE THAT MEETING.
TAKA TAKA
SORRY I'M LATE- CIGARETTE BREAK!
FUCK!
BUZZ!
MEETING INVITE: CATCH-UP
QWERTY
UIOPAS
DFGHJK
YOU'RE FIRED.

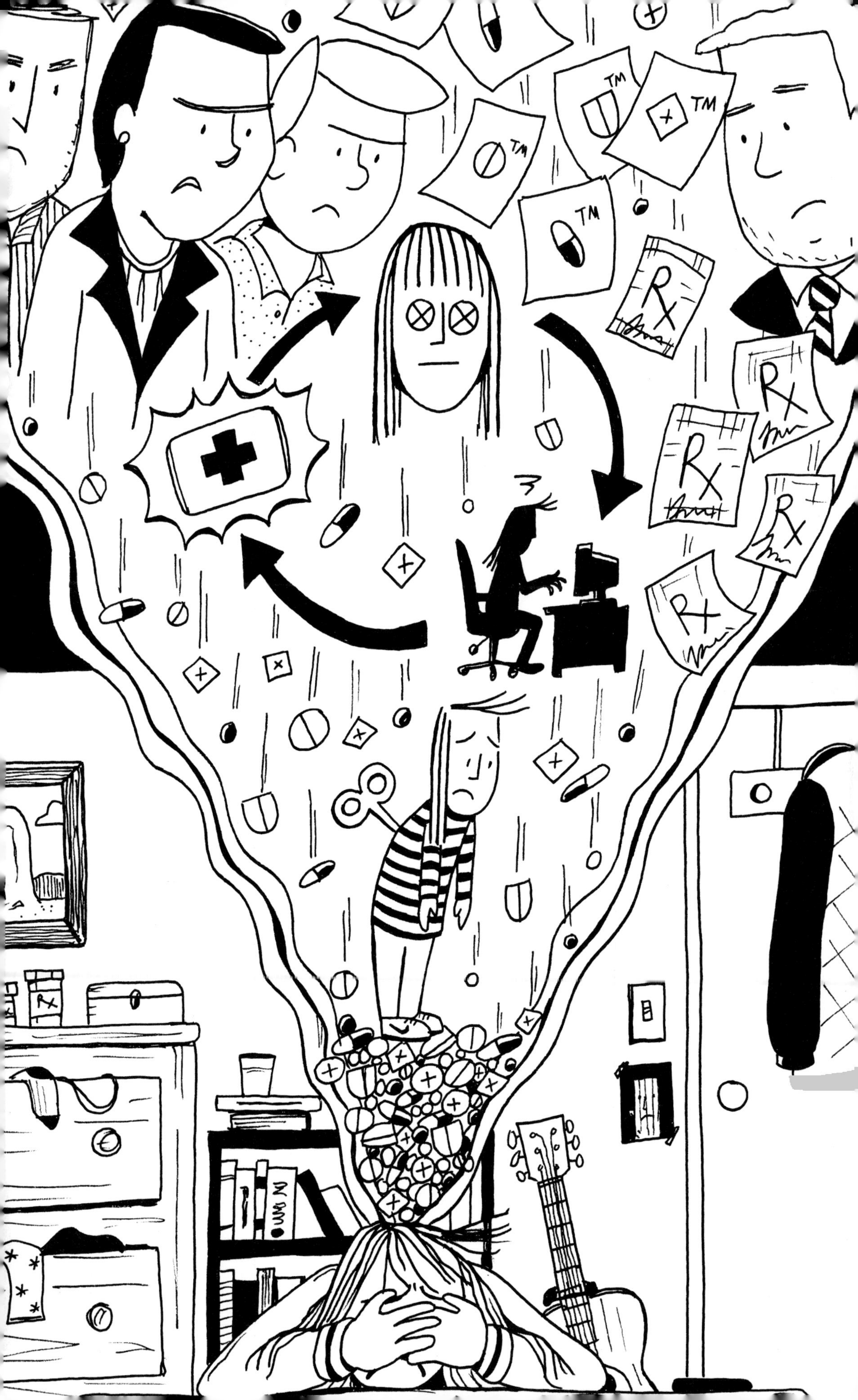
TM
TM
TM
TM
Rx
Rx
Rx
Rx
Rx
Rx

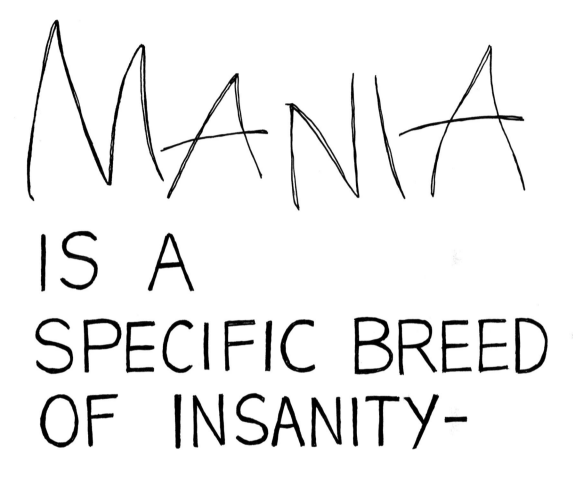

MANIA
IS A
SPECIFIC BREED
OF INSANITY-

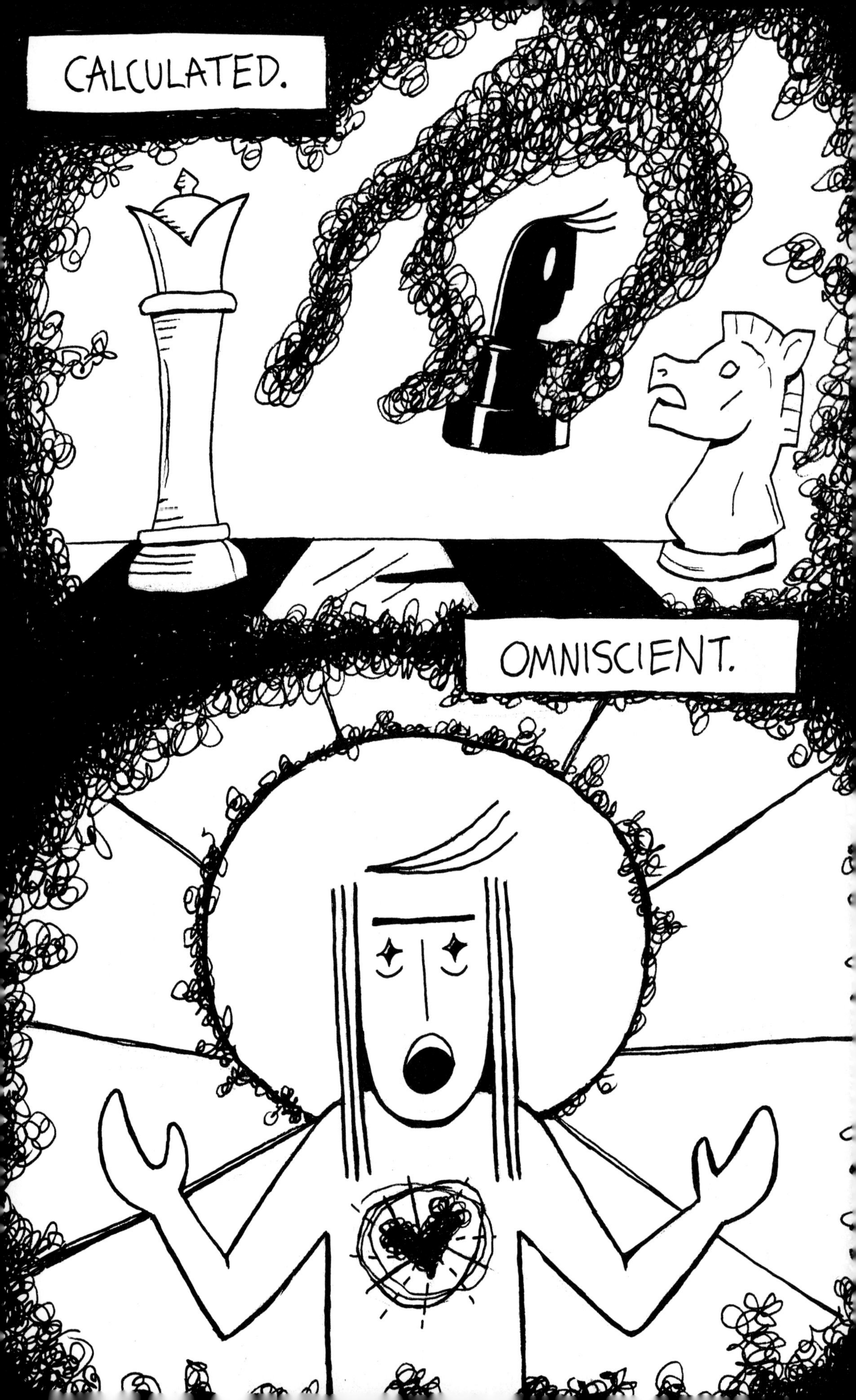
CALCULATED.
OMNISCIENT.

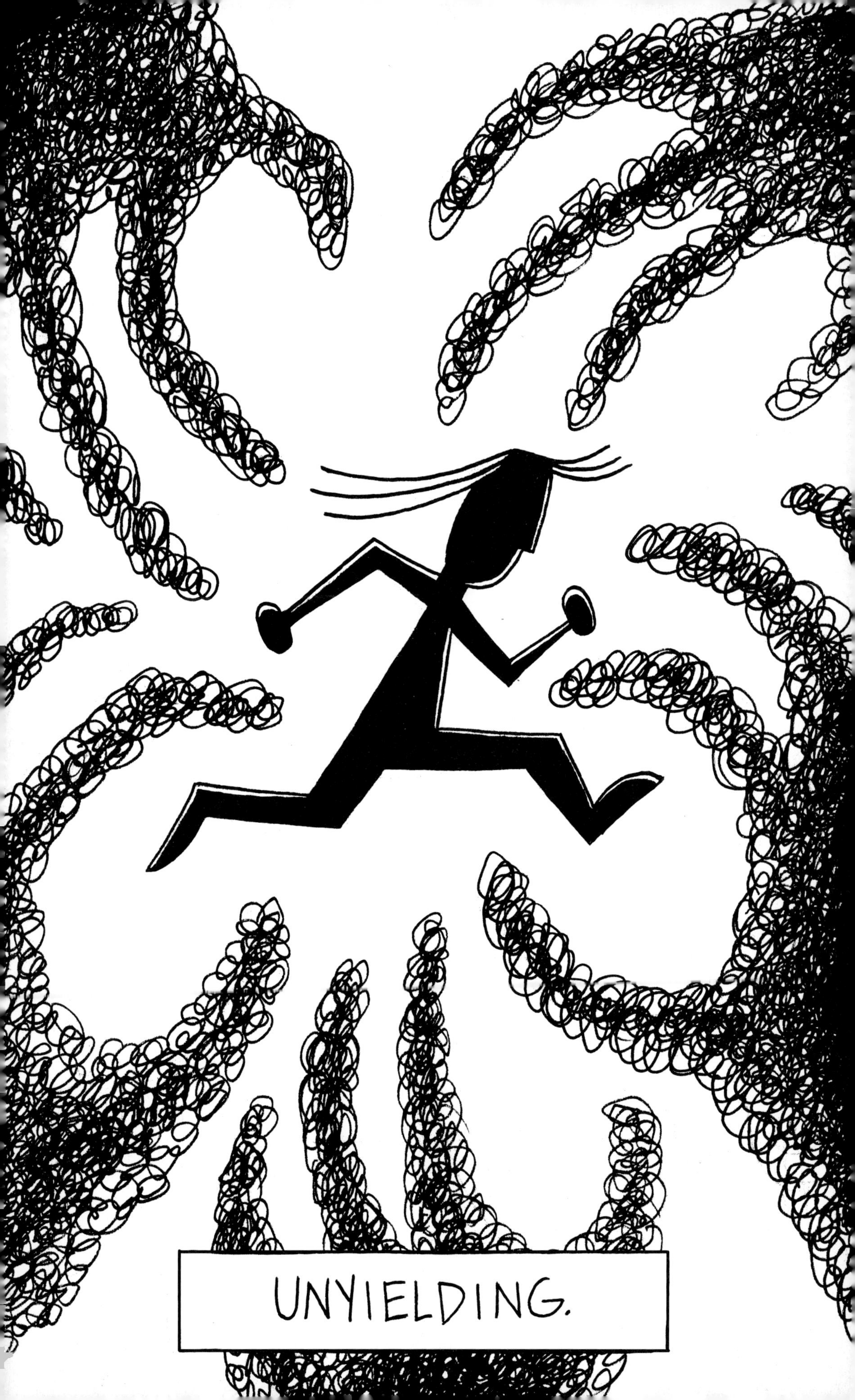
UNYIELDING.

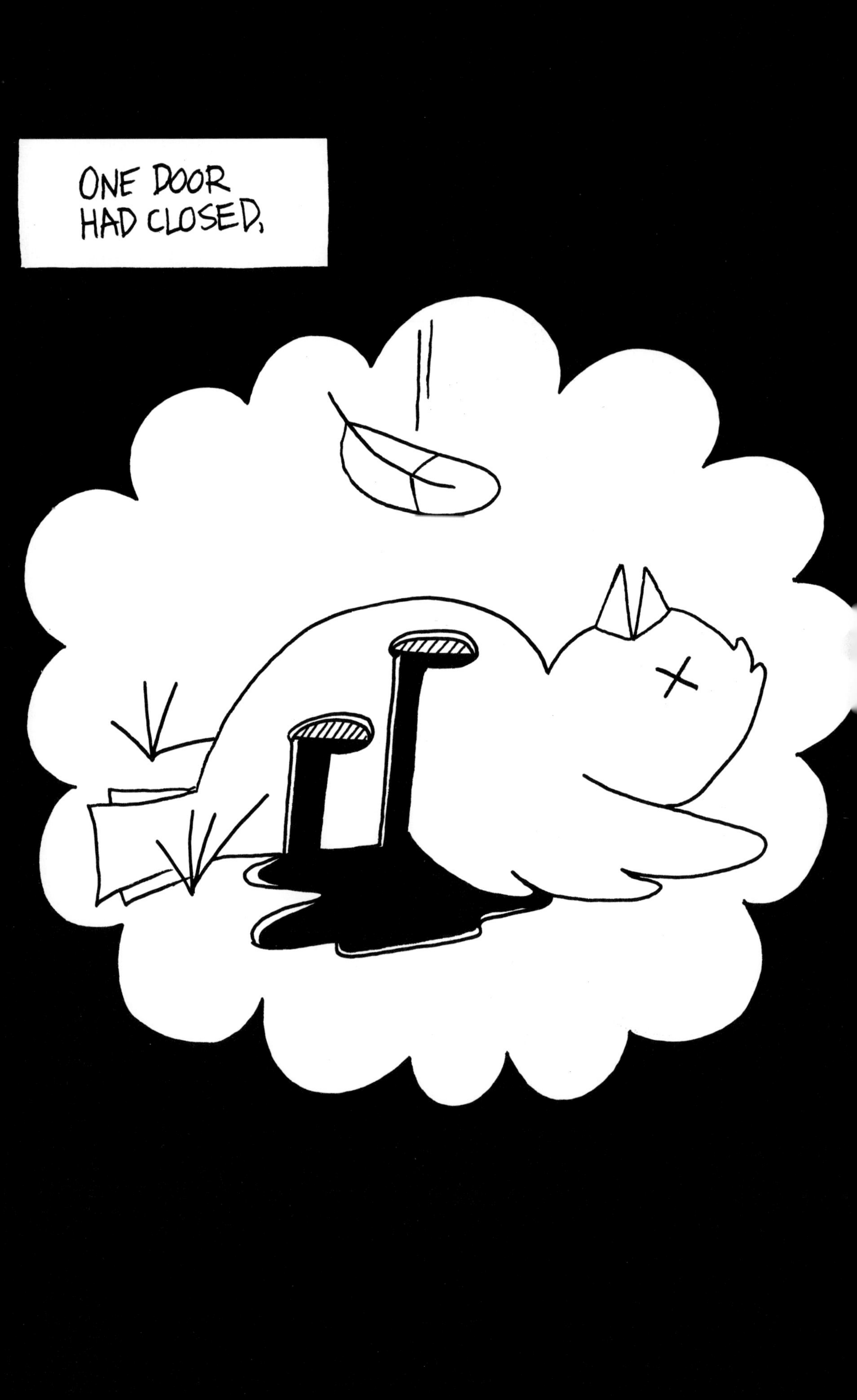
ONE DOOR HAD CLOSED.

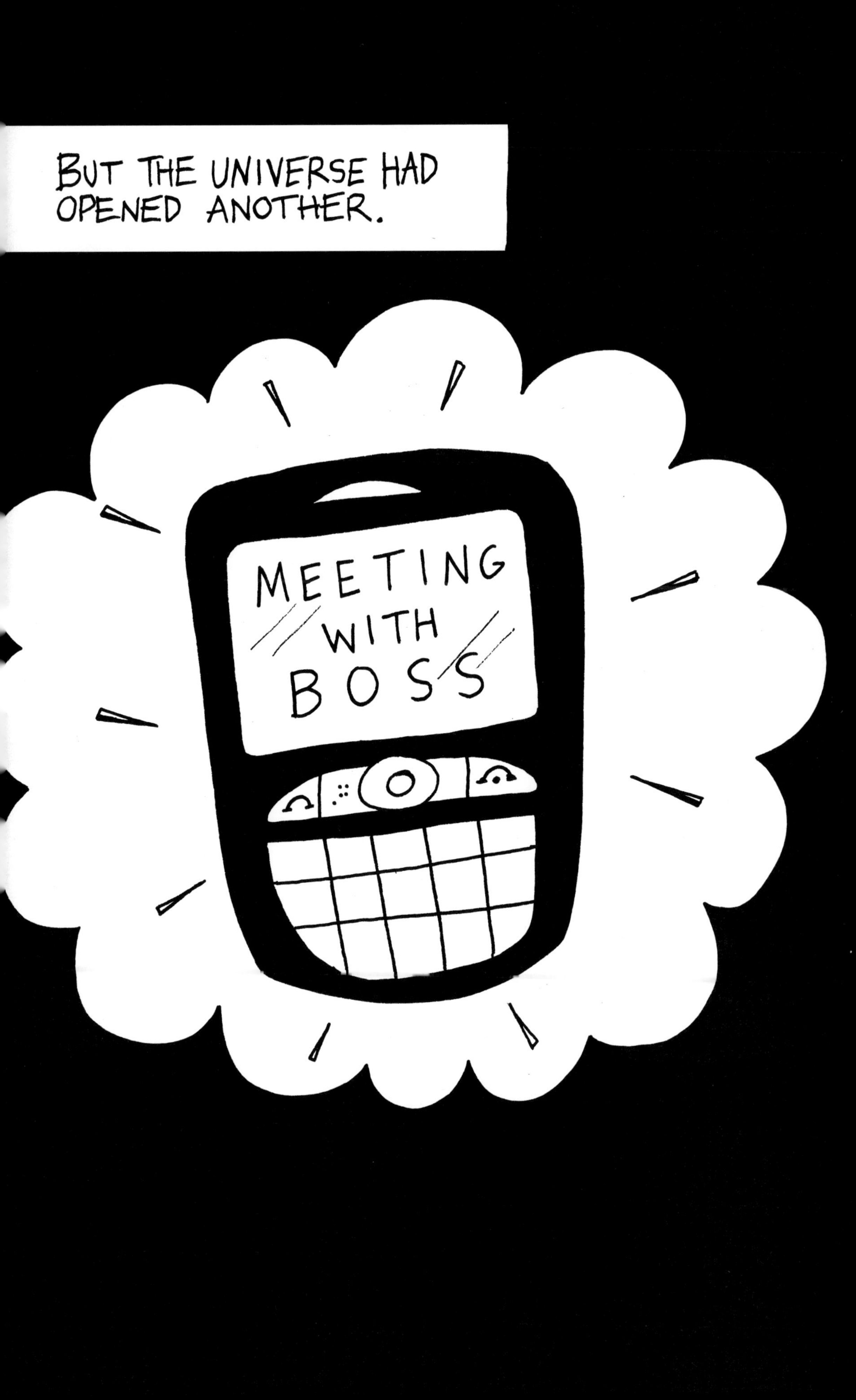
BUT THE UNIVERSE HAD OPENED ANOTHER.
MEETING WITH BOSS

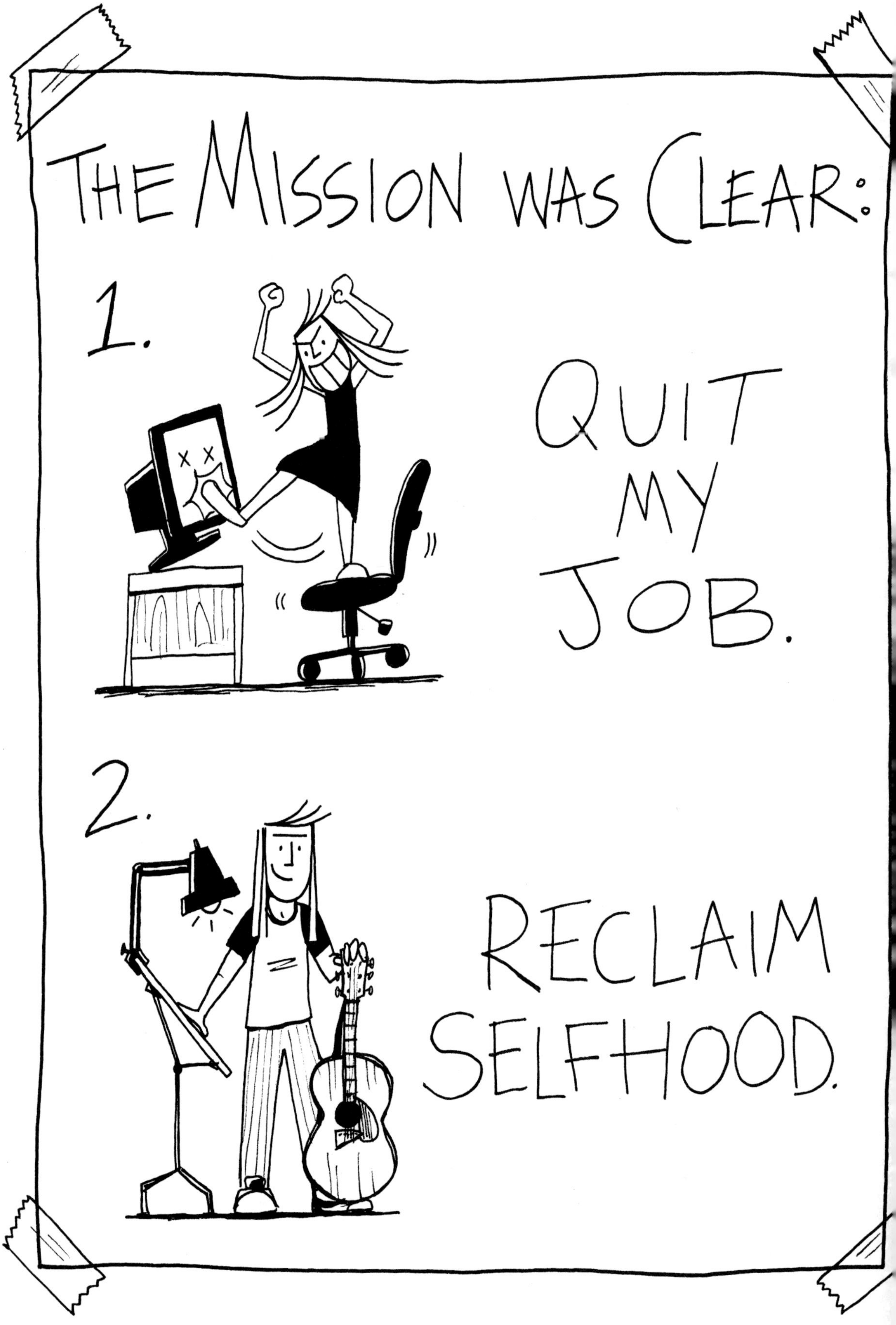
THE MISSION WAS CLEAR:
1.
QUIT MY JOB.
2.
RECLAIM SELFHOOD.

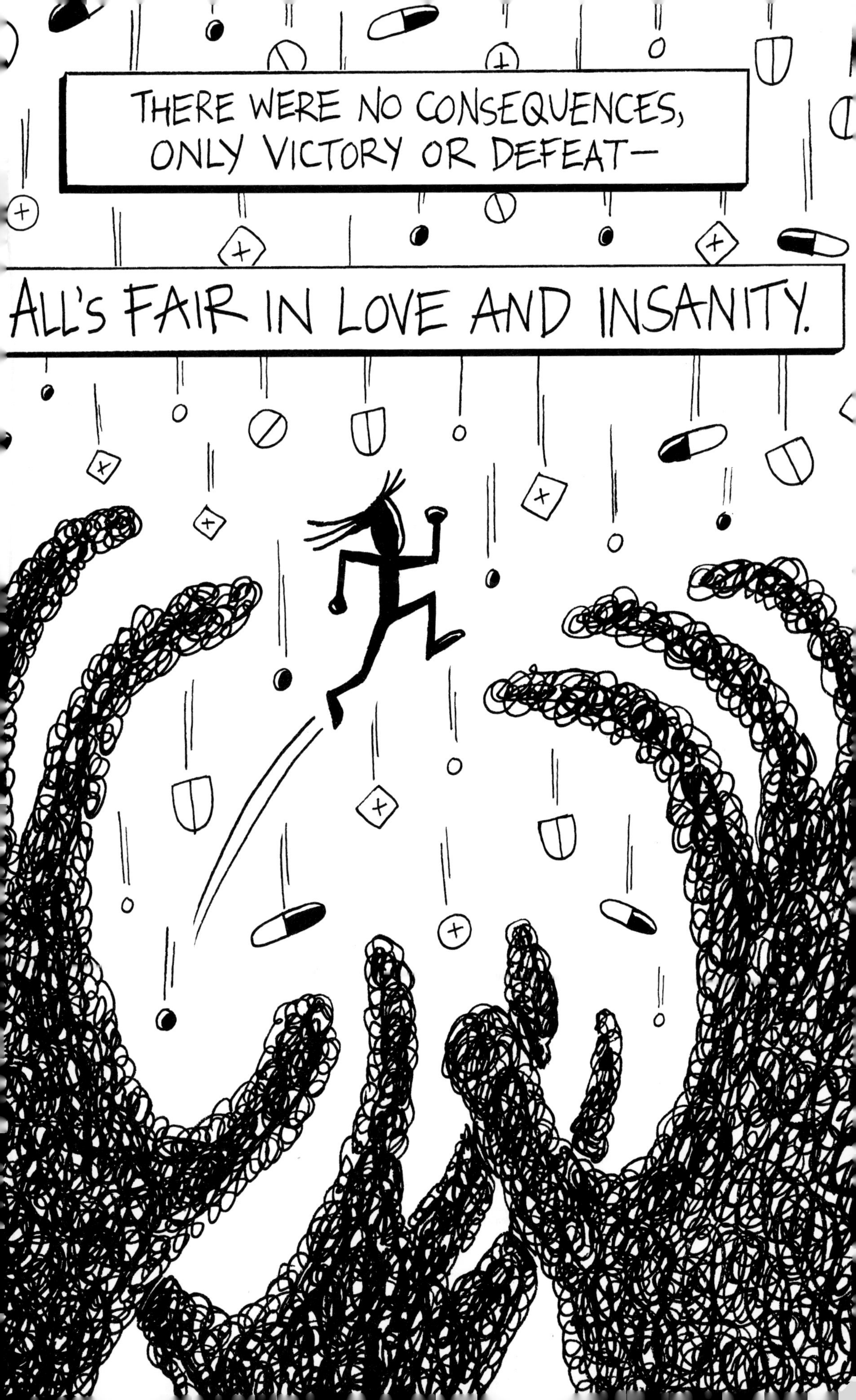
THERE WERE NO CONSEQUENCES, ONLY VICTORY OR DEFEAT—
ALL'S FAIR IN LOVE AND INSANITY.

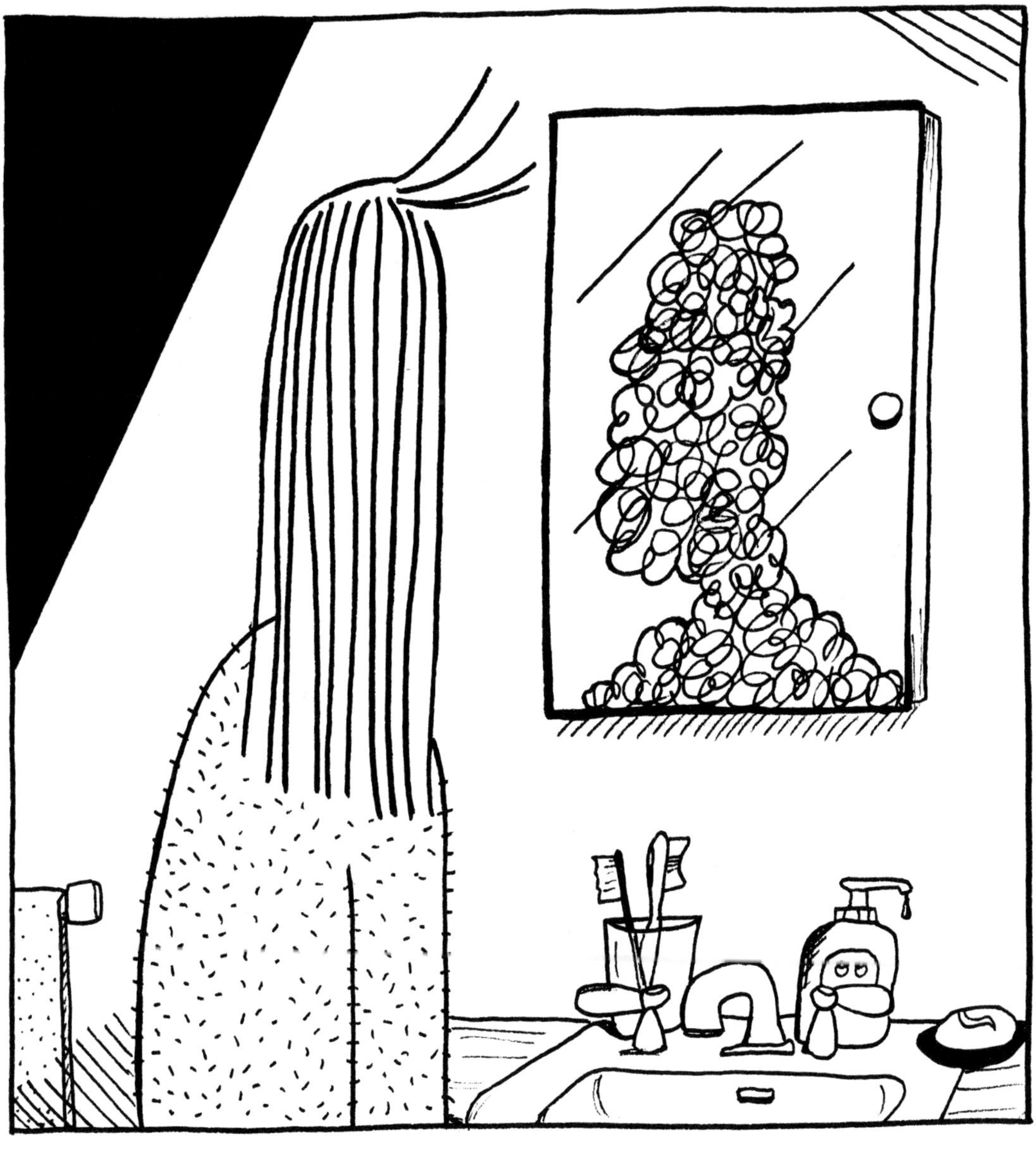

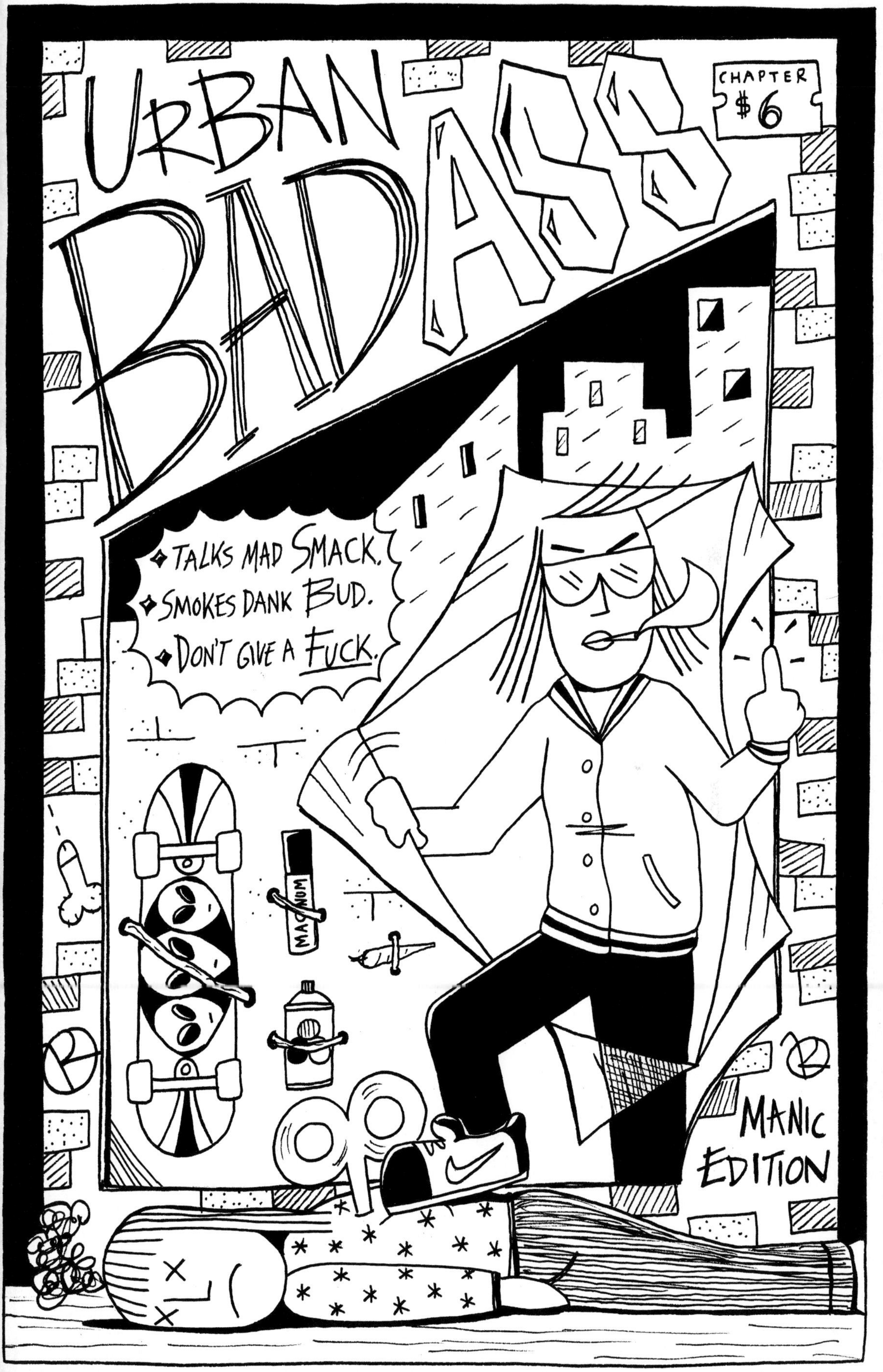
URBAN BADASS
CHAPTER $6
TALKS MAD SMACK.
SMOKES DANK BUD.
DON'T GIVE A FUCK.
MAGNUM
MANIC EDITION

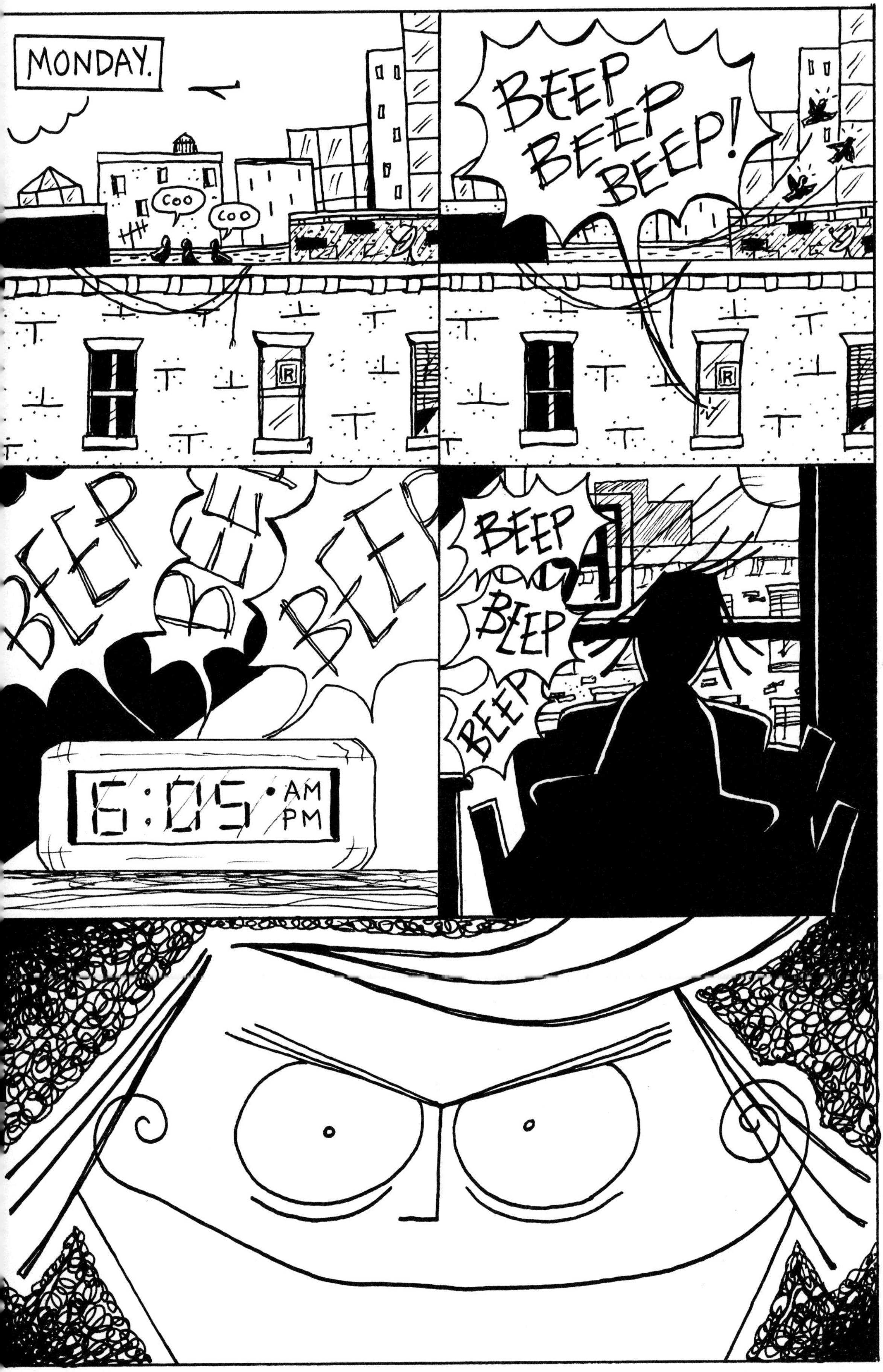
MONDAY.
COO
COO
BEEP BEEP BEEP!
6:05 AM PM
BEEP BEEP BEEP

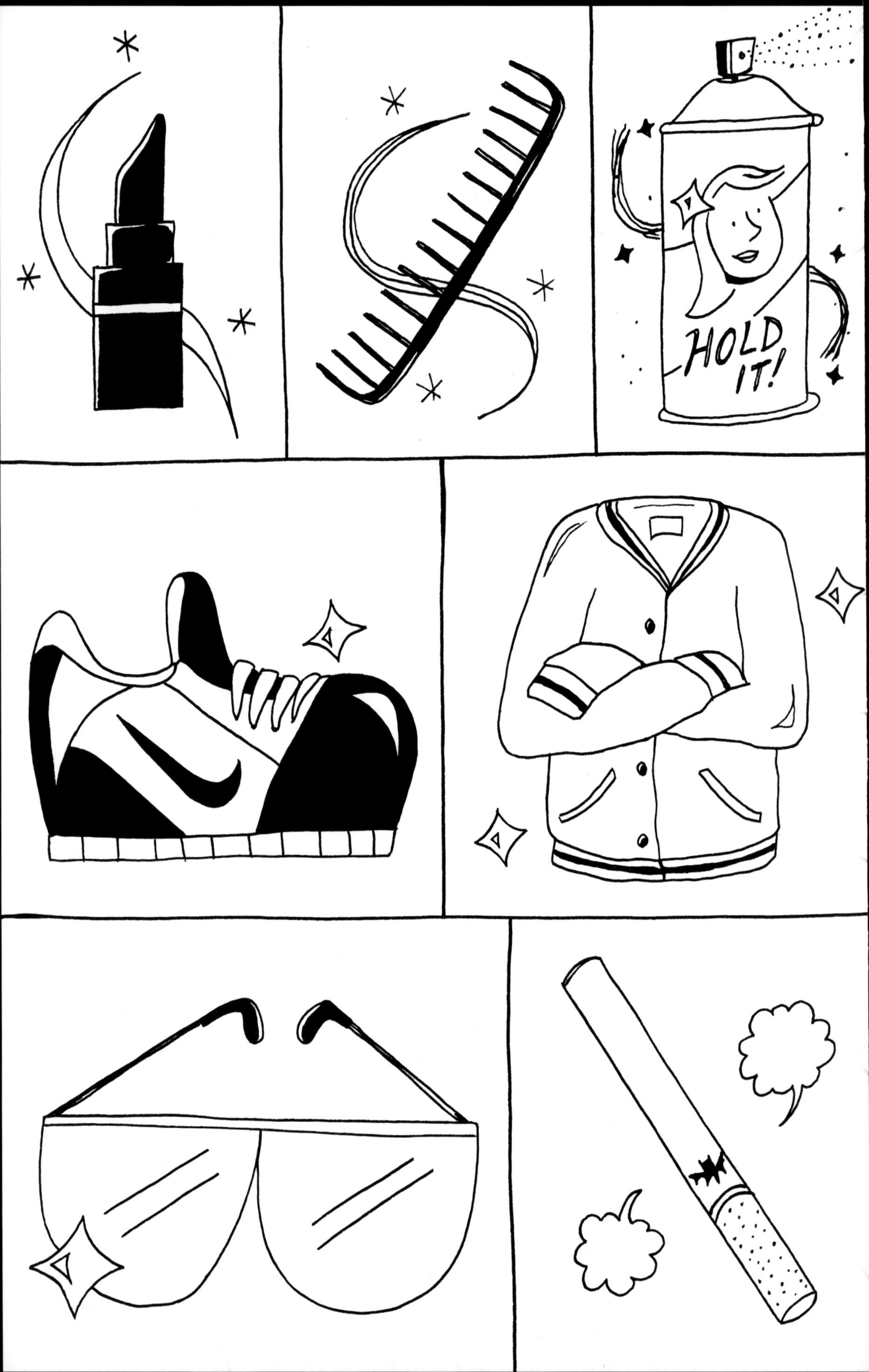
HOLD IT!

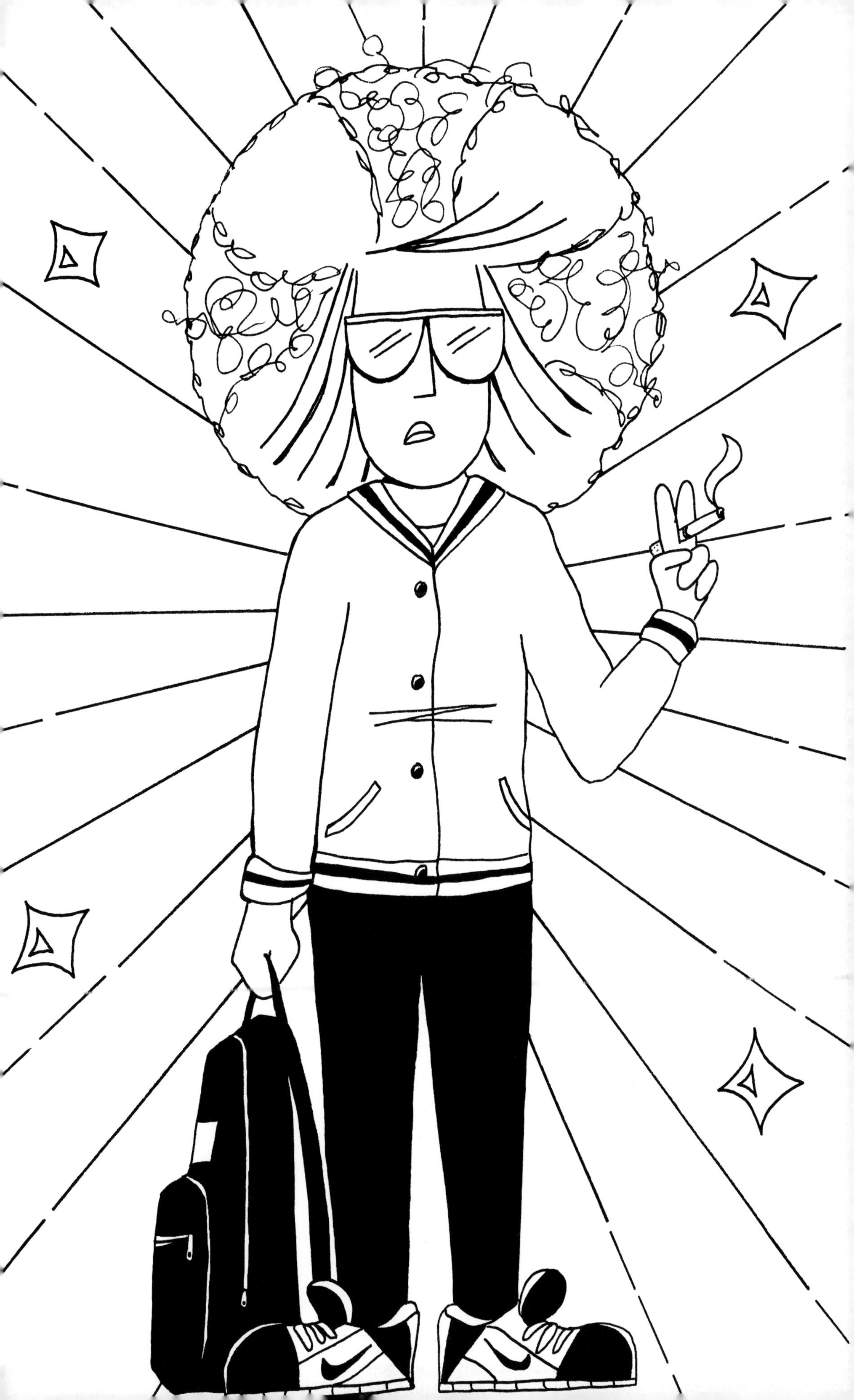

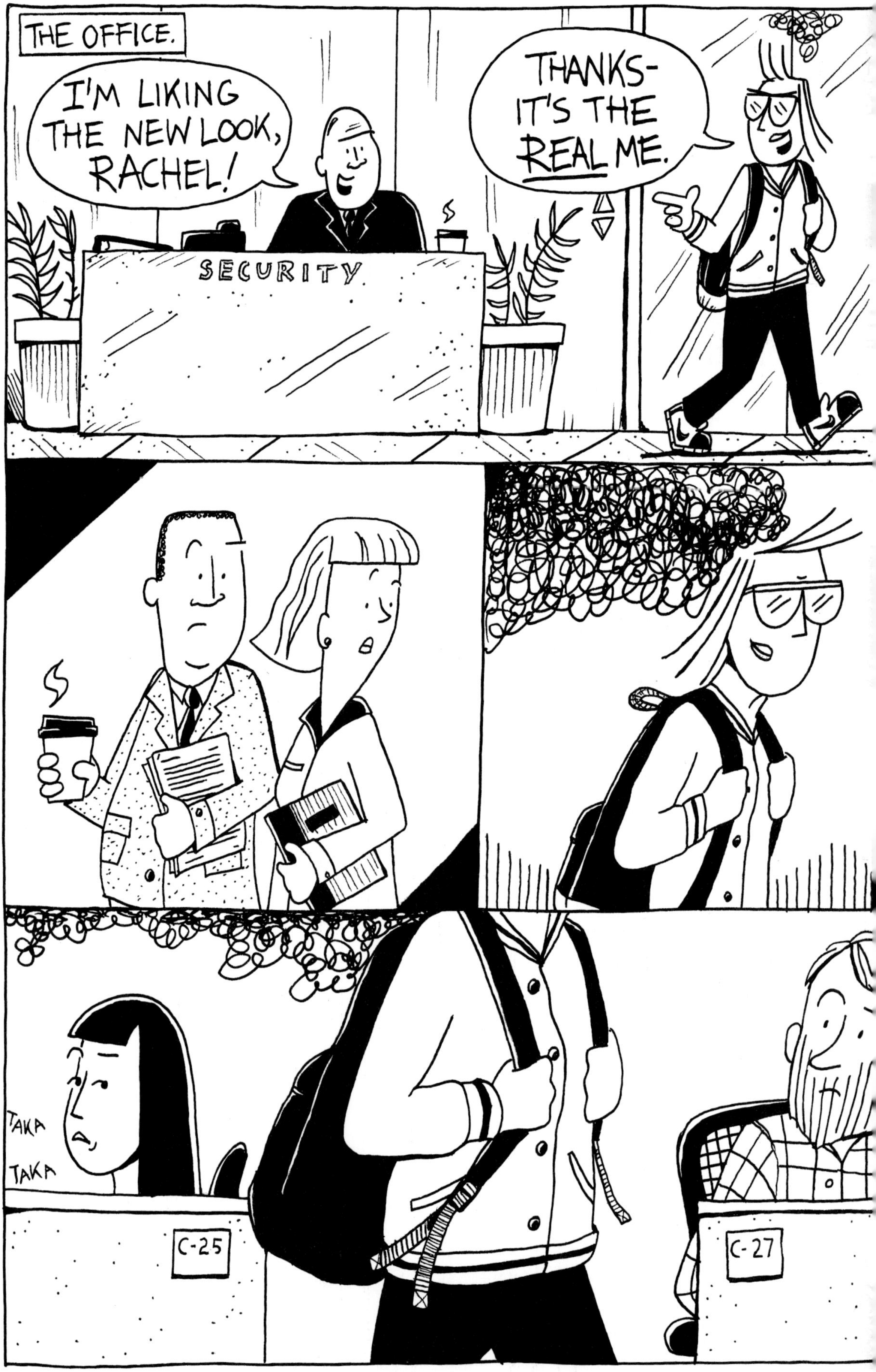
THE OFFICE.
I'M LIKING THE NEW LOOK, RACHEL!
SECURITY
THANKS- IT'S THE REAL ME.
TAKA TAKA
C-25
C-27

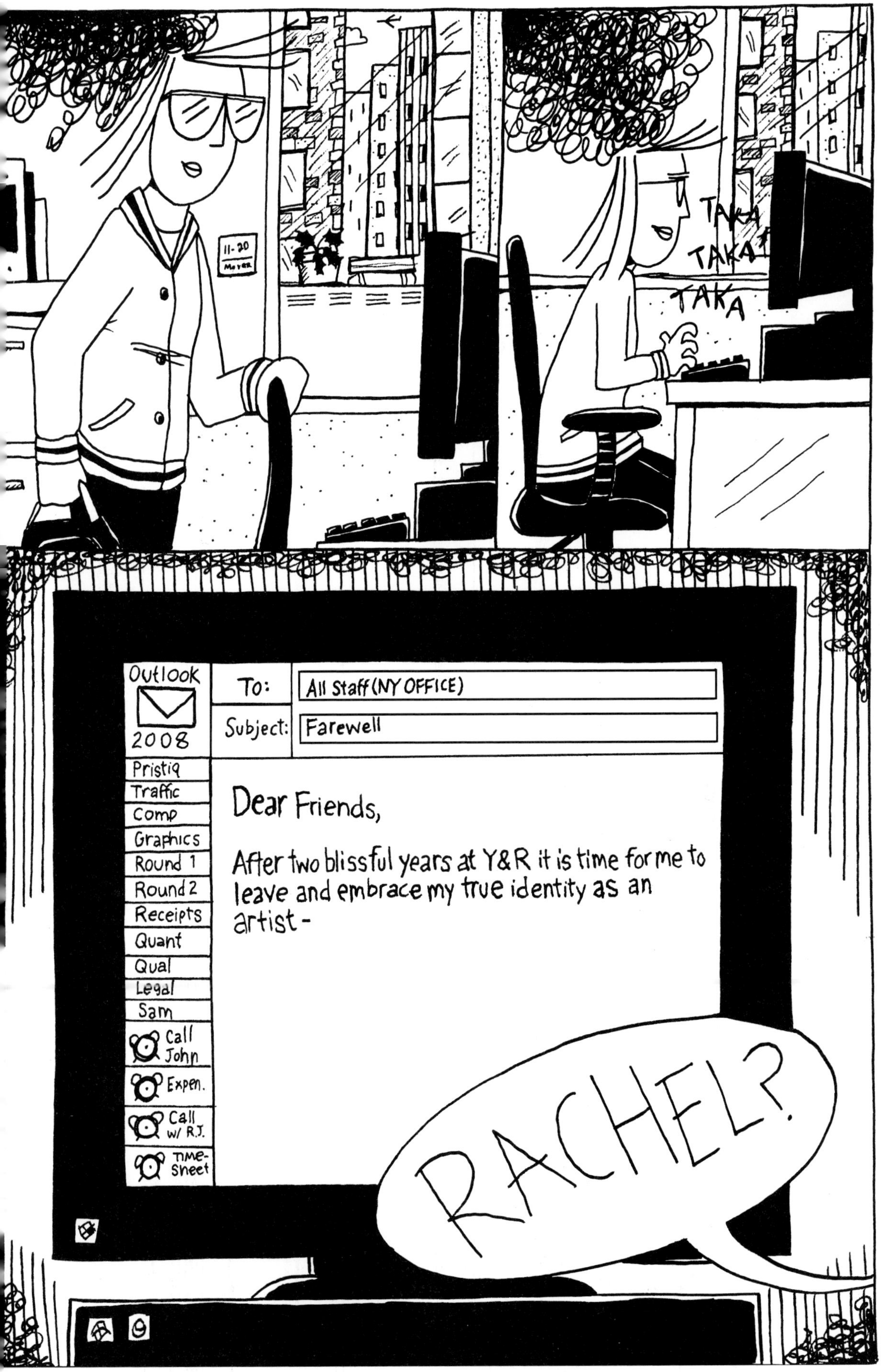
11-20
TAKA
TAKA
TAKA
Outlook
2008
To:
All Staff (NY OFFICE)
Subject:
Farewell
Pristiq
Traffic
Comp
Graphics
Round 1
Round 2
Receipts
Quant
Qual
Legal
Sam
Call John
Expen.
Call w/ R.J.
Time-sheet
Dear Friends,
After two blissful years at Y&R it is time for me to leave and embrace my true identity as an artist -
RACHEL?

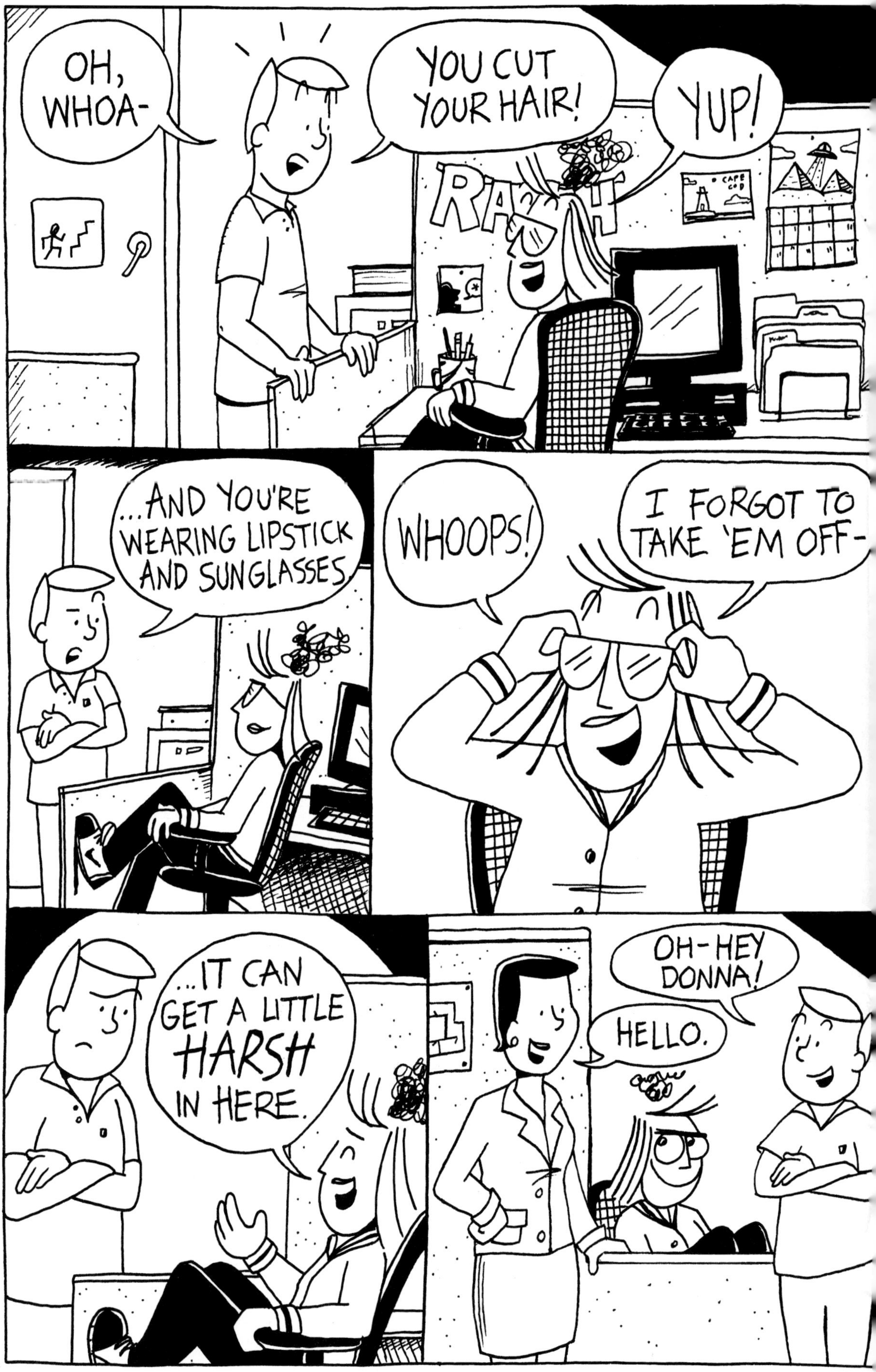
OH, WHOA-
YOU CUT YOUR HAIR!
YUP!
RAWR
...AND YOU'RE WEARING LIPSTICK AND SUNGLASSES.
WHOOPS!
I FORGOT TO TAKE 'EM OFF-
...IT CAN GET A LITTLE HARSH IN HERE.
OH-HEY DONNA!
HELLO.

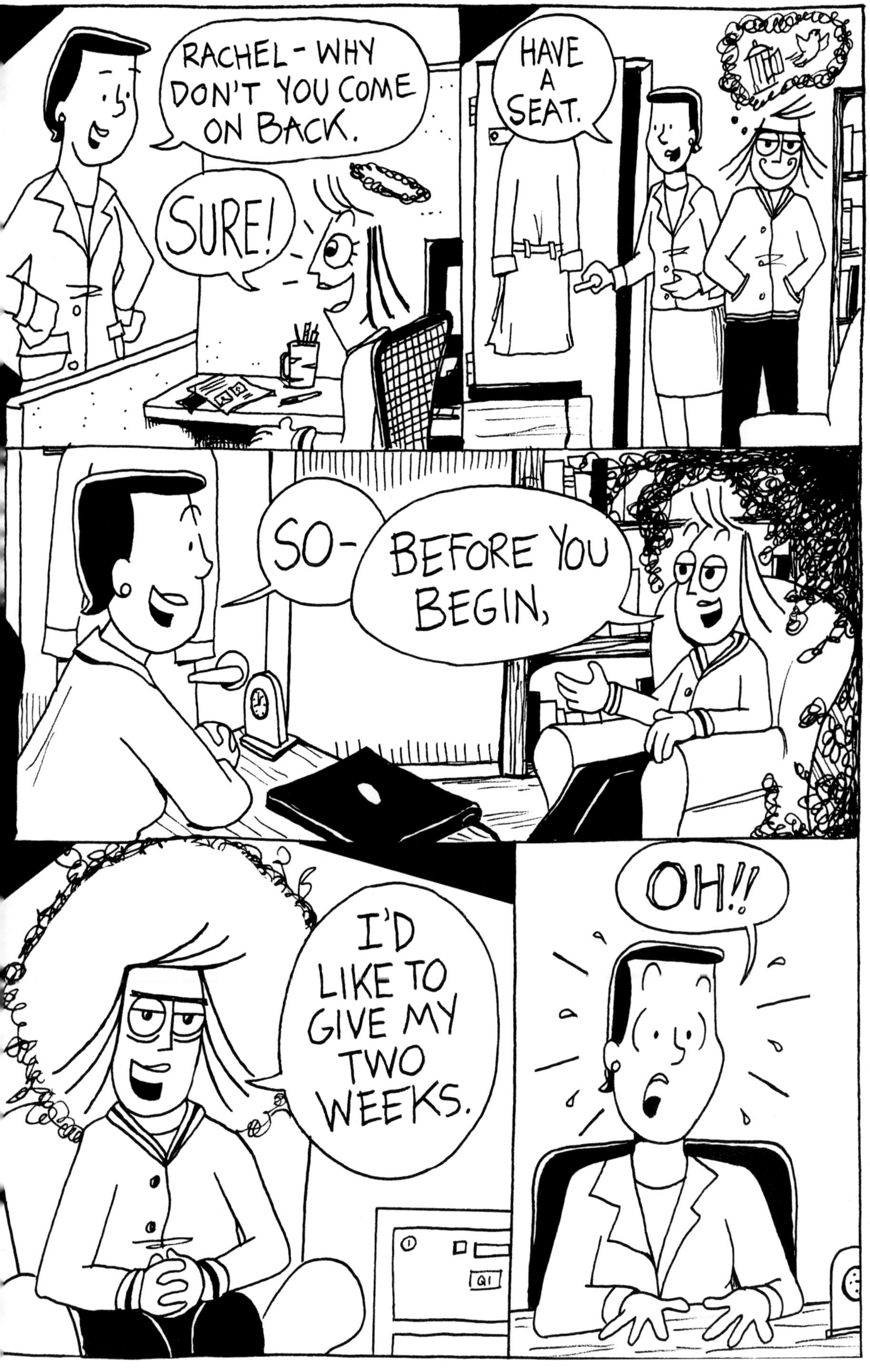
RACHEL- WHY DON'T YOU COME ON BACK.
SURE!
HAVE A SEAT.
SO-
BEFORE YOU BEGIN,
I'D LIKE TO GIVE MY TWO WEEKS.
OH!!

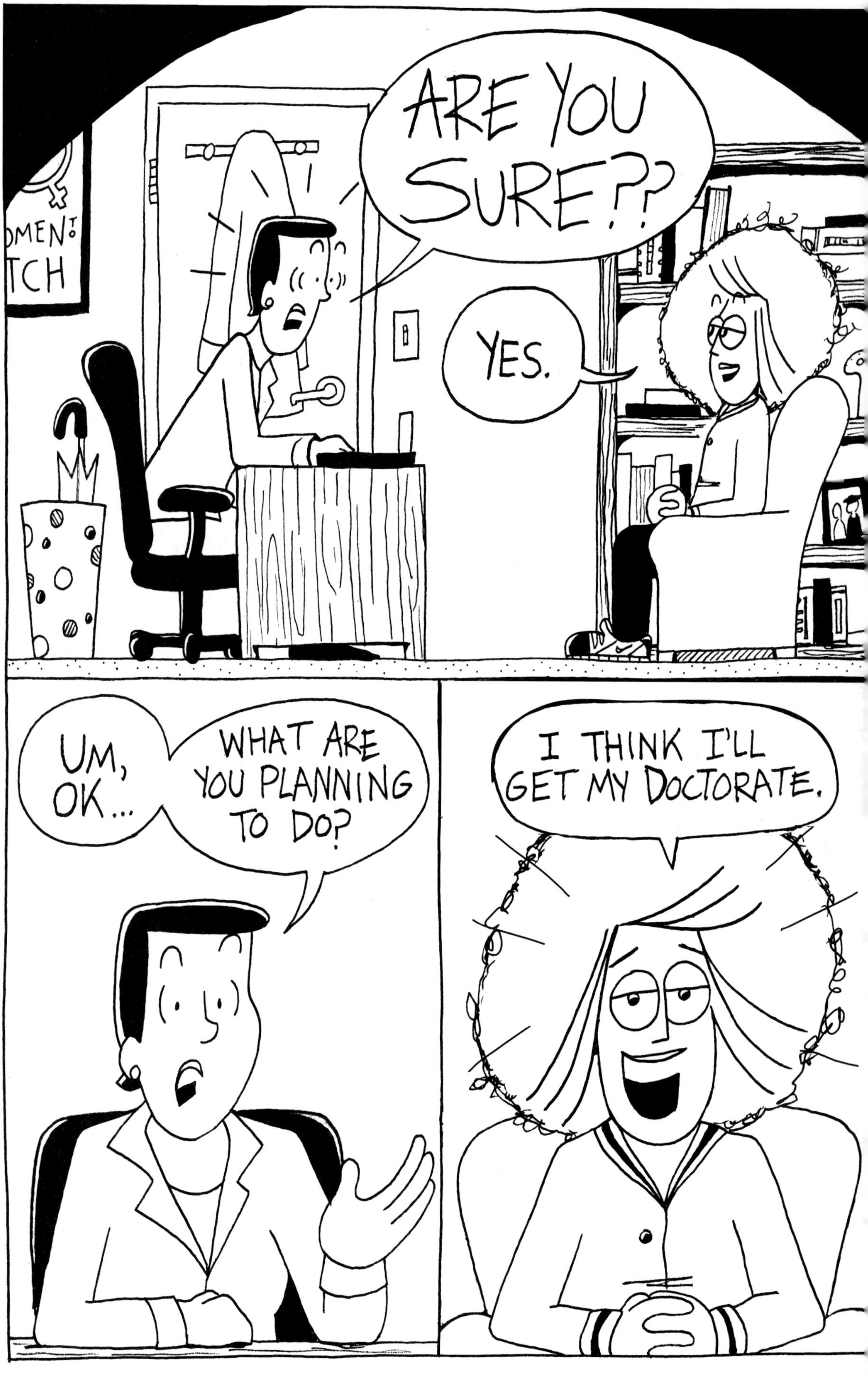
ARE YOU SURE??
YES.
UM, OK...
WHAT ARE YOU PLANNING TO DO?
I THINK I'LL GET MY DOCTORATE.

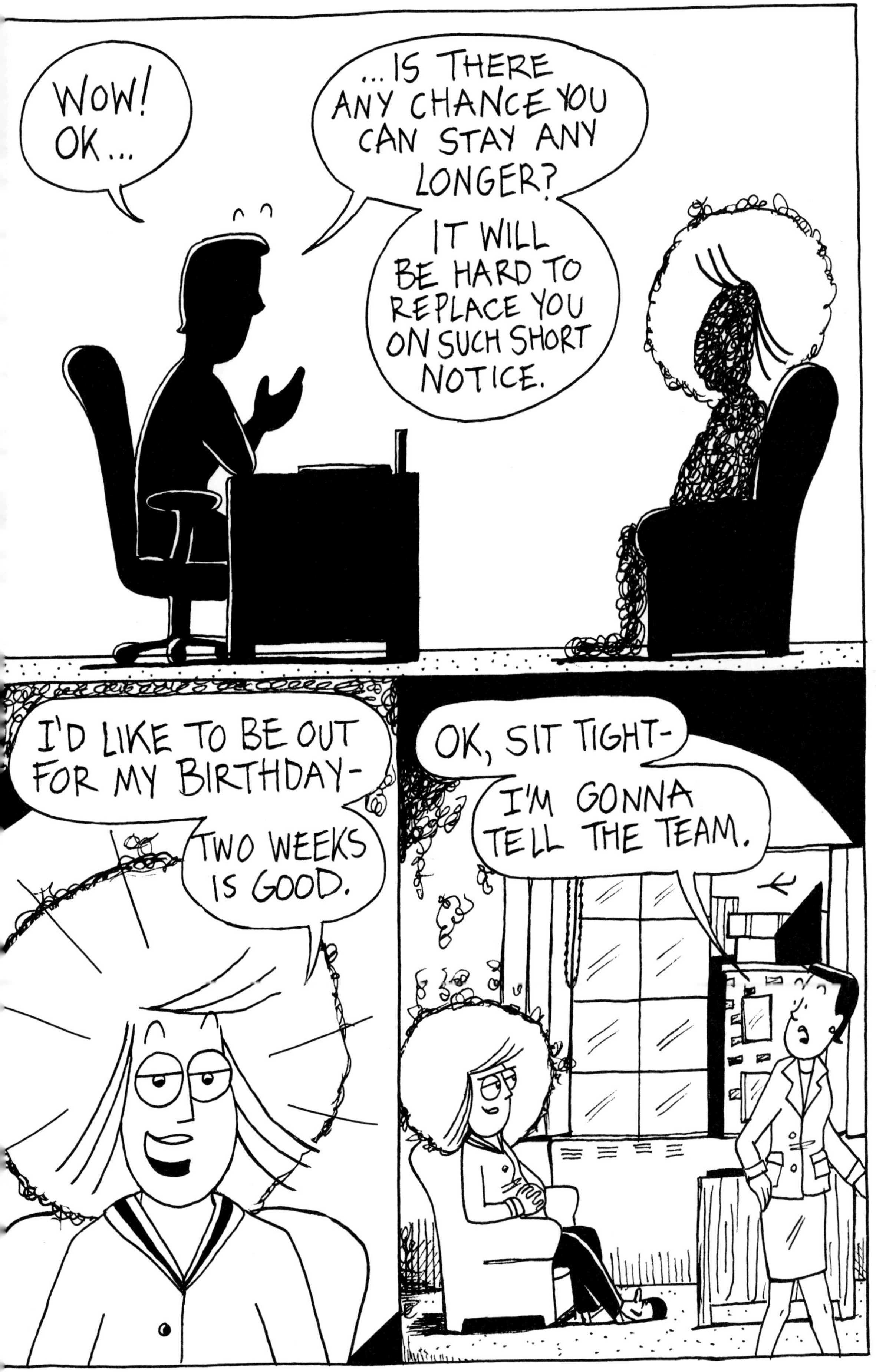
WOW! OK...
...IS THERE ANY CHANCE YOU CAN STAY ANY LONGER?
IT WILL BE HARD TO REPLACE YOU ON SUCH SHORT NOTICE.
I'D LIKE TO BE OUT FOR MY BIRTHDAY-
TWO WEEKS IS GOOD.
OK, SIT TIGHT-
I'M GONNA TELL THE TEAM.

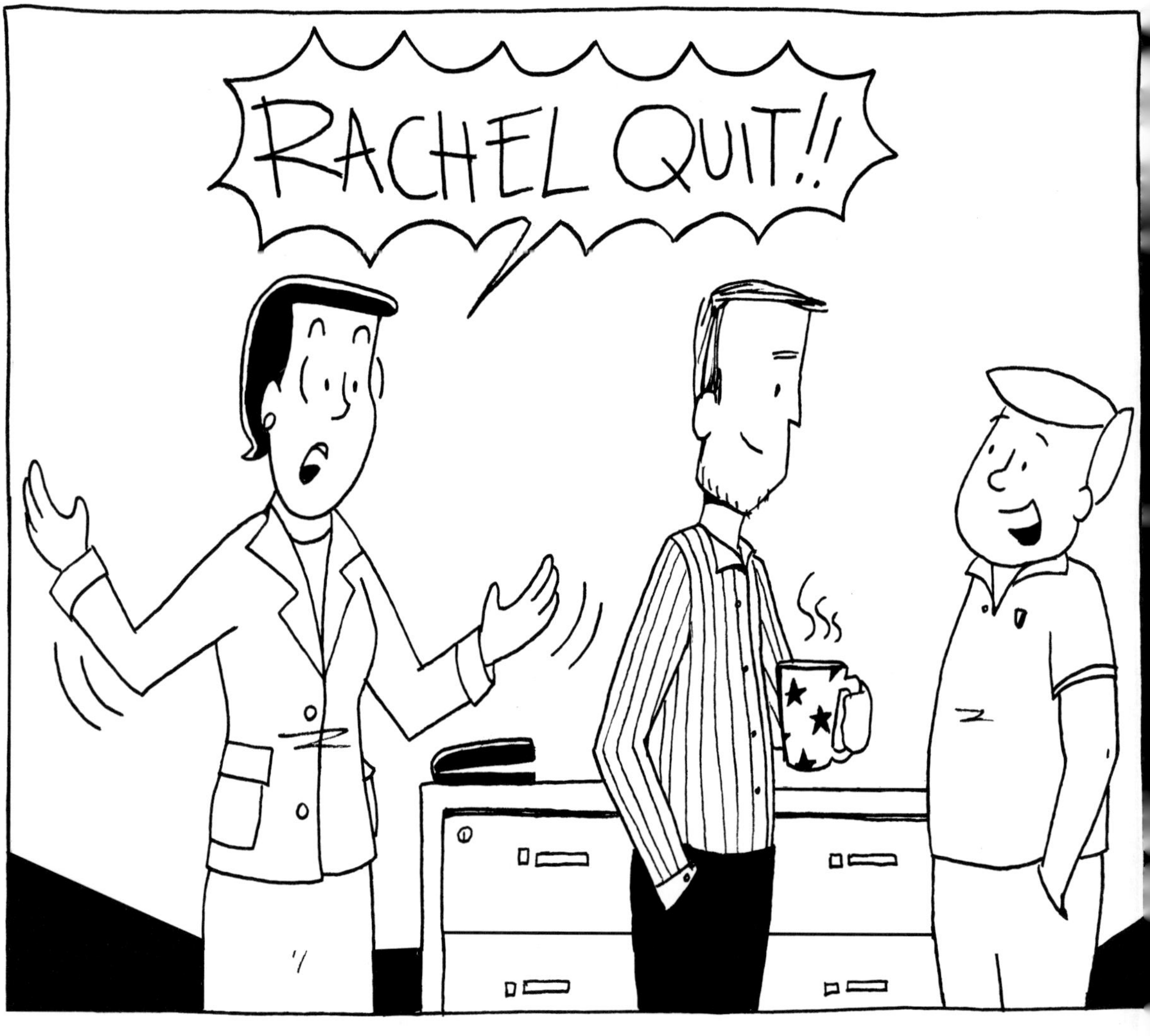
RACHEL QUIT!!

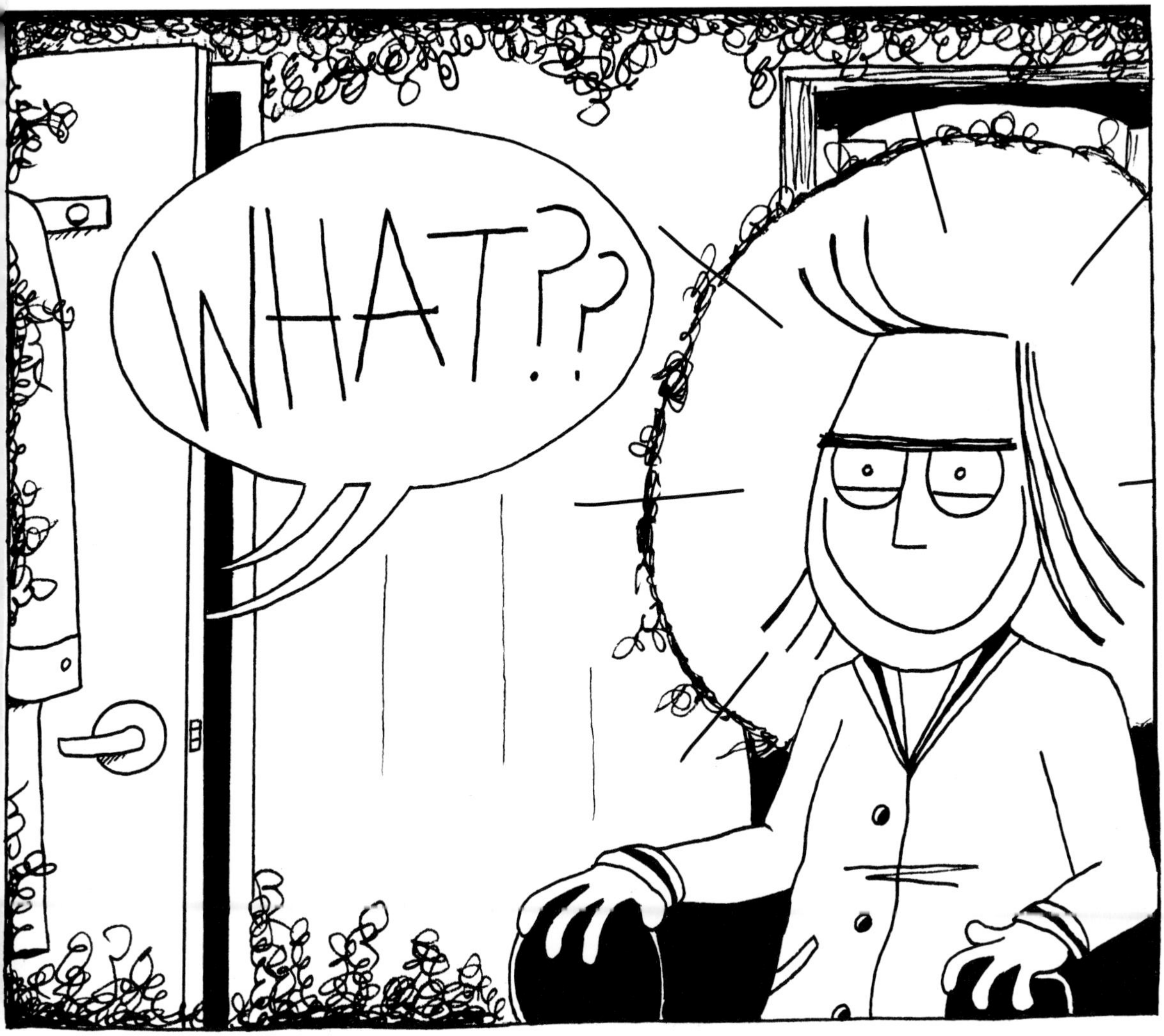
WHAT?!?

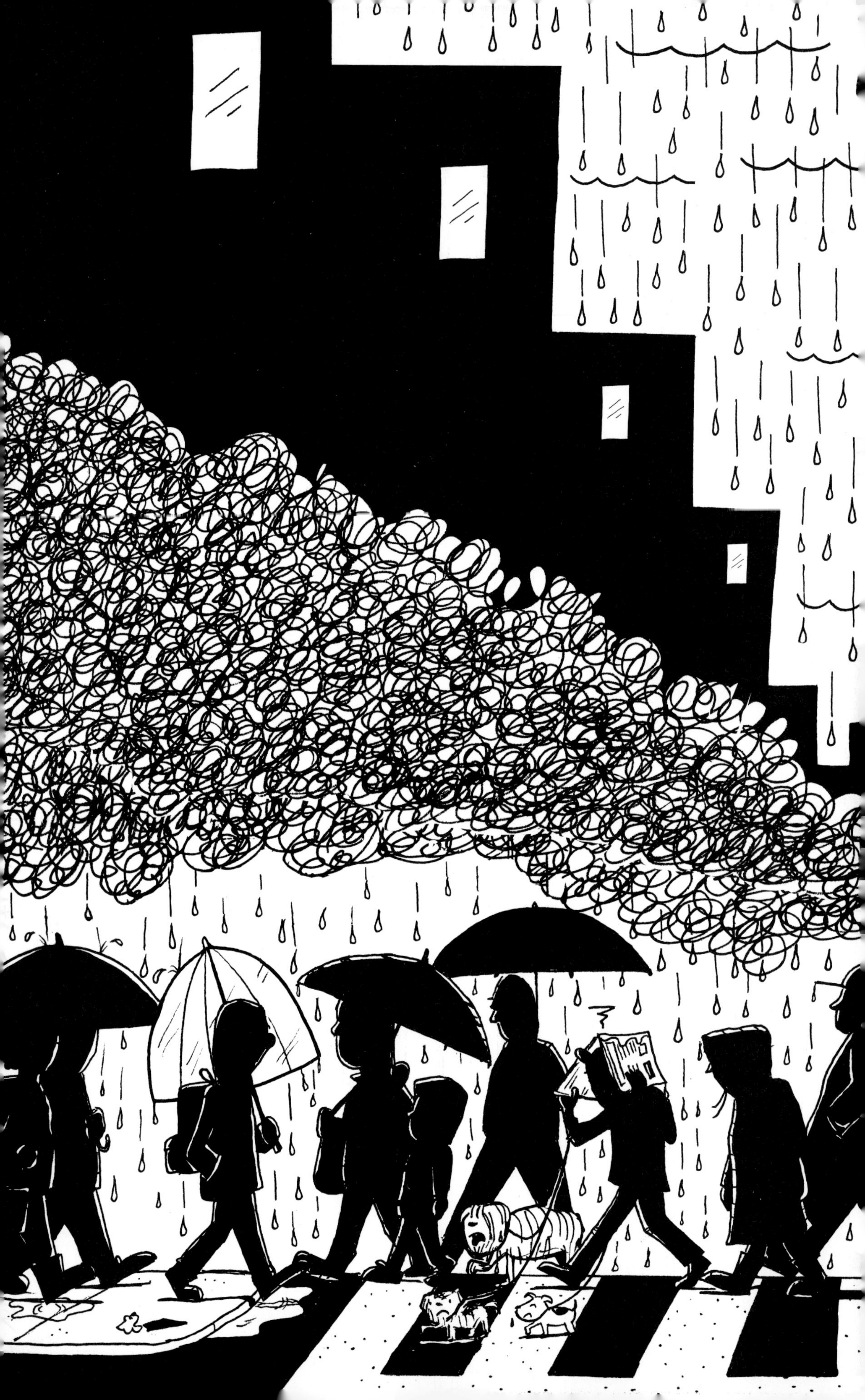

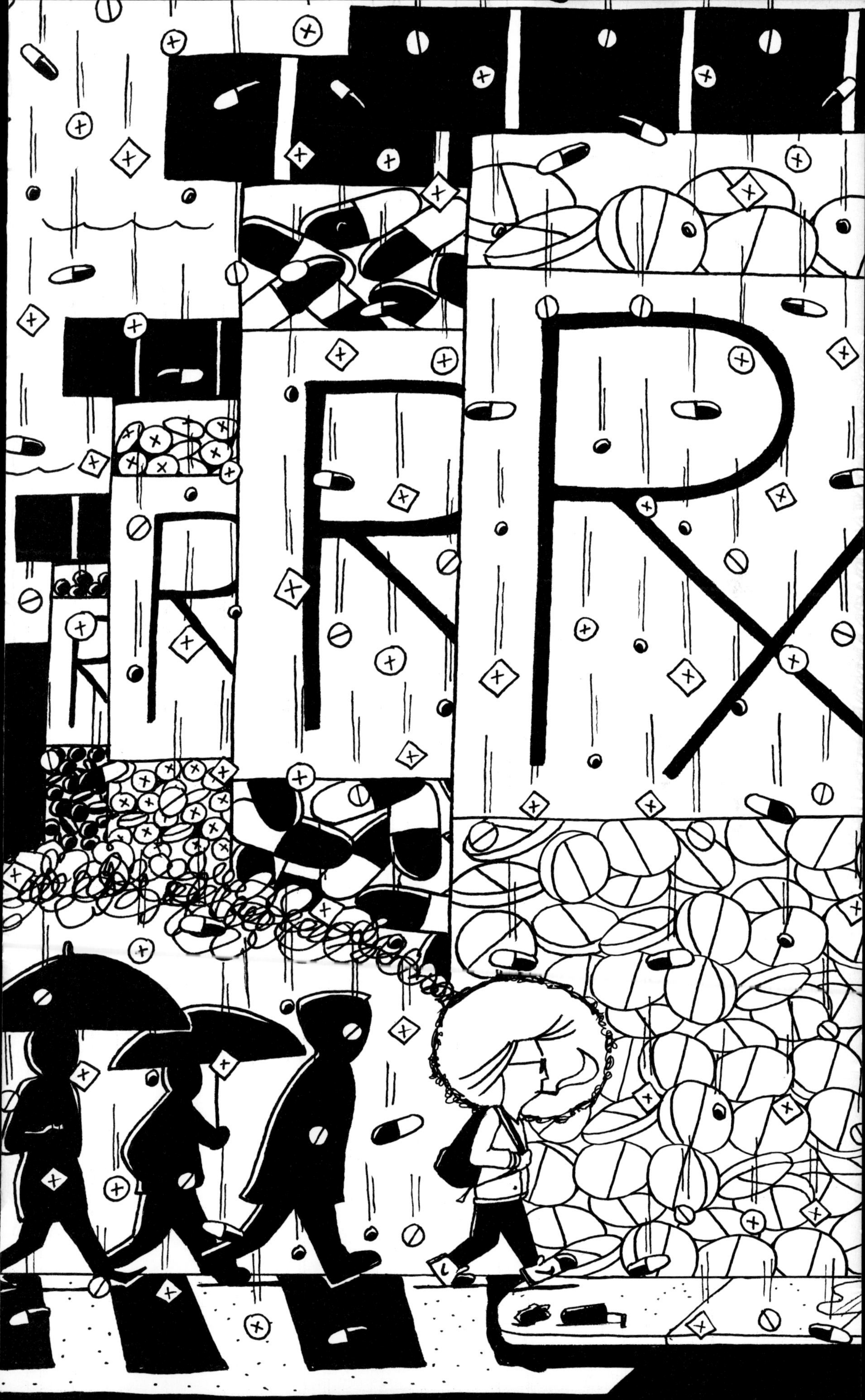
Rx

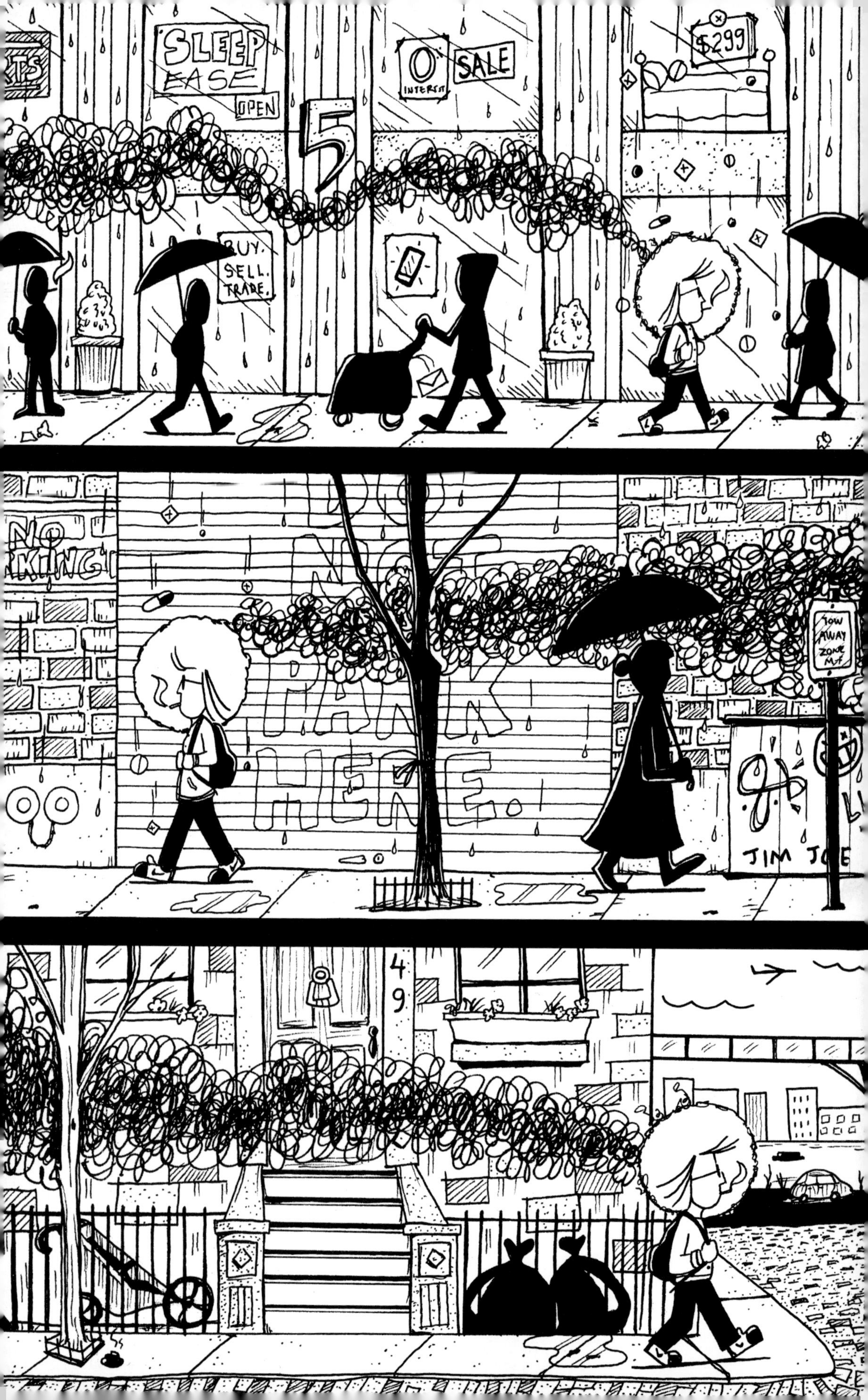
SLEEP EASE
OPEN
5
0 INTEREST
SALE
$299
BUY. SELL. TRADE.
TOW AWAY ZONE
JIM JOE
49

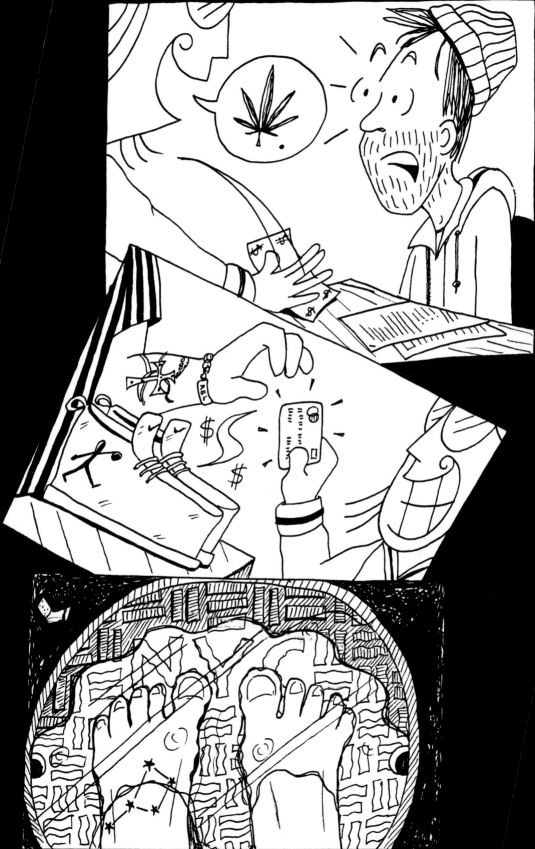

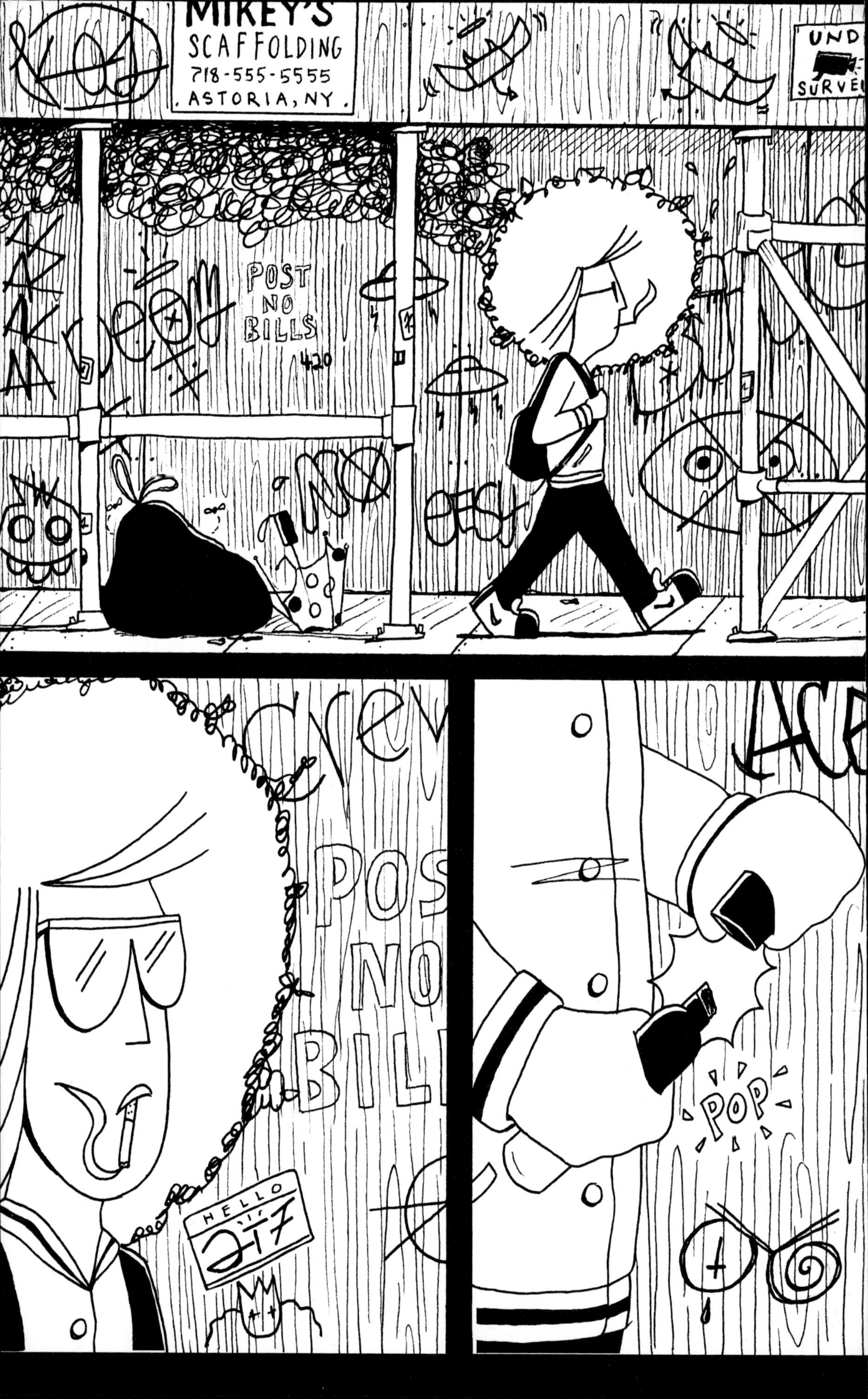
MIKEY'S
SCAFFOLDING
718-555-5555
ASTORIA, NY
POST NO BILLS
420
HELLO
POP

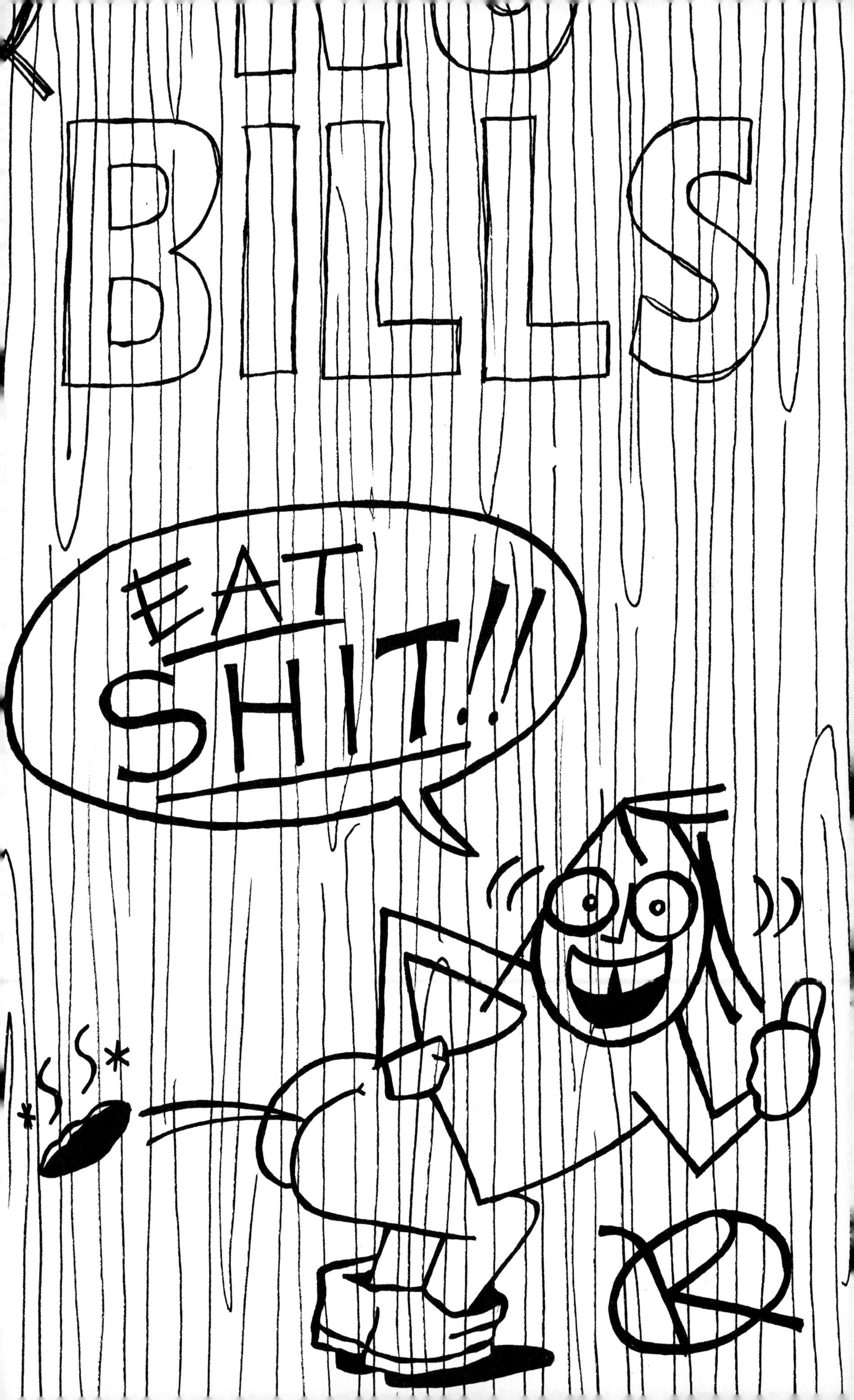
BILLS
EAT SHIT!!

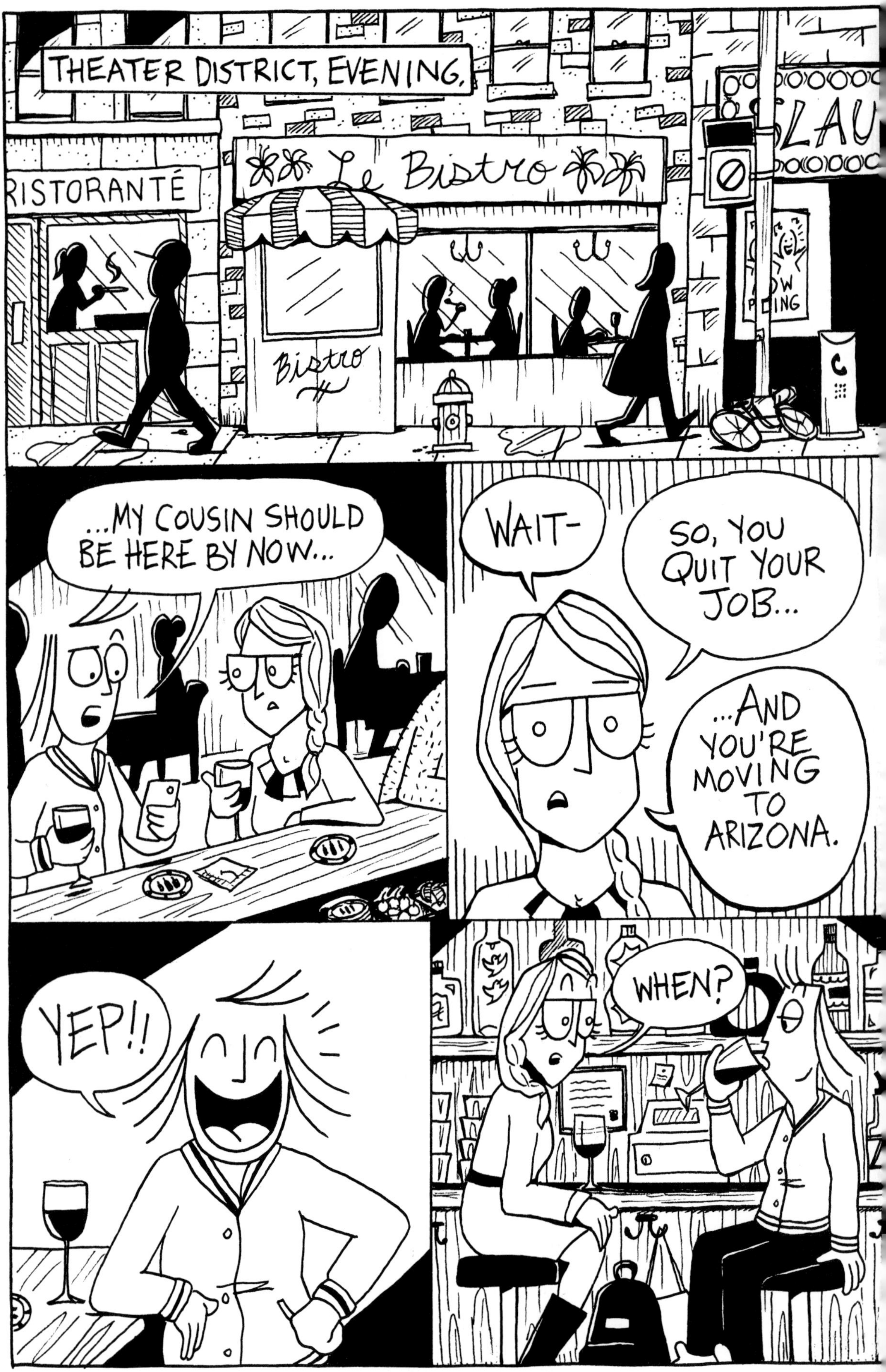
THEATER DISTRICT, EVENING.
RISTORANTÉ
Le Bistro
Bistro
...MY COUSIN SHOULD BE HERE BY NOW...
WAIT-
SO, YOU QUIT YOUR JOB...
...AND YOU'RE MOVING TO ARIZONA.
YEP!!
WHEN?

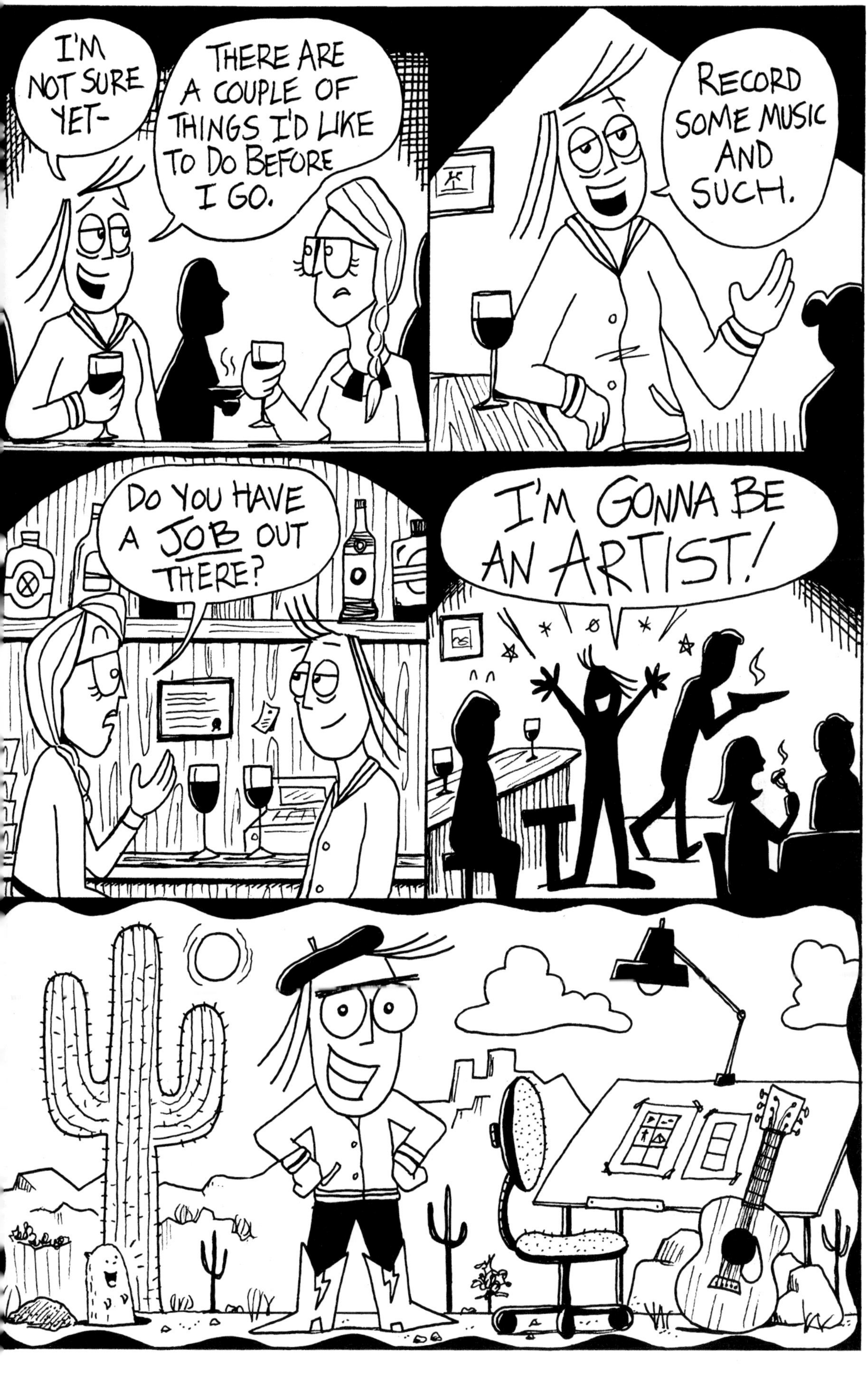
I'M NOT SURE YET-
THERE ARE A COUPLE OF THINGS I'D LIKE TO DO BEFORE I GO.
RECORD SOME MUSIC AND SUCH.
DO YOU HAVE A JOB OUT THERE?
I'M GONNA BE AN ARTIST!

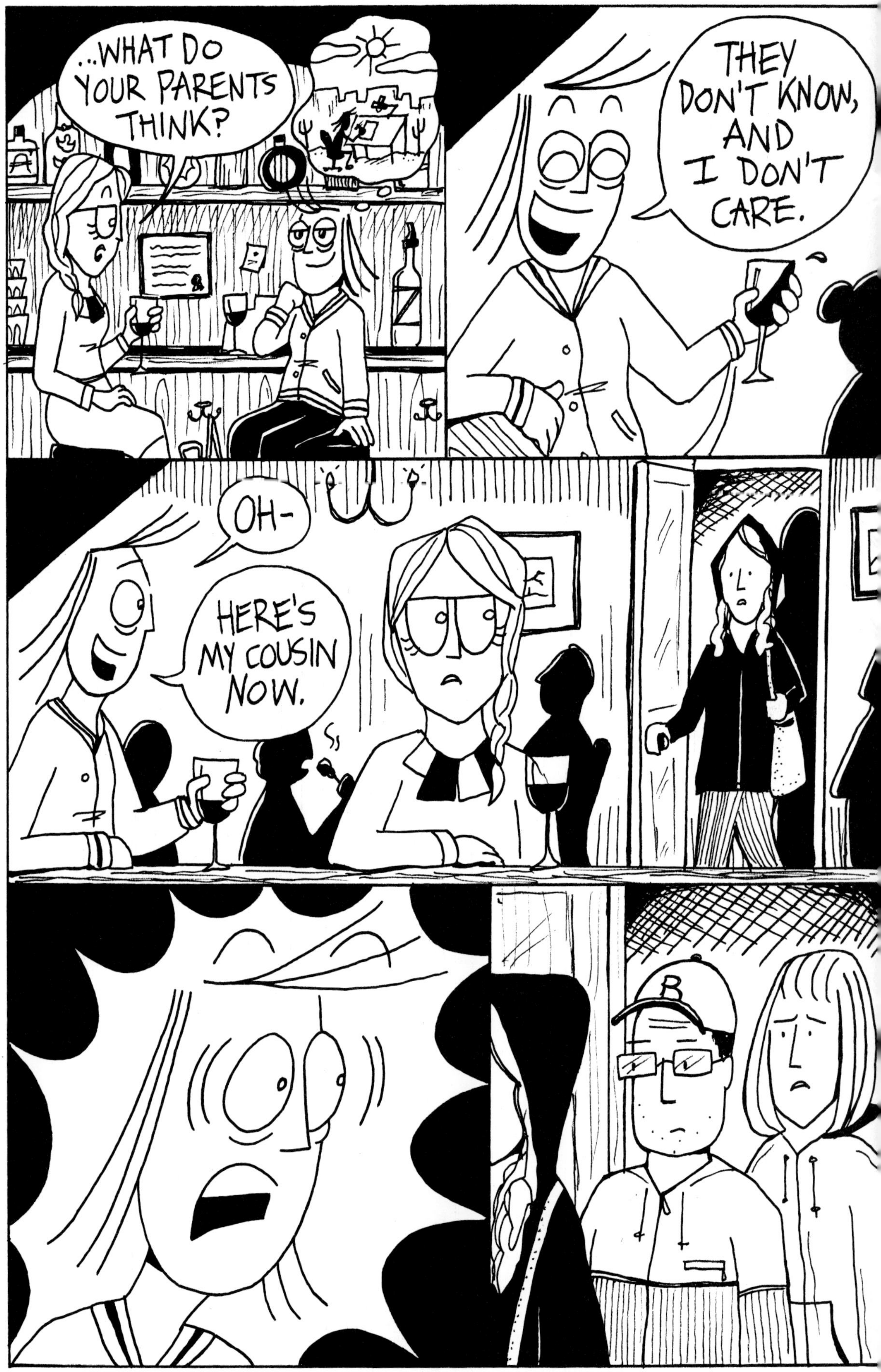
...WHAT DO YOUR PARENTS THINK?
THEY DON'T KNOW, AND I DON'T CARE.
OH-
HERE'S MY COUSIN NOW.

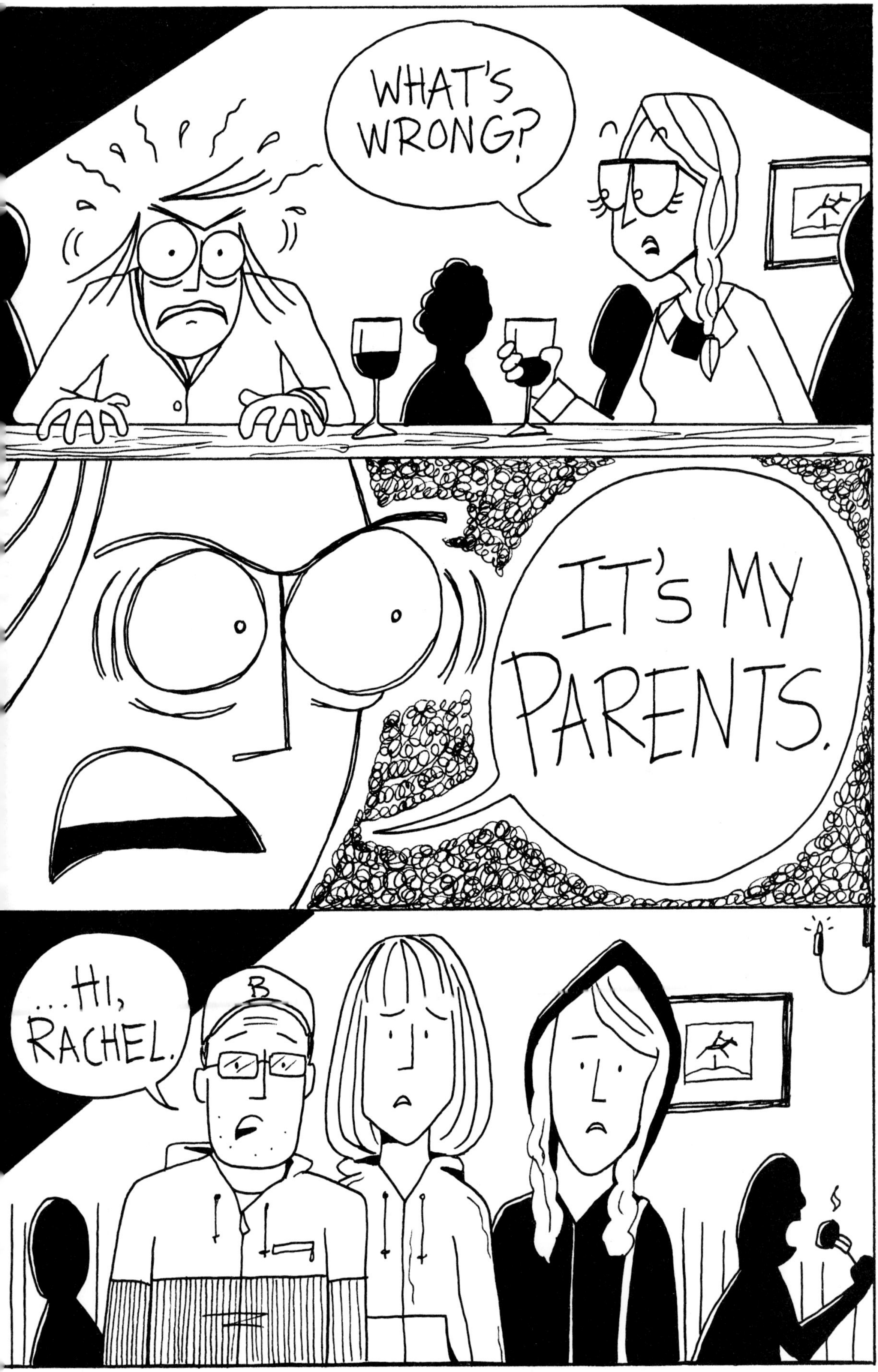
WHAT'S WRONG?
IT'S MY PARENTS.
...HI, RACHEL.

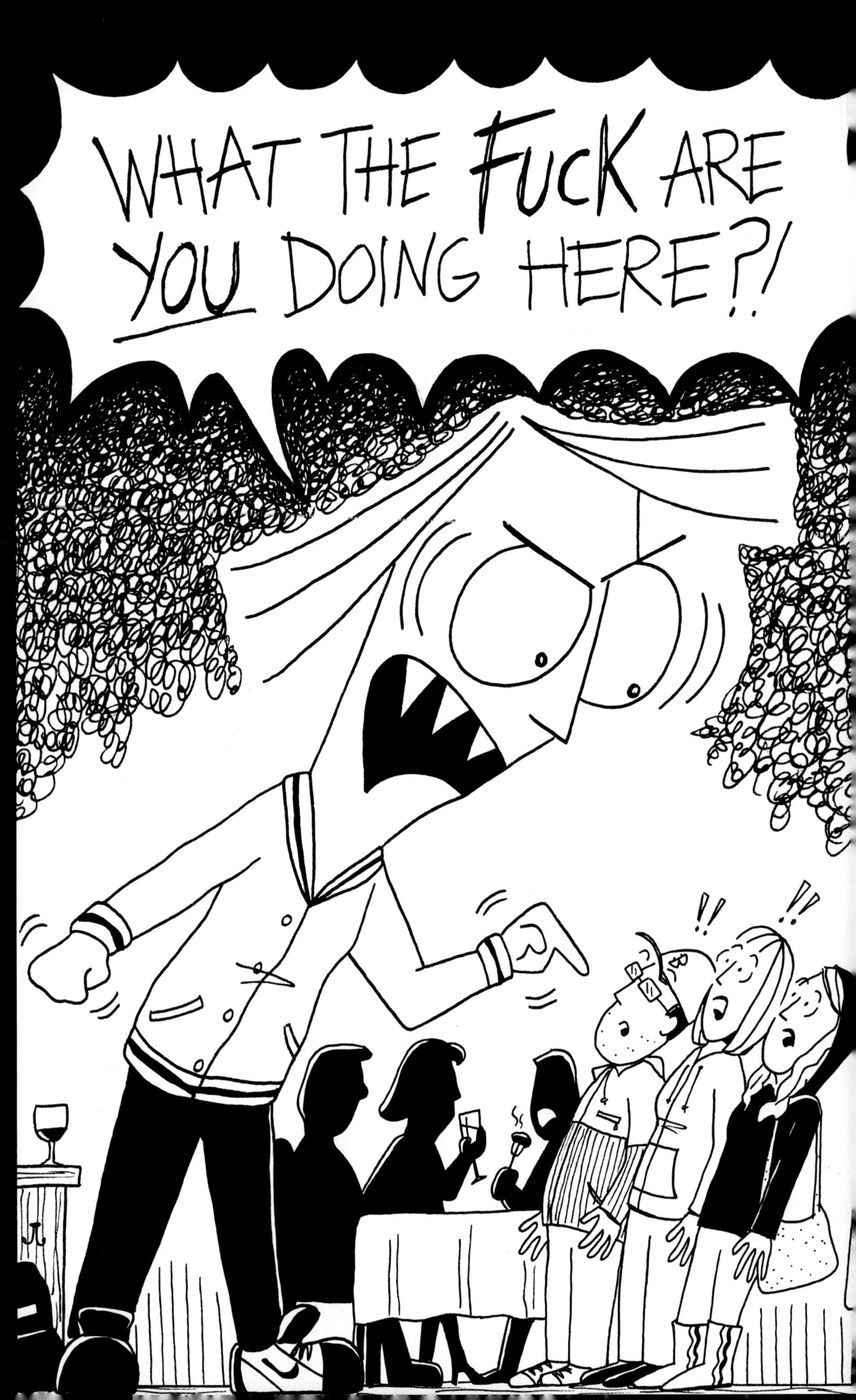
WHAT THE FUCK ARE YOU DOING HERE?!
!!
!!

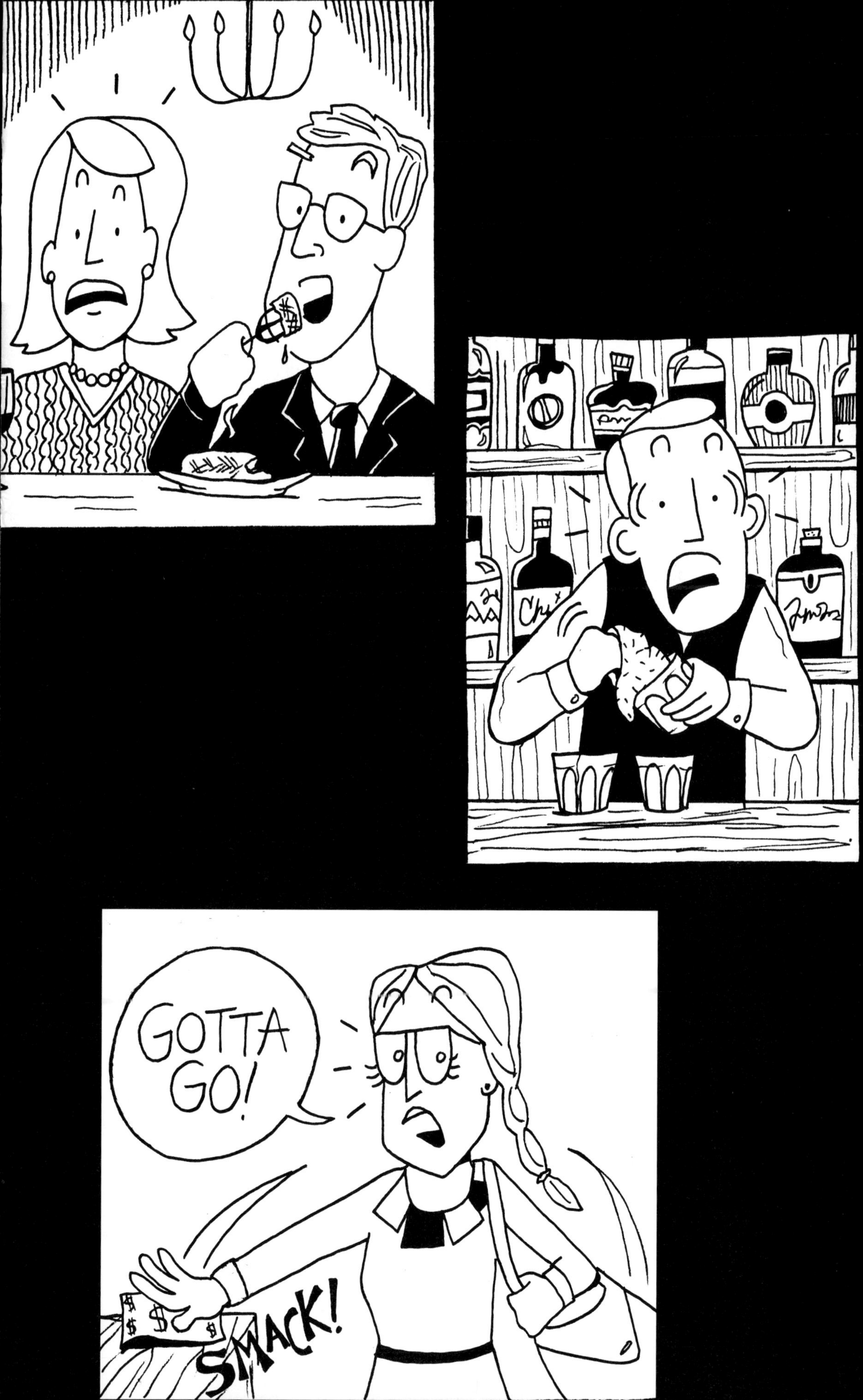
GOTTA GO!
SMACK!

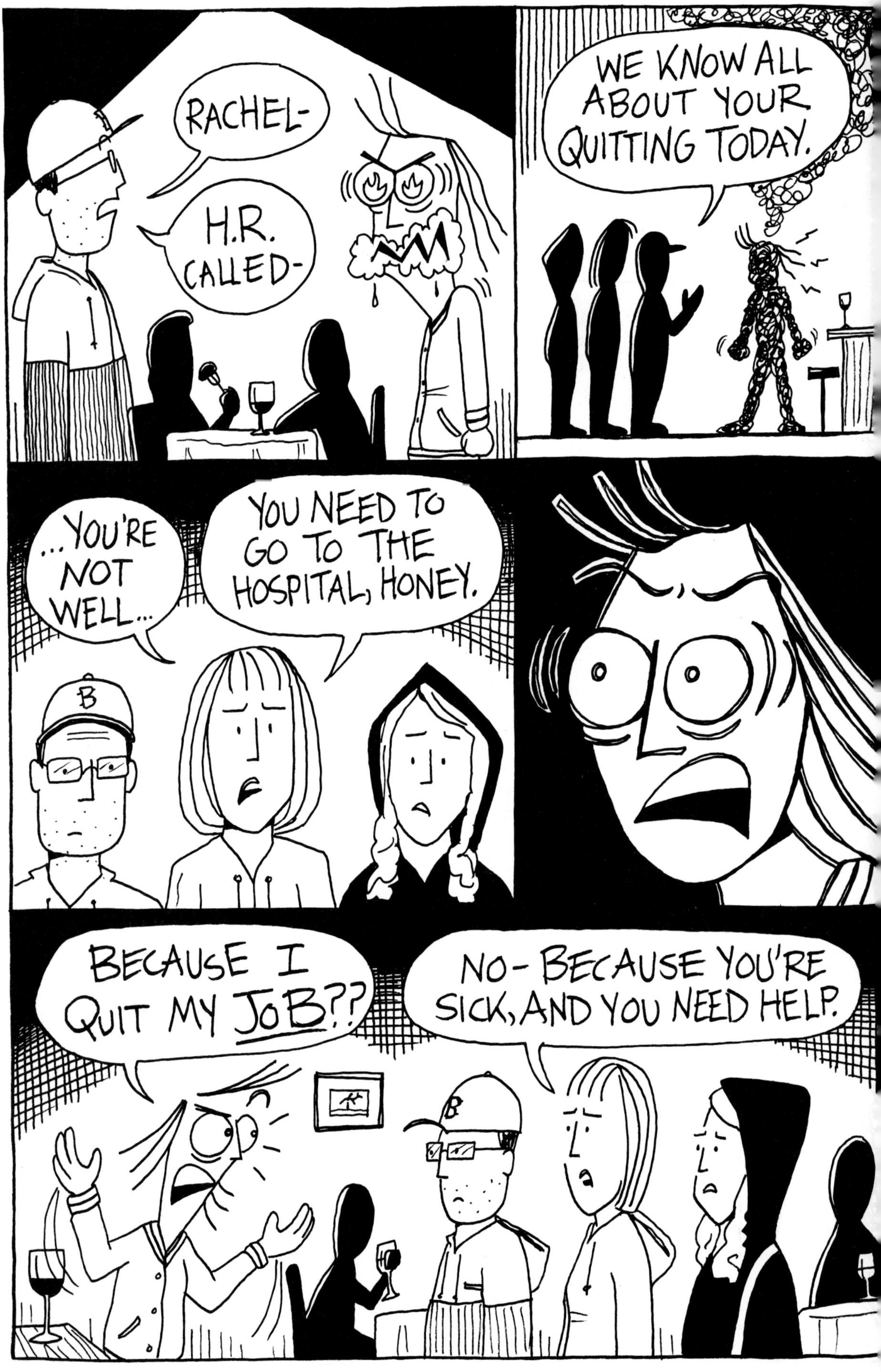
RACHEL-
H.R. CALLED-
WE KNOW ALL ABOUT YOUR QUITTING TODAY.
...YOU'RE NOT WELL...
YOU NEED TO GO TO THE HOSPITAL, HONEY.
BECAUSE I QUIT MY JOB??
NO- BECAUSE YOU'RE SICK, AND YOU NEED HELP.

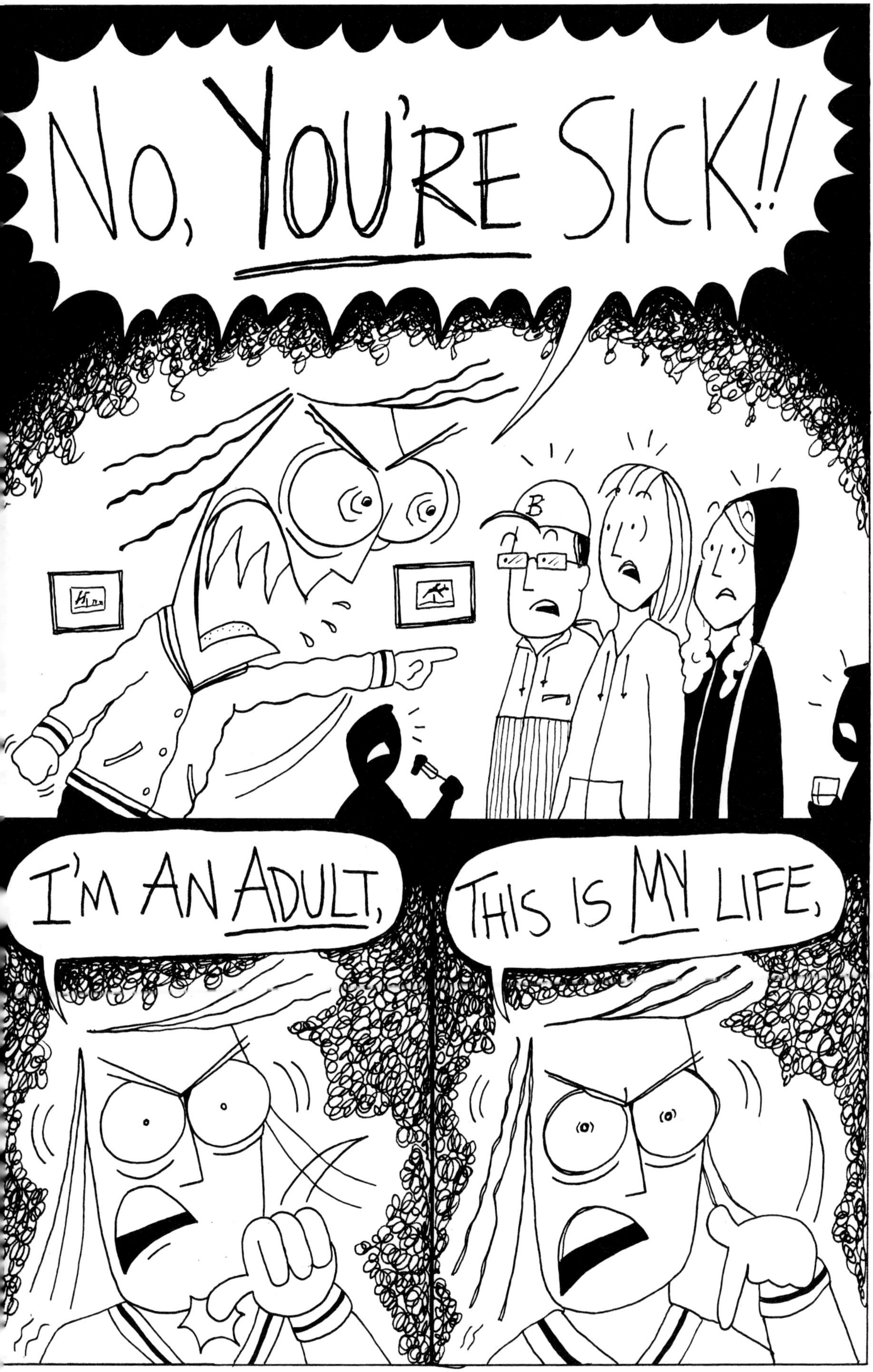
NO, YOU'RE SICK!!
I'M AN ADULT,
THIS IS MY LIFE,

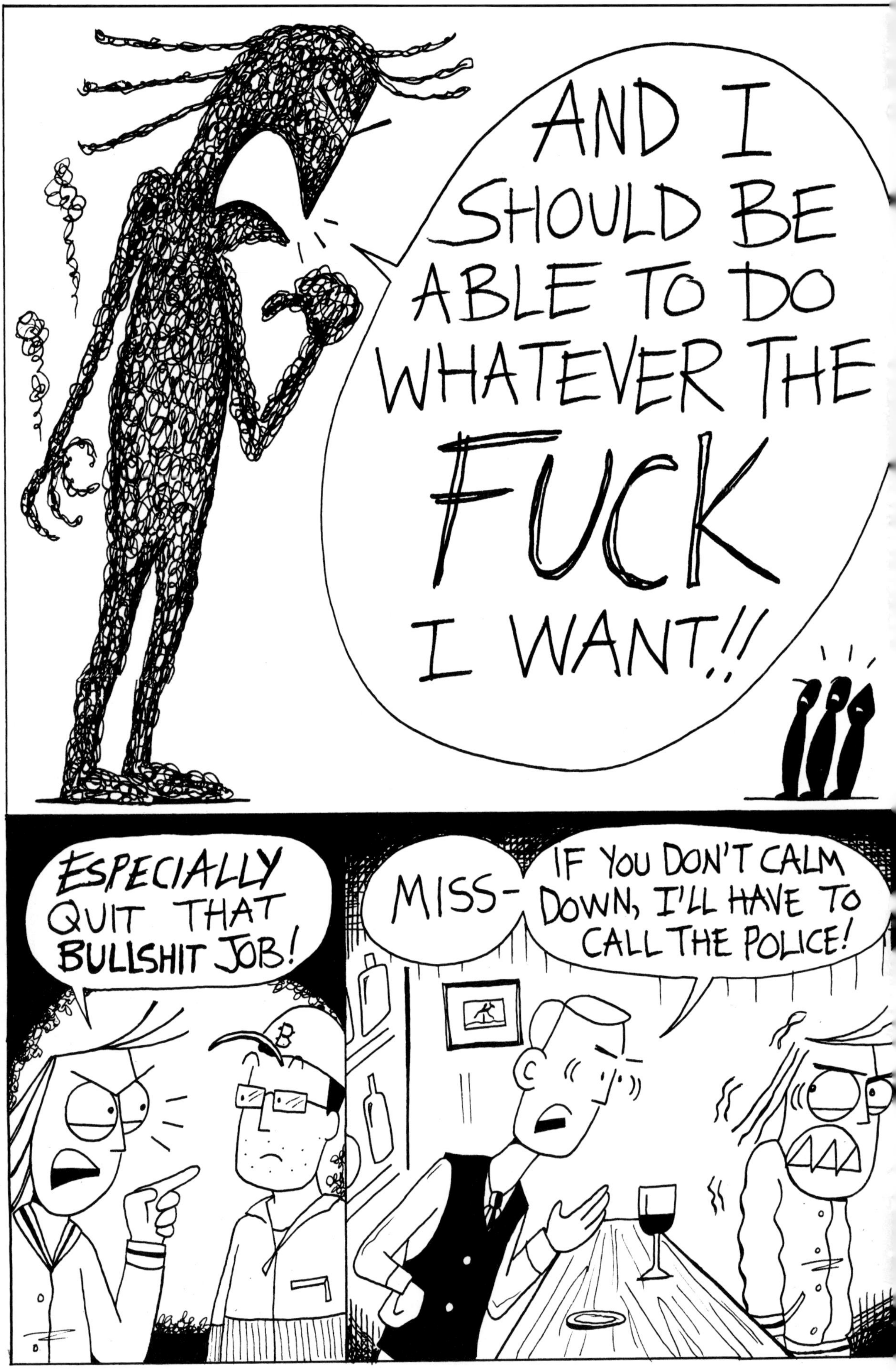
AND I SHOULD BE ABLE TO DO WHATEVER THE FUCK I WANT!!
ESPECIALLY QUIT THAT BULLSHIT JOB!
MISS-
IF YOU DON'T CALM DOWN, I'LL HAVE TO CALL THE POLICE!

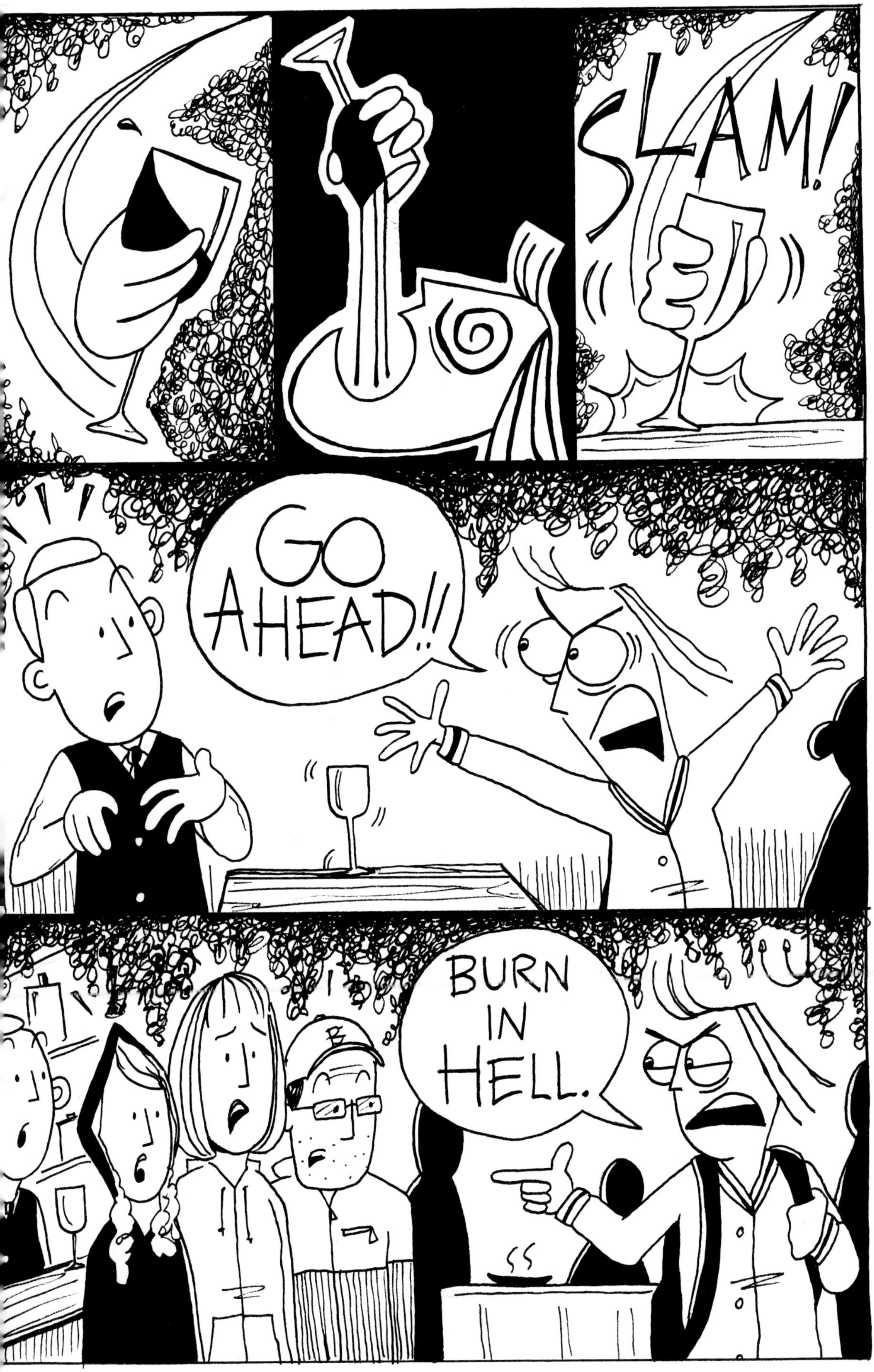
SLAM!
GO AHEAD!!
BURN IN HELL.

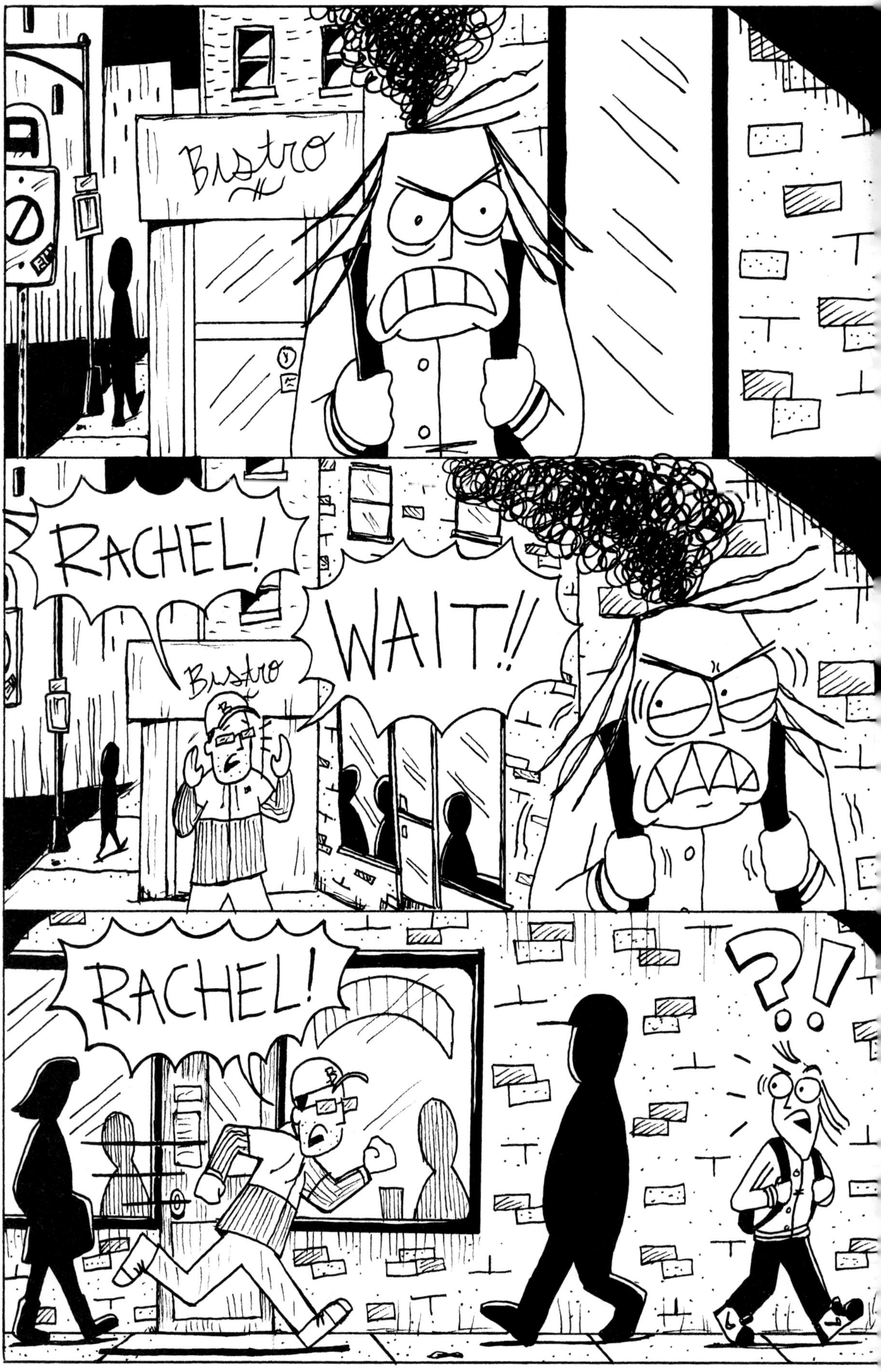
Bistro
RACHEL!
WAIT!!
RACHEL!
?!

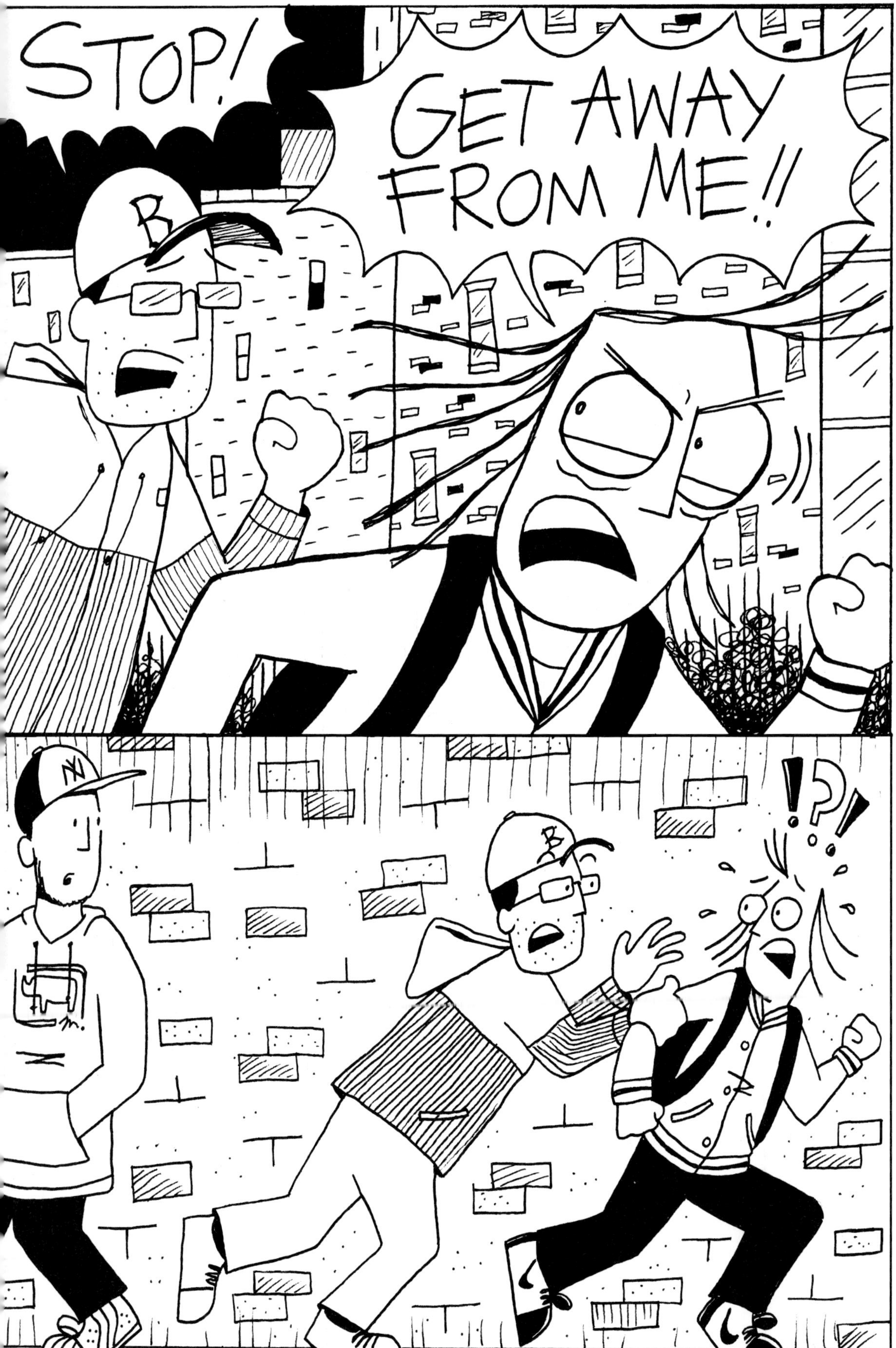
STOP!
GET AWAY FROM ME!!
!?!

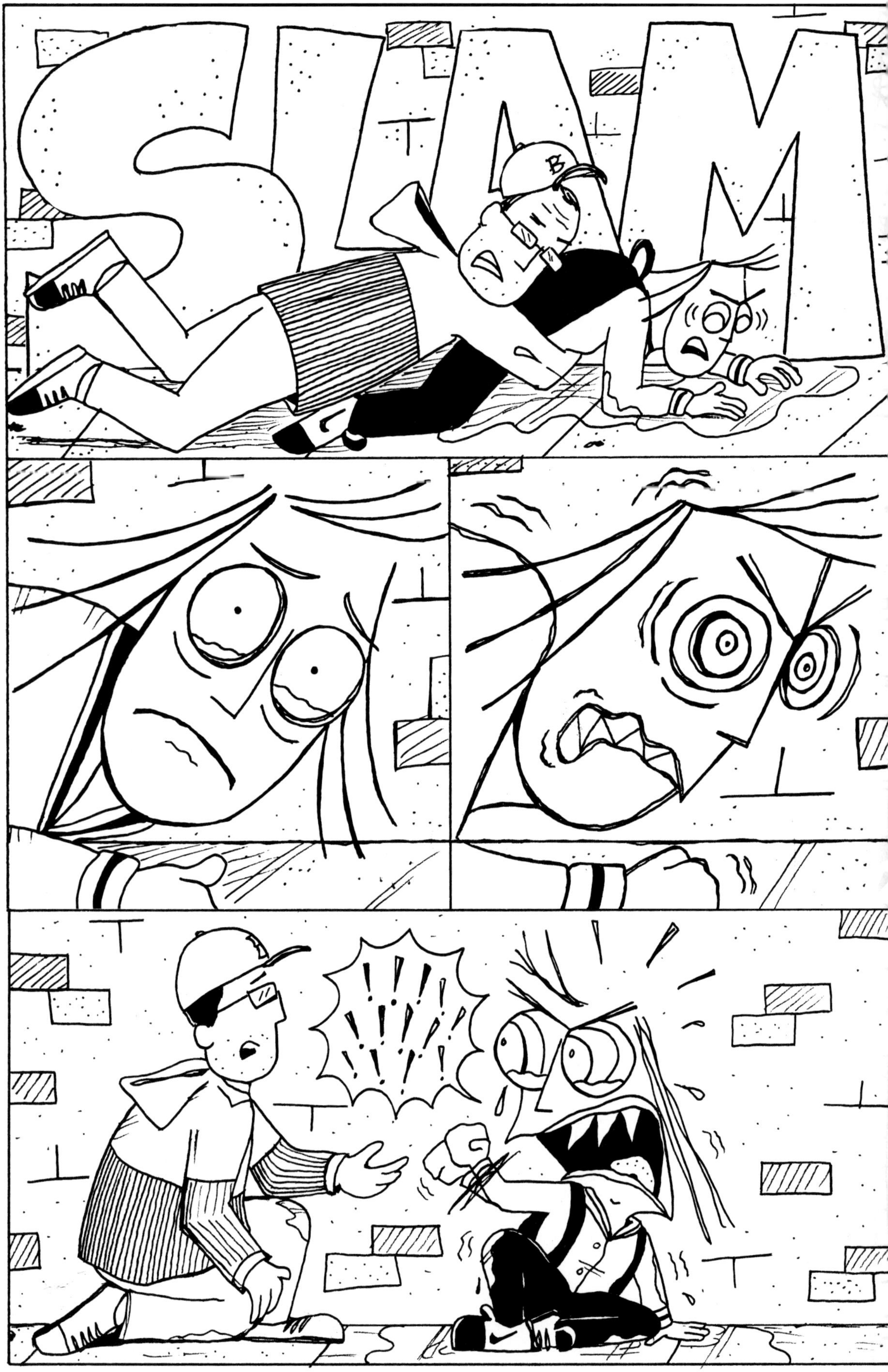
SLAM

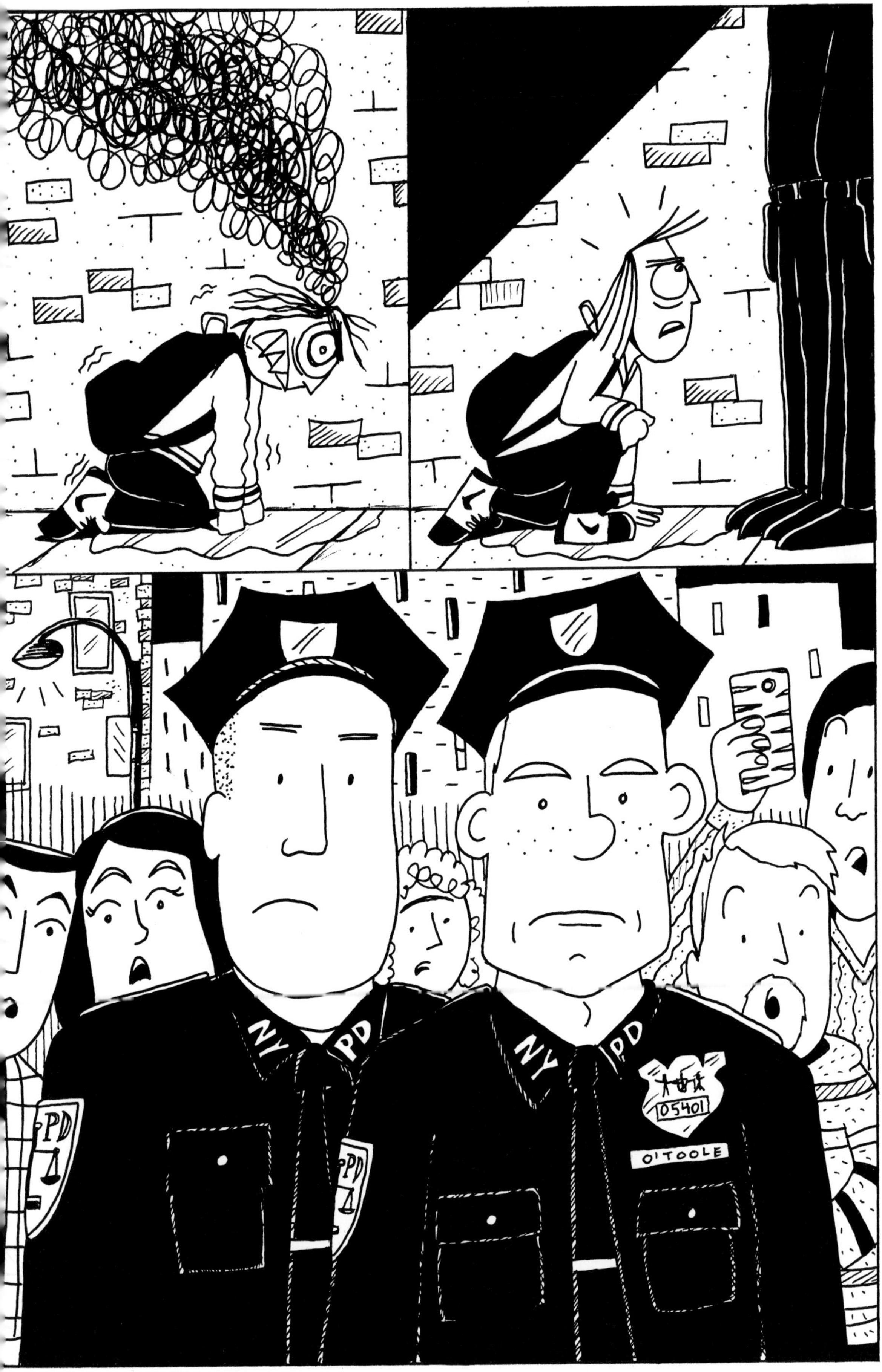

NY
PD
NY
PD
PD
PD
05401
O'TOOLE

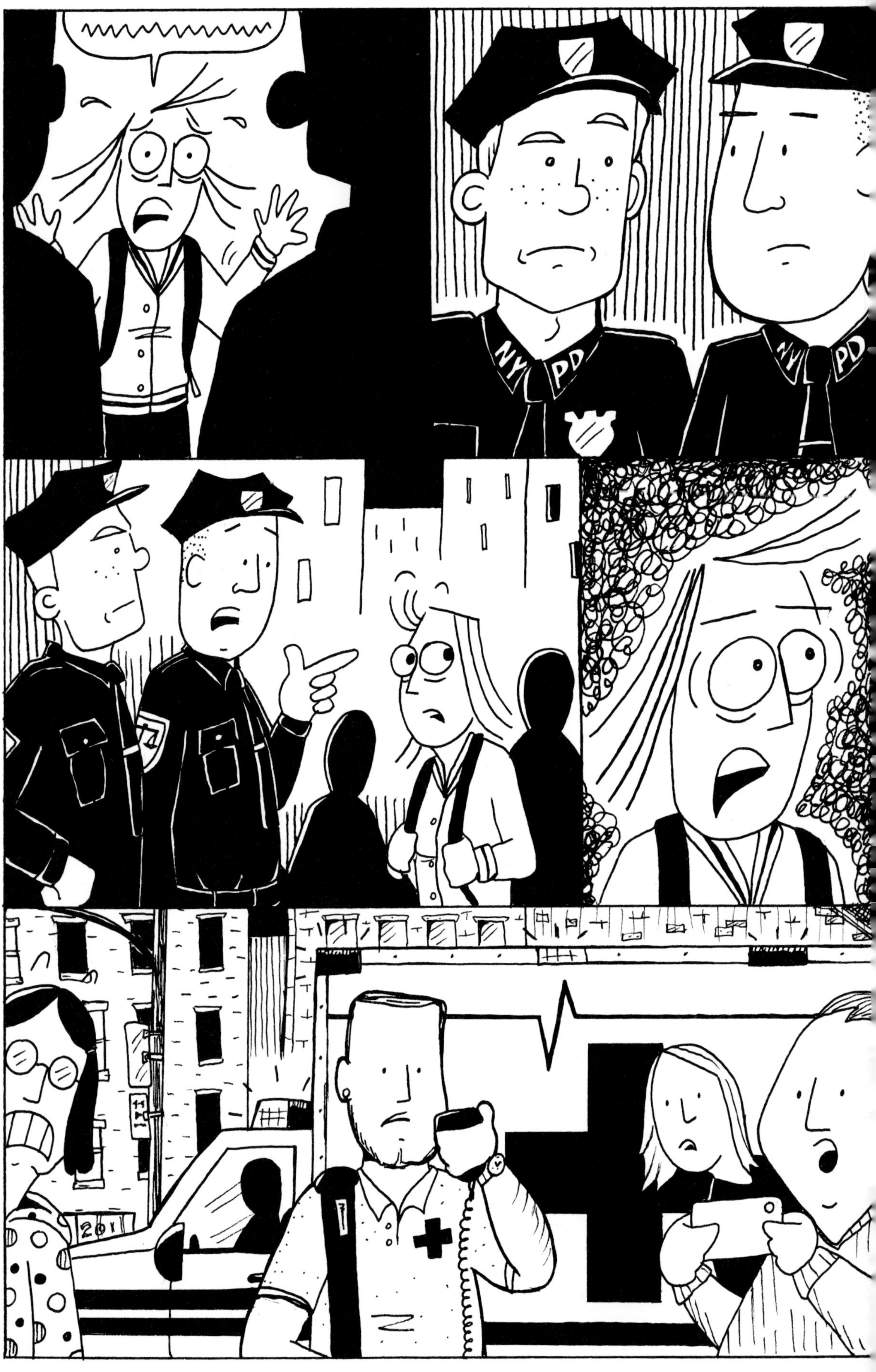
NY PD
NY PD
201

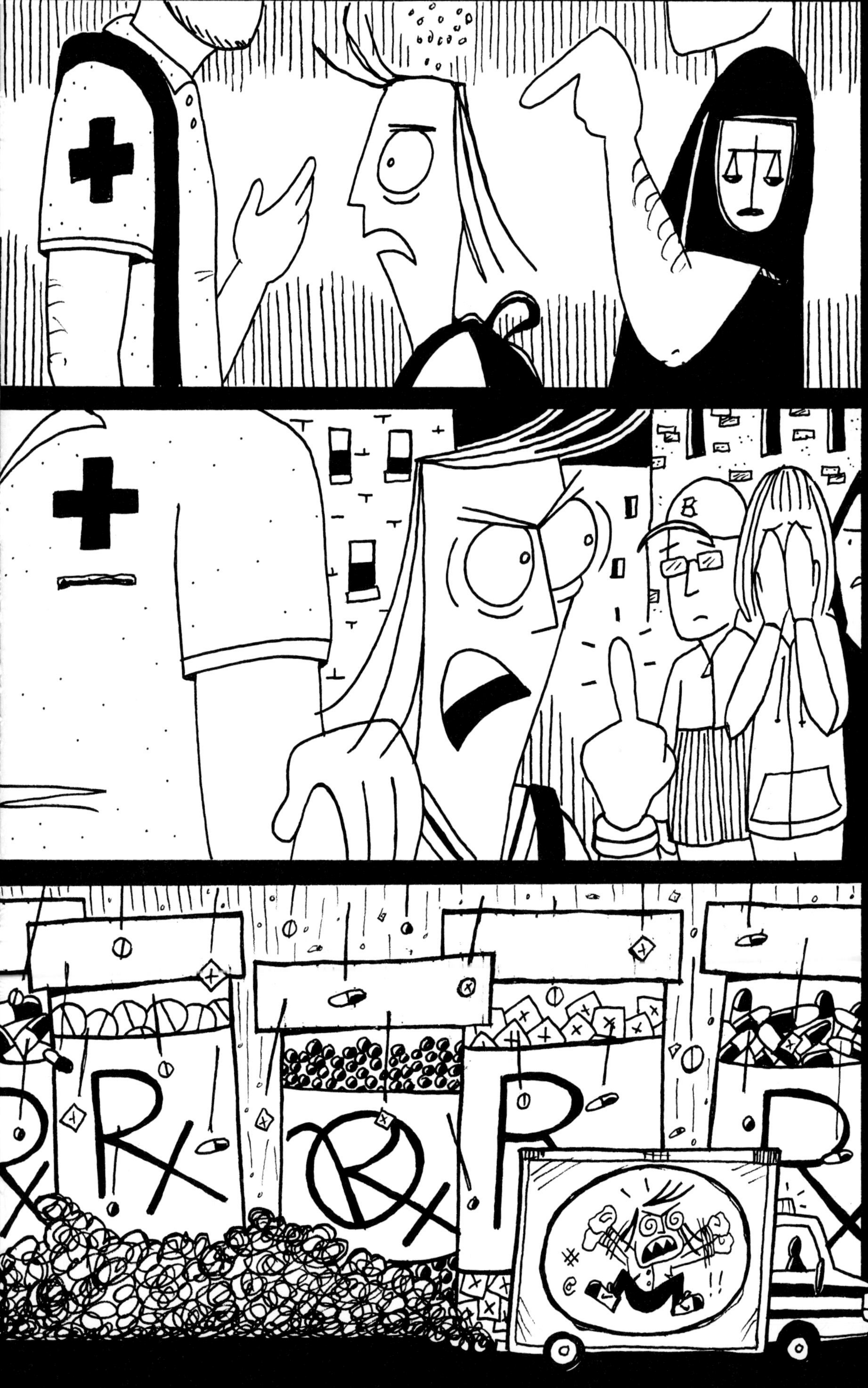
RX
RX

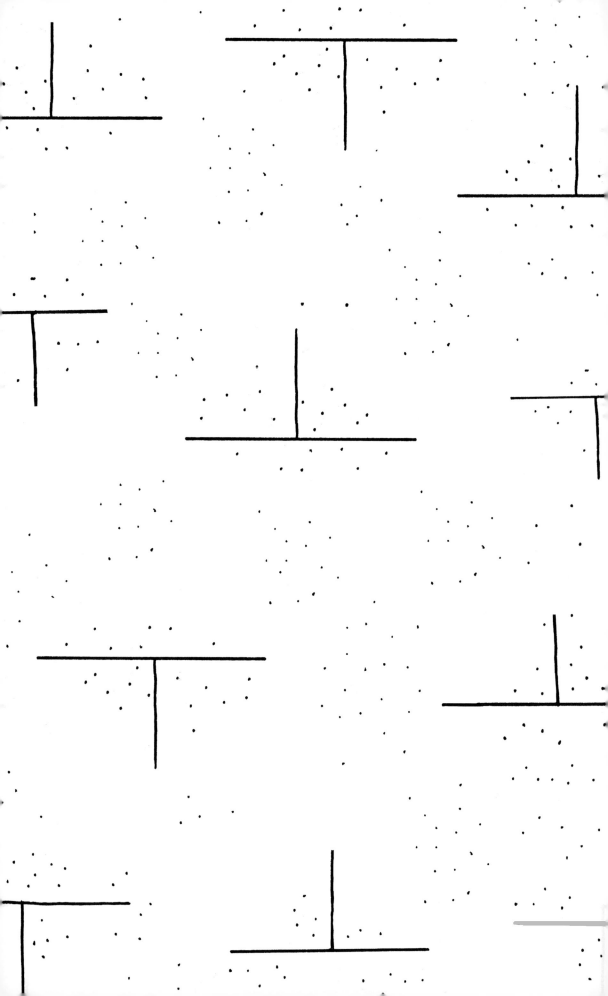

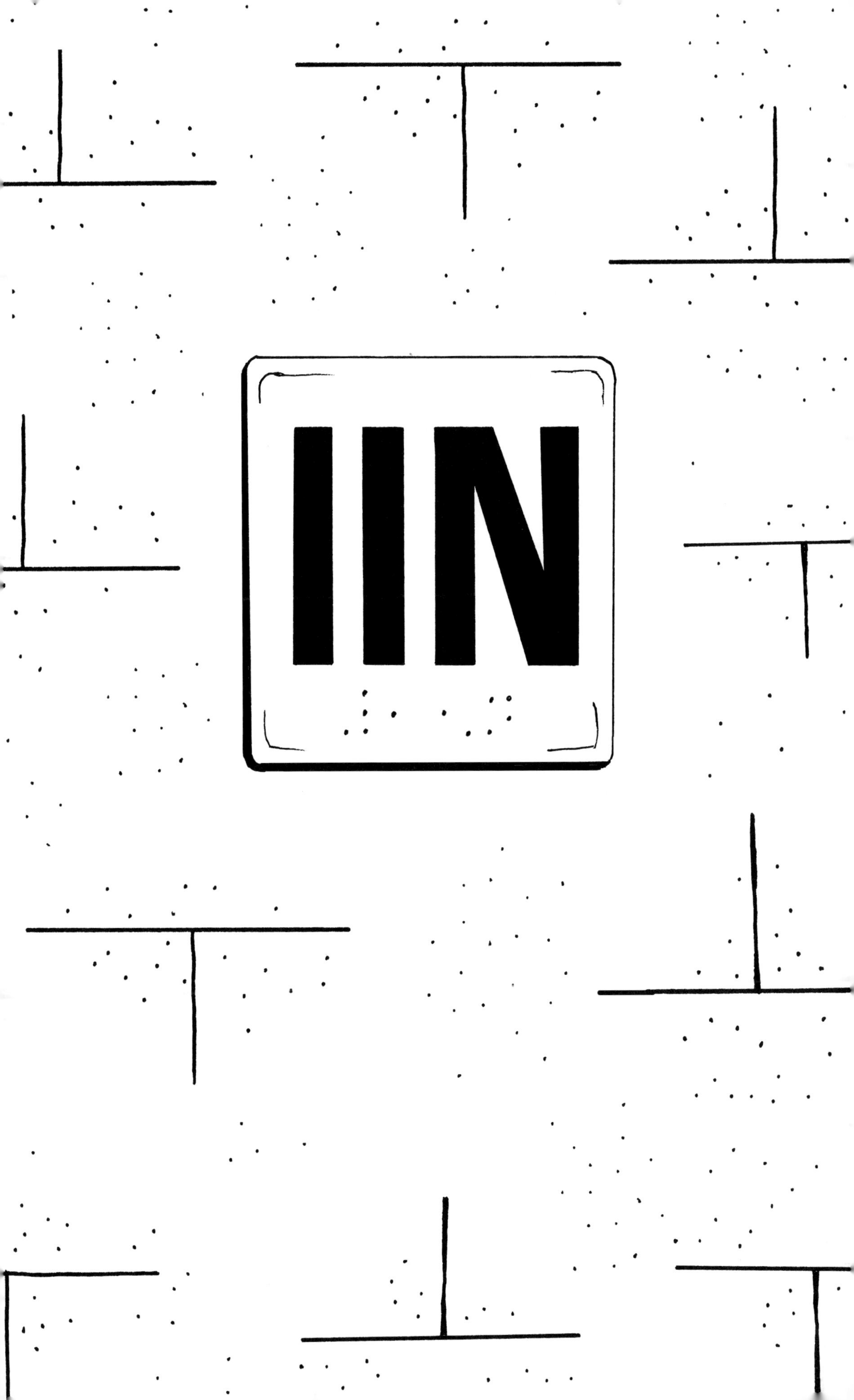
IIN

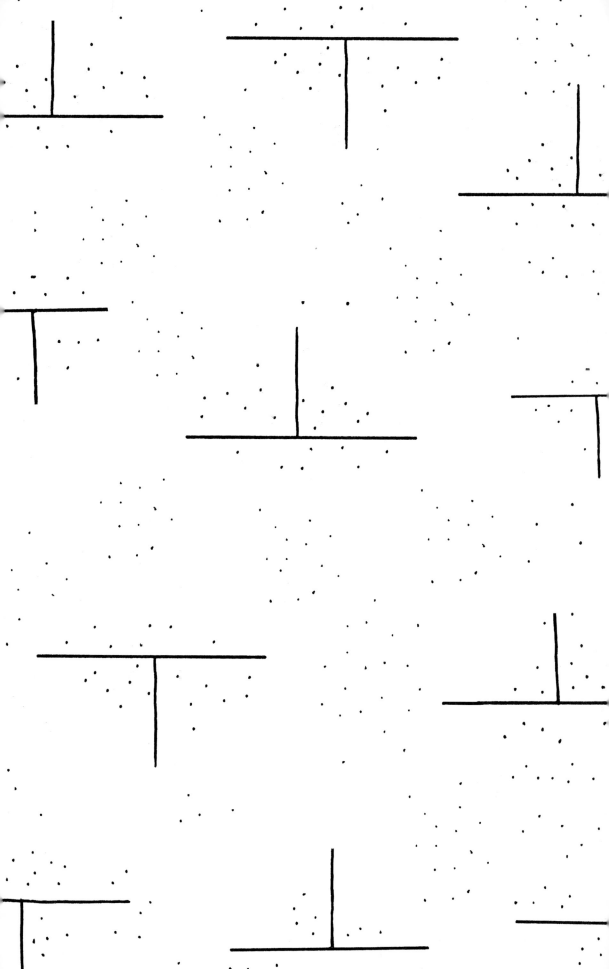

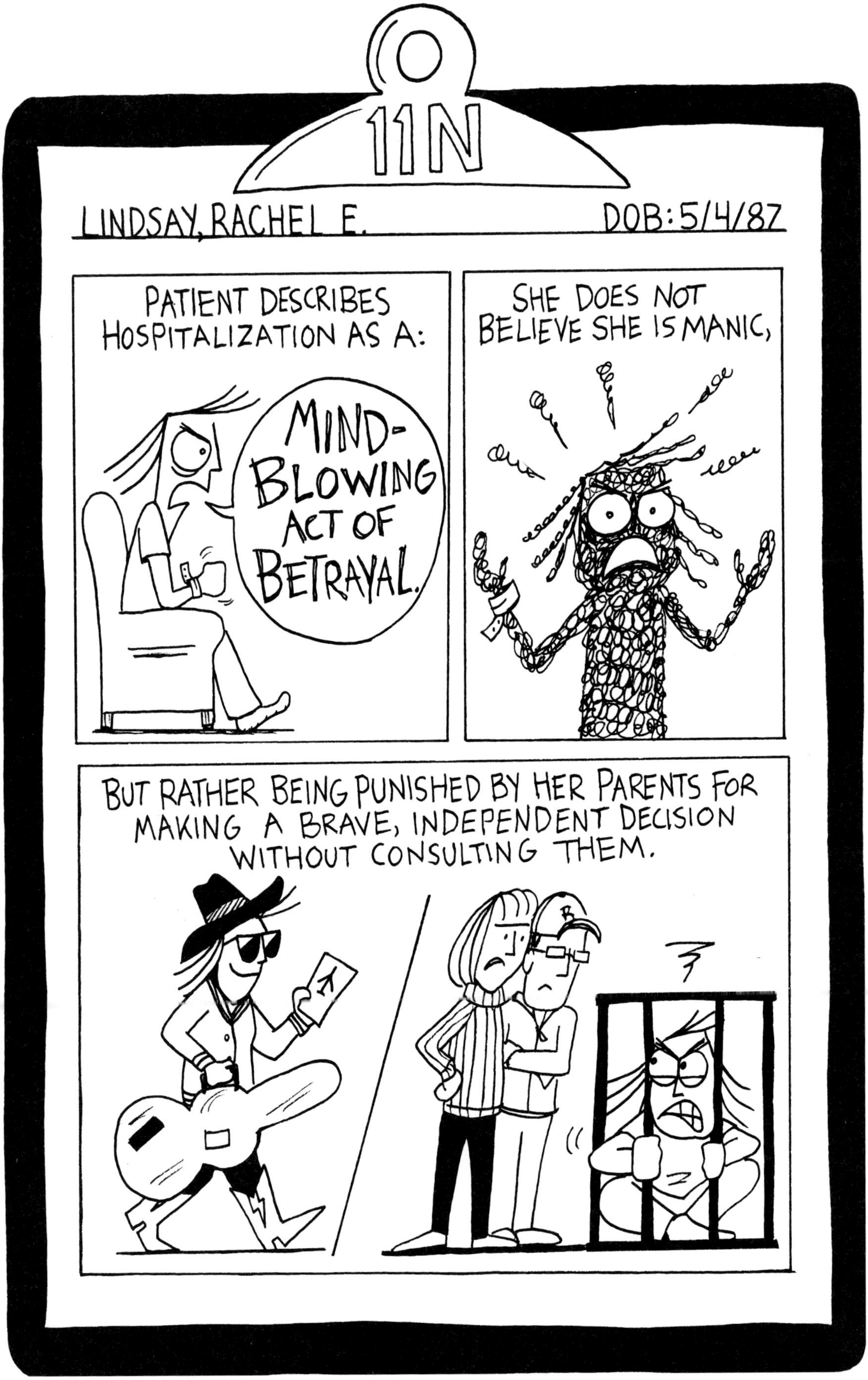
11N
LINDSAY, RACHEL E.
DOB: 5/4/87
PATIENT DESCRIBES HOSPITALIZATION AS A:
MIND-BLOWING ACT OF BETRAYAL.
SHE DOES NOT BELIEVE SHE IS MANIC,
BUT RATHER BEING PUNISHED BY HER PARENTS FOR MAKING A BRAVE, INDEPENDENT DECISION WITHOUT CONSULTING THEM.

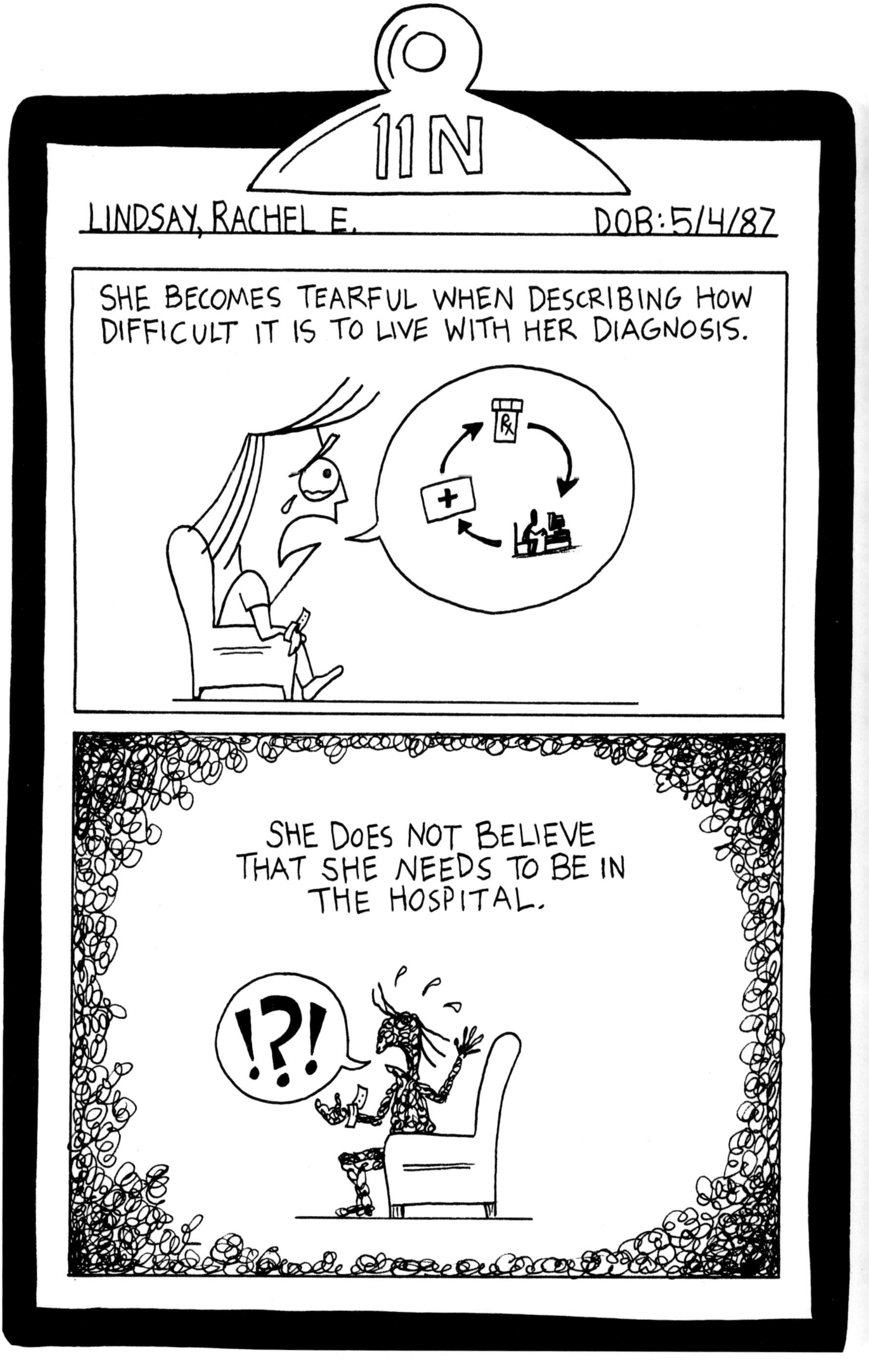
11N
LINDSAY, RACHEL E.
DOB: 5/4/87
SHE BECOMES TEARFUL WHEN DESCRIBING HOW DIFFICULT IT IS TO LIVE WITH HER DIAGNOSIS.
Rx
SHE DOES NOT BELIEVE THAT SHE NEEDS TO BE IN THE HOSPITAL.
!?!

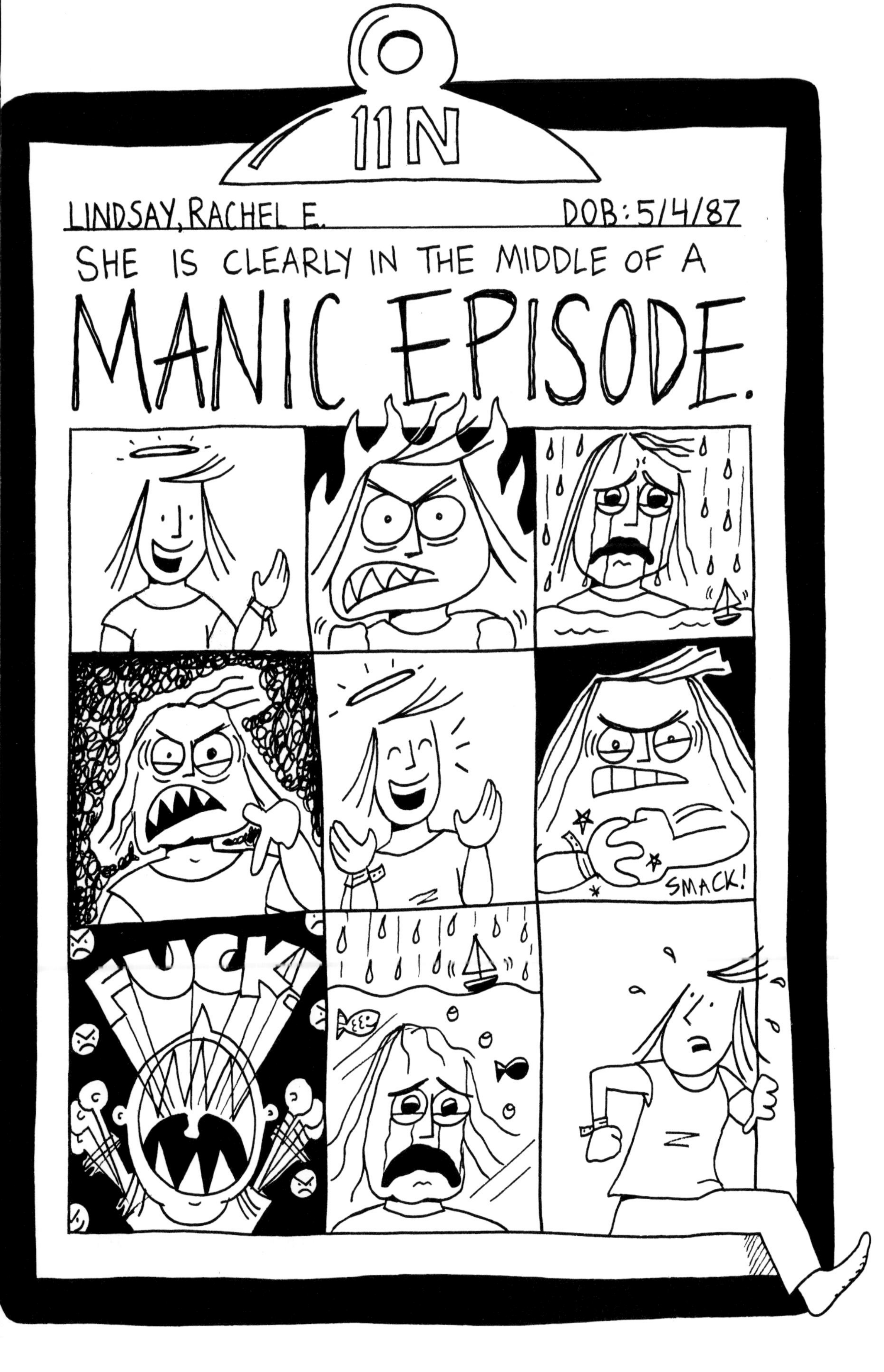
11N
LINDSAY, RACHEL E.
DOB: 5/4/87
SHE IS CLEARLY IN THE MIDDLE OF A
MANIC EPISODE.
SMACK!
FUCK

GIVEN HER WISH TO MAKE DECISIONS WITH SIGNIFICANT IMPAC ON HER FUTURE WHILE IN THIS STATE,

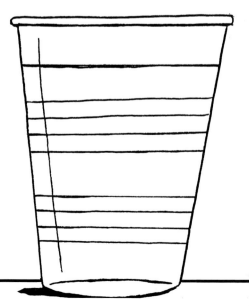

...AS WELL AS HER PSYCHIATRIST'S INABILITY TO MANAGE HER AS AN OUTPATIENT,

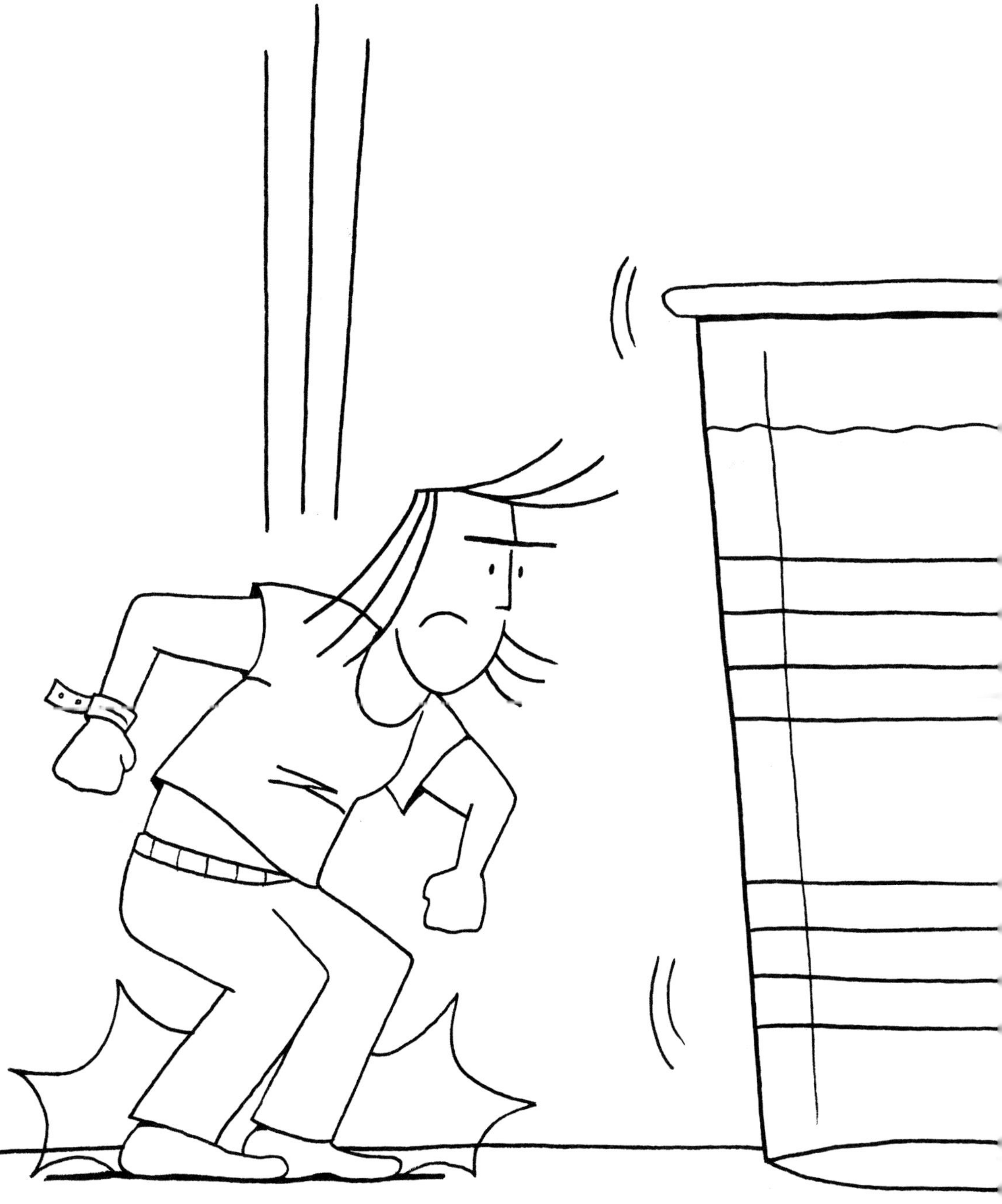

HOSPITALIZATION IS INDICATED FOR STABILIZATION AND MEDICATION ADJUSTMENT.

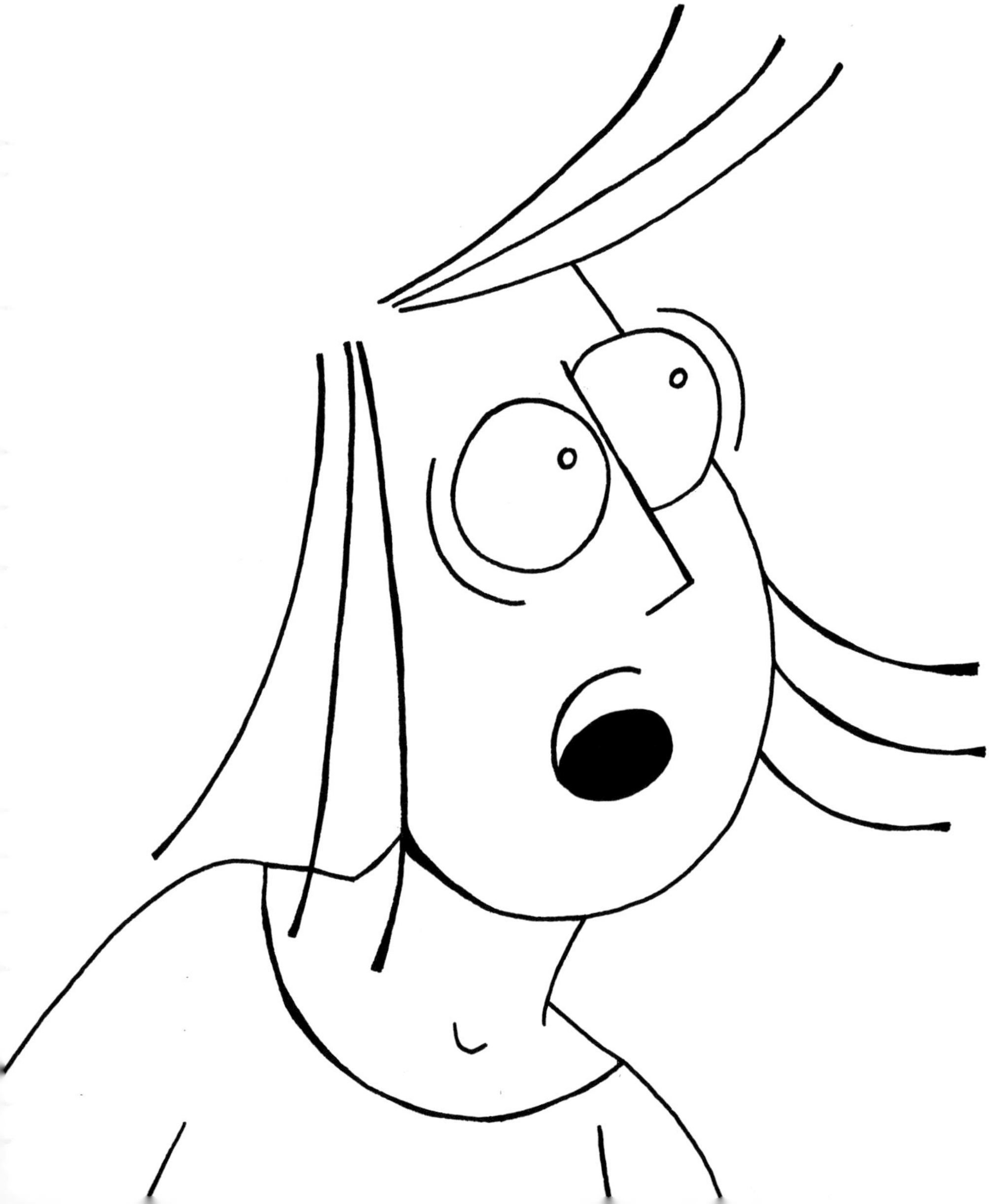

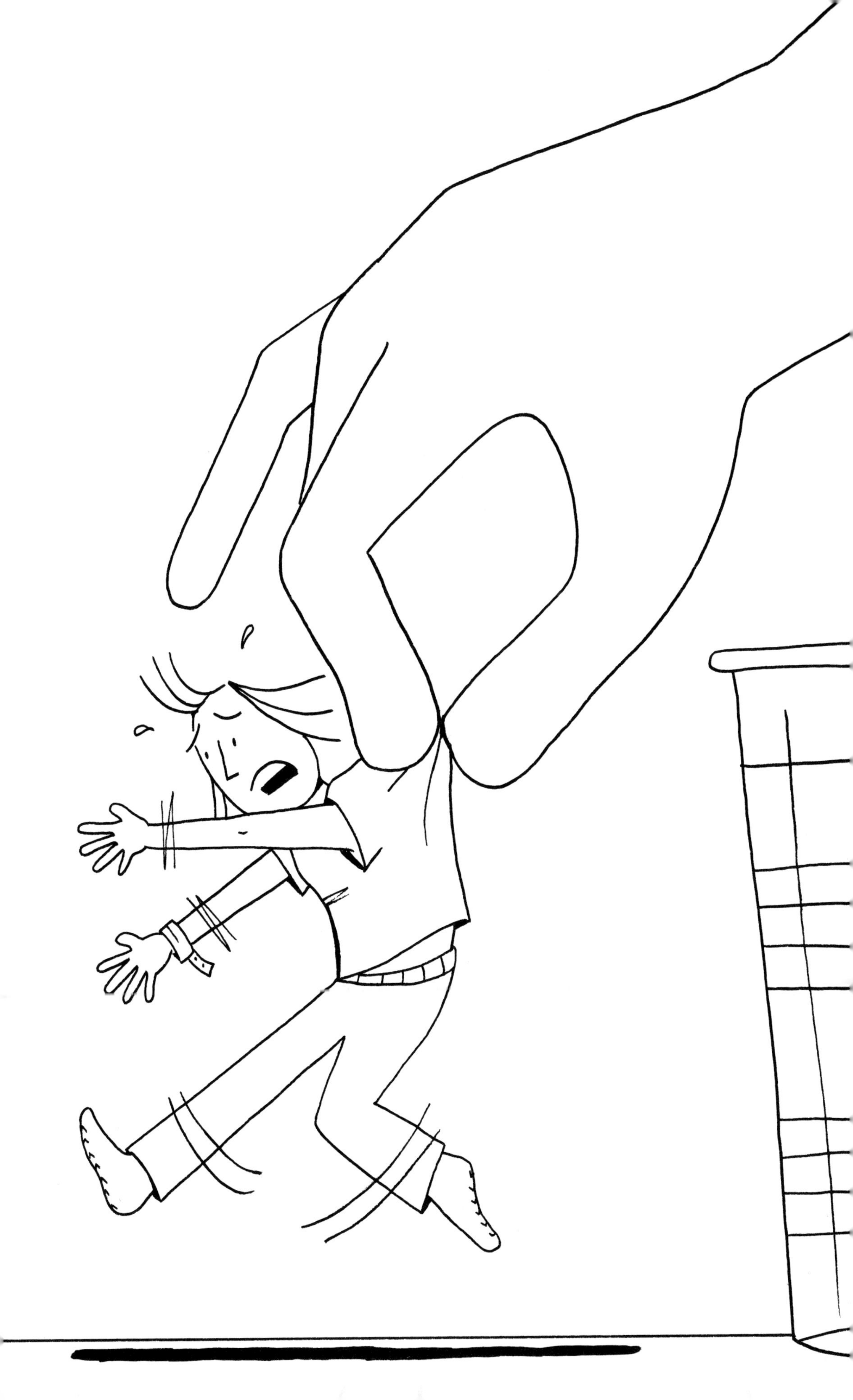

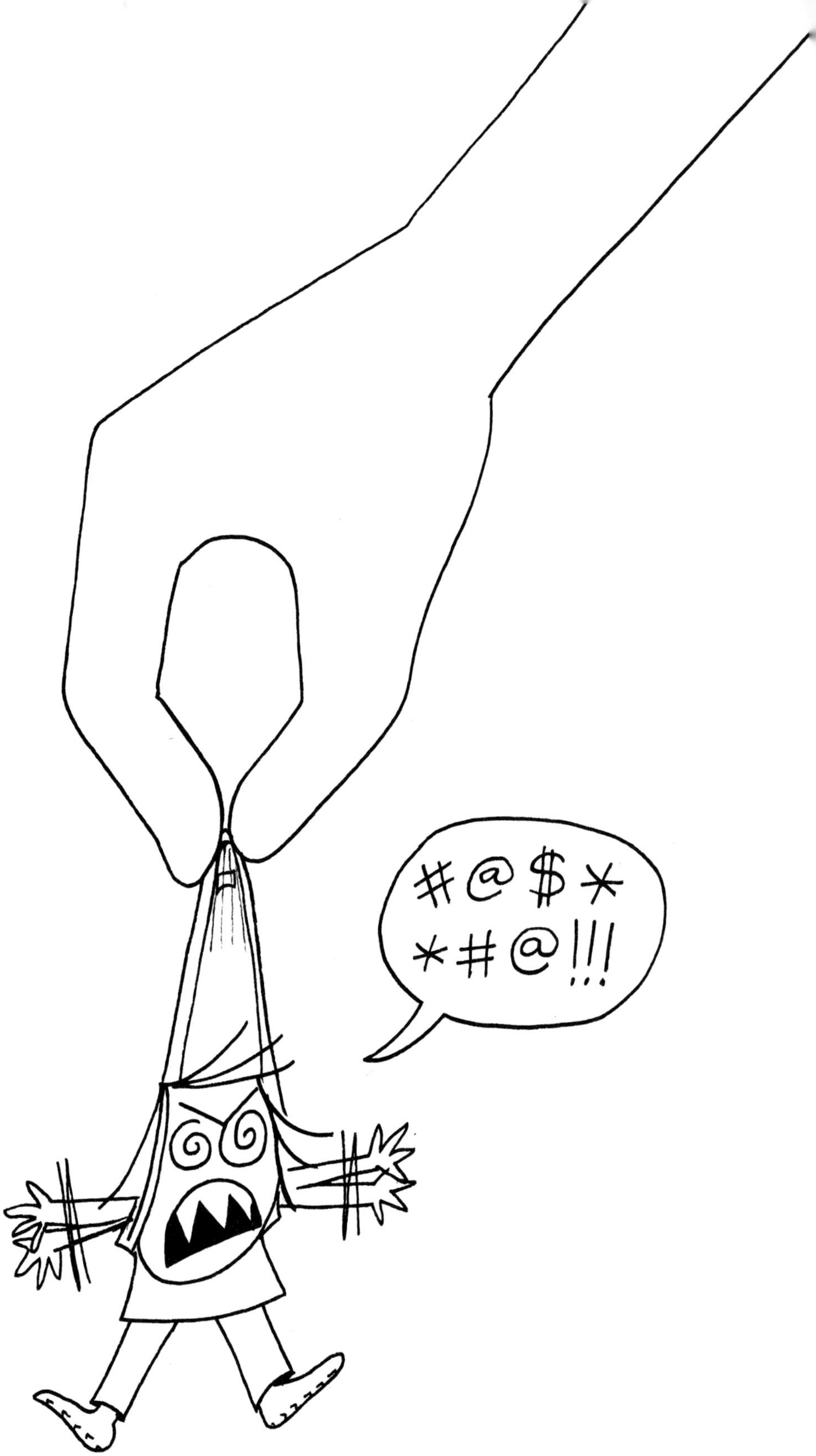
#@$*
*#@!!!

IN

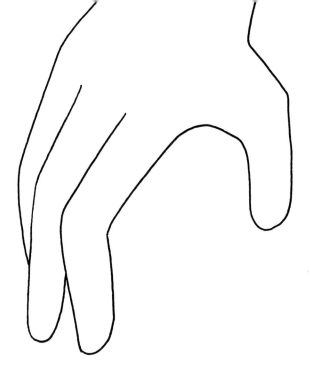

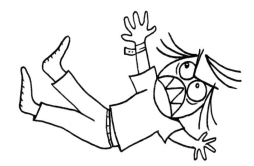

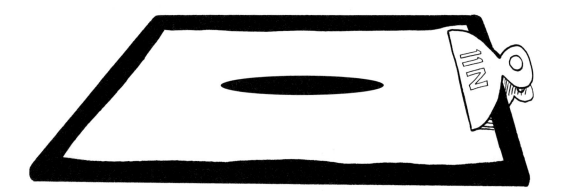

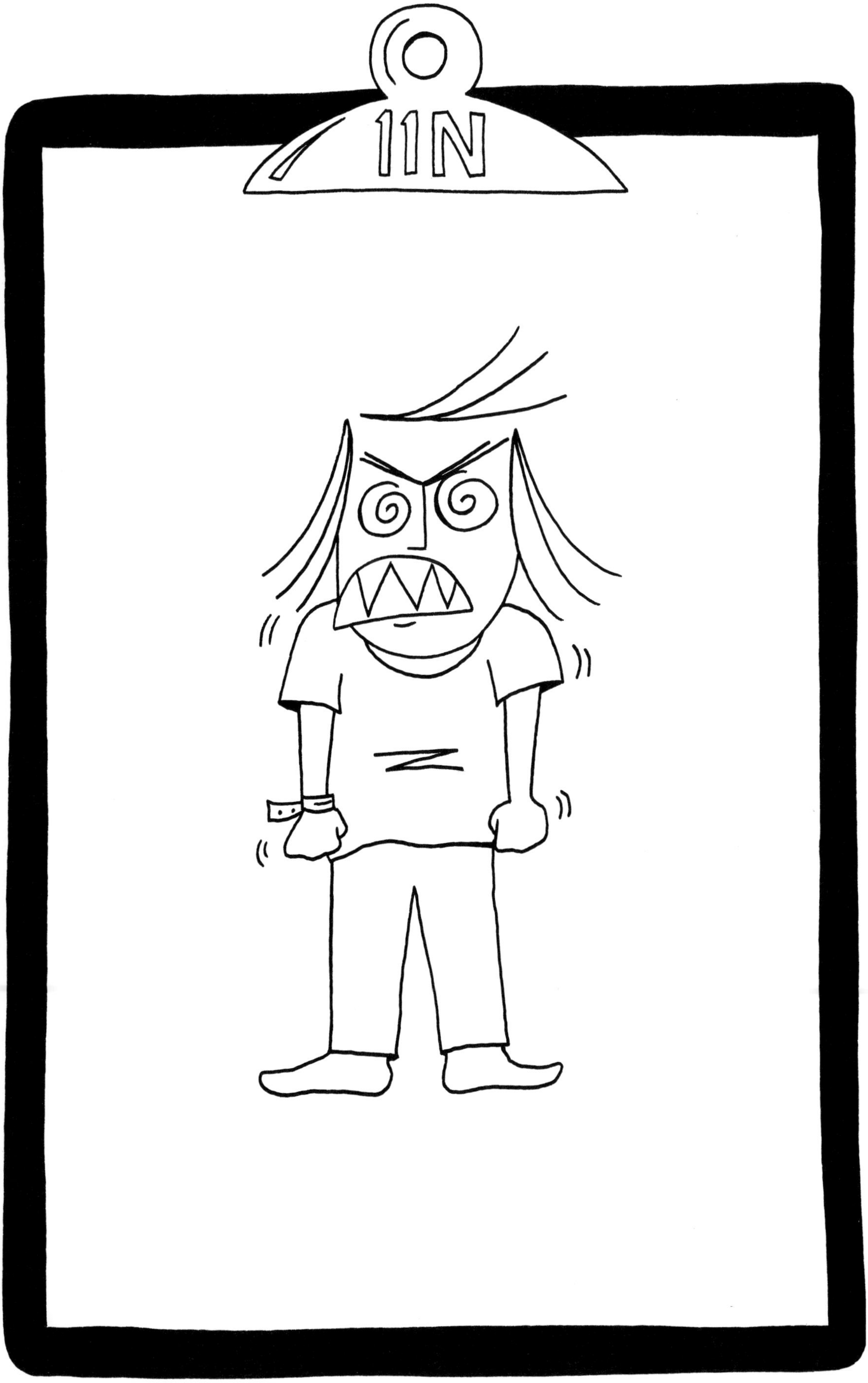
11N

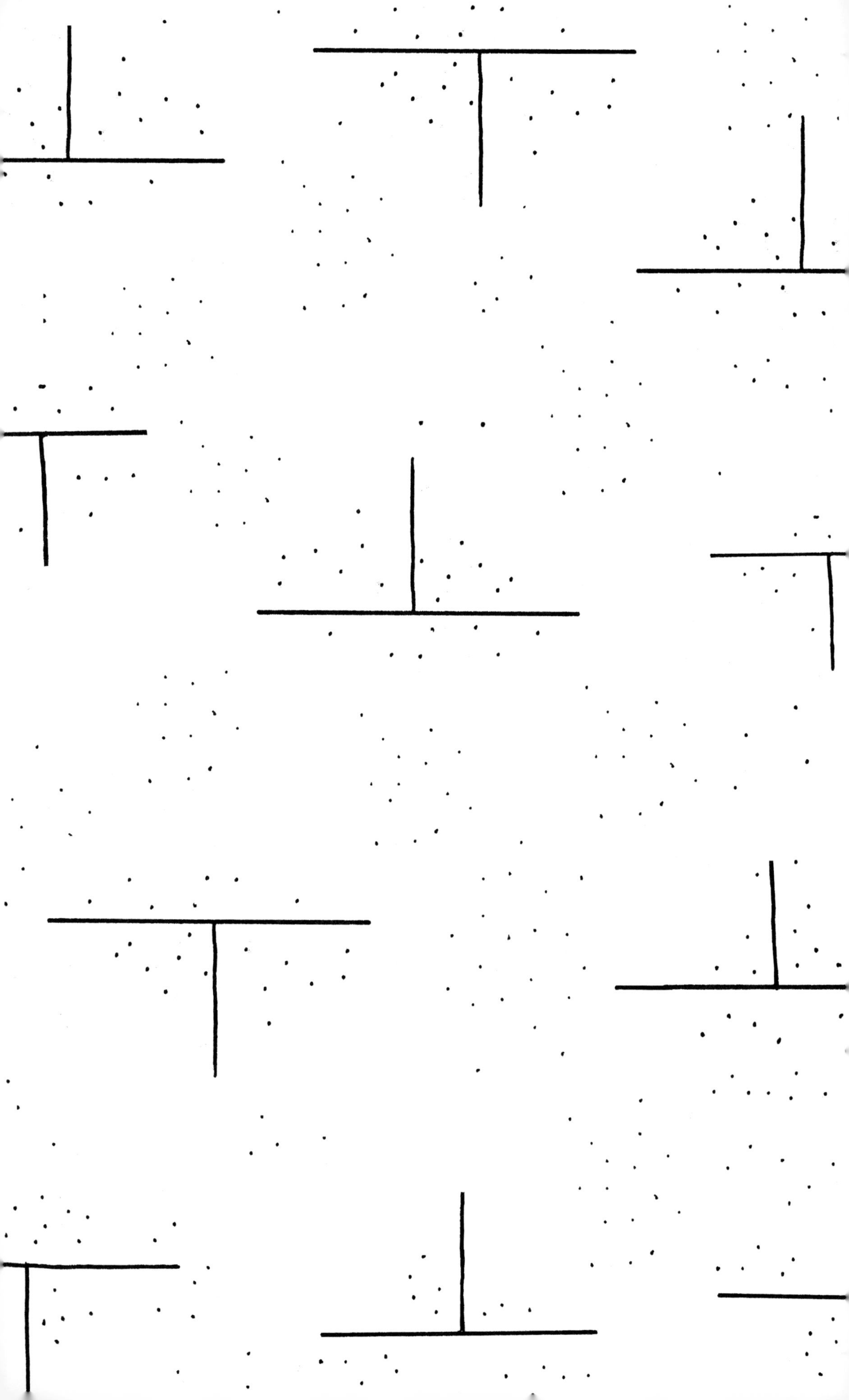

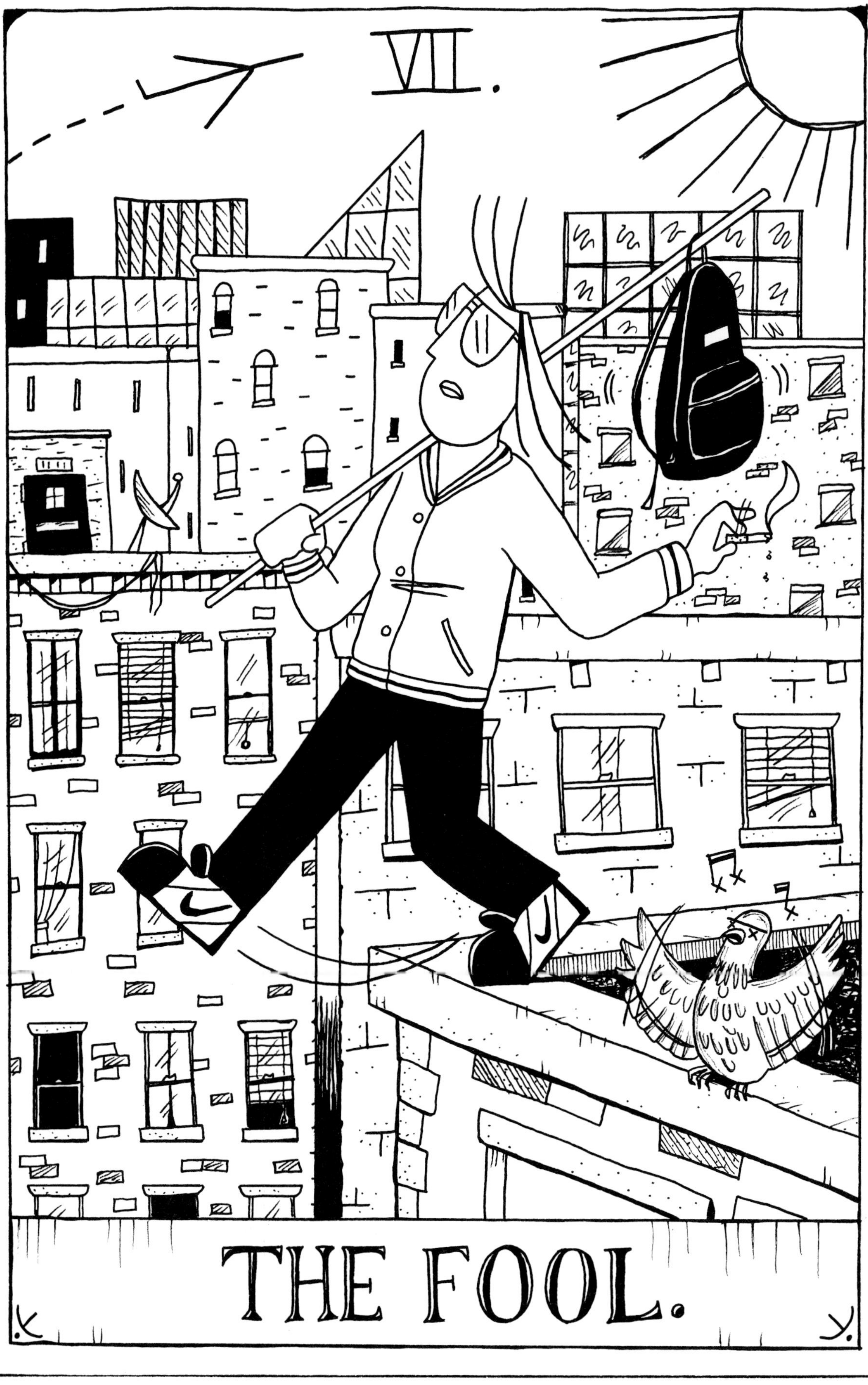
VII.
THE FOOL.

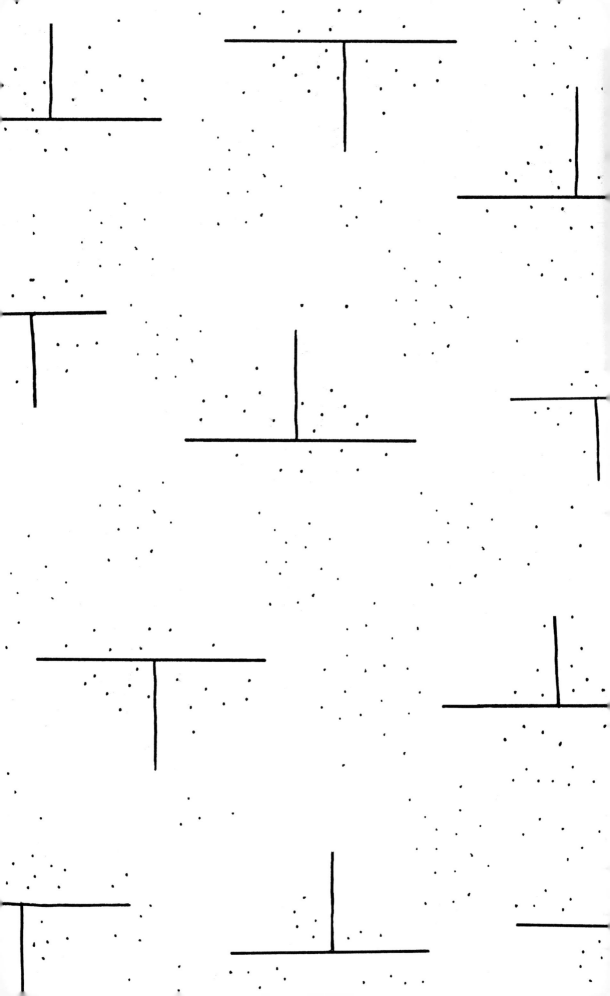

IT'S EASIER TO BE ANGRY THAN SAD.
THAT FIRST MORNING, I AWOKE INTO A NIGHTMARE THAT HAD LESS TO DO WITH MY SURROUNDINGS
...THAN THE COMPLETE FAILURE OF THE SYSTEM I HAD BEEN LED TO BELIEVE WOULD PROTECT ME FROM THIS FATE.

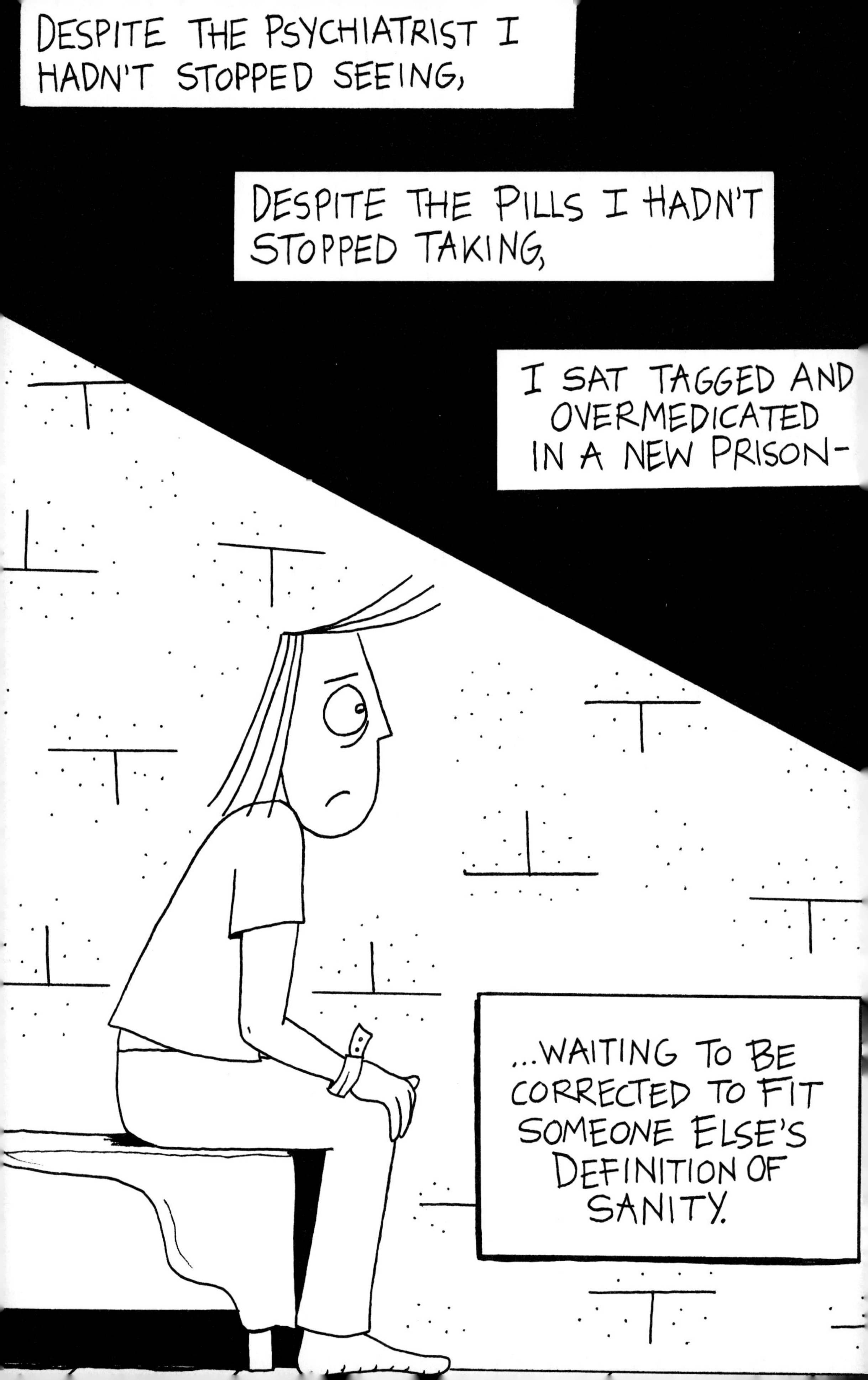
DESPITE THE PSYCHIATRIST I HADN'T STOPPED SEEING,
DESPITE THE PILLS I HADN'T STOPPED TAKING,
I SAT TAGGED AND OVERMEDICATED IN A NEW PRISON-
...WAITING TO BE CORRECTED TO FIT SOMEONE ELSE'S DEFINITION OF SANITY.

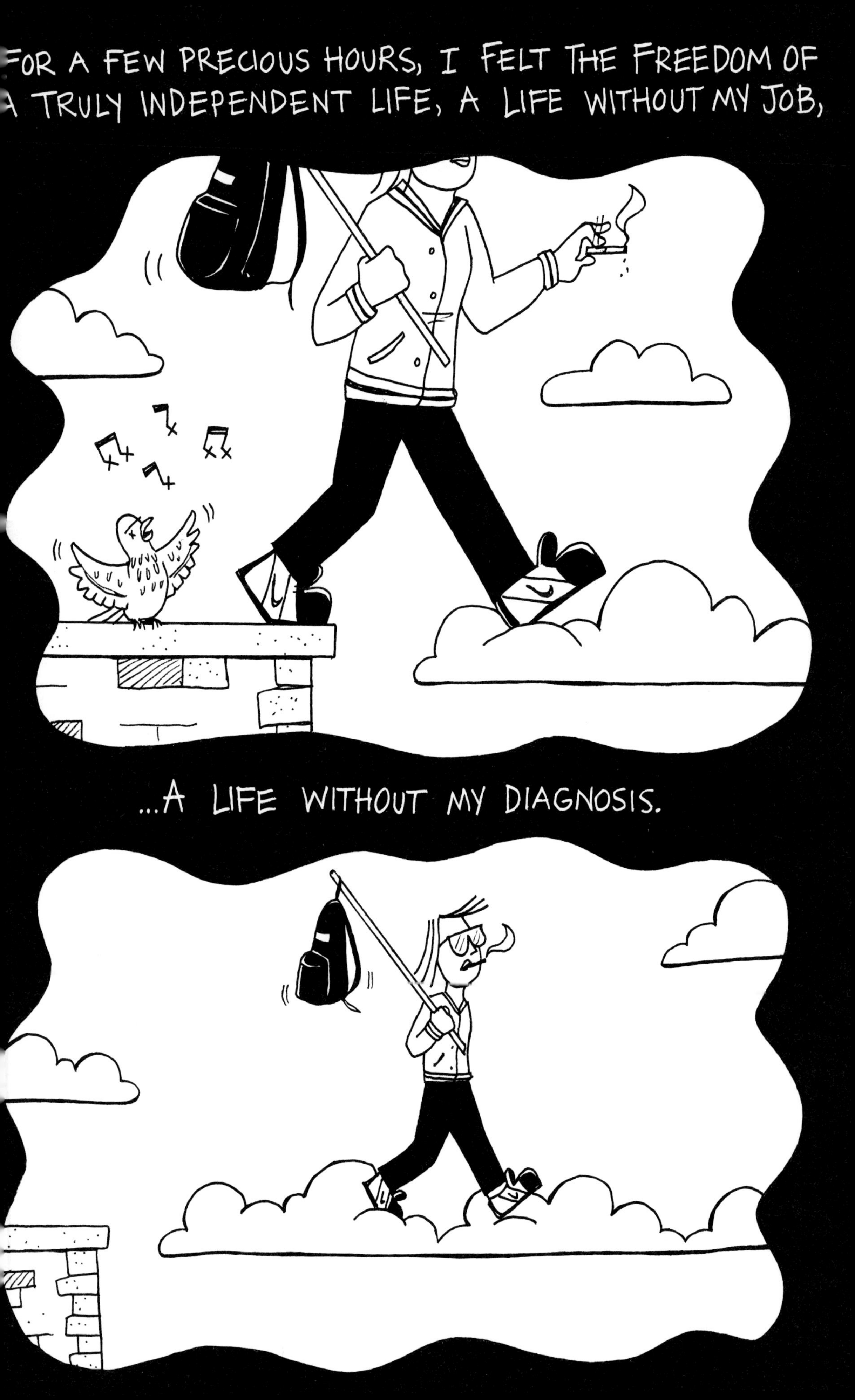
FOR A FEW PRECIOUS HOURS, I FELT THE FREEDOM OF A TRULY INDEPENDENT LIFE, A LIFE WITHOUT MY JOB,
...A LIFE WITHOUT MY DIAGNOSIS.

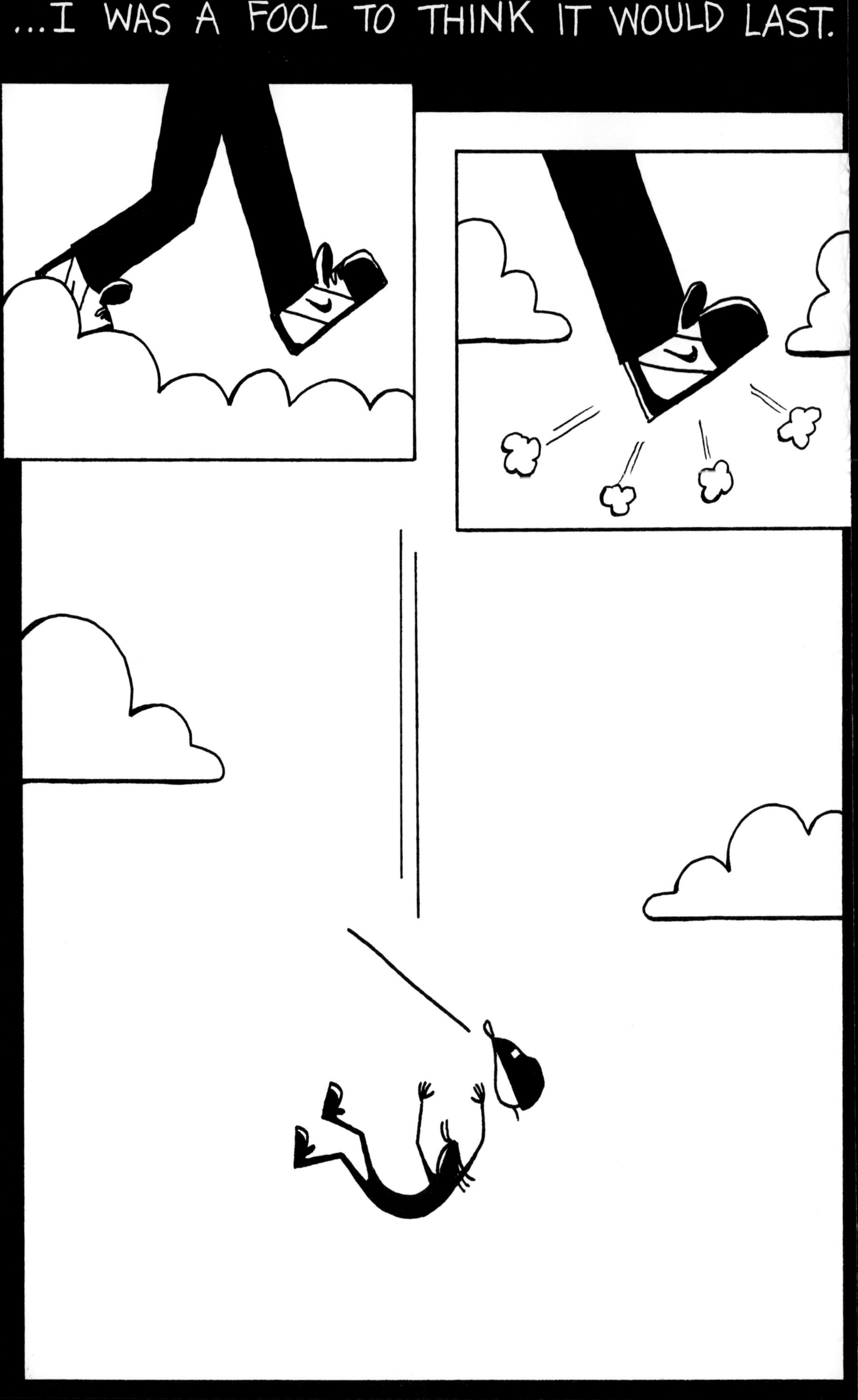
...I WAS A FOOL TO THINK IT WOULD LAST.

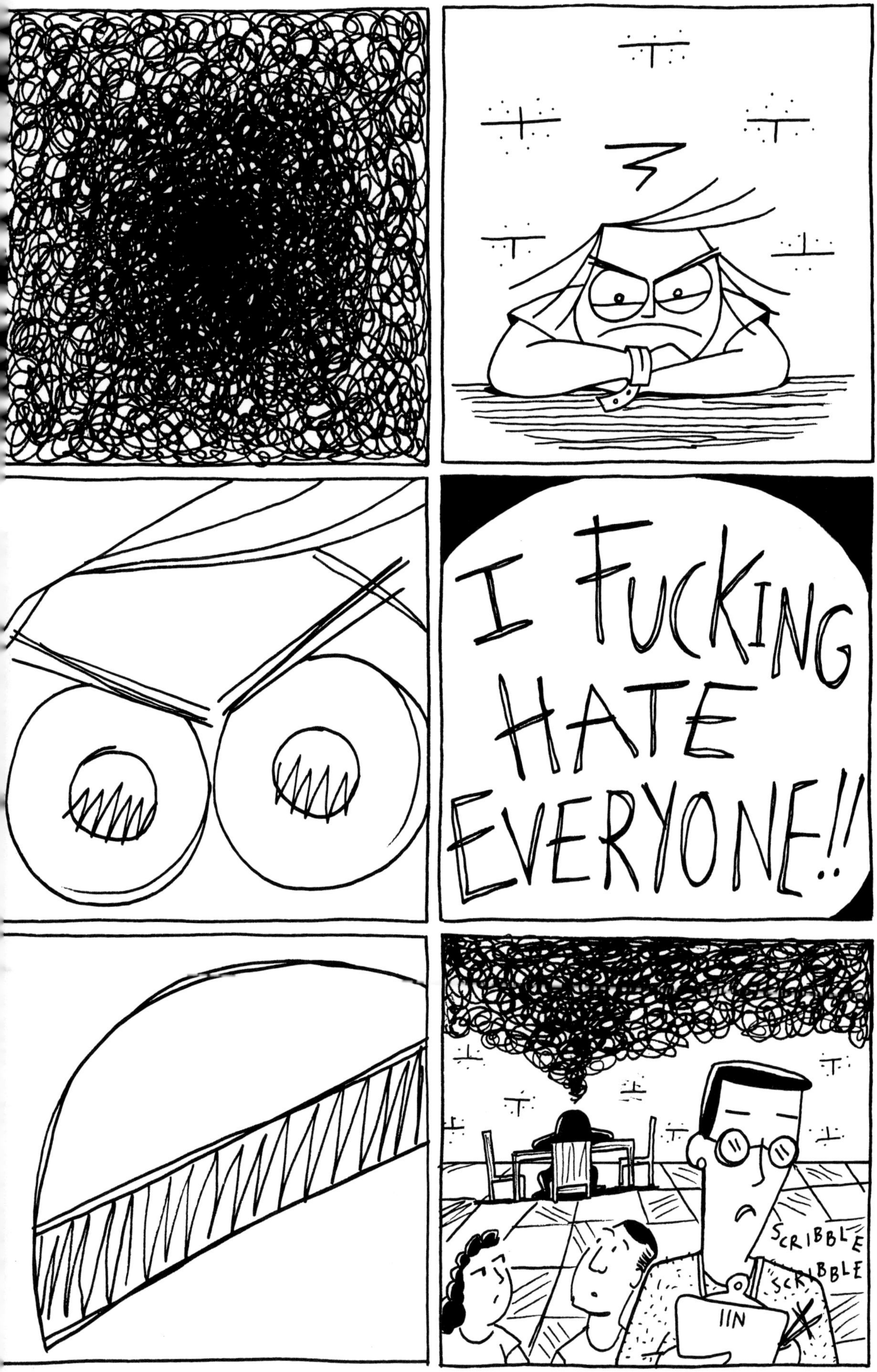
I FUCKING HATE EVERYONE!!
SCRIBBLE
SCRIBBLE

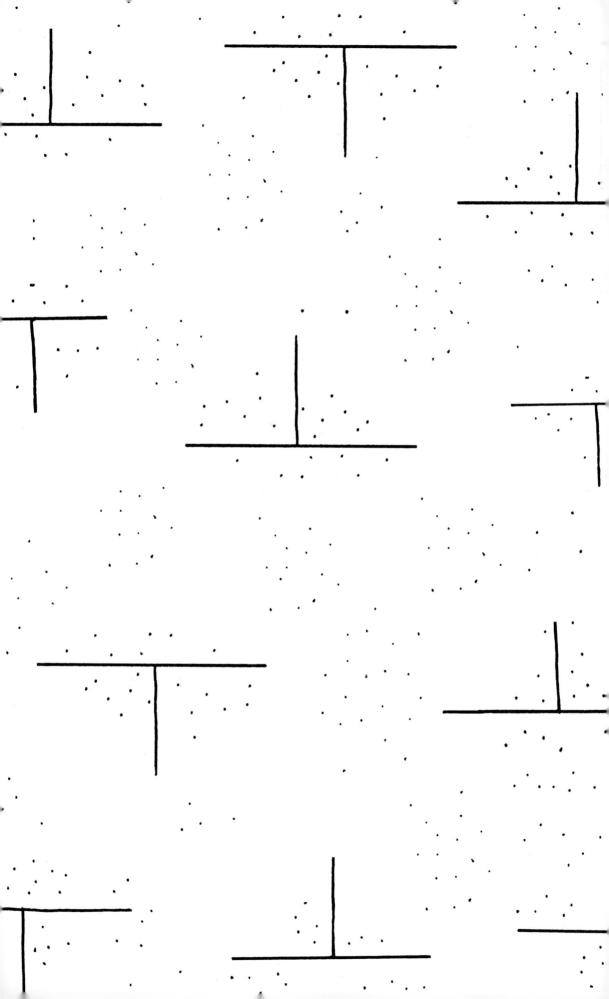

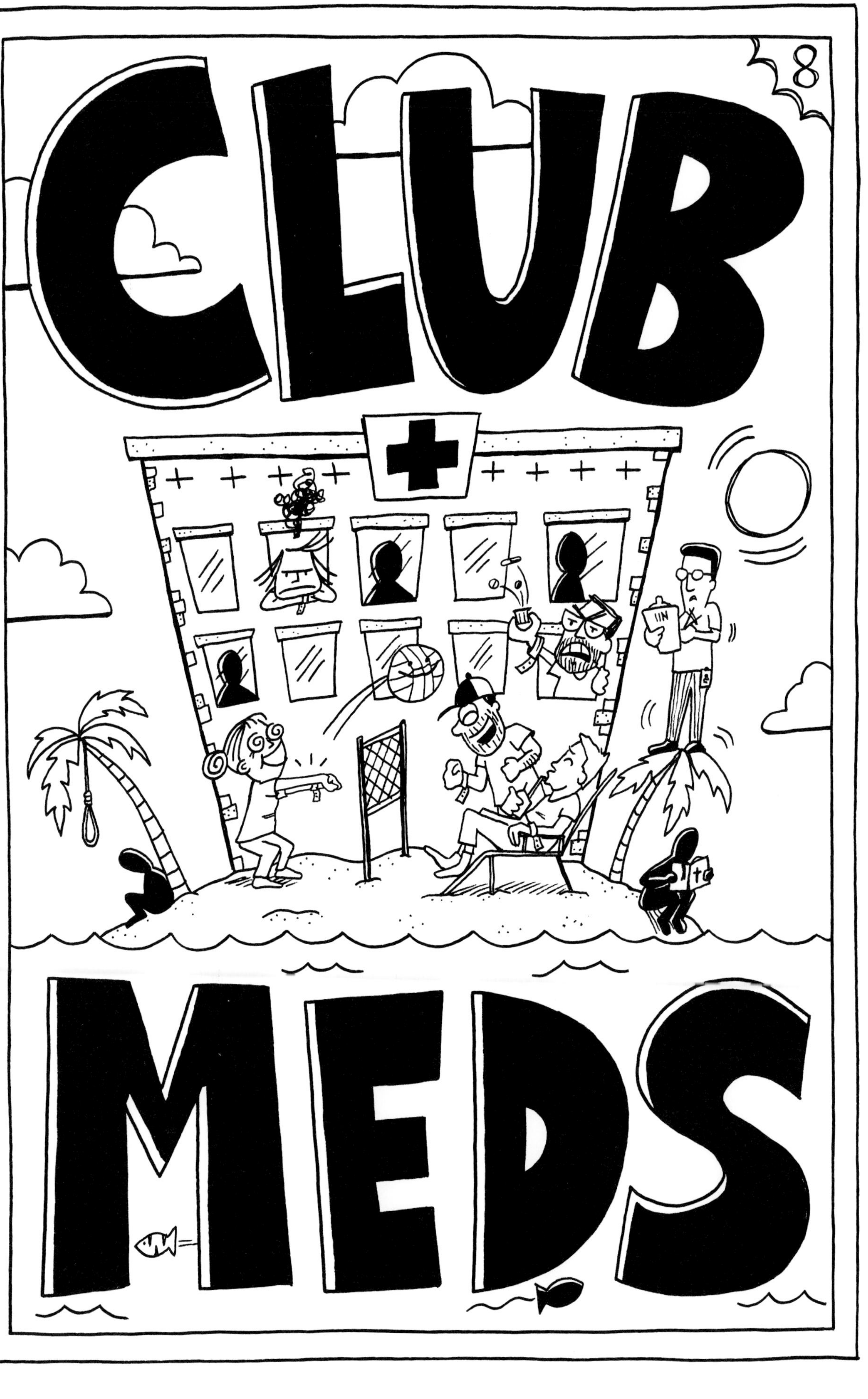
8
CLUB
MEDS

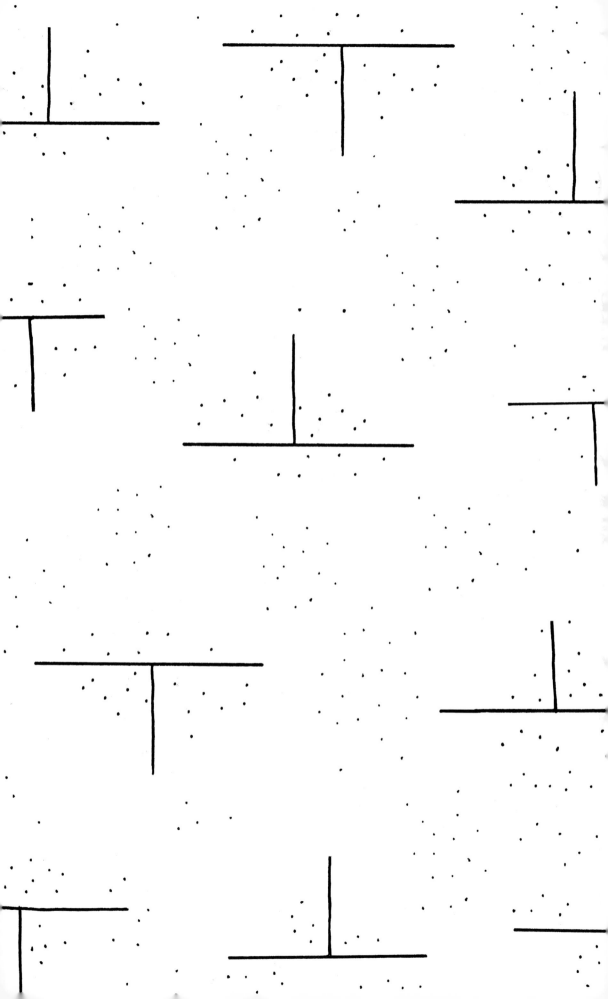

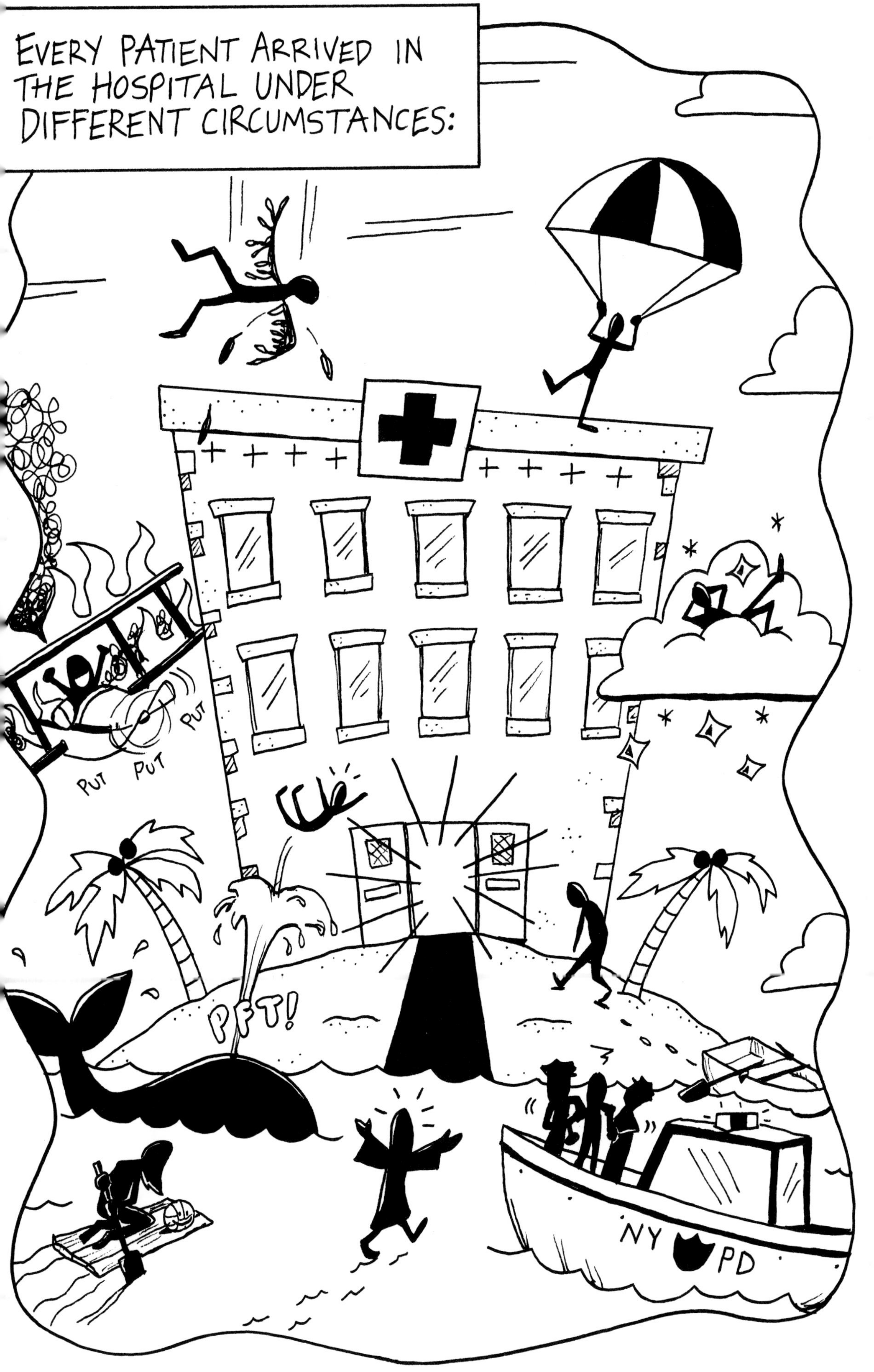
EVERY PATIENT ARRIVED IN THE HOSPITAL UNDER DIFFERENT CIRCUMSTANCES:
PUT PUT PUT
PFFT!
NY PD

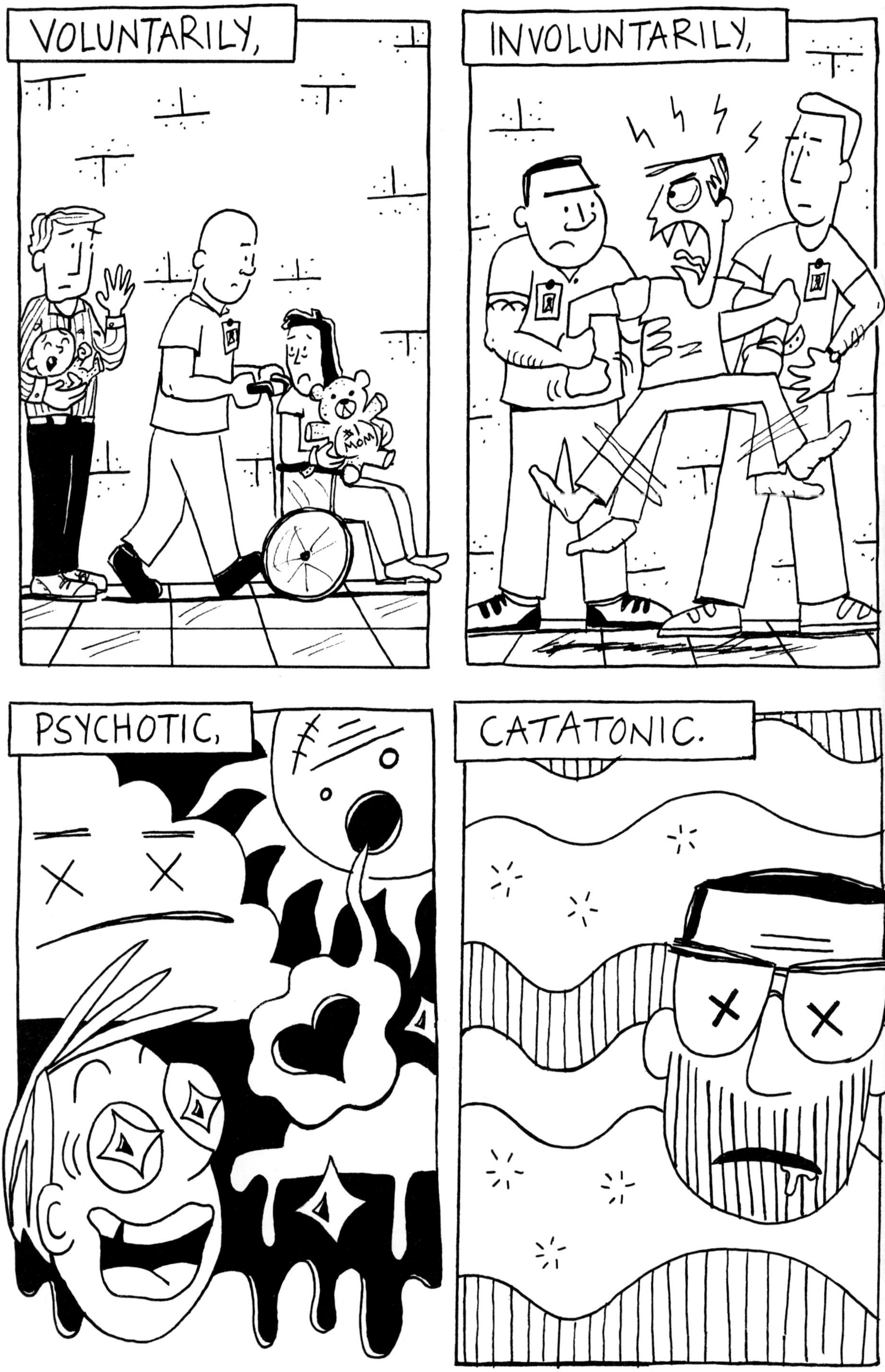
VOLUNTARILY,
#1 MOM
INVOLUNTARILY,
PSYCHOTIC,
CATATONIC.

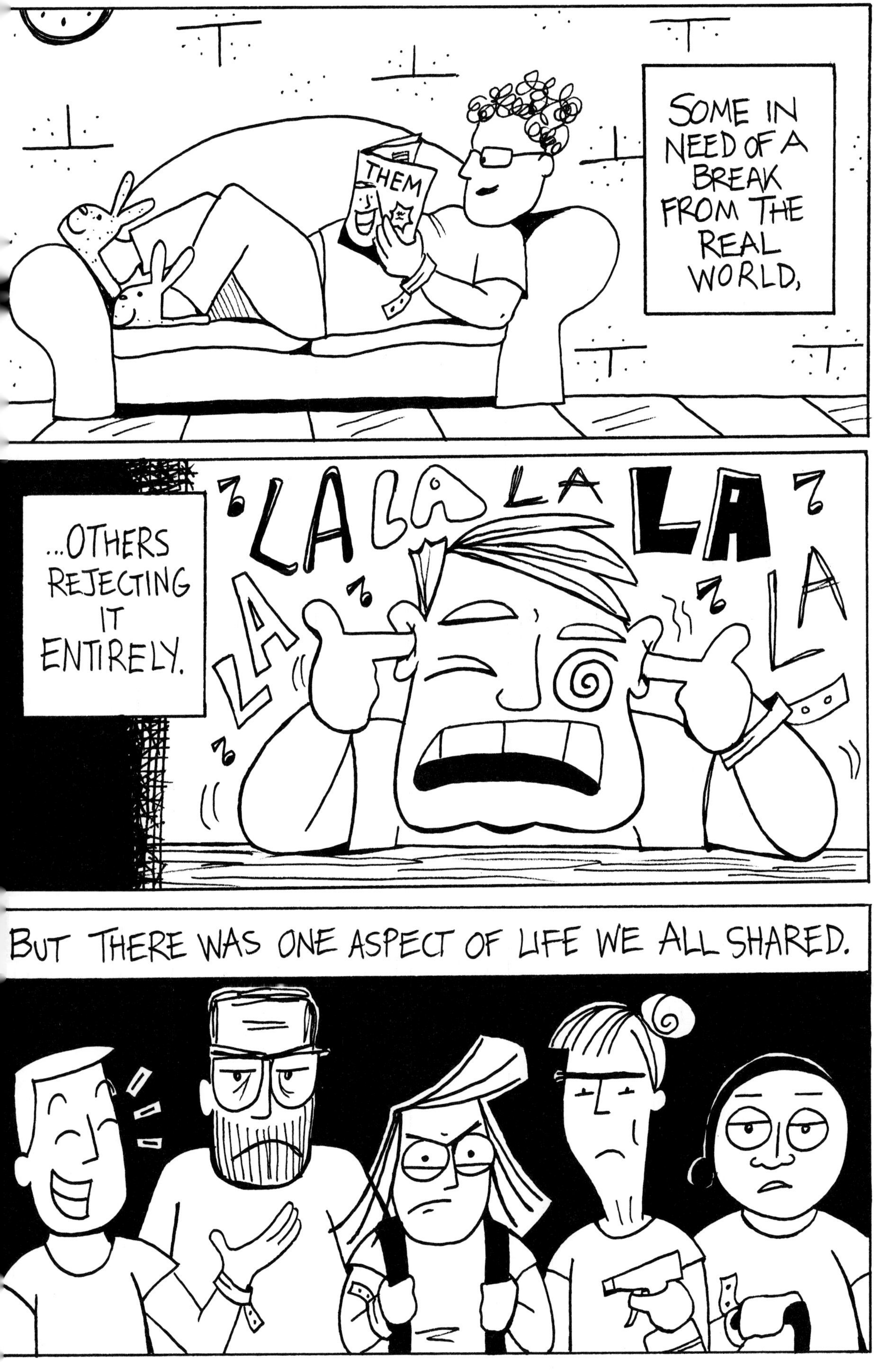
SOME IN NEED OF A BREAK FROM THE REAL WORLD,
THEM
...OTHERS REJECTING IT ENTIRELY.
LA LA LA LA LA LA LA
BUT THERE WAS ONE ASPECT OF LIFE WE ALL SHARED.

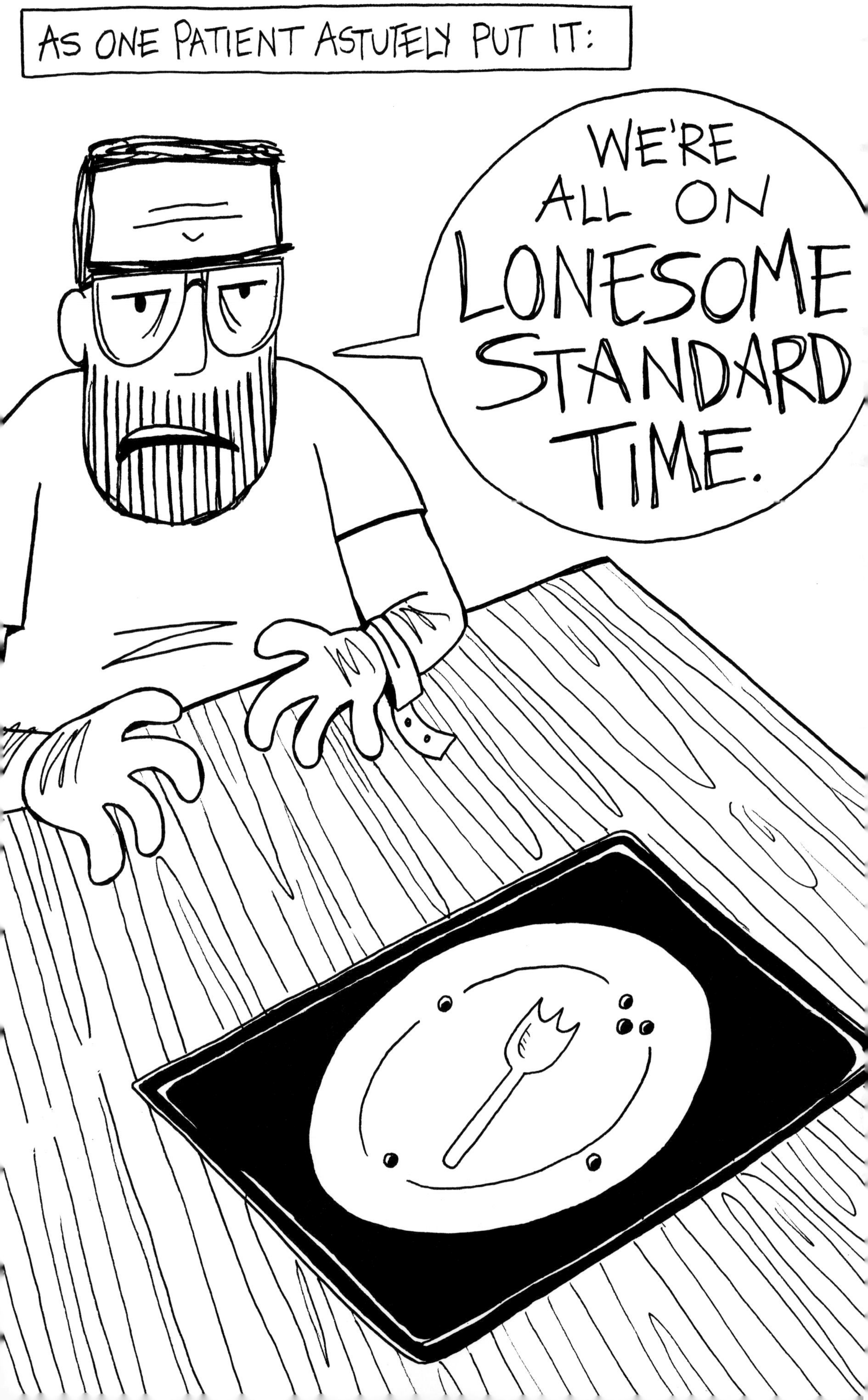
AS ONE PATIENT ASTUTELY PUT IT:
WE'RE ALL ON LONESOME STANDARD TIME.

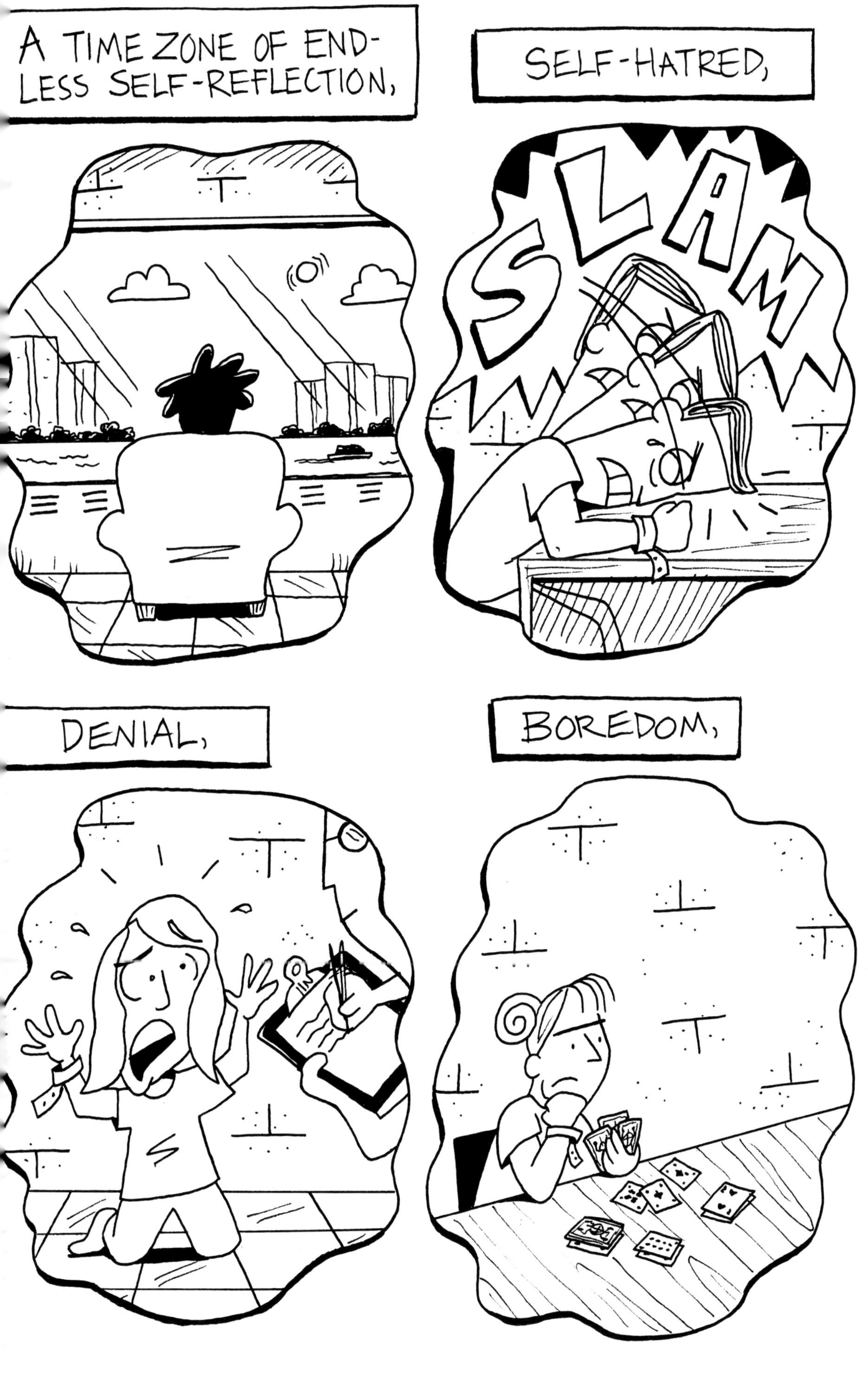
A TIME ZONE OF END-
LESS SELF-REFLECTION,
SELF-HATRED,
SLAM
DENIAL,
BOREDOM,

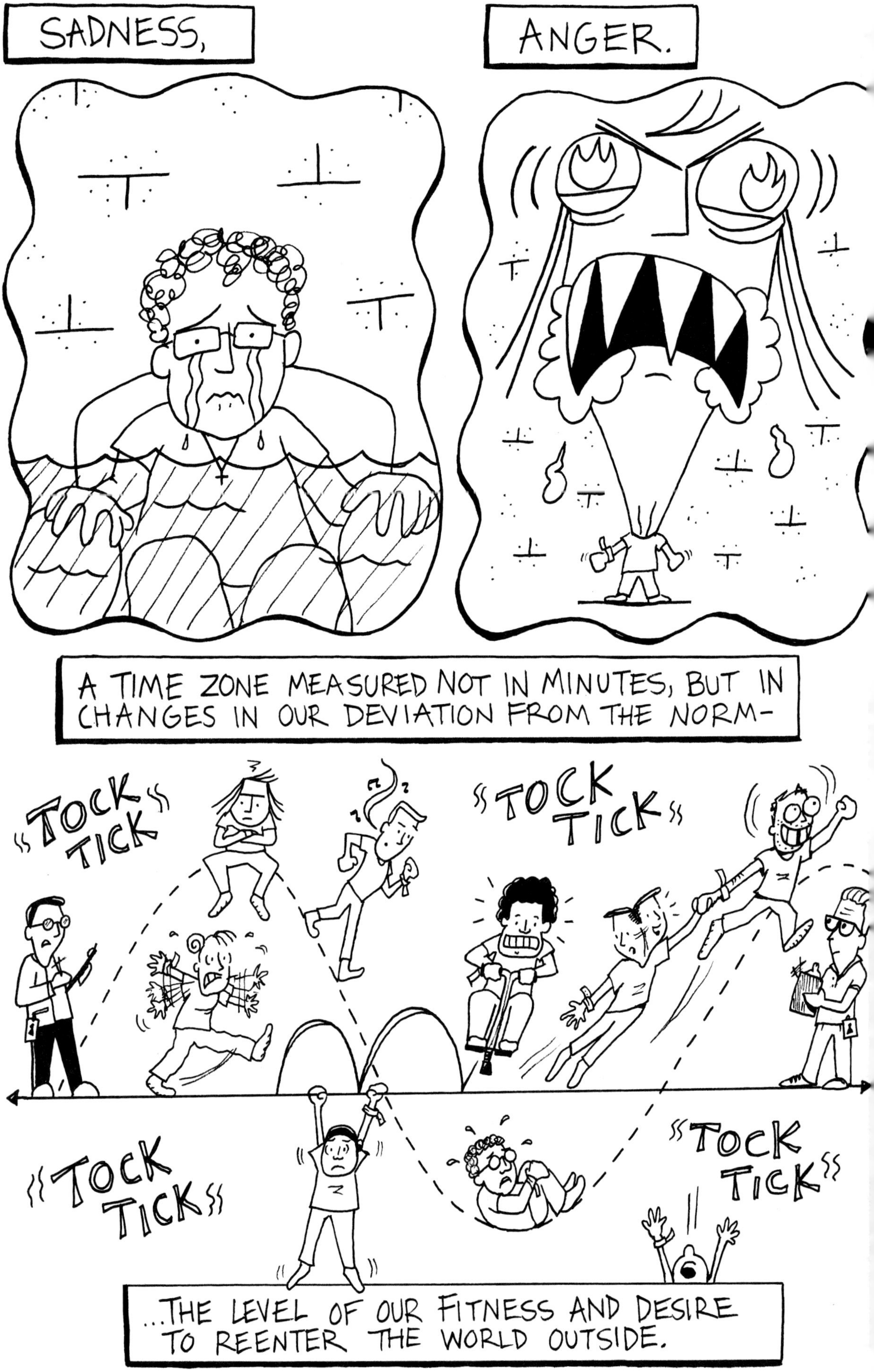
SADNESS,
ANGER.
A TIME ZONE MEASURED NOT IN MINUTES, BUT IN CHANGES IN OUR DEVIATION FROM THE NORM-
TOCK TICK
TOCK TICK
TOCK TICK
TOCK TICK
...THE LEVEL OF OUR FITNESS AND DESIRE TO REENTER THE WORLD OUTSIDE.

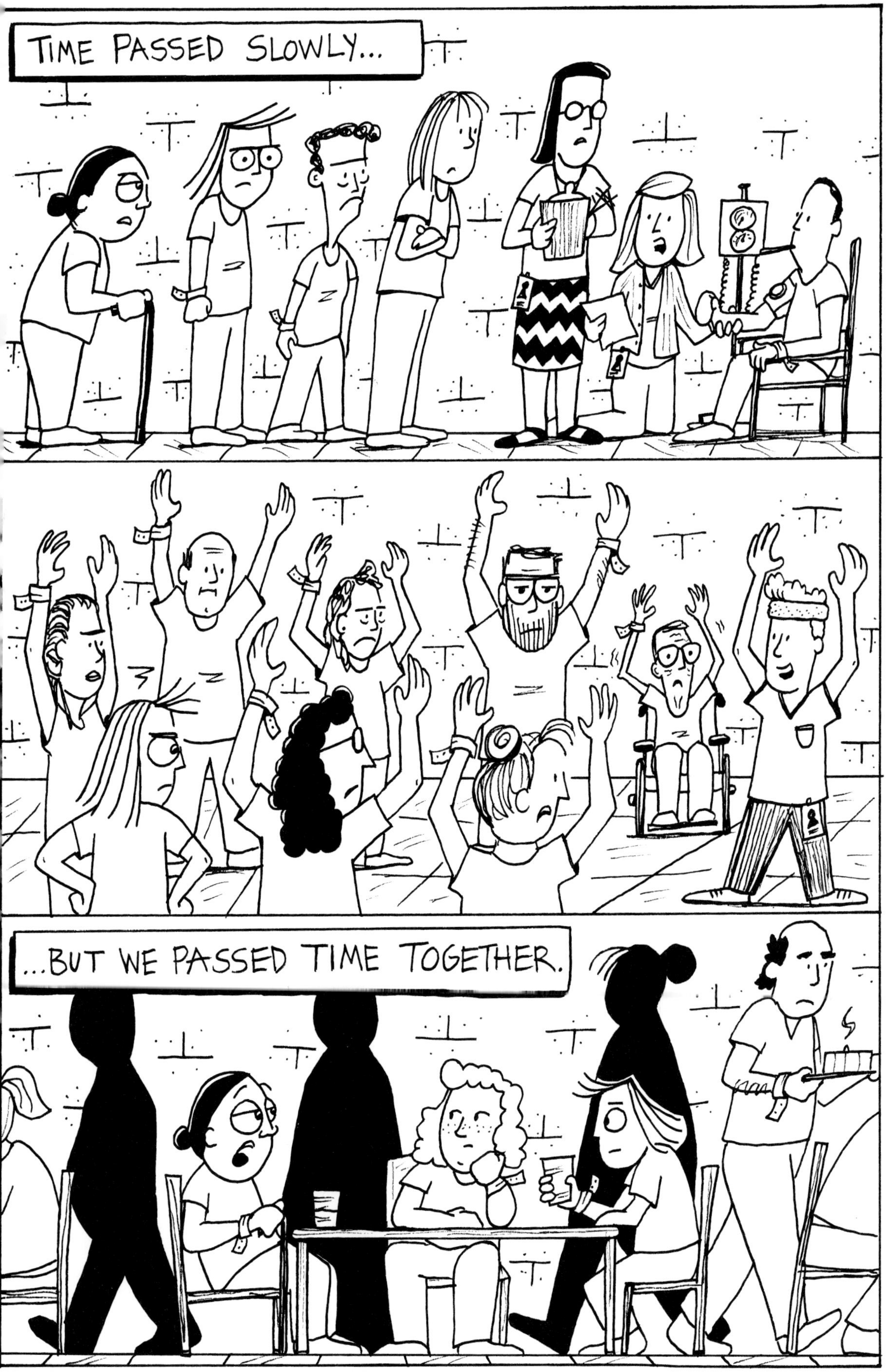
TIME PASSED SLOWLY...
...BUT WE PASSED TIME TOGETHER.

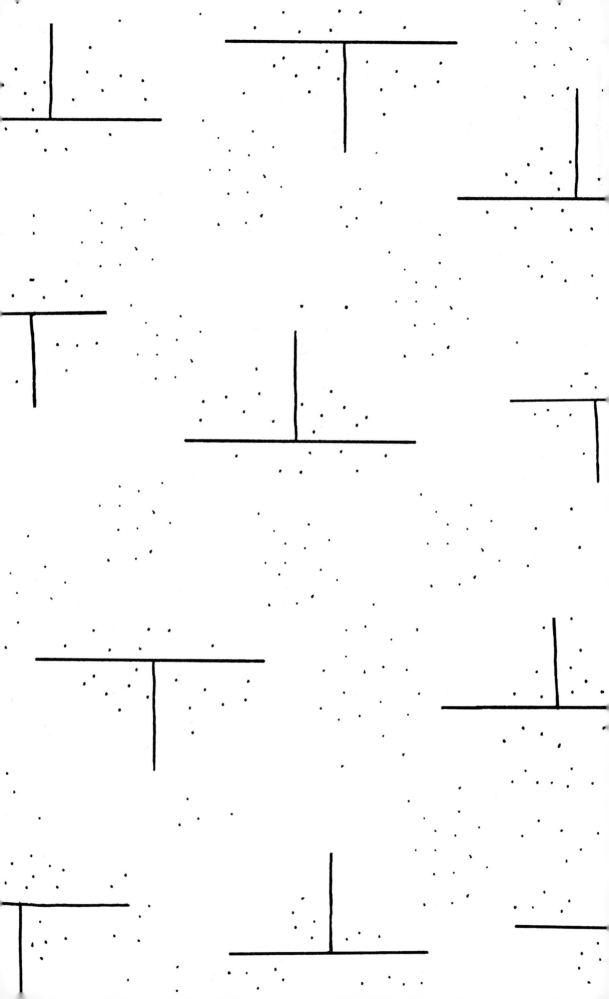

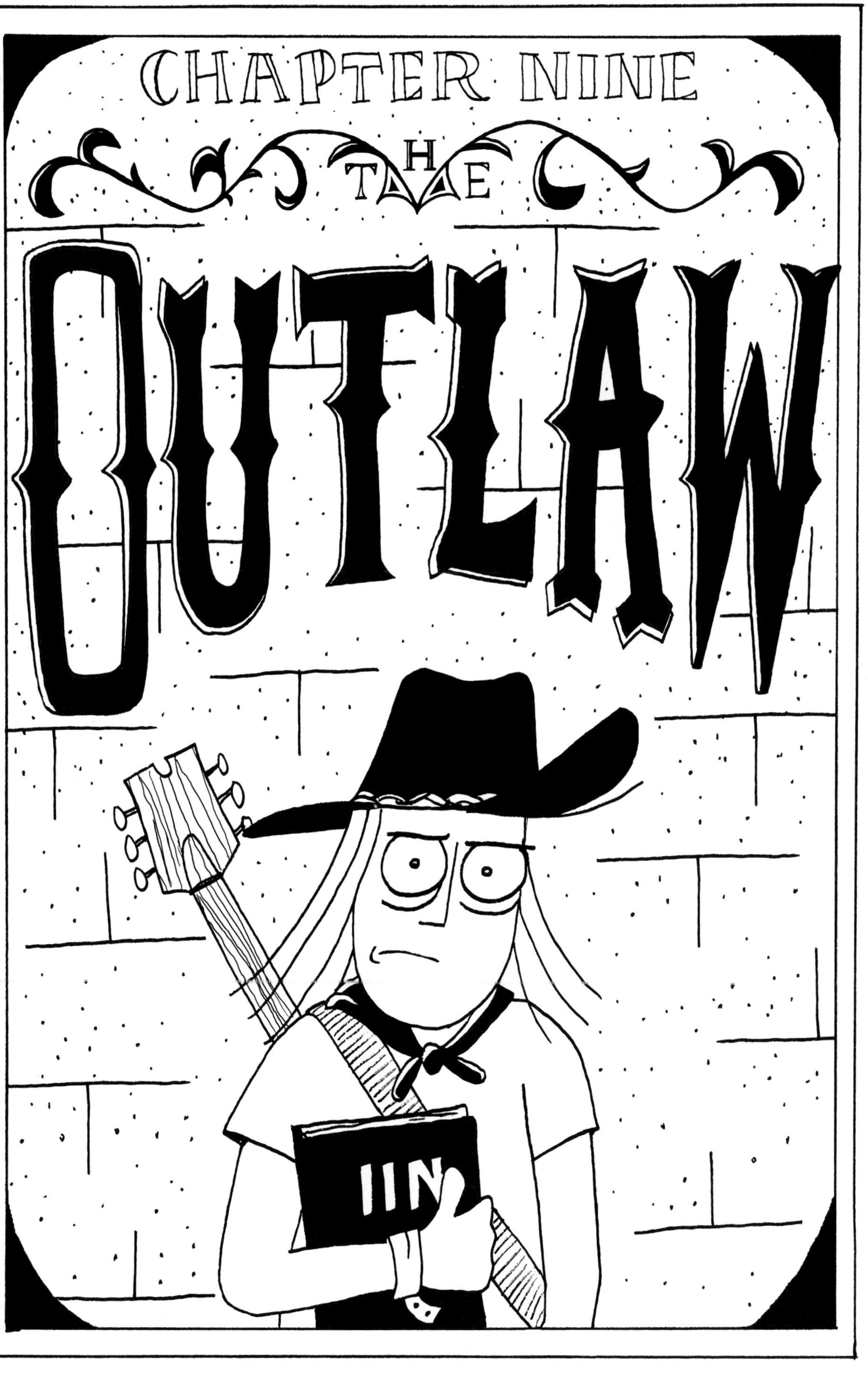
CHAPTER NINE
THE
OUTLAW

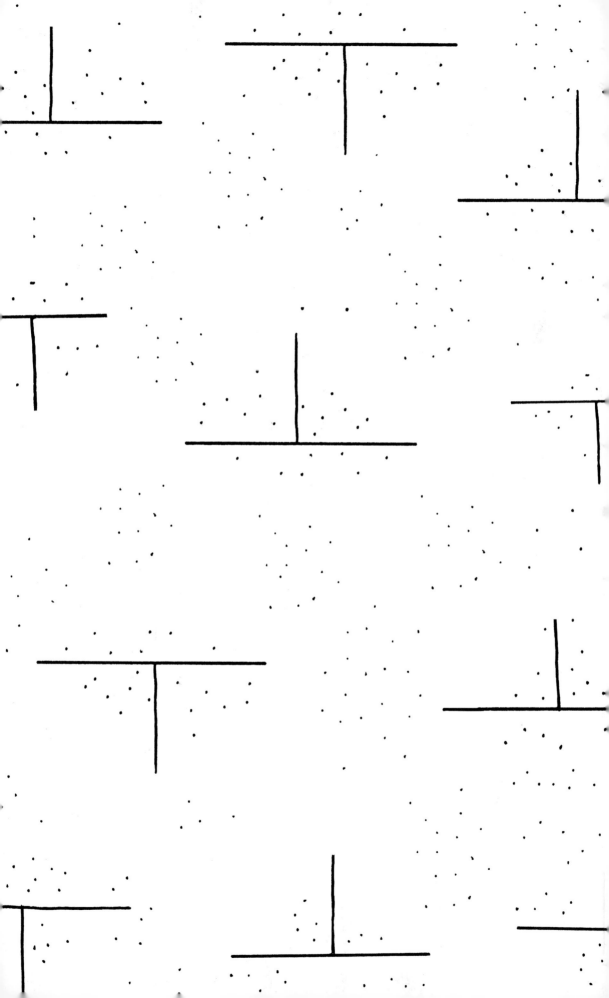

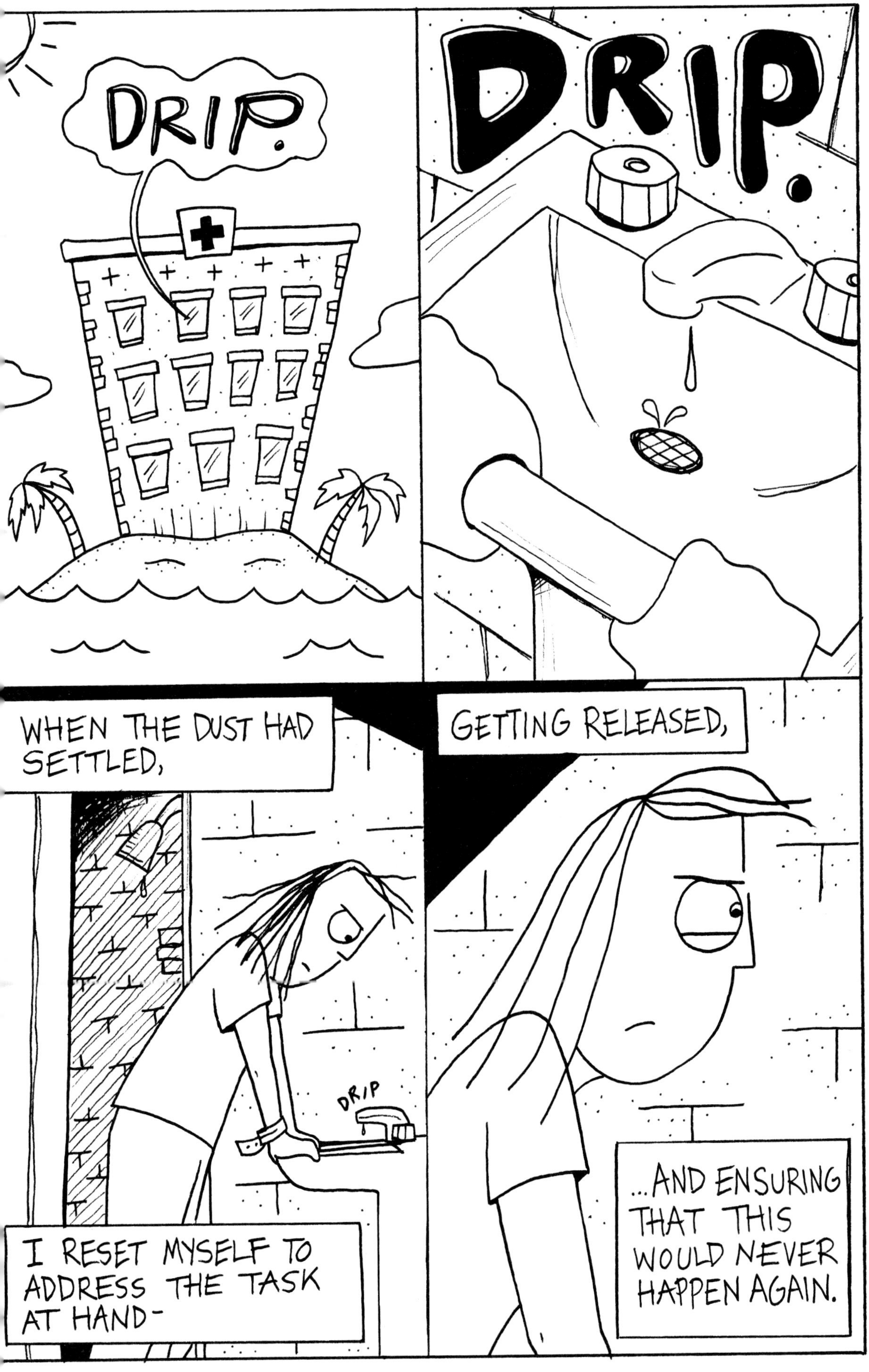
DRIP.
DRIP.
WHEN THE DUST HAD SETTLED,
DRIP
I RESET MYSELF TO ADDRESS THE TASK AT HAND-
GETTING RELEASED,
...AND ENSURING THAT THIS WOULD NEVER HAPPEN AGAIN.

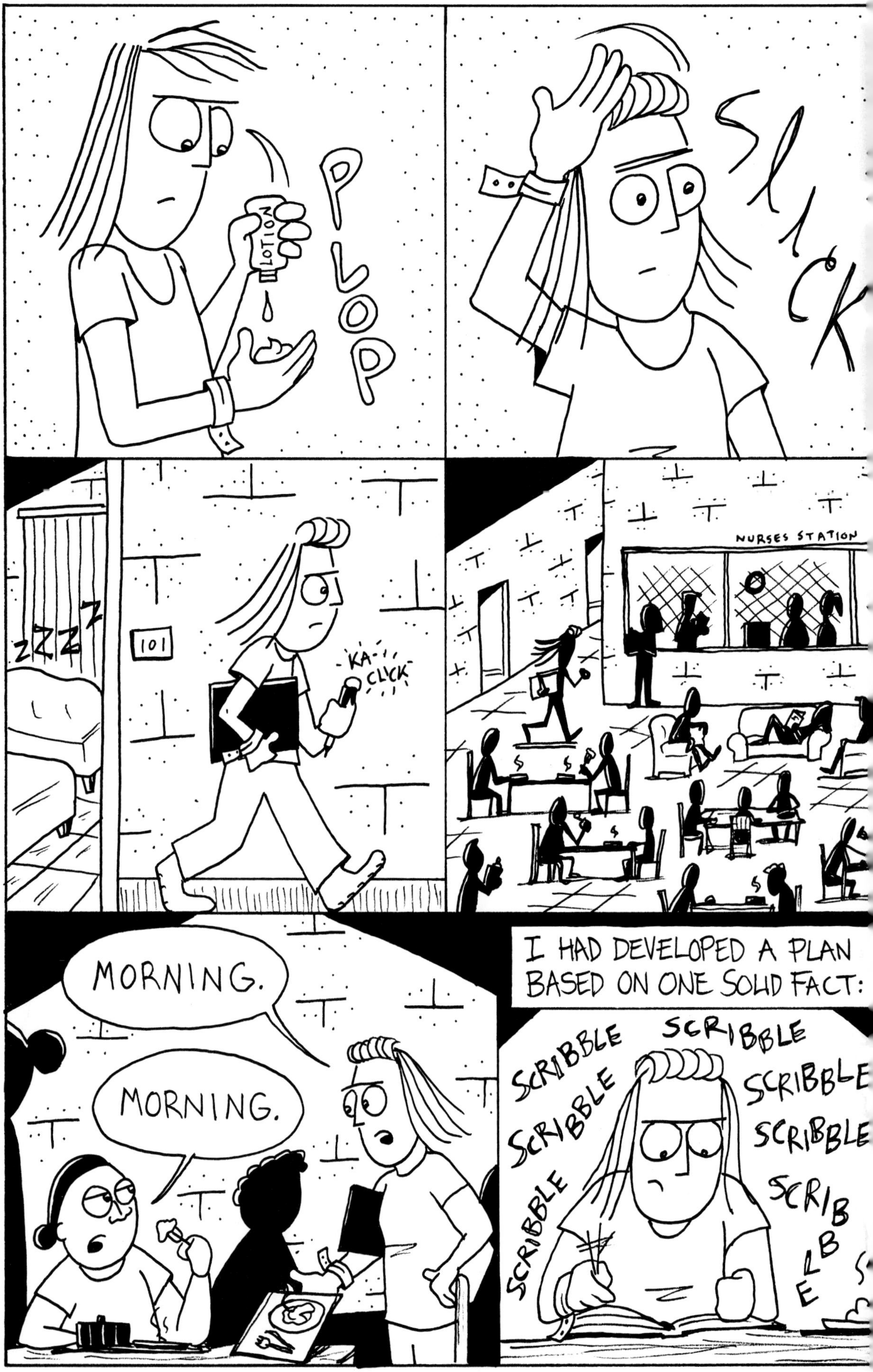
LOTION
PLOP
SLICK
ZZZZ
101
KA-CLICK
NURSES STATION
MORNING.
MORNING.
I HAD DEVELOPED A PLAN BASED ON ONE SOLID FACT:
SCRIBBLE SCRIBBLE
SCRIBBLE SCRIBBLE
SCRIBBLE SCRIBBLE
SCRIBBLE
SCRIBBLE

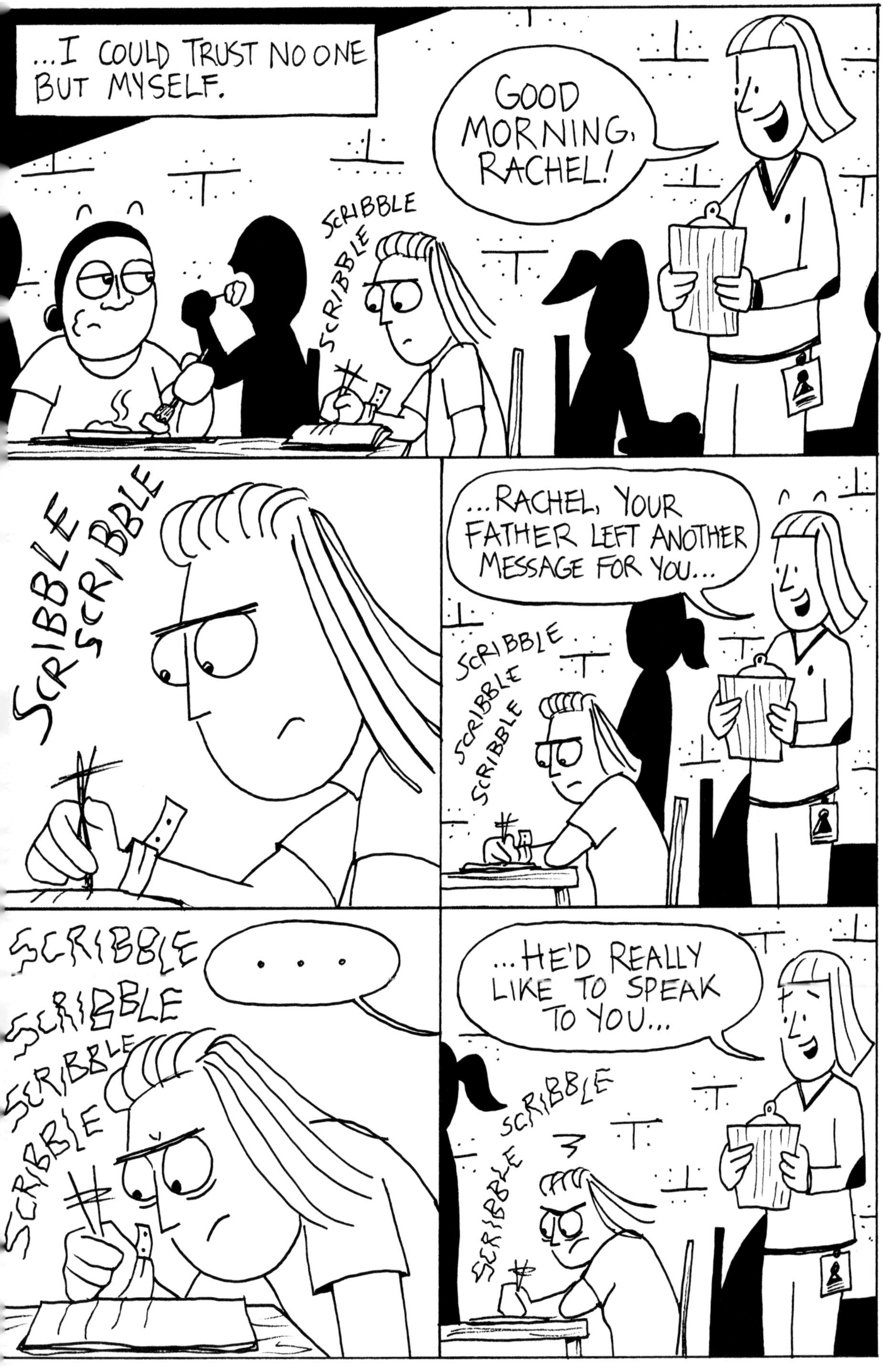
...I COULD TRUST NO ONE BUT MYSELF.
GOOD MORNING, RACHEL!
SCRIBBLE SCRIBBLE SCRIBBLE
SCRIBBLE SCRIBBLE
...RACHEL, YOUR FATHER LEFT ANOTHER MESSAGE FOR YOU...
SCRIBBLE SCRIBBLE SCRIBBLE
SCRIBBLE SCRIBBLE SCRIBBLE SCRIBBLE
. . .
...HE'D REALLY LIKE TO SPEAK TO YOU...
SCRIBBLE SCRIBBLE

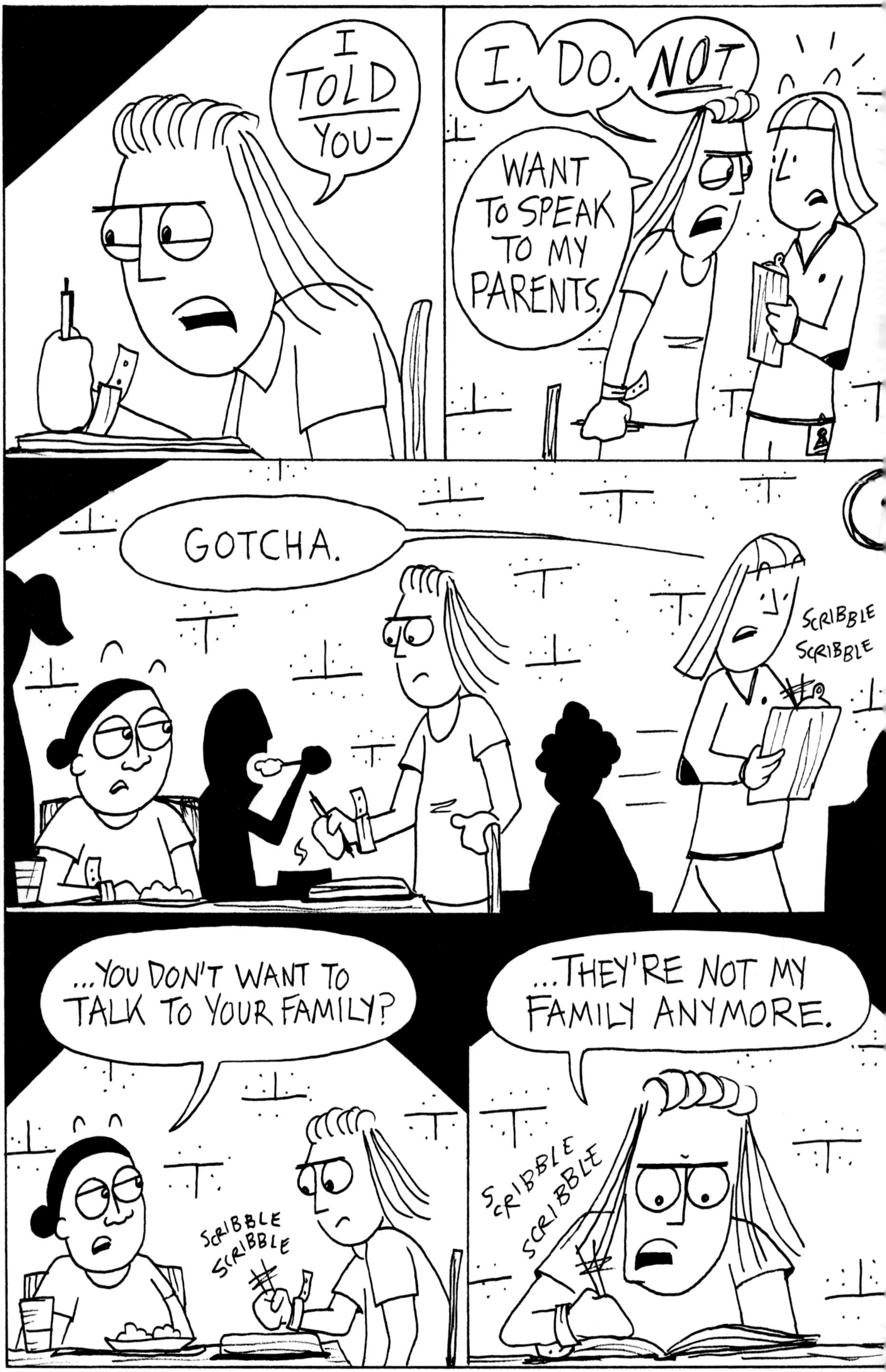
I TOLD YOU-
I. DO. NOT
WANT TO SPEAK TO MY PARENTS.
GOTCHA.
SCRIBBLE SCRIBBLE
...YOU DON'T WANT TO TALK TO YOUR FAMILY?
SCRIBBLE SCRIBBLE
...THEY'RE NOT MY FAMILY ANYMORE.
SCRIBBLE SCRIBBLE

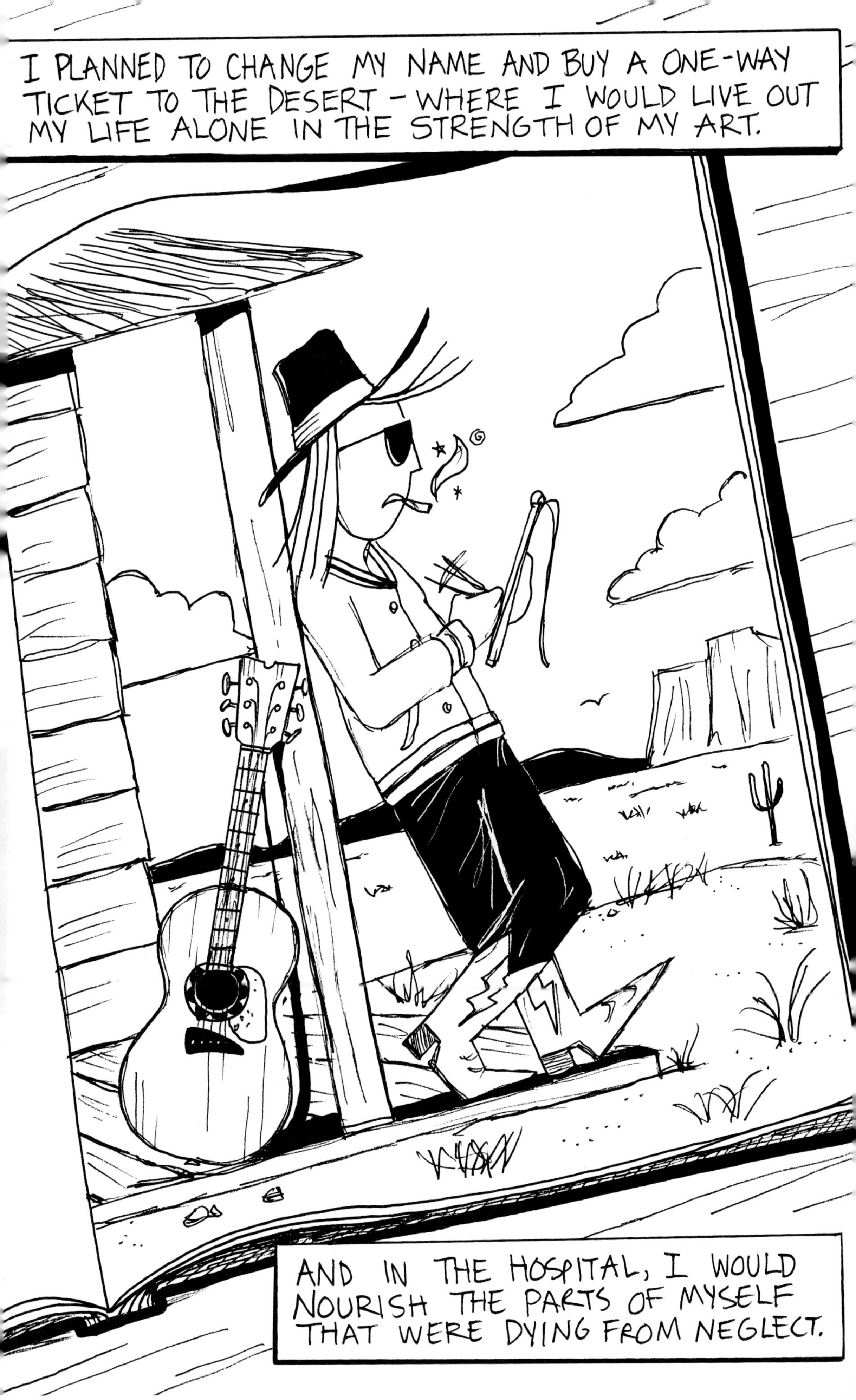
I PLANNED TO CHANGE MY NAME AND BUY A ONE-WAY TICKET TO THE DESERT - WHERE I WOULD LIVE OUT MY LIFE ALONE IN THE STRENGTH OF MY ART.
AND IN THE HOSPITAL, I WOULD NOURISH THE PARTS OF MYSELF THAT WERE DYING FROM NEGLECT.

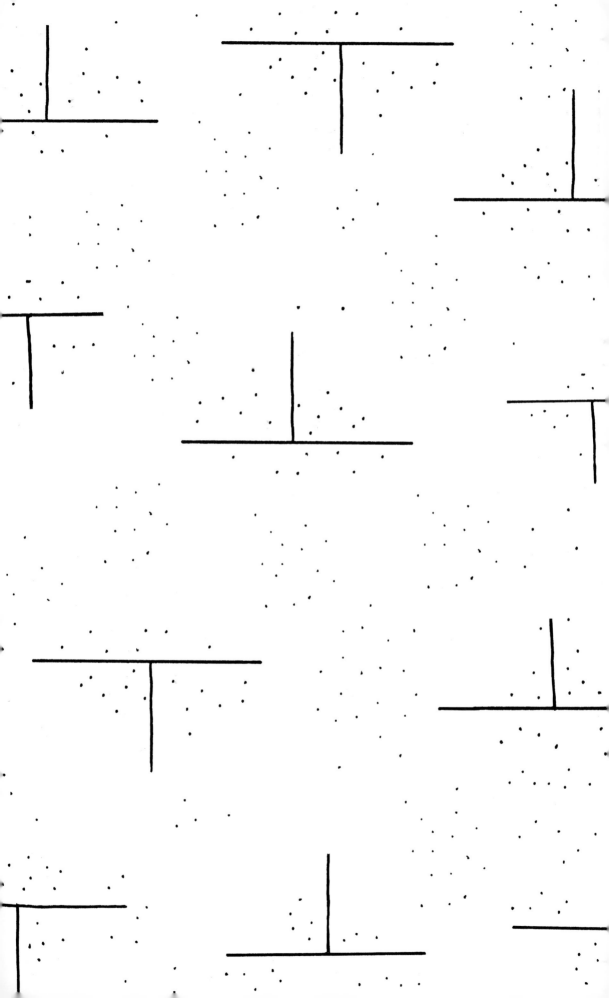

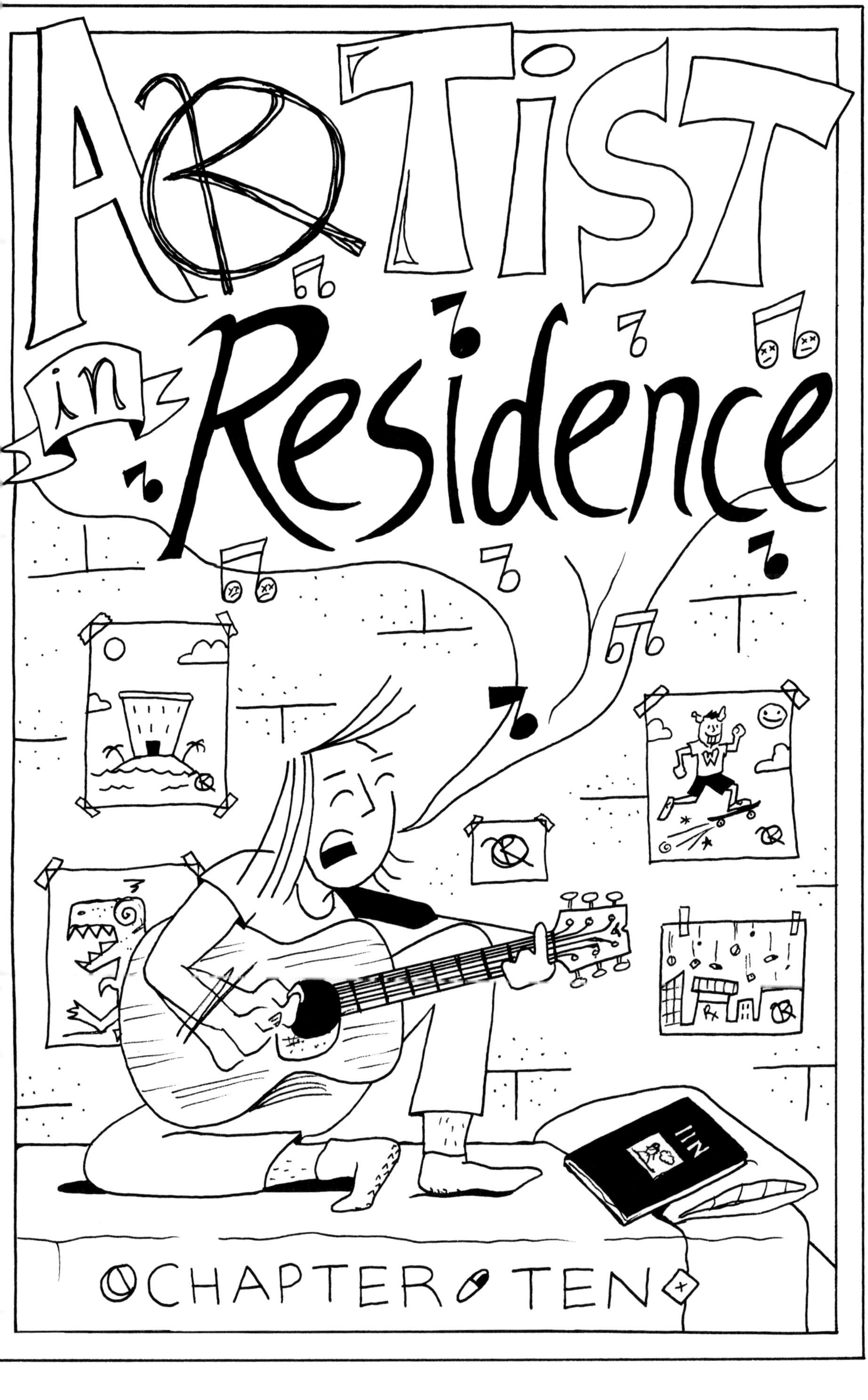

ARTIST in Residence
CHAPTER TEN

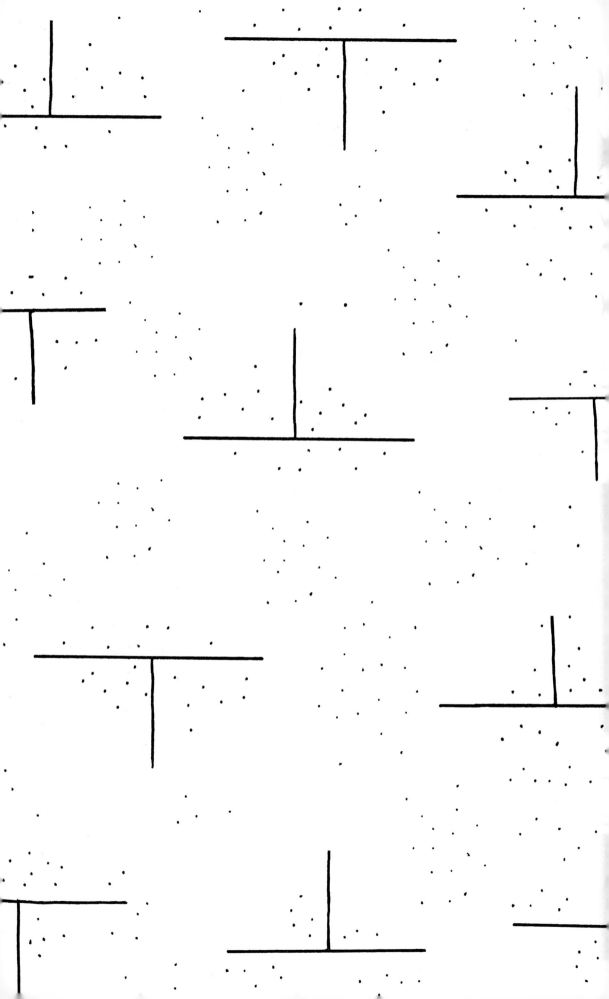

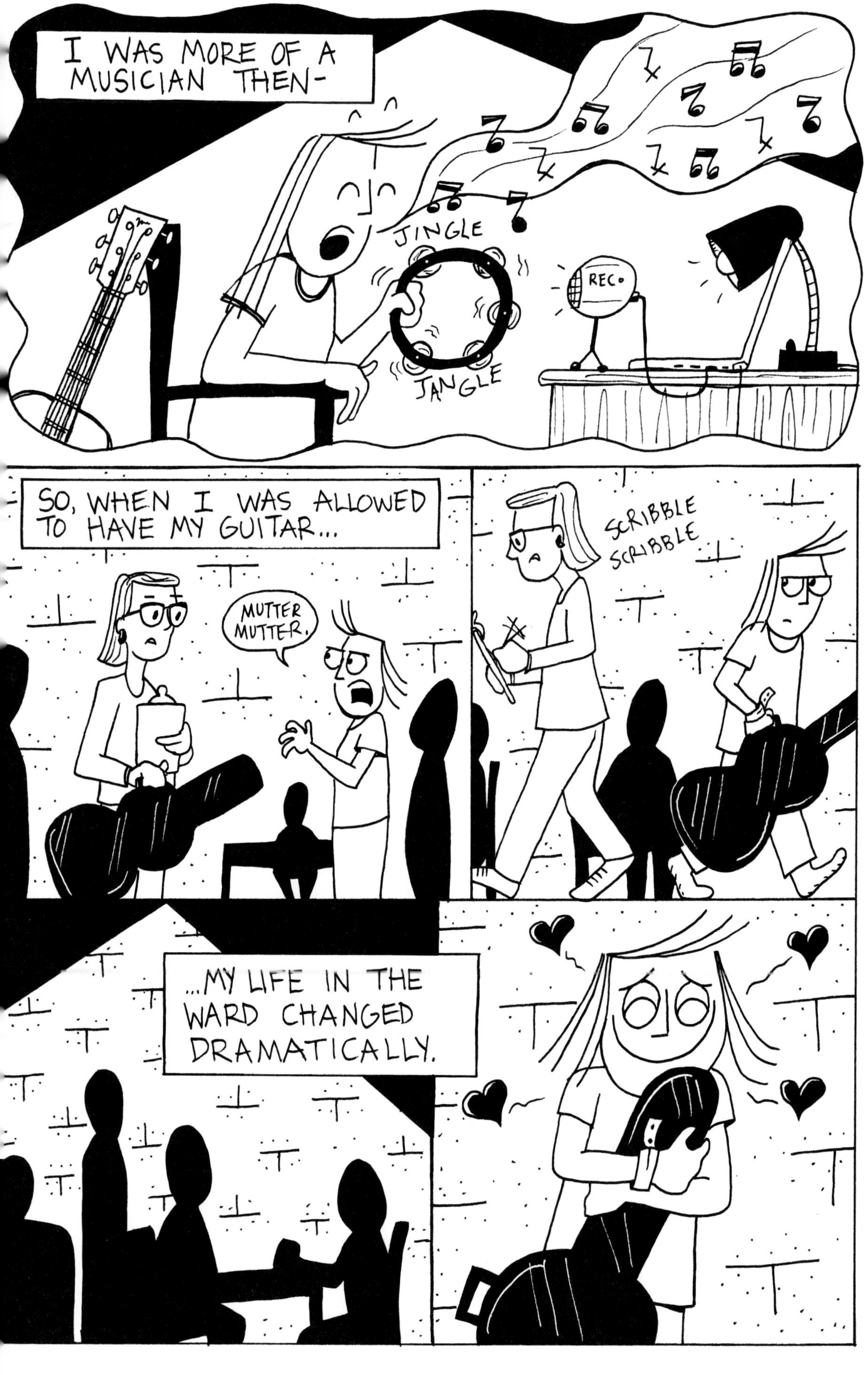

I WAS MORE OF A MUSICIAN THEN-
JINGLE
JANGLE
REC.
SO, WHEN I WAS ALLOWED TO HAVE MY GUITAR...
MUTTER MUTTER.
SCRIBBLE SCRIBBLE
...MY LIFE IN THE WARD CHANGED DRAMATICALLY.

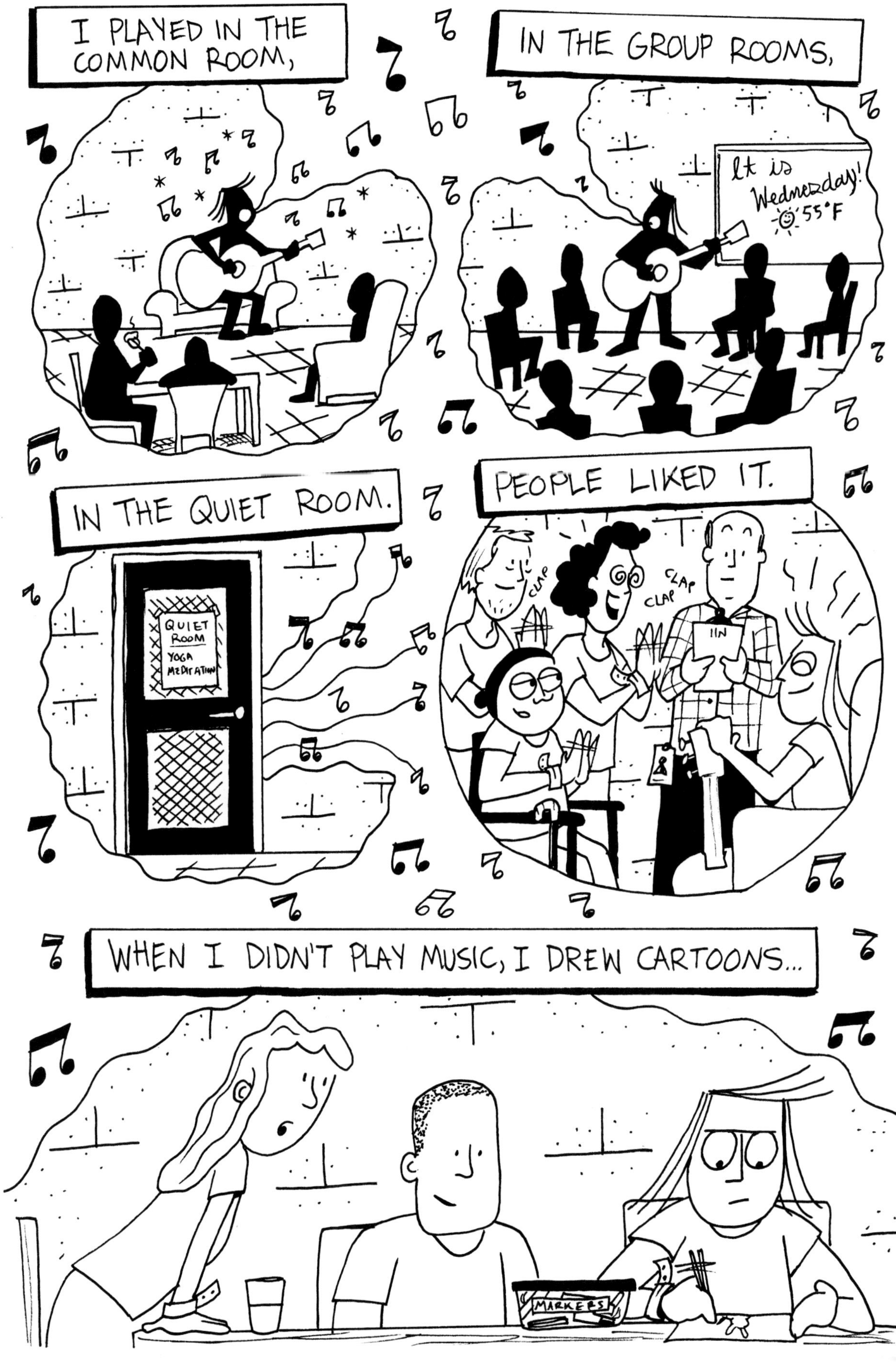
I PLAYED IN THE COMMON ROOM,
IN THE GROUP ROOMS,
It is Wednesday!
55°F
IN THE QUIET ROOM.
QUIET ROOM
YOGA
MEDITATION
PEOPLE LIKED IT.
CLAP
CLAP
CLAP
WHEN I DIDN'T PLAY MUSIC, I DREW CARTOONS...
MARKERS

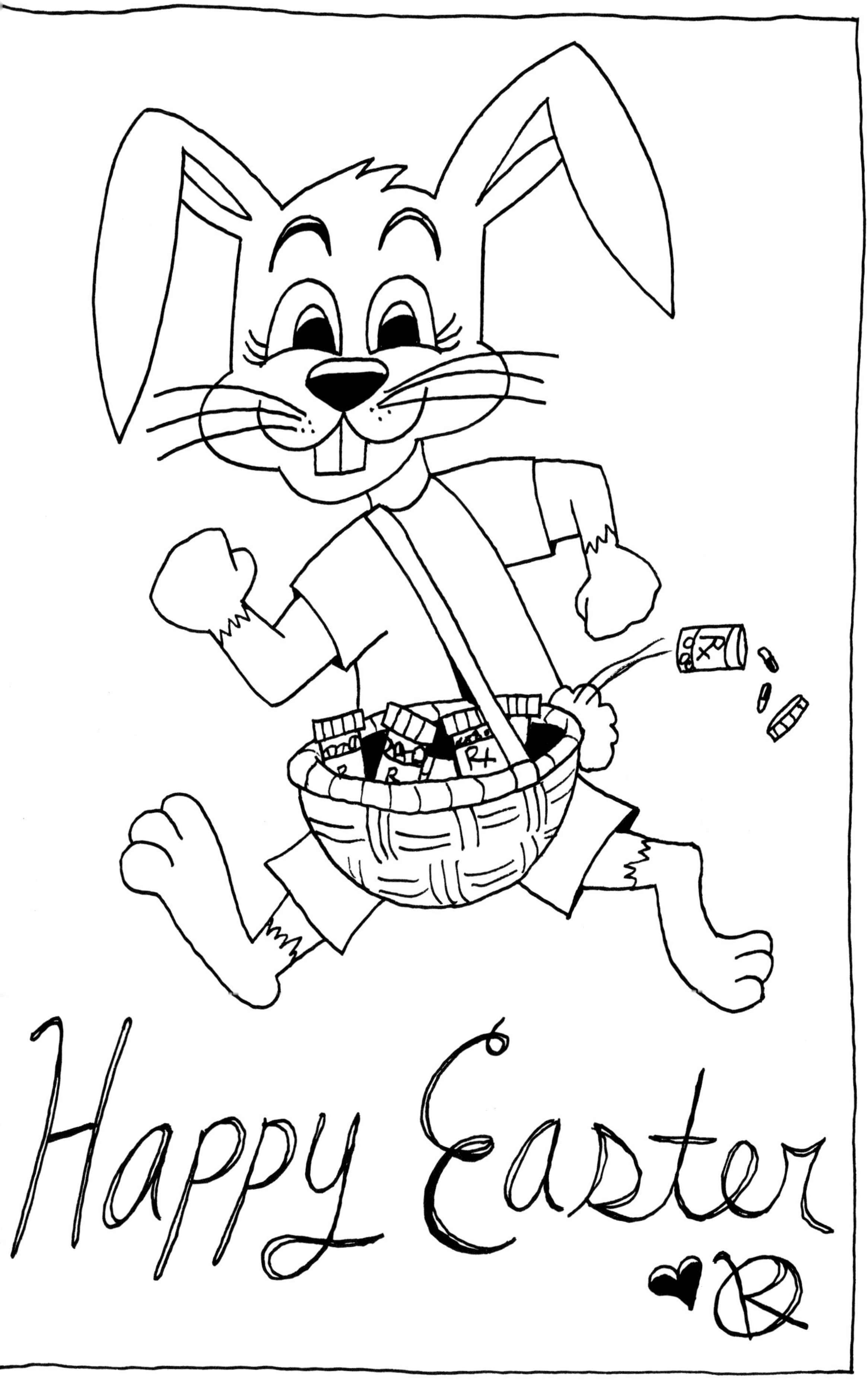
Rx
Happy Easter

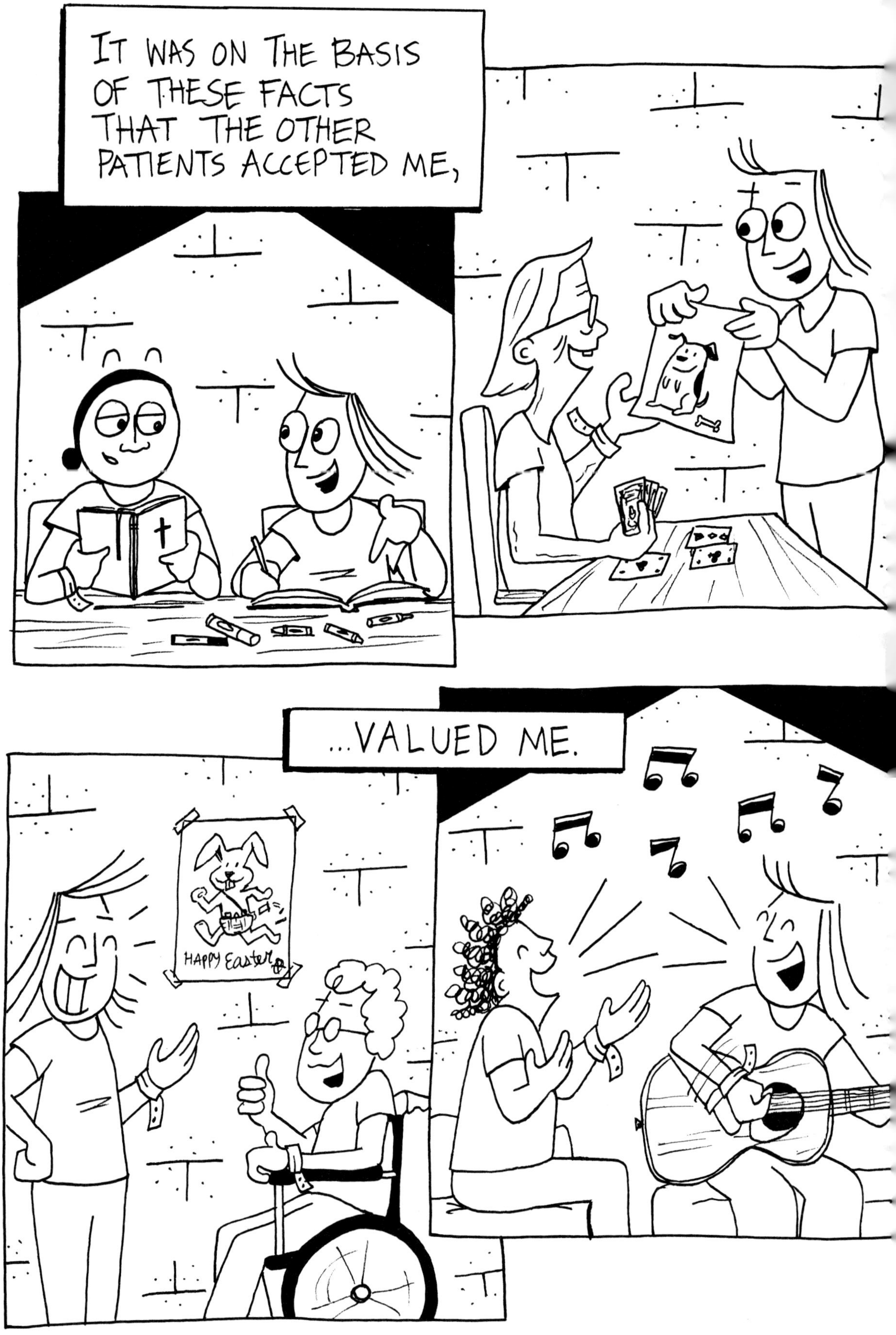
IT WAS ON THE BASIS OF THESE FACTS THAT THE OTHER PATIENTS ACCEPTED ME,
...VALUED ME.
HAPPY Easter

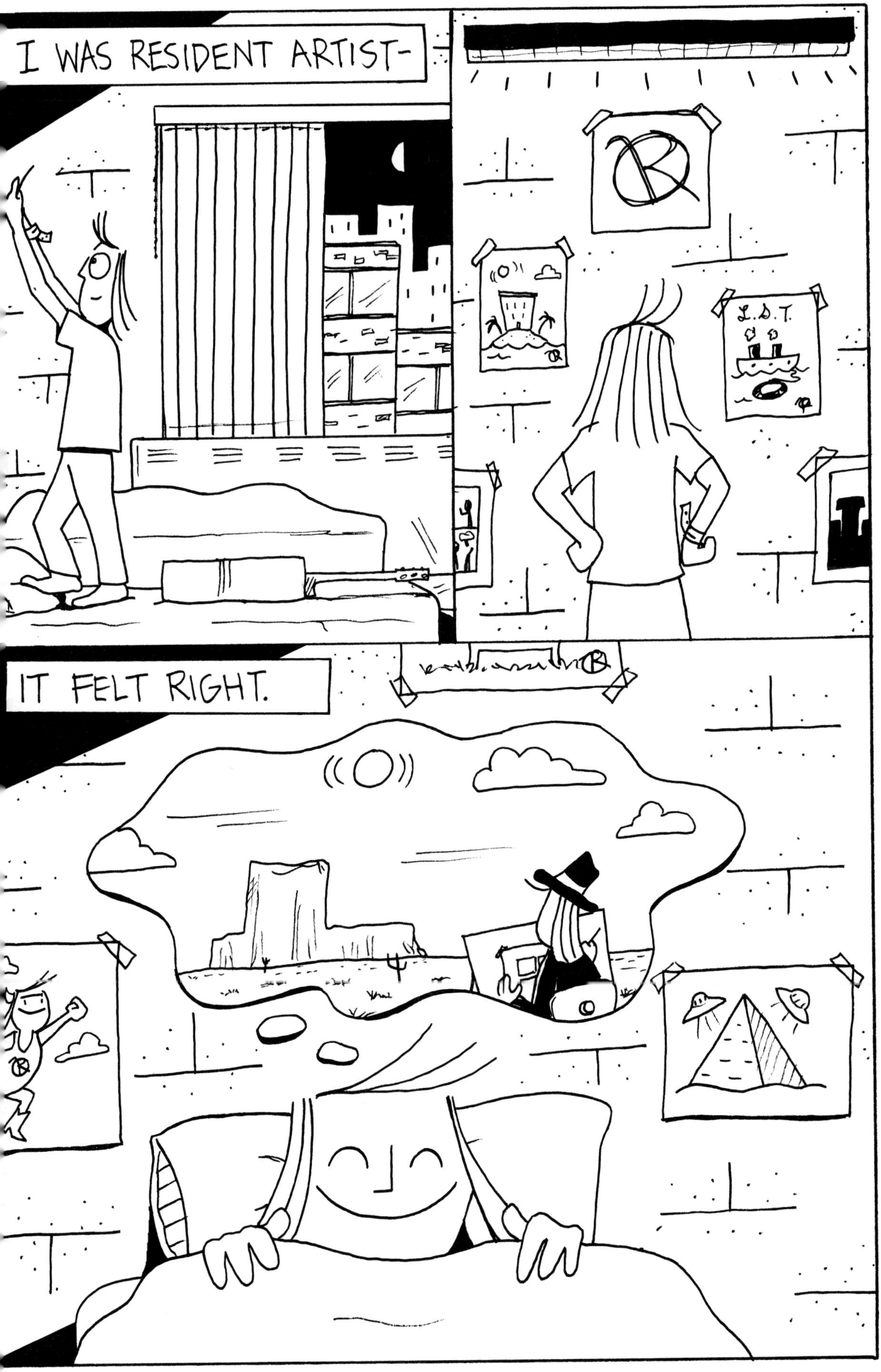
I WAS RESIDENT ARTIST-
L.S.T.
IT FELT RIGHT.

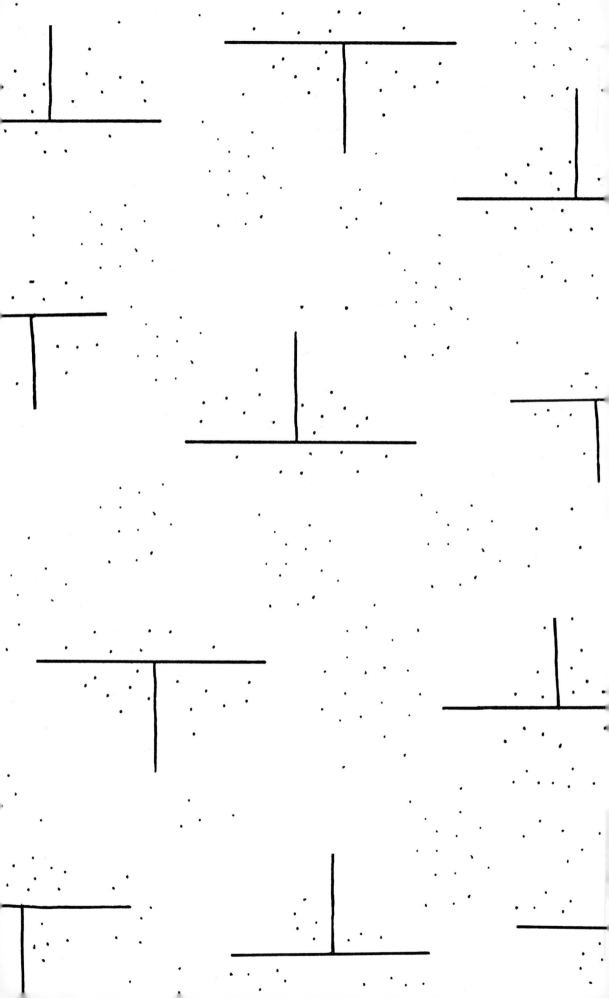

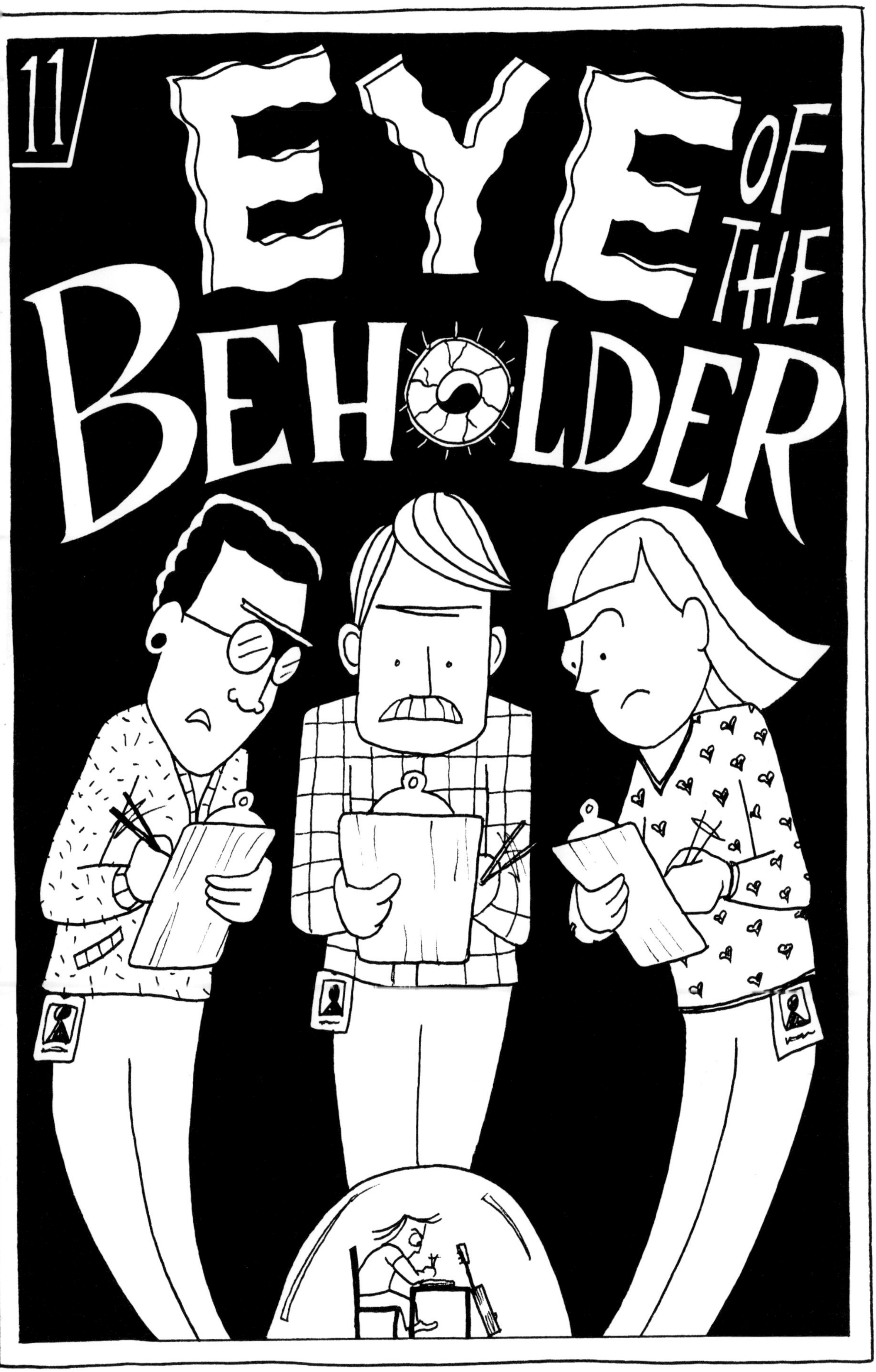

11
EYE OF THE BEHOLDER

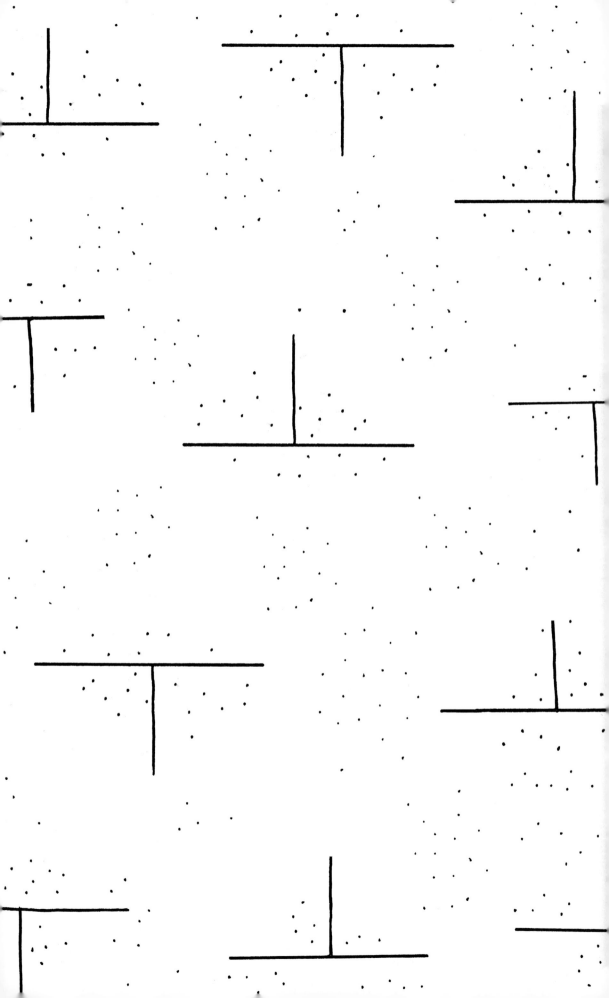

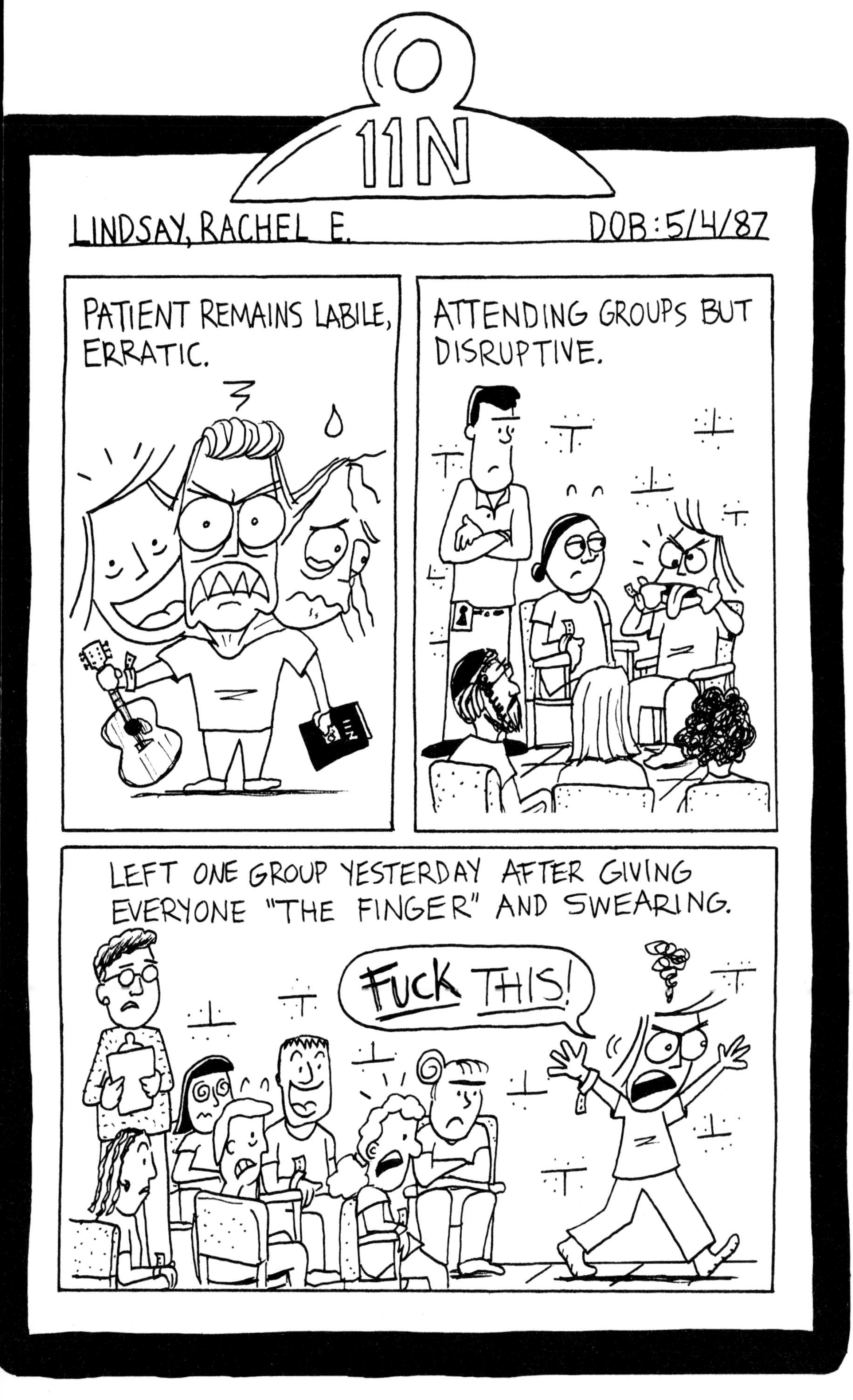
11N
LINDSAY, RACHEL E.
DOB: 5/4/87
PATIENT REMAINS LABILE, ERRATIC.
ATTENDING GROUPS BUT DISRUPTIVE.
LEFT ONE GROUP YESTERDAY AFTER GIVING EVERYONE "THE FINGER" AND SWEARING.
FUCK THIS!

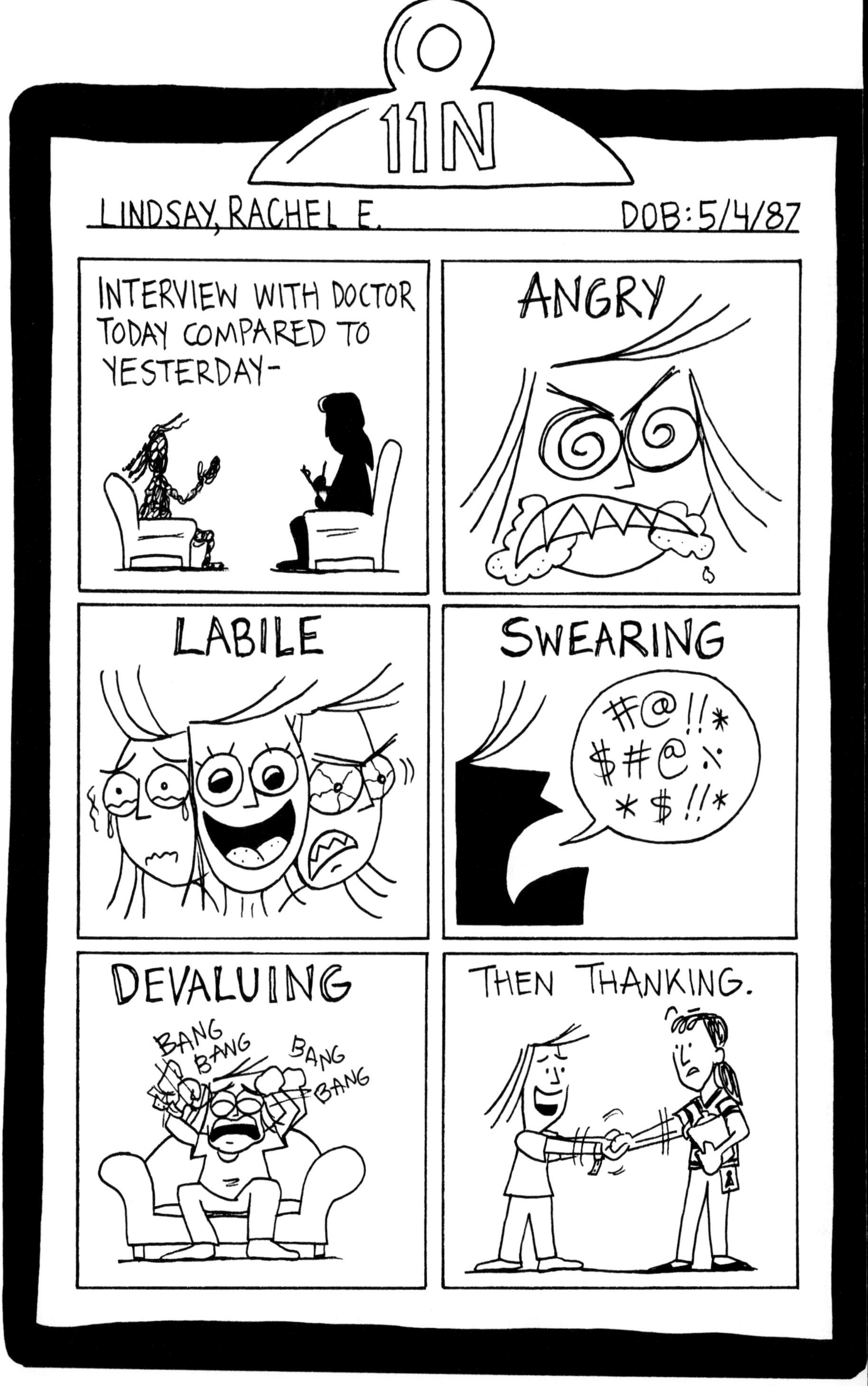
11N
LINDSAY, RACHEL E.
DOB: 5/4/87
INTERVIEW WITH DOCTOR TODAY COMPARED TO YESTERDAY-
ANGRY
LABILE
SWEARING
#@!!*
$#@%
$!!
DEVALUING
BANG BANG
BANG BANG
THEN THANKING.

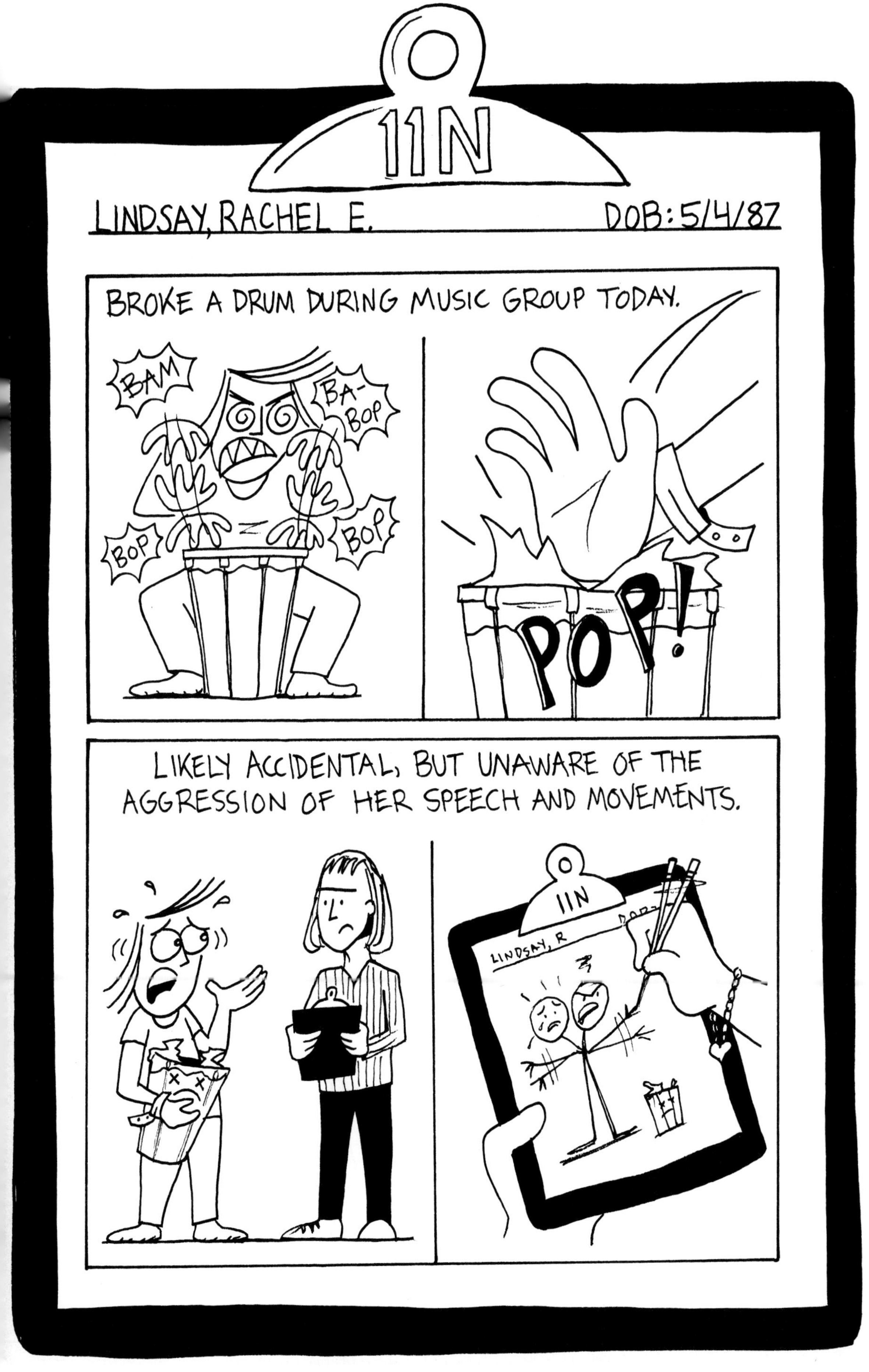
11N
LINDSAY, RACHEL E.
DOB: 5/4/87
BROKE A DRUM DURING MUSIC GROUP TODAY.
BAM
BA-BOP
BOP
BOP
POP!
LIKELY ACCIDENTAL, BUT UNAWARE OF THE AGGRESSION OF HER SPEECH AND MOVEMENTS.
11N
LINDSAY, R

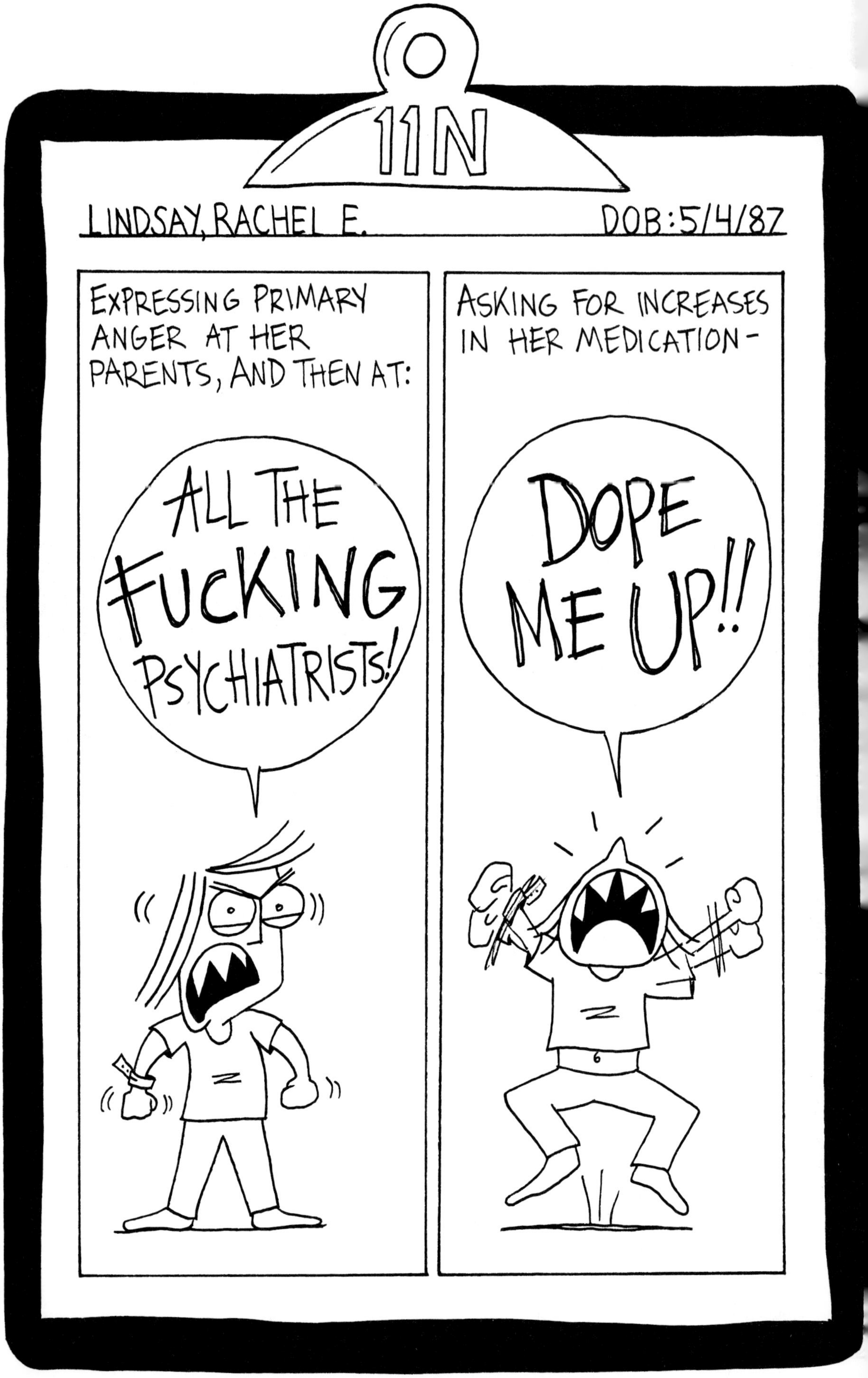
11N
LINDSAY, RACHEL E.
DOB: 5/4/87
EXPRESSING PRIMARY ANGER AT HER PARENTS, AND THEN AT:
ALL THE FUCKING PSYCHIATRISTS!
ASKING FOR INCREASES IN HER MEDICATION-
DOPE ME UP!!

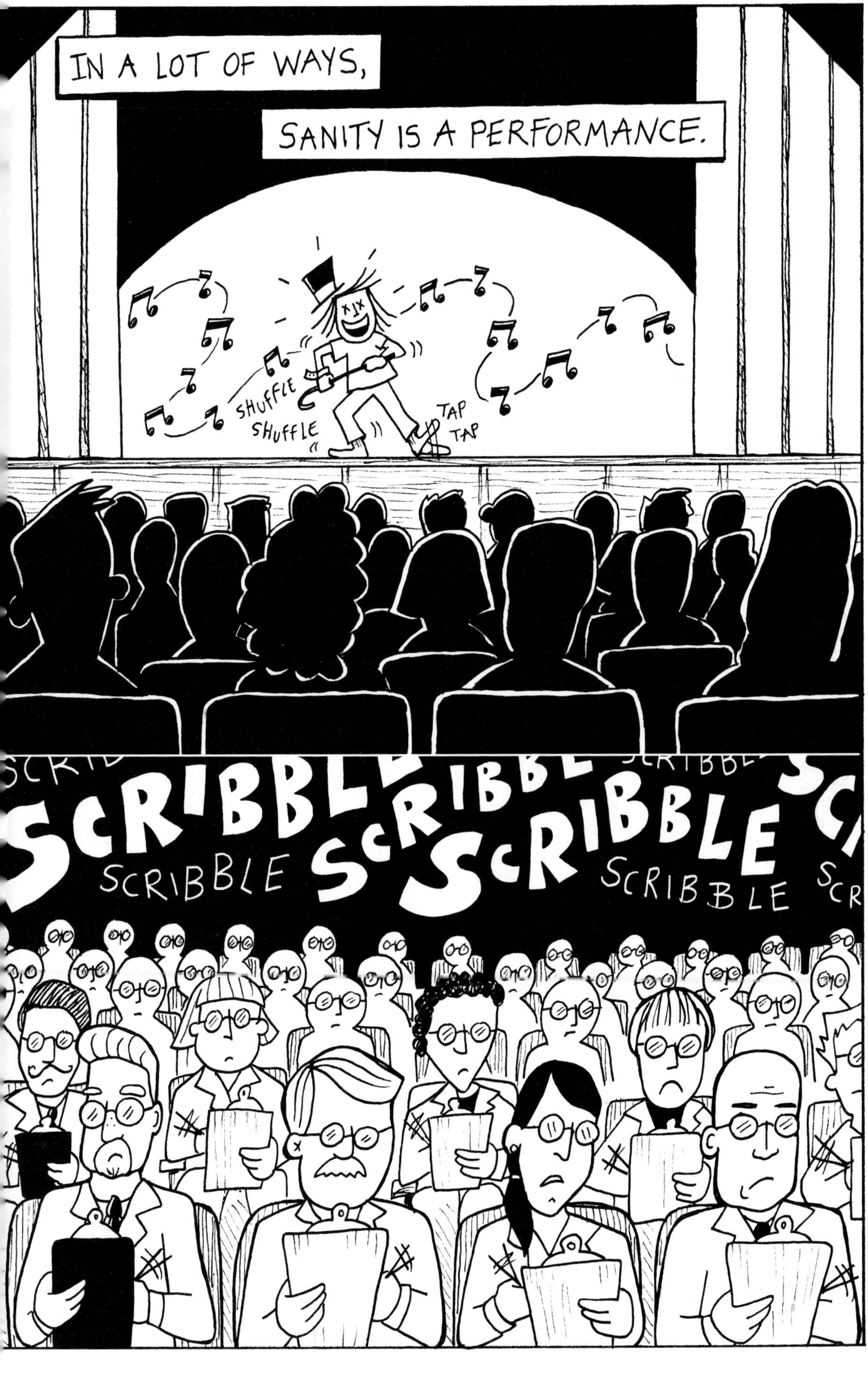
IN A LOT OF WAYS,
SANITY IS A PERFORMANCE.
SHUFFLE
SHUFFLE
TAP
TAP
SCRIBBLE
SCRIBBLE
SCRIBBLE
SCRIBBLE
SCRIBBLE

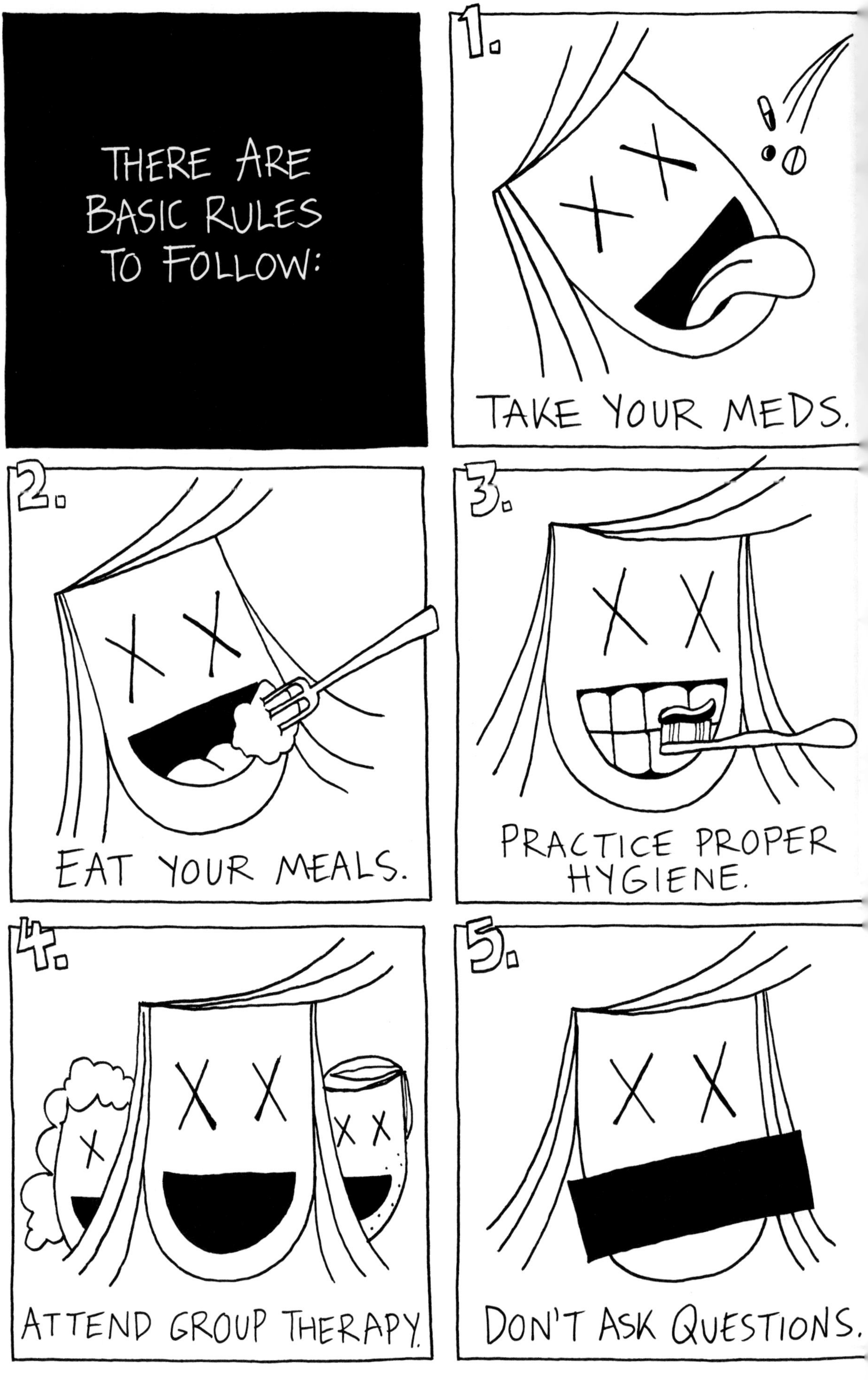
THERE ARE BASIC RULES TO FOLLOW:
1.
TAKE YOUR MEDS.
2.
EAT YOUR MEALS.
3.
PRACTICE PROPER HYGIENE.
4.
ATTEND GROUP THERAPY.
5.
DON'T ASK QUESTIONS.

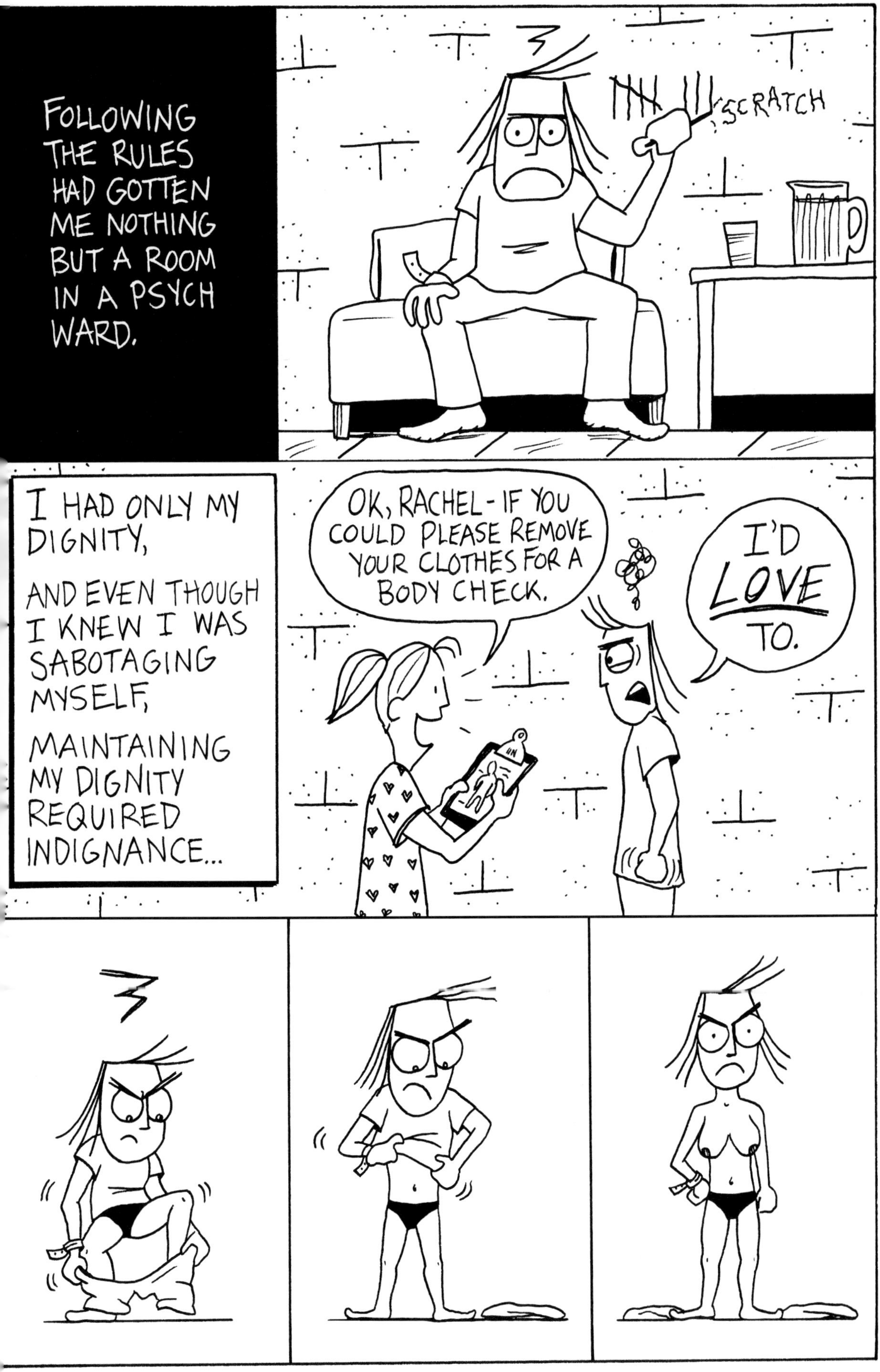
FOLLOWING THE RULES HAD GOTTEN ME NOTHING BUT A ROOM IN A PSYCH WARD.
SCRATCH
I HAD ONLY MY DIGNITY,
AND EVEN THOUGH I KNEW I WAS SABOTAGING MYSELF,
MAINTAINING MY DIGNITY REQUIRED INDIGNANCE...
OK, RACHEL - IF YOU COULD PLEASE REMOVE YOUR CLOTHES FOR A BODY CHECK.
I'D LOVE TO.

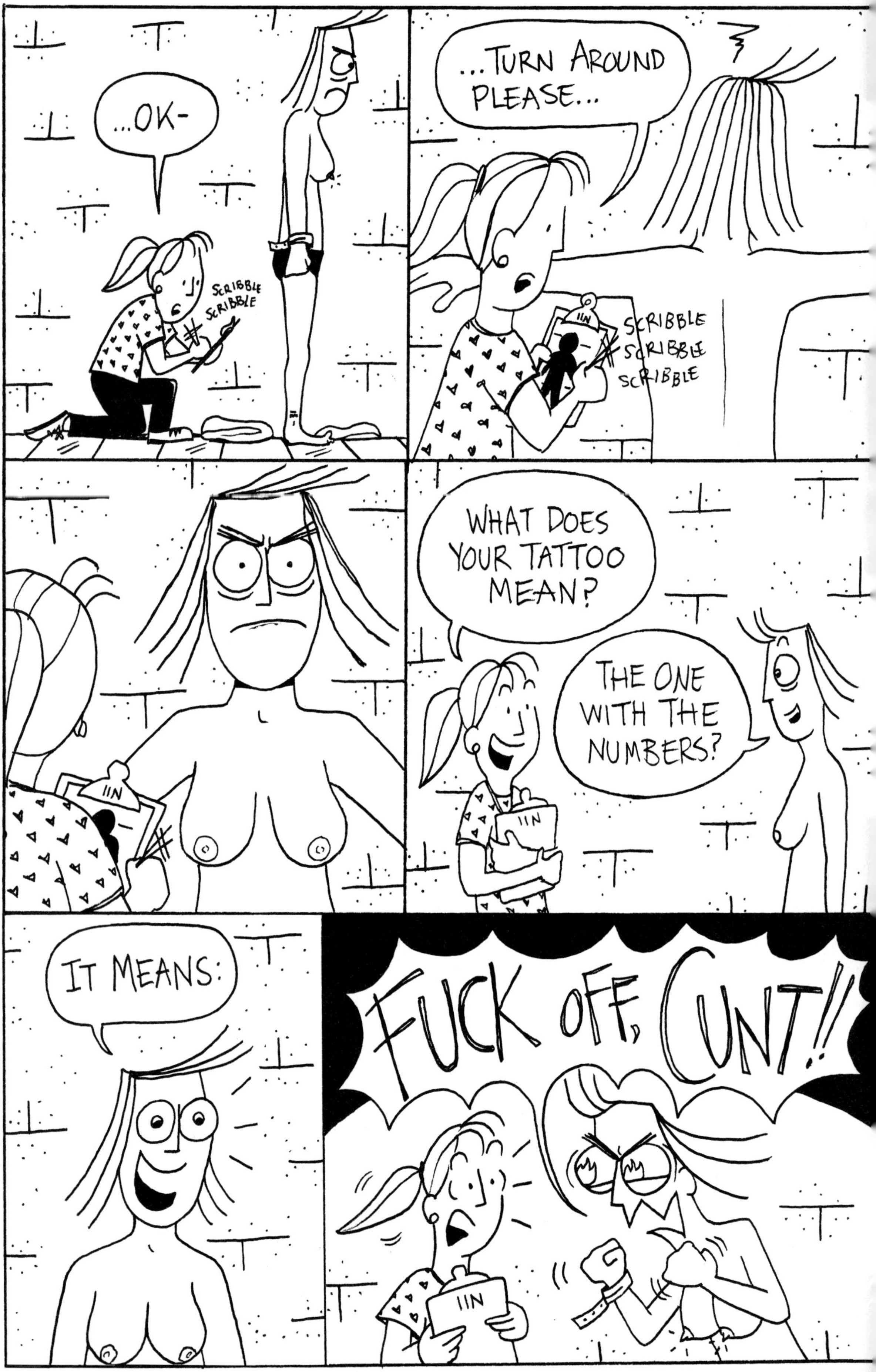
...OK-
SCRIBBLE SCRIBBLE
...TURN AROUND PLEASE...
IIN
SCRIBBLE SCRIBBLE SCRIBBLE
IIN
WHAT DOES YOUR TATTOO MEAN?
THE ONE WITH THE NUMBERS?
IIN
IT MEANS:
FUCK OFF, CUNT!!
IIN

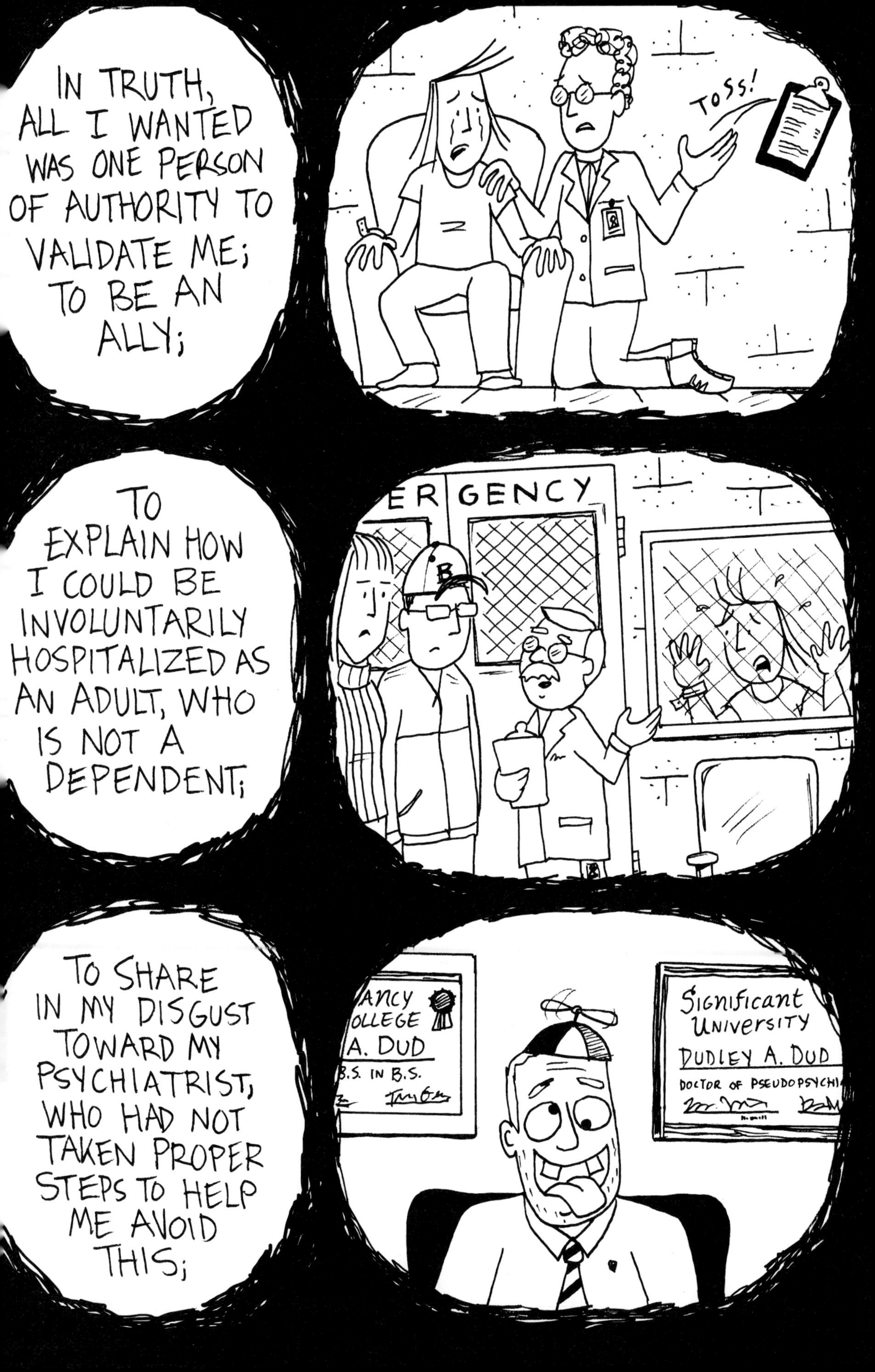
IN TRUTH, ALL I WANTED WAS ONE PERSON OF AUTHORITY TO VALIDATE ME; TO BE AN ALLY;
TOSS!
TO EXPLAIN HOW I COULD BE INVOLUNTARILY HOSPITALIZED AS AN ADULT, WHO IS NOT A DEPENDENT;
ER GENCY
TO SHARE IN MY DISGUST TOWARD MY PSYCHIATRIST, WHO HAD NOT TAKEN PROPER STEPS TO HELP ME AVOID THIS;
ANCY
OLLEGE
A. DUD
B.S. IN B.S.
Significant University
DUDLEY A. DUD
DOCTOR OF PSEUDOPSYCHI

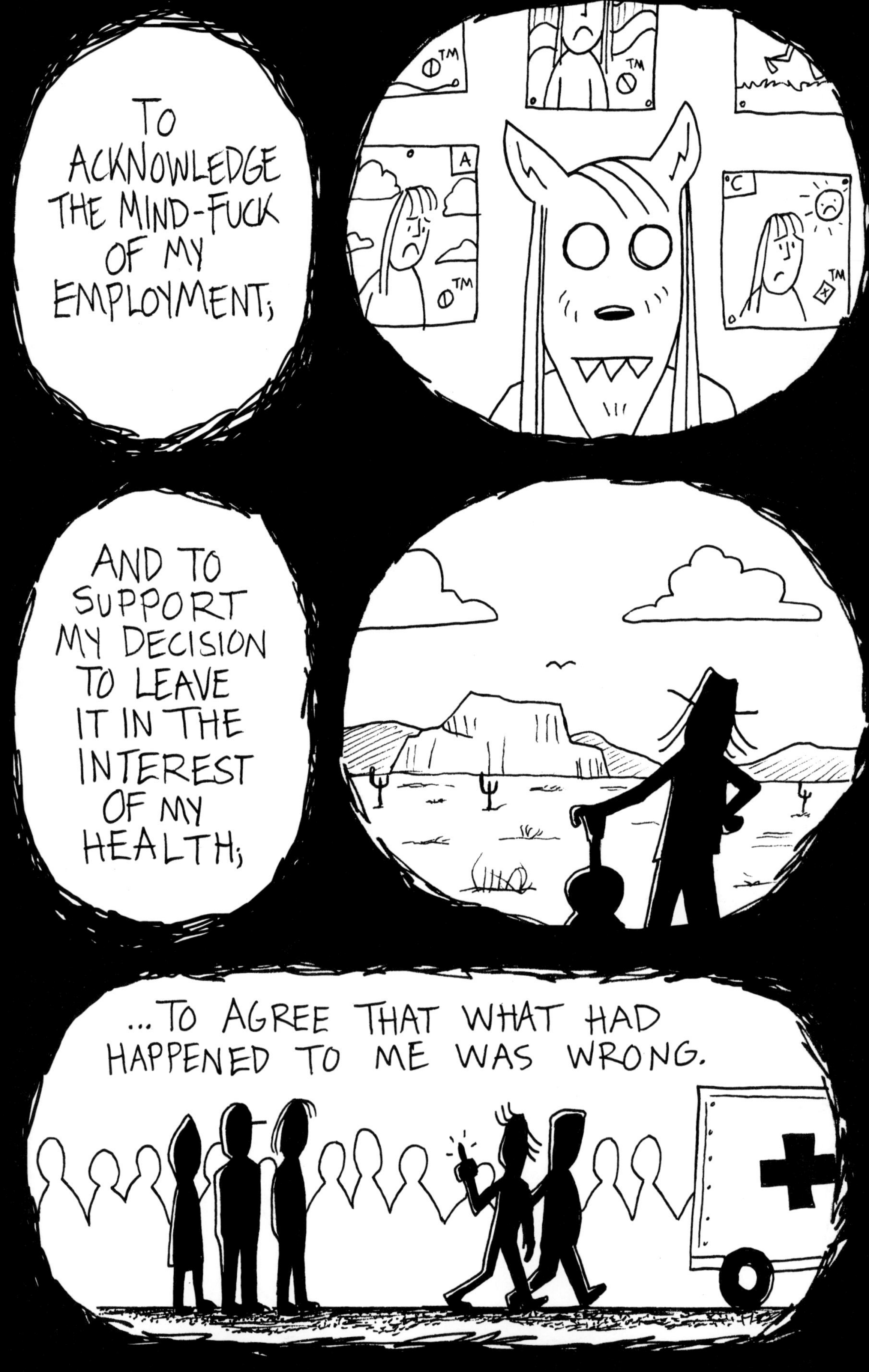
TO ACKNOWLEDGE THE MIND-FUCK OF MY EMPLOYMENT;
AND TO SUPPORT MY DECISION TO LEAVE IT IN THE INTEREST OF MY HEALTH;
...TO AGREE THAT WHAT HAD HAPPENED TO ME WAS WRONG.

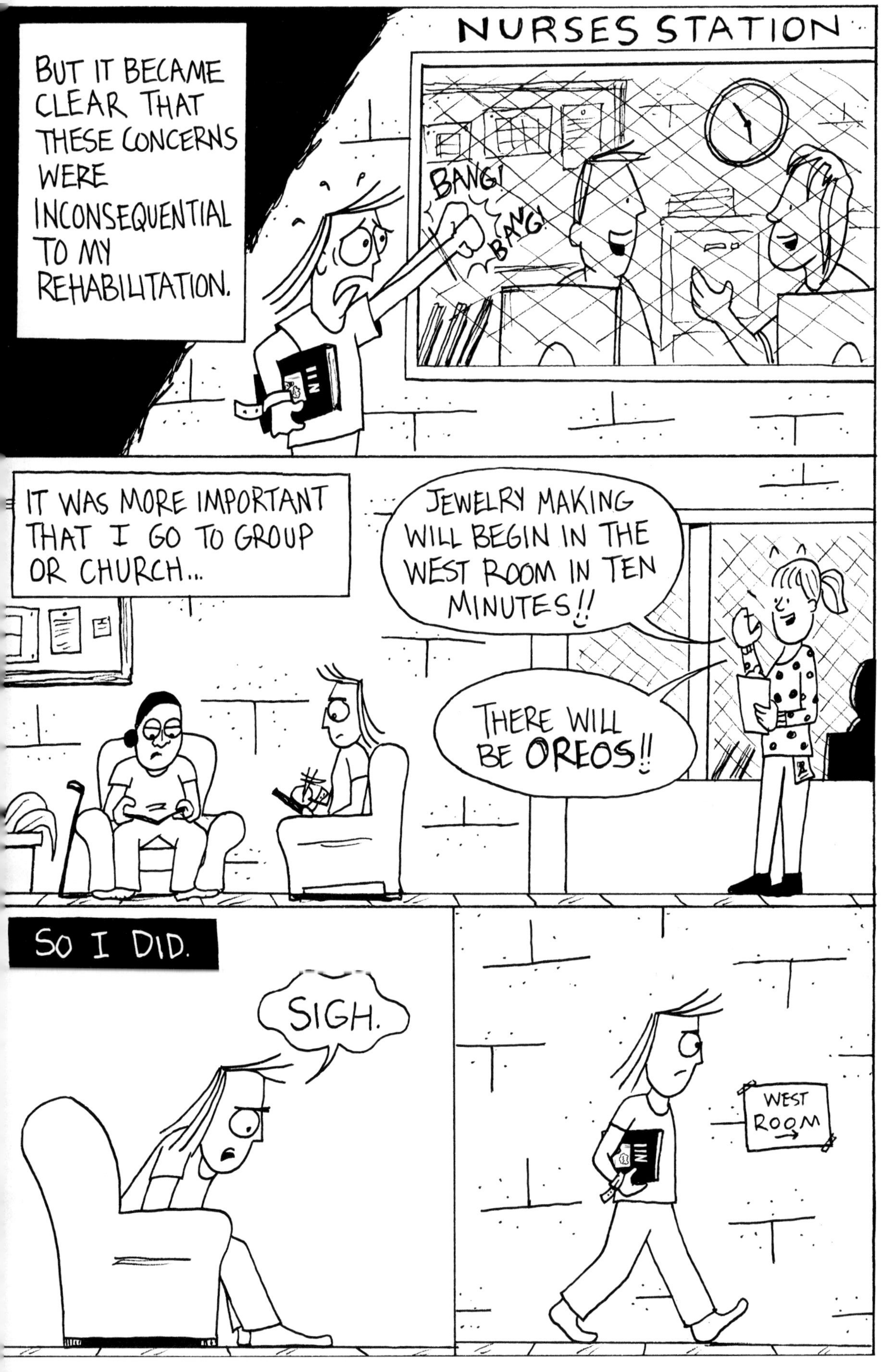
NURSES STATION
BUT IT BECAME CLEAR THAT THESE CONCERNS WERE INCONSEQUENTIAL TO MY REHABILITATION.
BANG!
BANG!
IT WAS MORE IMPORTANT THAT I GO TO GROUP OR CHURCH...
JEWELRY MAKING WILL BEGIN IN THE WEST ROOM IN TEN MINUTES!!
THERE WILL BE OREOS!!
SO I DID.
SIGH.
WEST ROOM

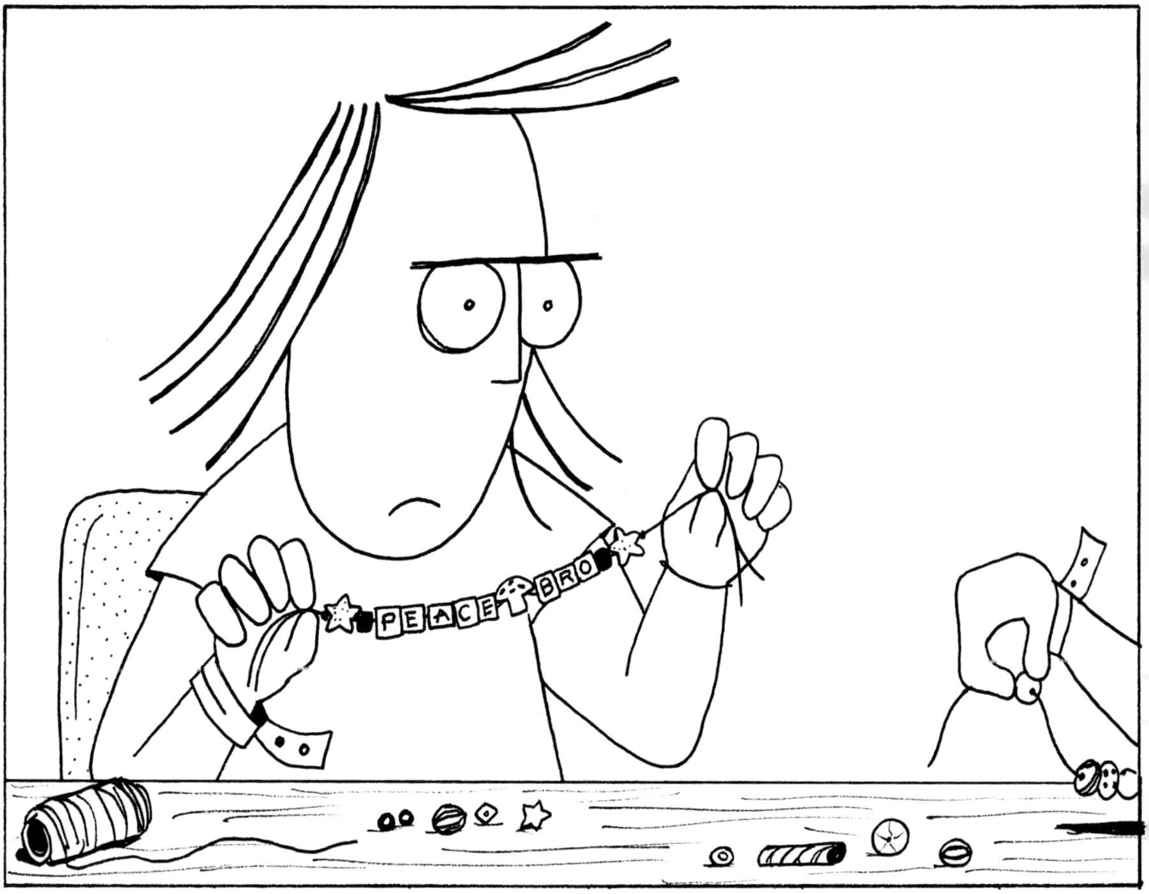
PEACE BRO

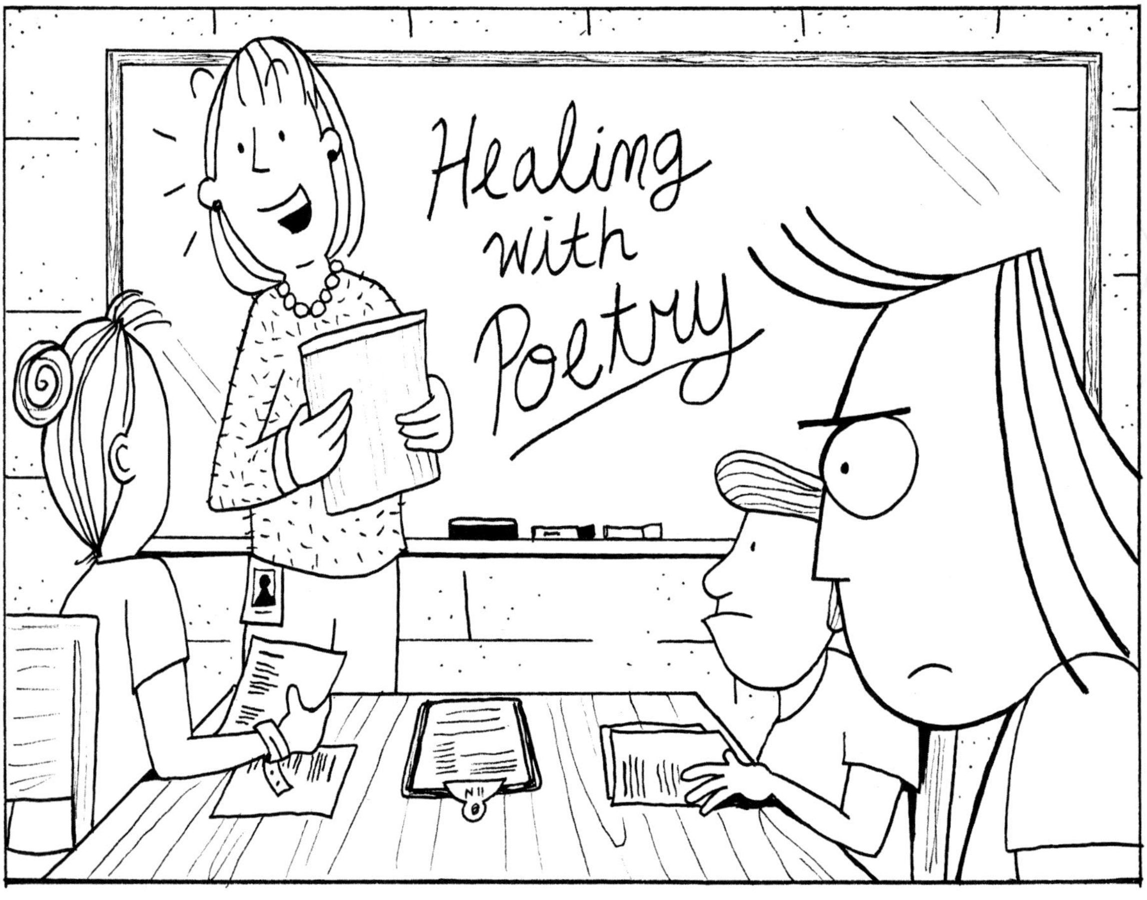
Healing with Poetry

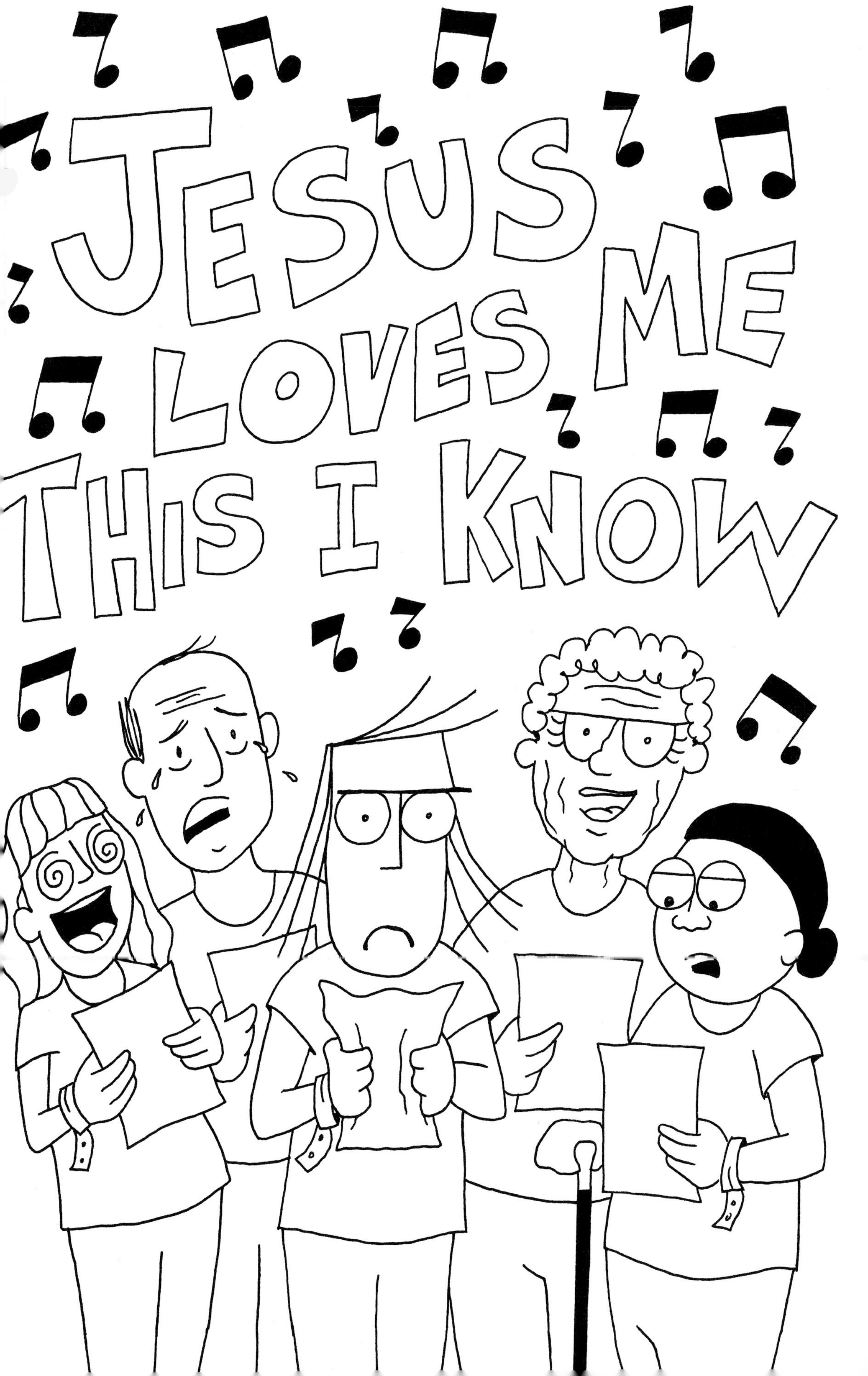
JESUS LOVES ME THIS I KNOW

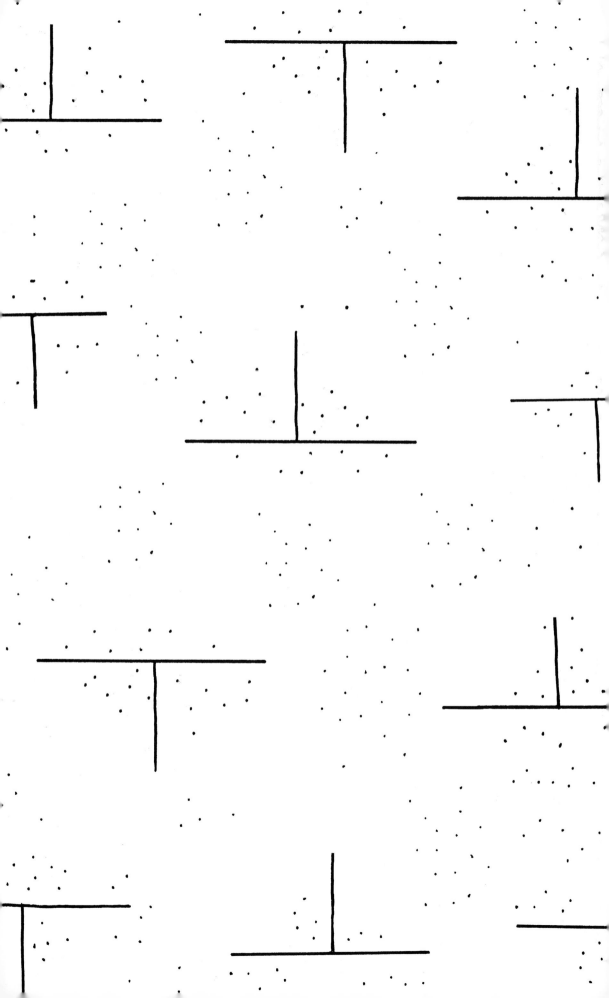

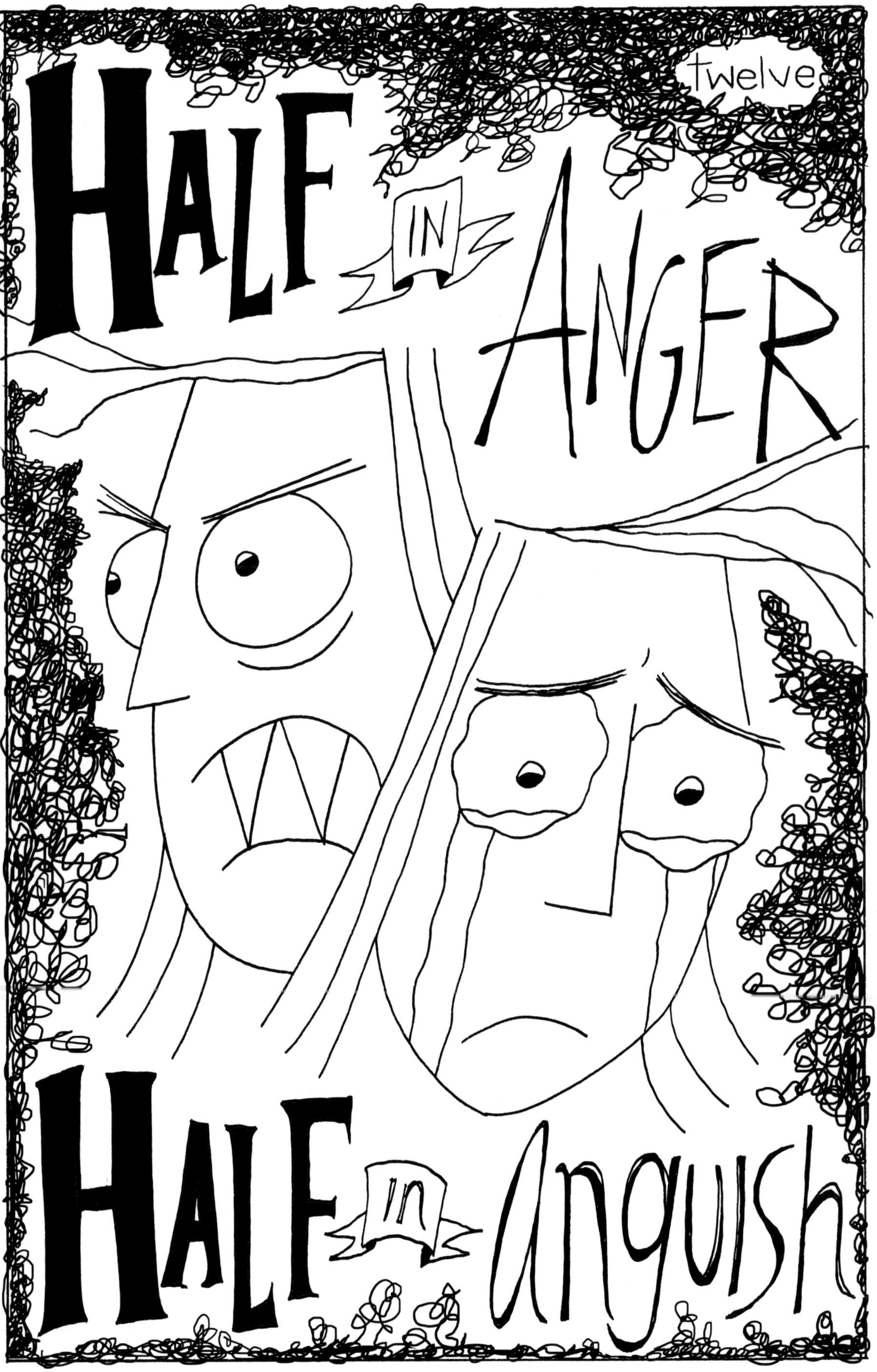
twelve
HALF IN ANGER
HALF in Anguish

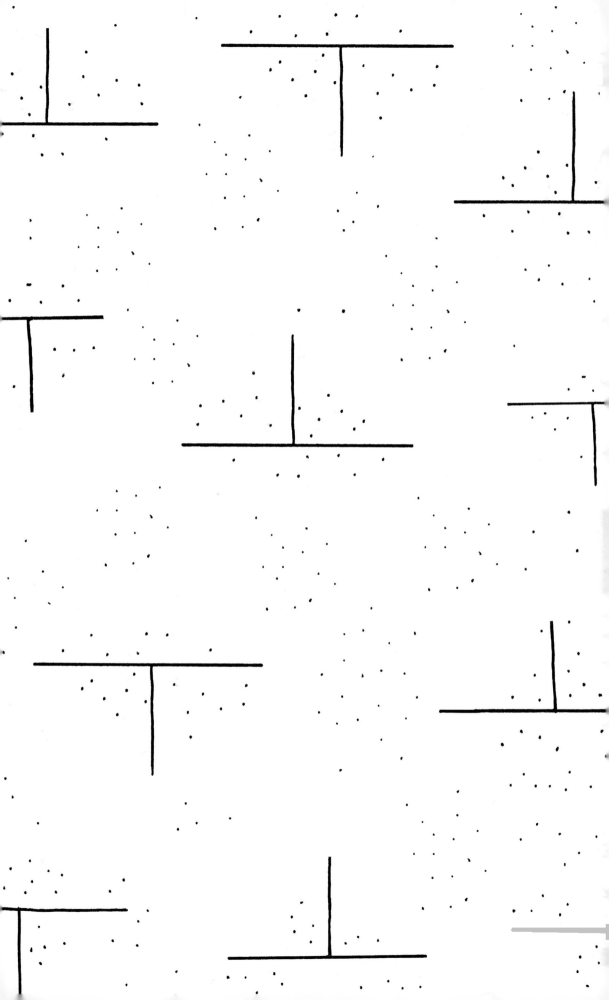

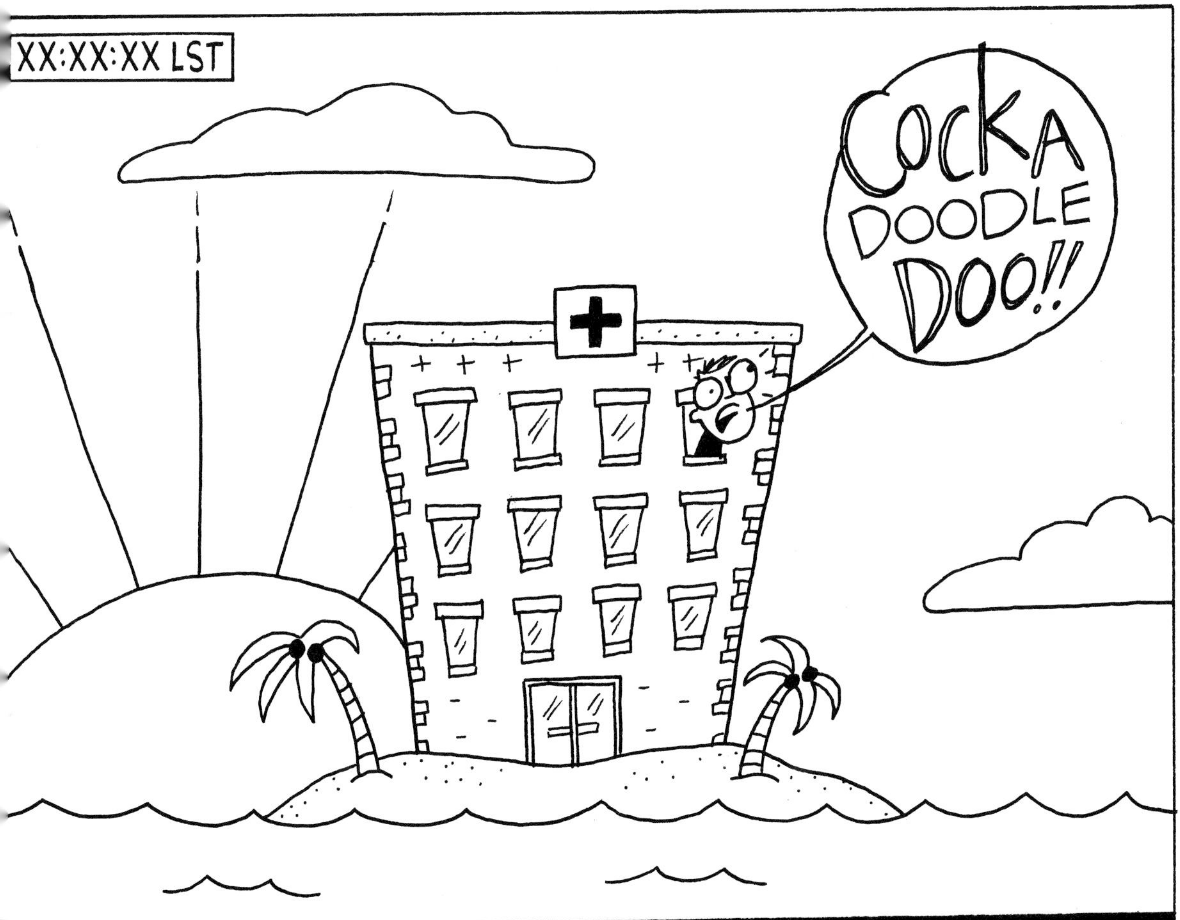
XX:XX:XX LST
COCKA DOODLE DOO!!

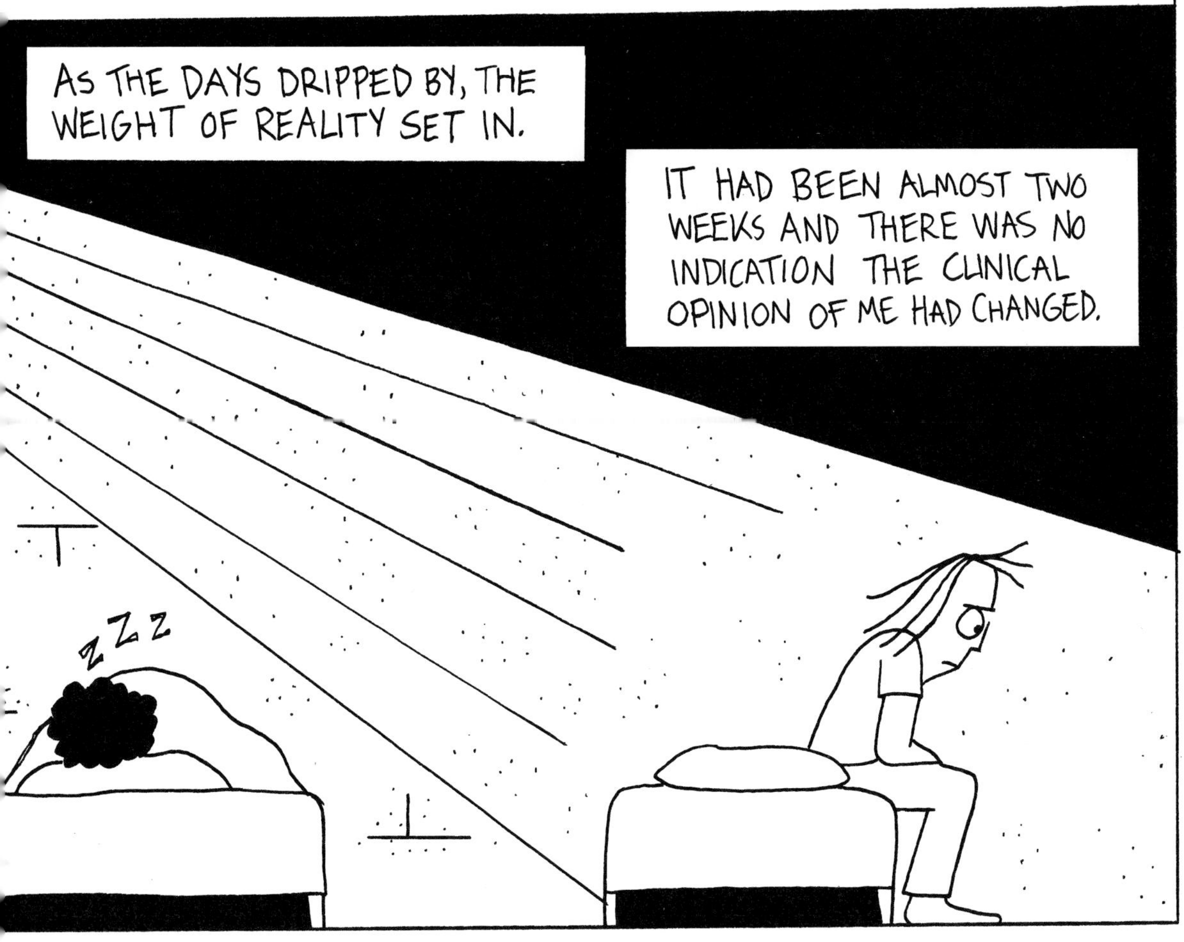
AS THE DAYS DRIPPED BY, THE WEIGHT OF REALITY SET IN.
IT HAD BEEN ALMOST TWO WEEKS AND THERE WAS NO INDICATION THE CLINICAL OPINION OF ME HAD CHANGED.
Z Z Z

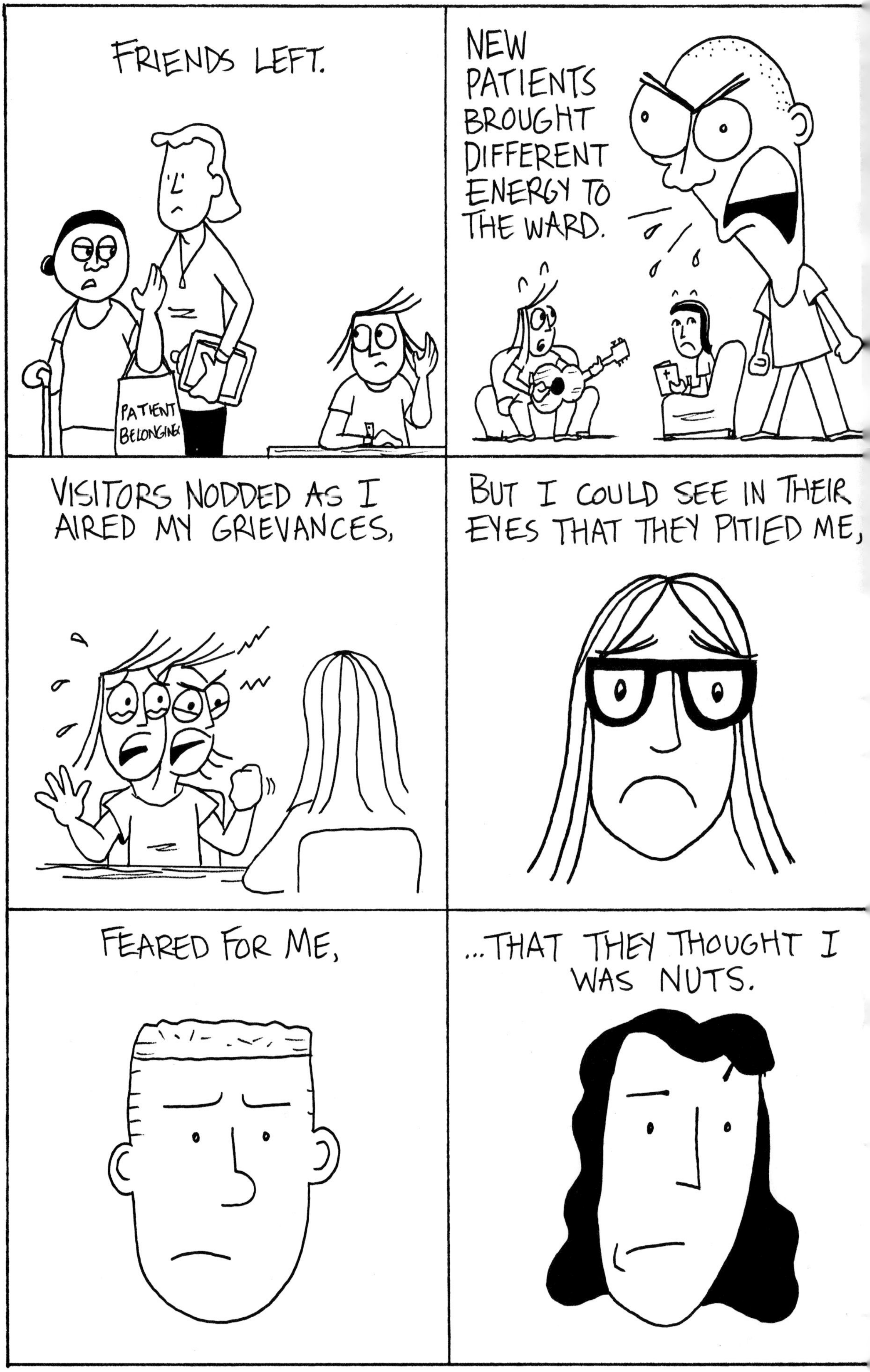
FRIENDS LEFT.
PATIENT BELONGINGS
NEW PATIENTS BROUGHT DIFFERENT ENERGY TO THE WARD.
VISITORS NODDED AS I AIRED MY GRIEVANCES,
BUT I COULD SEE IN THEIR EYES THAT THEY PITIED ME,
FEARED FOR ME,
...THAT THEY THOUGHT I WAS NUTS.

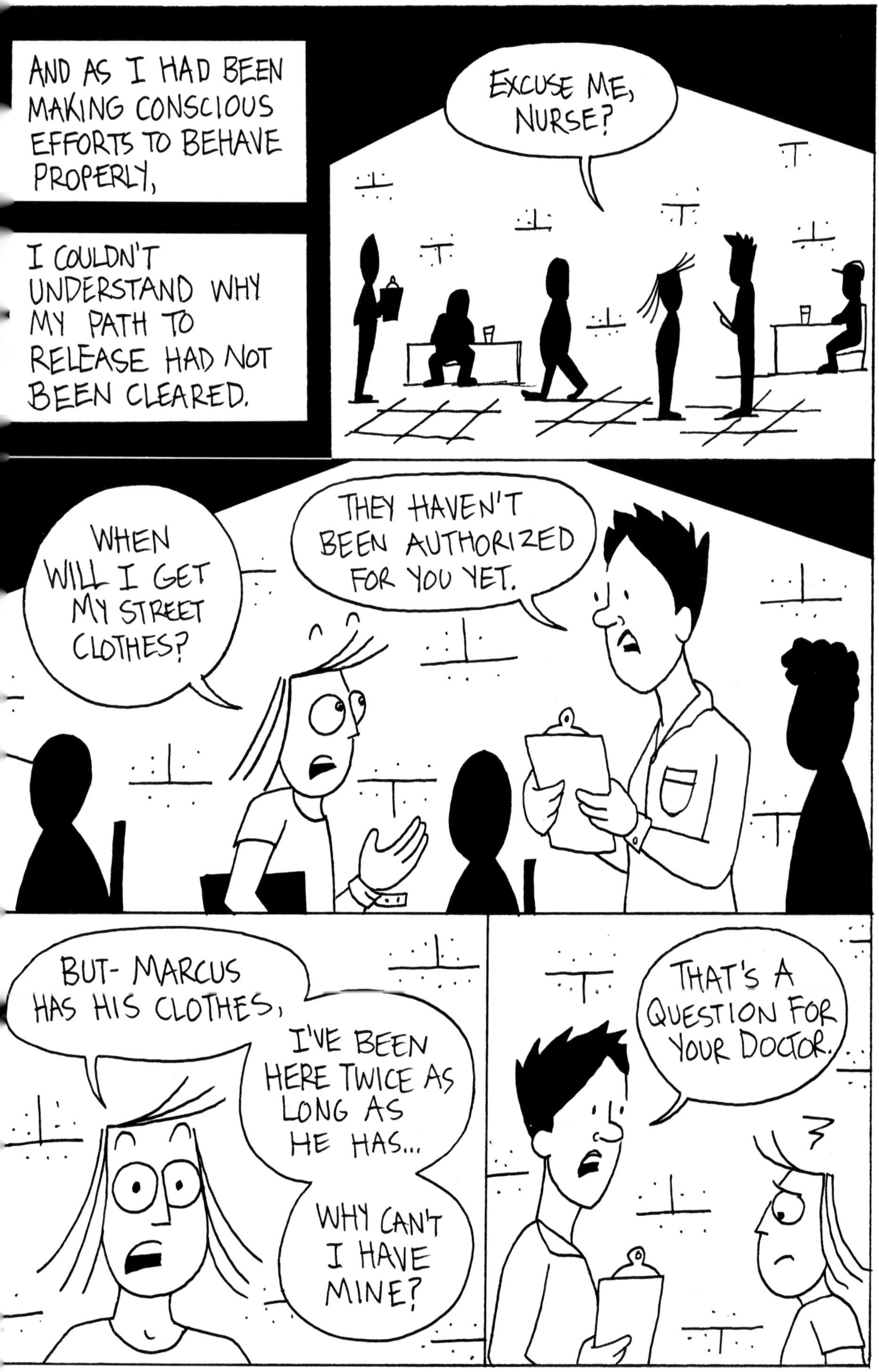
AND AS I HAD BEEN MAKING CONSCIOUS EFFORTS TO BEHAVE PROPERLY,
I COULDN'T UNDERSTAND WHY MY PATH TO RELEASE HAD NOT BEEN CLEARED.
EXCUSE ME, NURSE?
WHEN WILL I GET MY STREET CLOTHES?
THEY HAVEN'T BEEN AUTHORIZED FOR YOU YET.
BUT- MARCUS HAS HIS CLOTHES,
I'VE BEEN HERE TWICE AS LONG AS HE HAS...
WHY CAN'T I HAVE MINE?
THAT'S A QUESTION FOR YOUR DOCTOR.

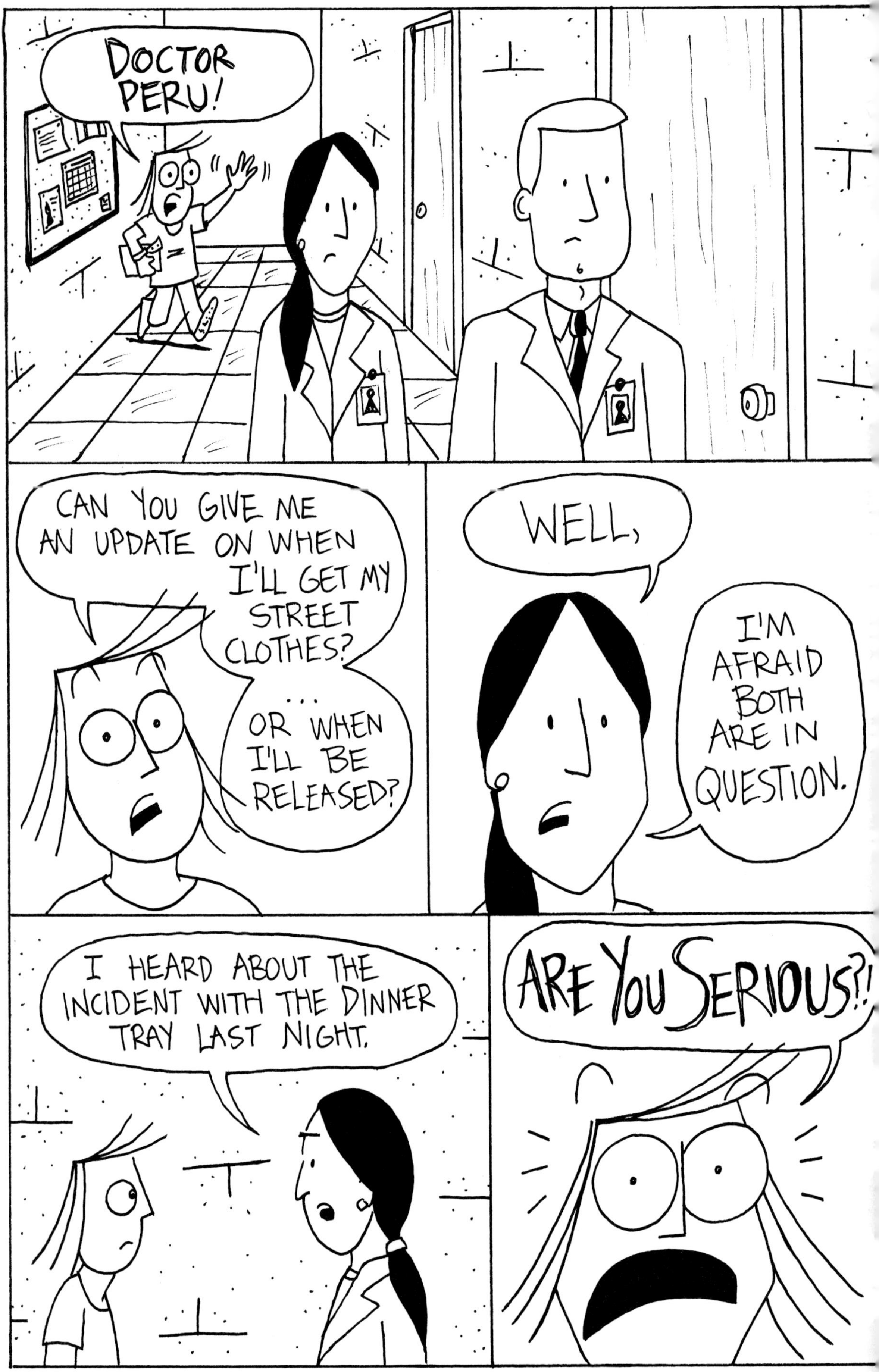
DOCTOR PERU!
CAN YOU GIVE ME AN UPDATE ON WHEN I'LL GET MY STREET CLOTHES?
... OR WHEN I'LL BE RELEASED?
WELL,
I'M AFRAID BOTH ARE IN QUESTION.
I HEARD ABOUT THE INCIDENT WITH THE DINNER TRAY LAST NIGHT.
ARE YOU SERIOUS?!

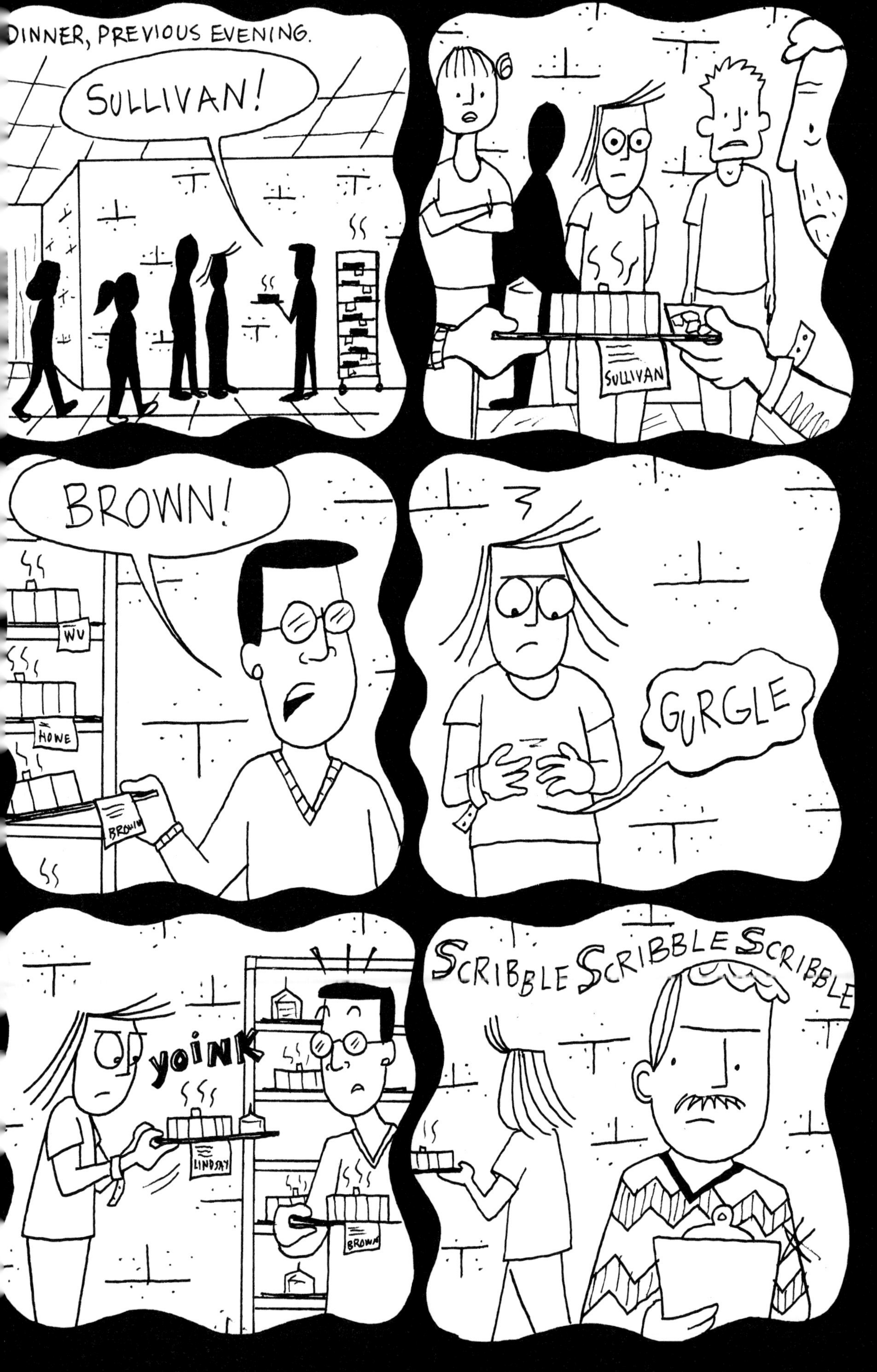
DINNER, PREVIOUS EVENING.
SULLIVAN!
SULLIVAN
BROWN!
WU
HOWE
BROWN
GURGLE
YOINK
LINDSAY
BROWN
SCRIBBLE SCRIBBLE SCRIBBLE

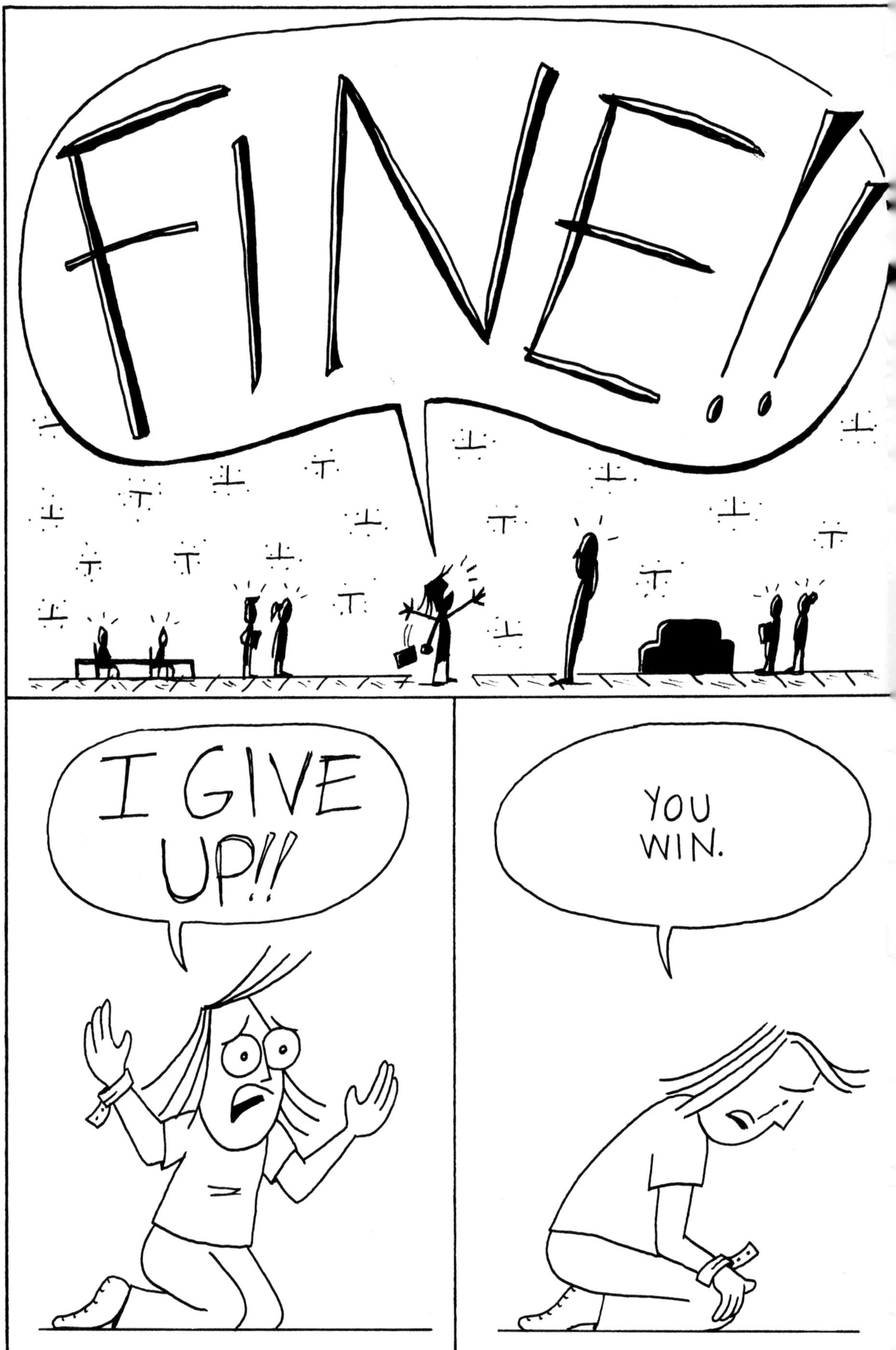
FINE!!
I GIVE UP!!
YOU WIN.

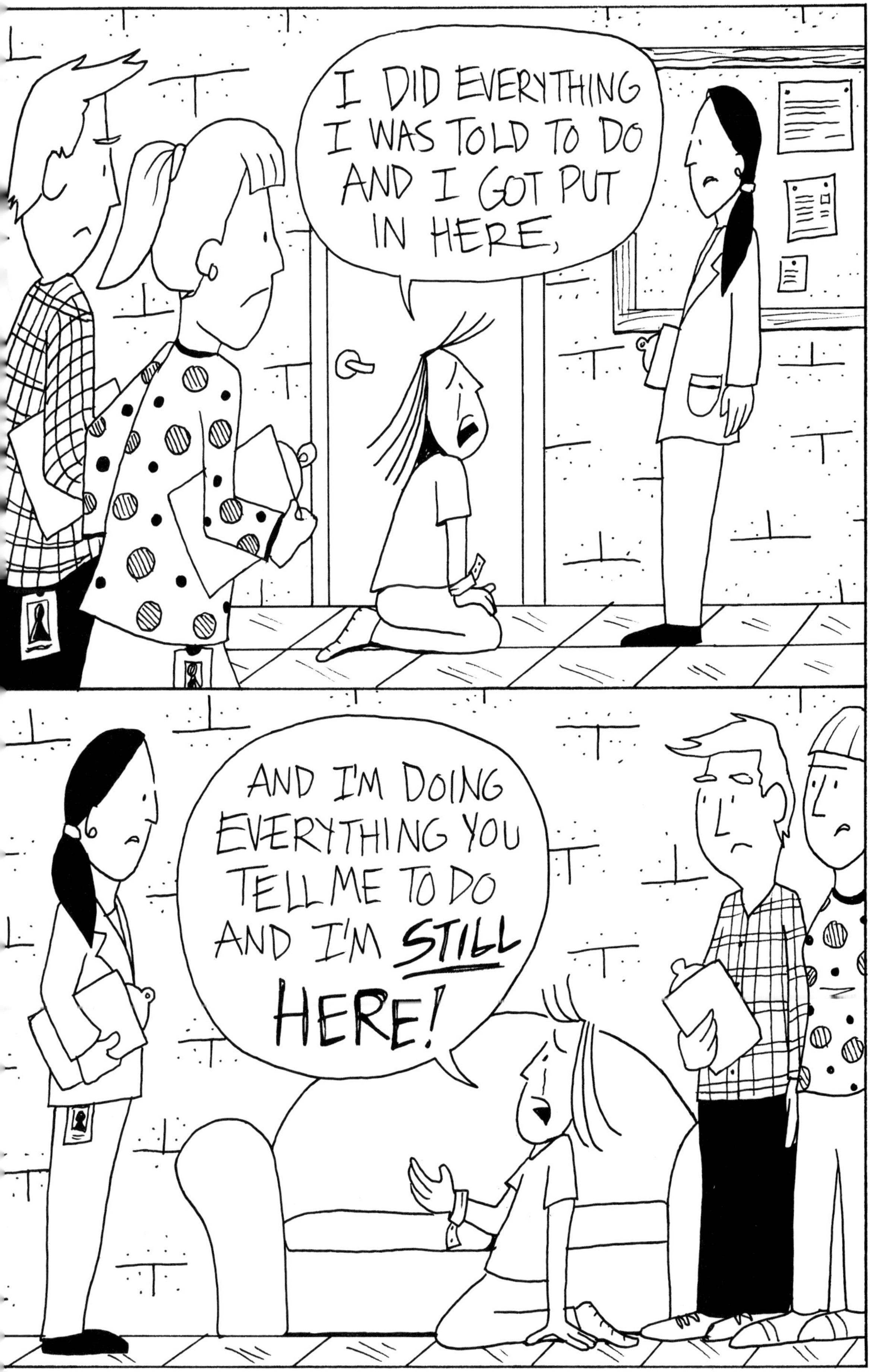
I DID EVERYTHING I WAS TOLD TO DO AND I GOT PUT IN HERE,
AND I'M DOING EVERYTHING YOU TELL ME TO DO AND I'M STILL HERE!

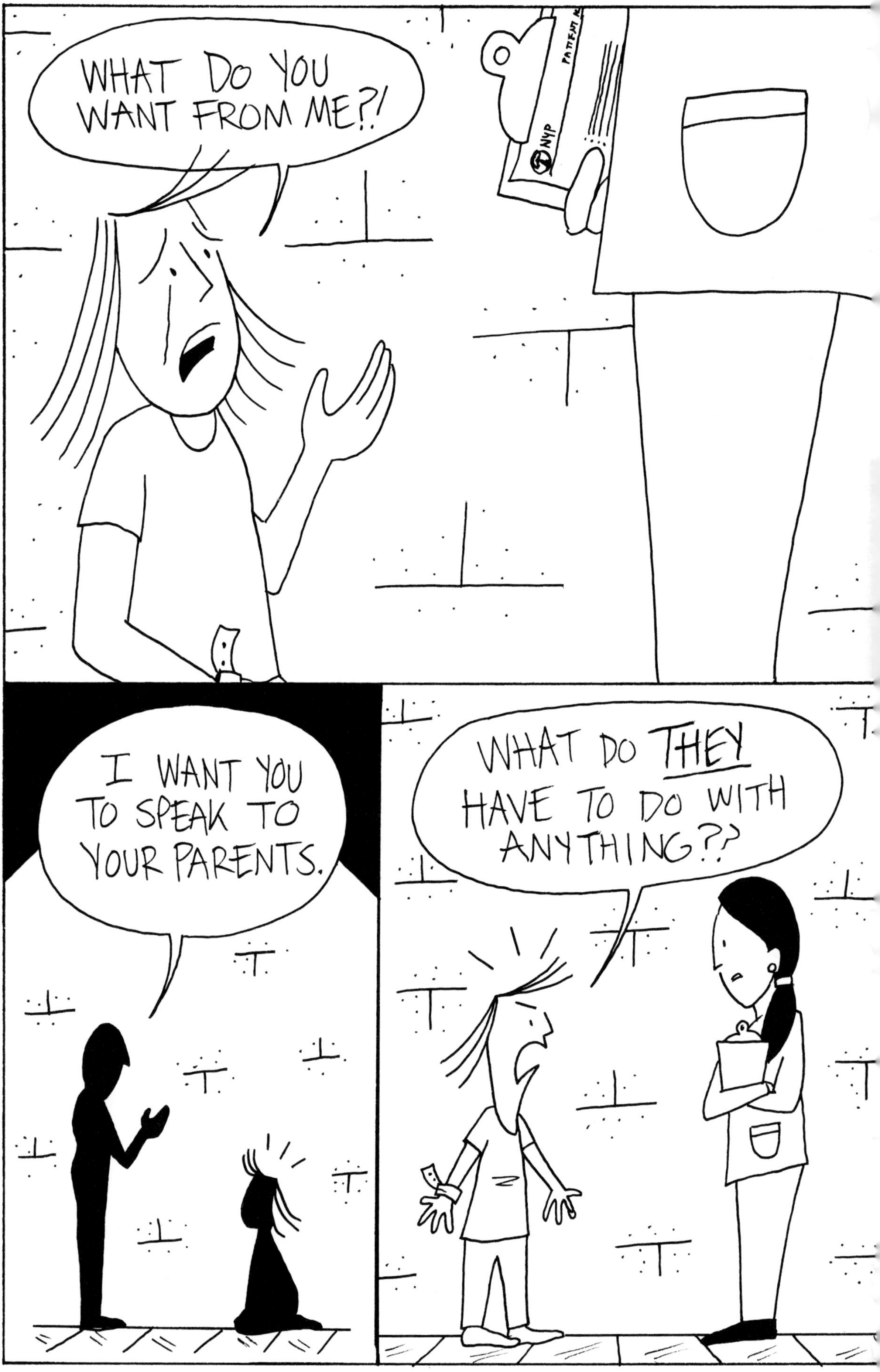
WHAT DO YOU WANT FROM ME?!
PATIENT N
NYP
I WANT YOU TO SPEAK TO YOUR PARENTS.
WHAT DO THEY HAVE TO DO WITH ANYTHING?!

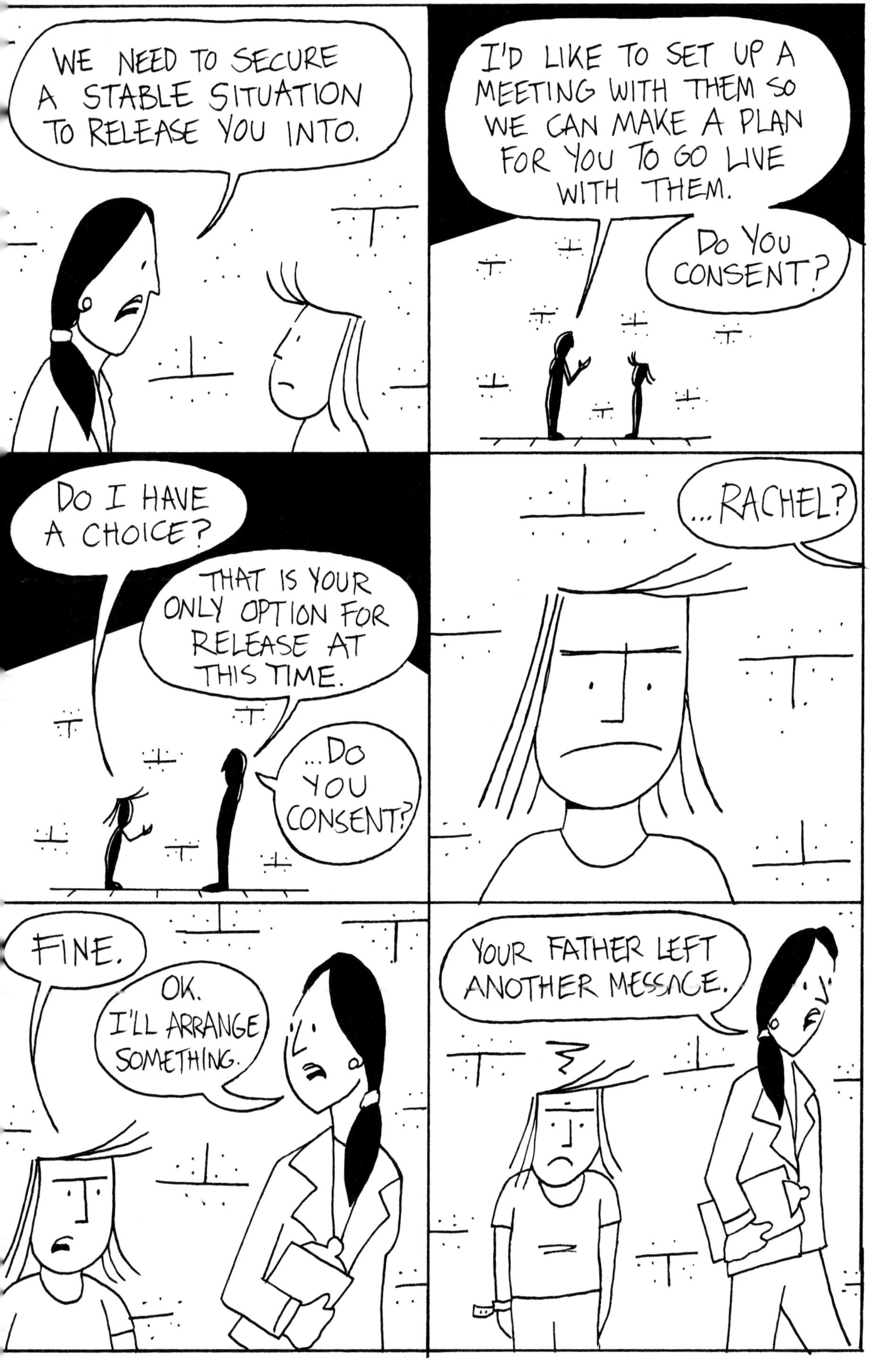
WE NEED TO SECURE A STABLE SITUATION TO RELEASE YOU INTO.
I'D LIKE TO SET UP A MEETING WITH THEM SO WE CAN MAKE A PLAN FOR YOU TO GO LIVE WITH THEM.
DO YOU CONSENT?
DO I HAVE A CHOICE?
THAT IS YOUR ONLY OPTION FOR RELEASE AT THIS TIME.
...DO YOU CONSENT?
...RACHEL?
FINE.
OK. I'LL ARRANGE SOMETHING.
YOUR FATHER LEFT ANOTHER MESSAGE.

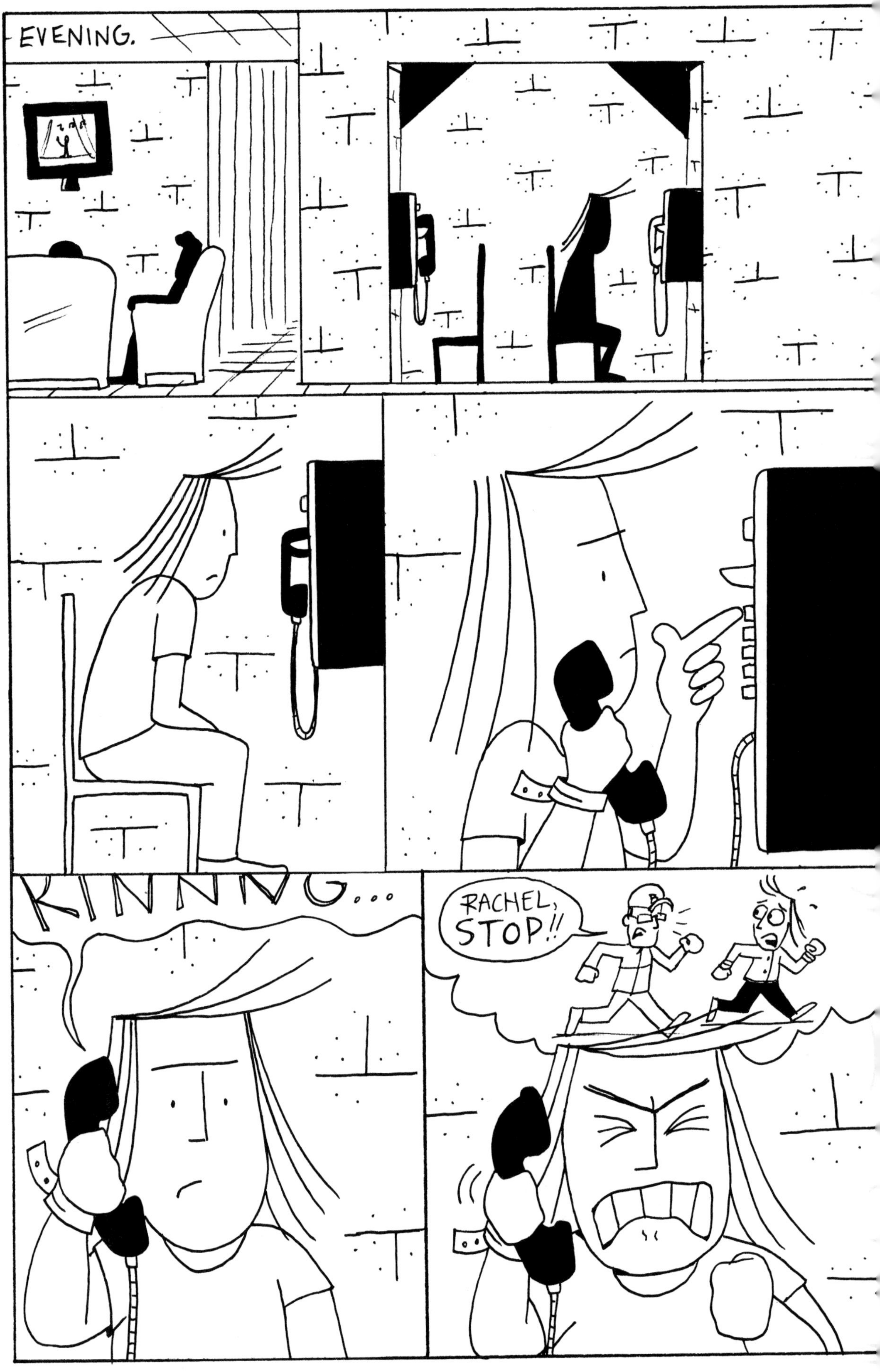
EVENING.
KINNNG...
RACHEL, STOP!!

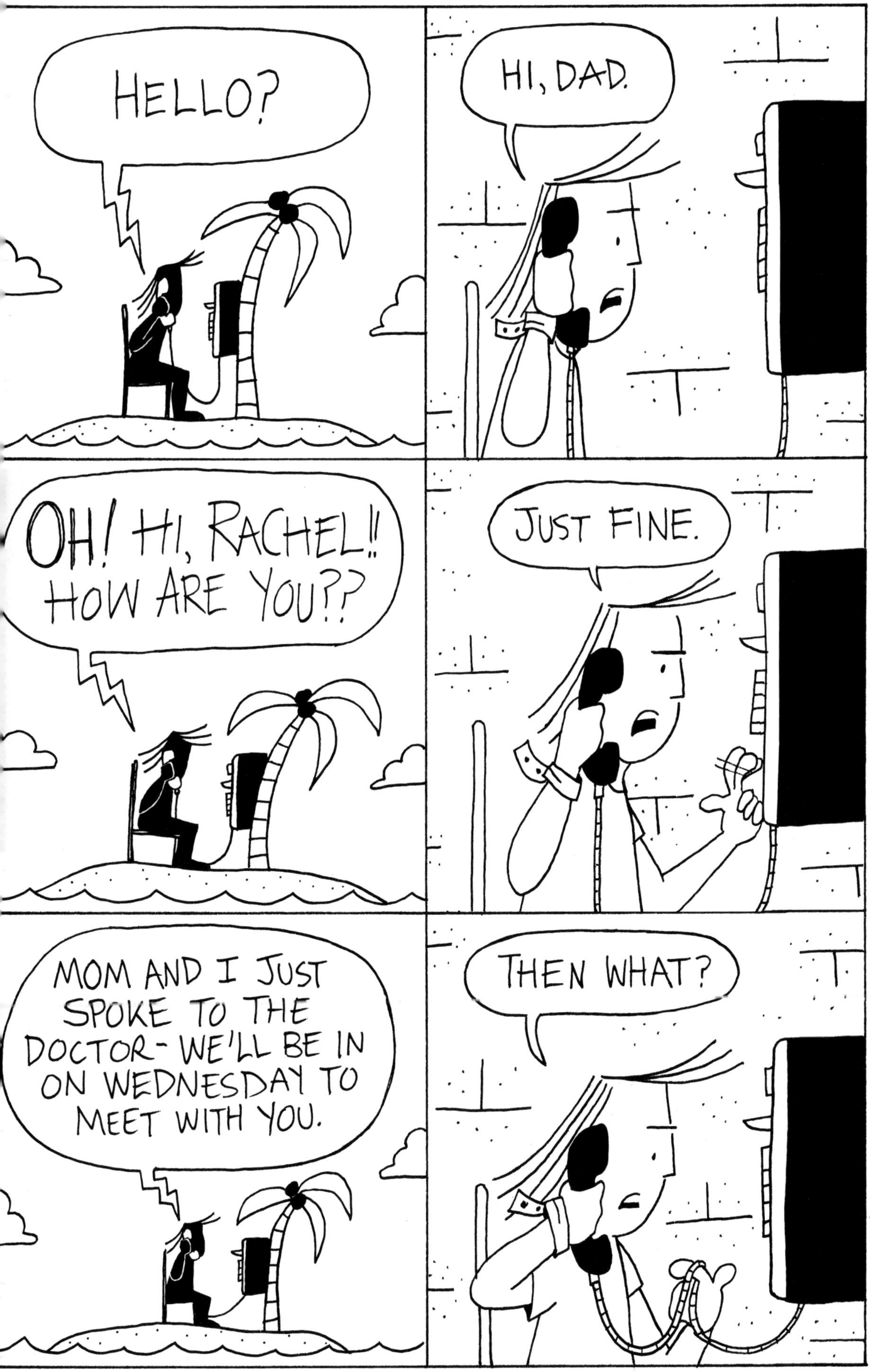
HELLO?
HI, DAD.
OH! HI, RACHEL!! HOW ARE YOU??
JUST FINE.
MOM AND I JUST SPOKE TO THE DOCTOR- WE'LL BE IN ON WEDNESDAY TO MEET WITH YOU.
THEN WHAT?

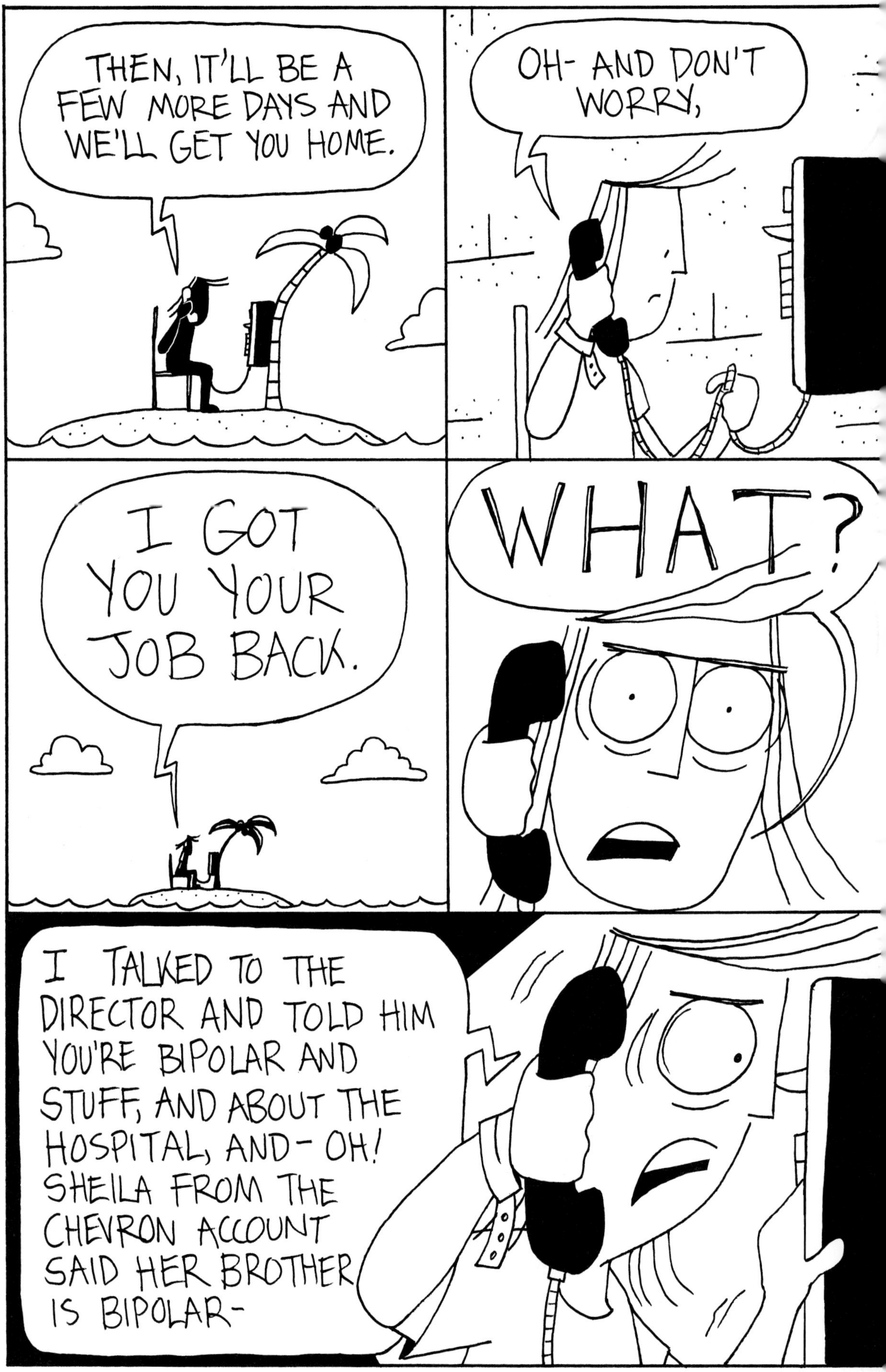
THEN, IT'LL BE A FEW MORE DAYS AND WE'LL GET YOU HOME.
OH- AND DON'T WORRY,
I GOT YOU YOUR JOB BACK.
WHAT?
I TALKED TO THE DIRECTOR AND TOLD HIM YOU'RE BIPOLAR AND STUFF, AND ABOUT THE HOSPITAL, AND- OH! SHEILA FROM THE CHEVRON ACCOUNT SAID HER BROTHER IS BIPOLAR-

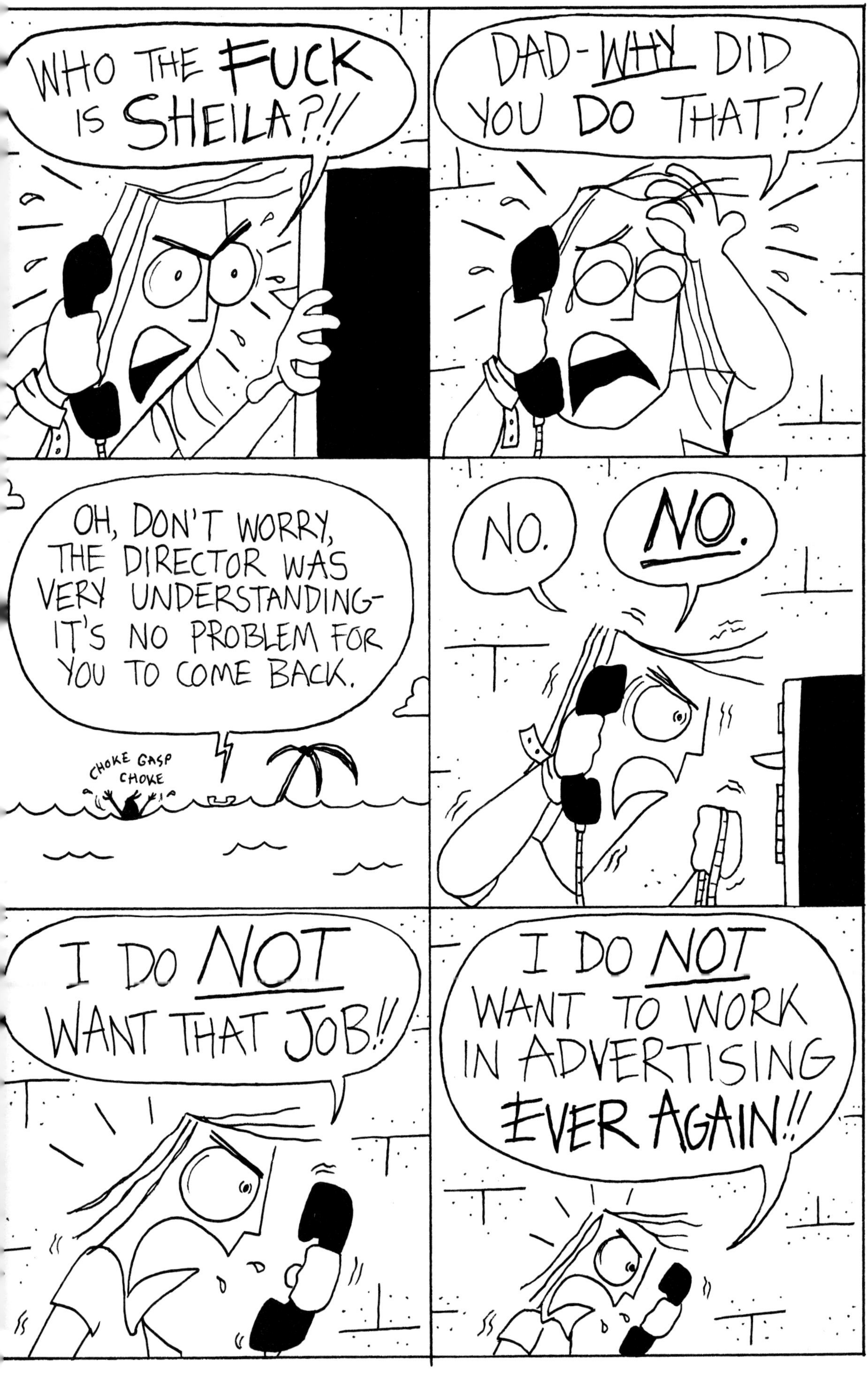
WHO THE FUCK IS SHEILA?!!
DAD- WHY DID YOU DO THAT?!
OH, DON'T WORRY, THE DIRECTOR WAS VERY UNDERSTANDING- IT'S NO PROBLEM FOR YOU TO COME BACK.
CHOKE GASP CHOKE
NO.
NO.
I DO NOT WANT THAT JOB!!
I DO NOT WANT TO WORK IN ADVERTISING EVER AGAIN!!

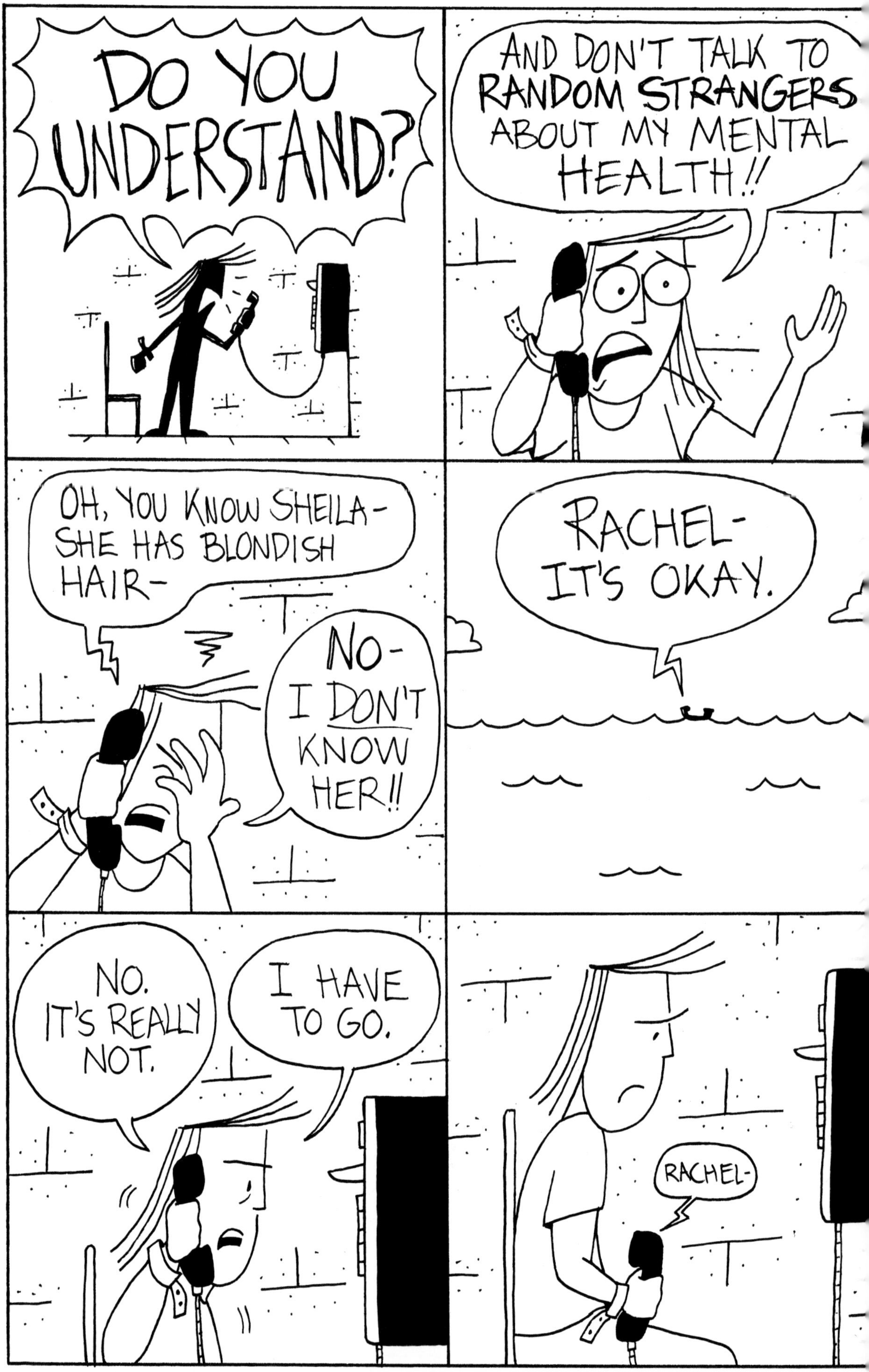
DO YOU UNDERSTAND?
AND DON'T TALK TO RANDOM STRANGERS ABOUT MY MENTAL HEALTH!!
OH, YOU KNOW SHEILA- SHE HAS BLONDISH HAIR-
NO- I DON'T KNOW HER!!
RACHEL- IT'S OKAY.
NO. IT'S REALLY NOT.
I HAVE TO GO.
RACHEL-

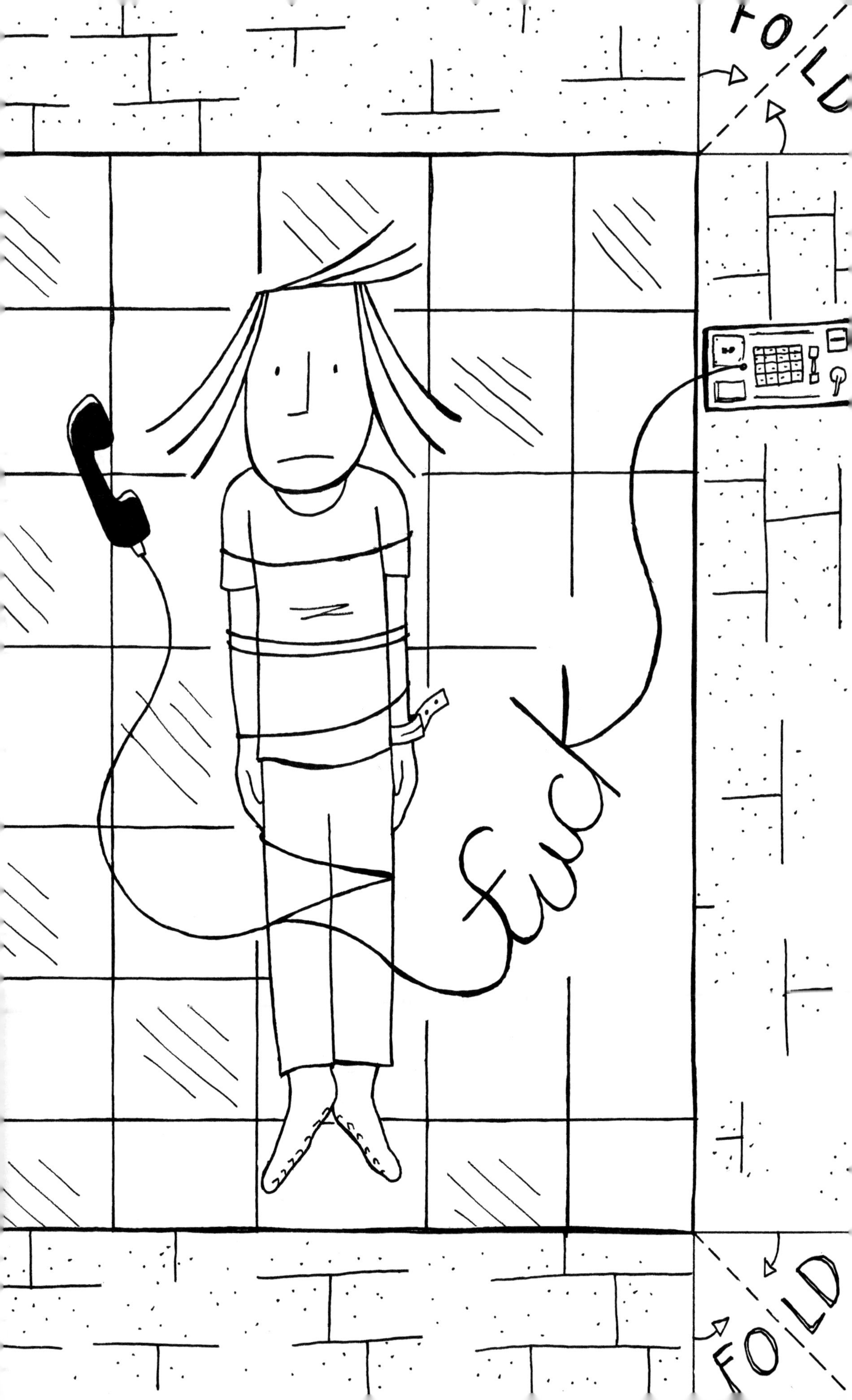
FOLD
FOLD

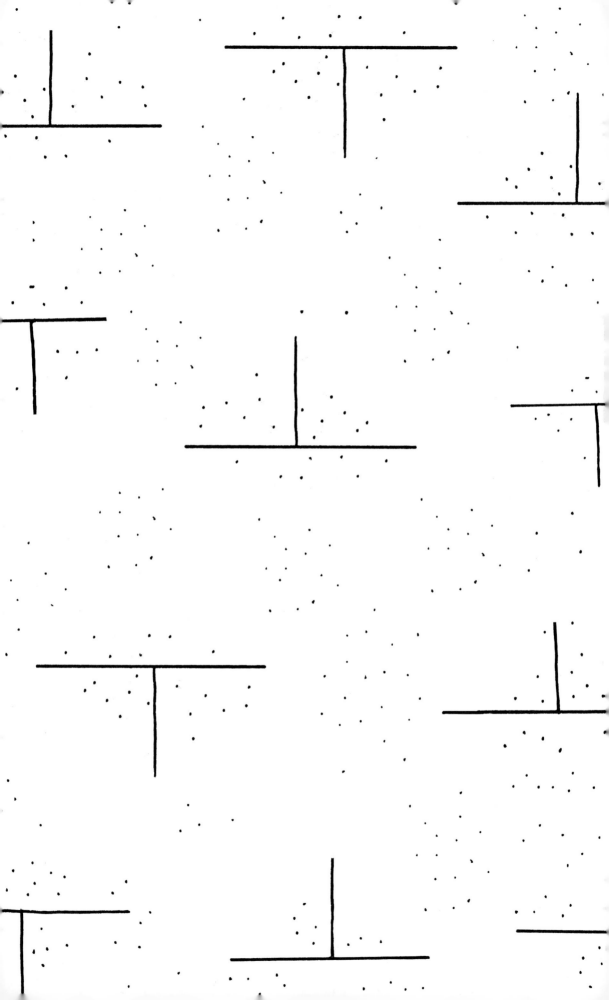

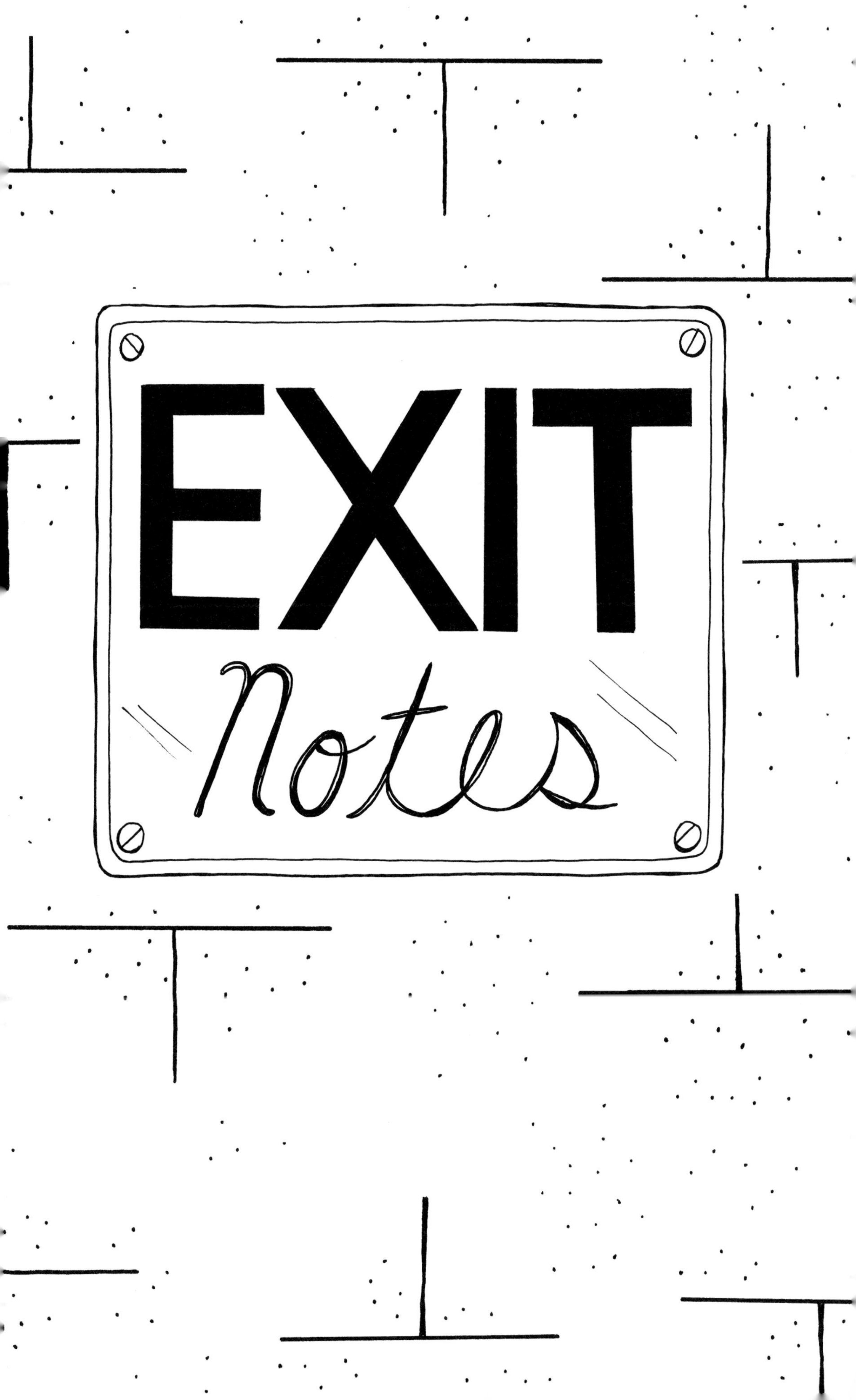
EXIT
Notes

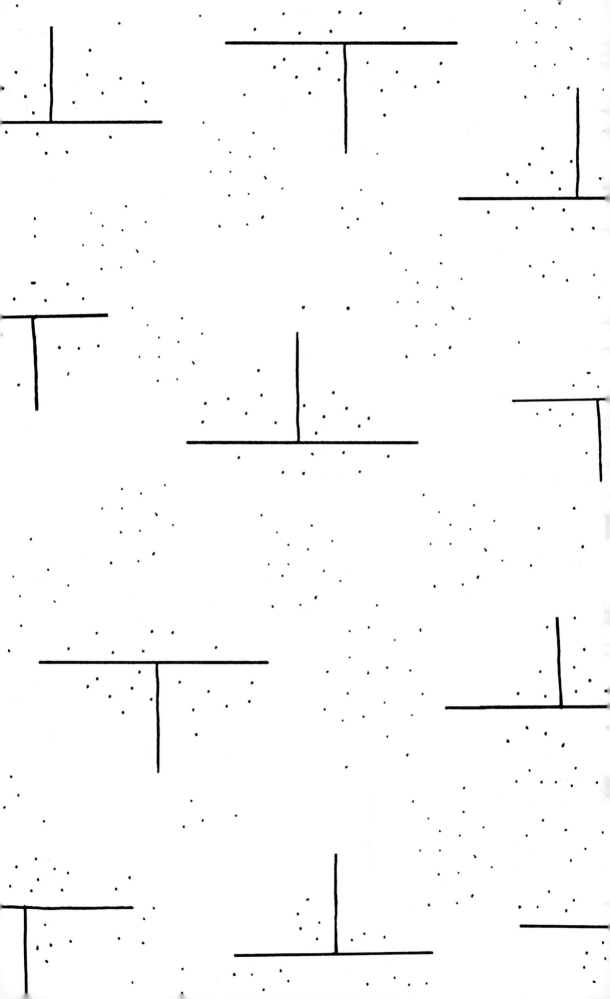

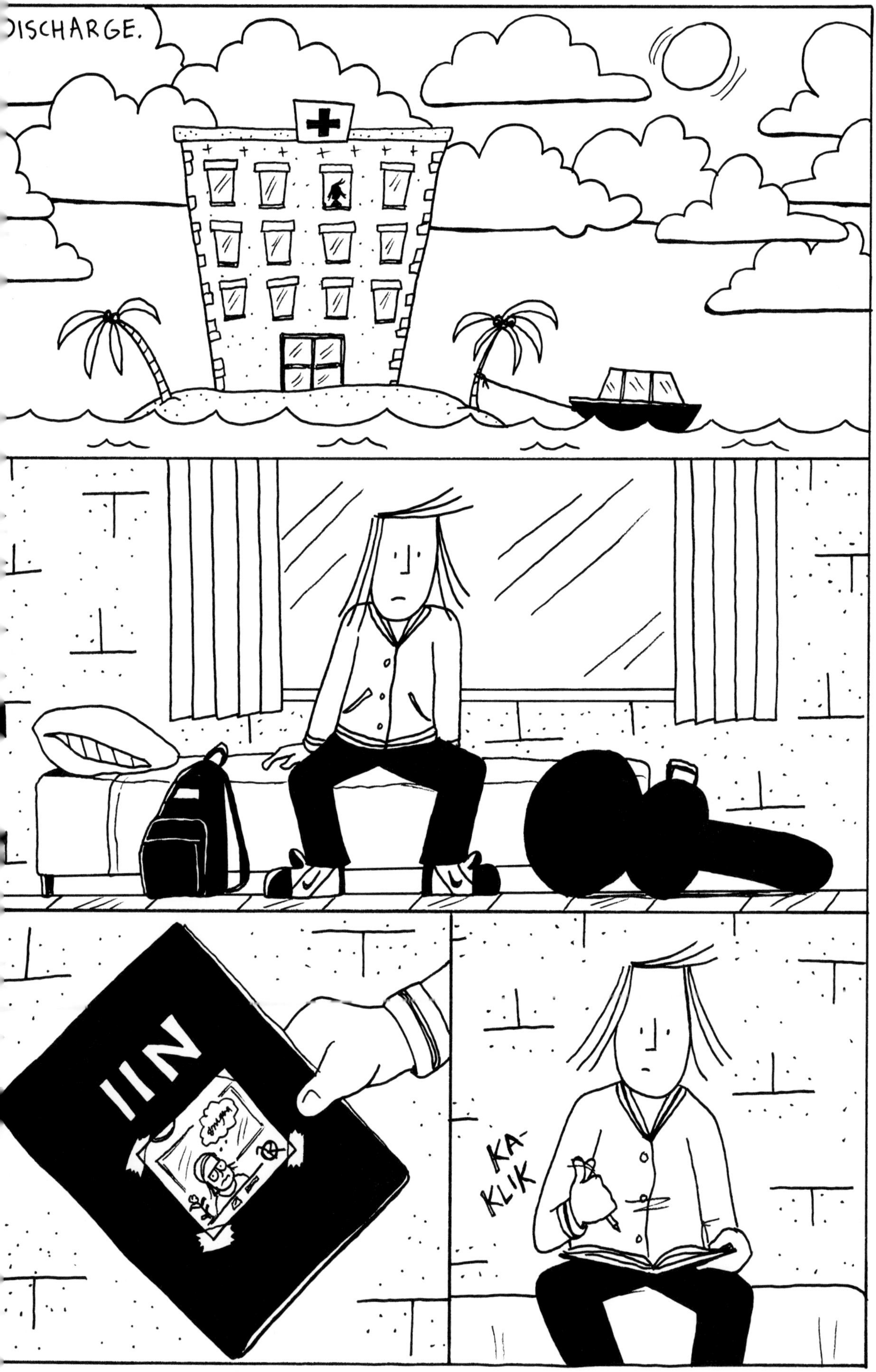
ISCHARGE.
IIN
KA-
KLIK

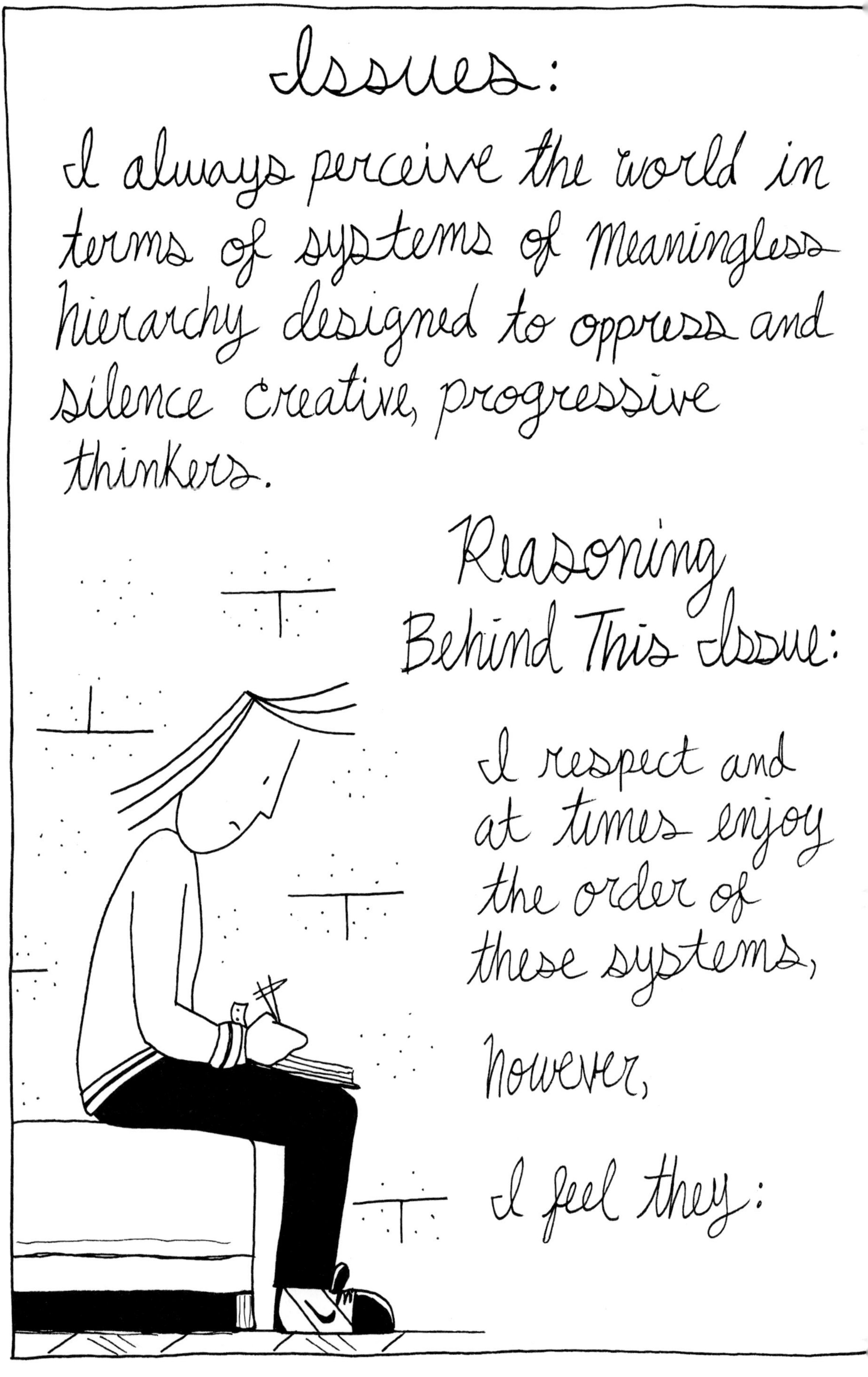
Issues:
I always perceive the world in terms of systems of meaningless hierarchy designed to oppress and silence creative, progressive thinkers.
Reasoning Behind This Issue:
I respect and at times enjoy the order of these systems,
however,
I feel they:

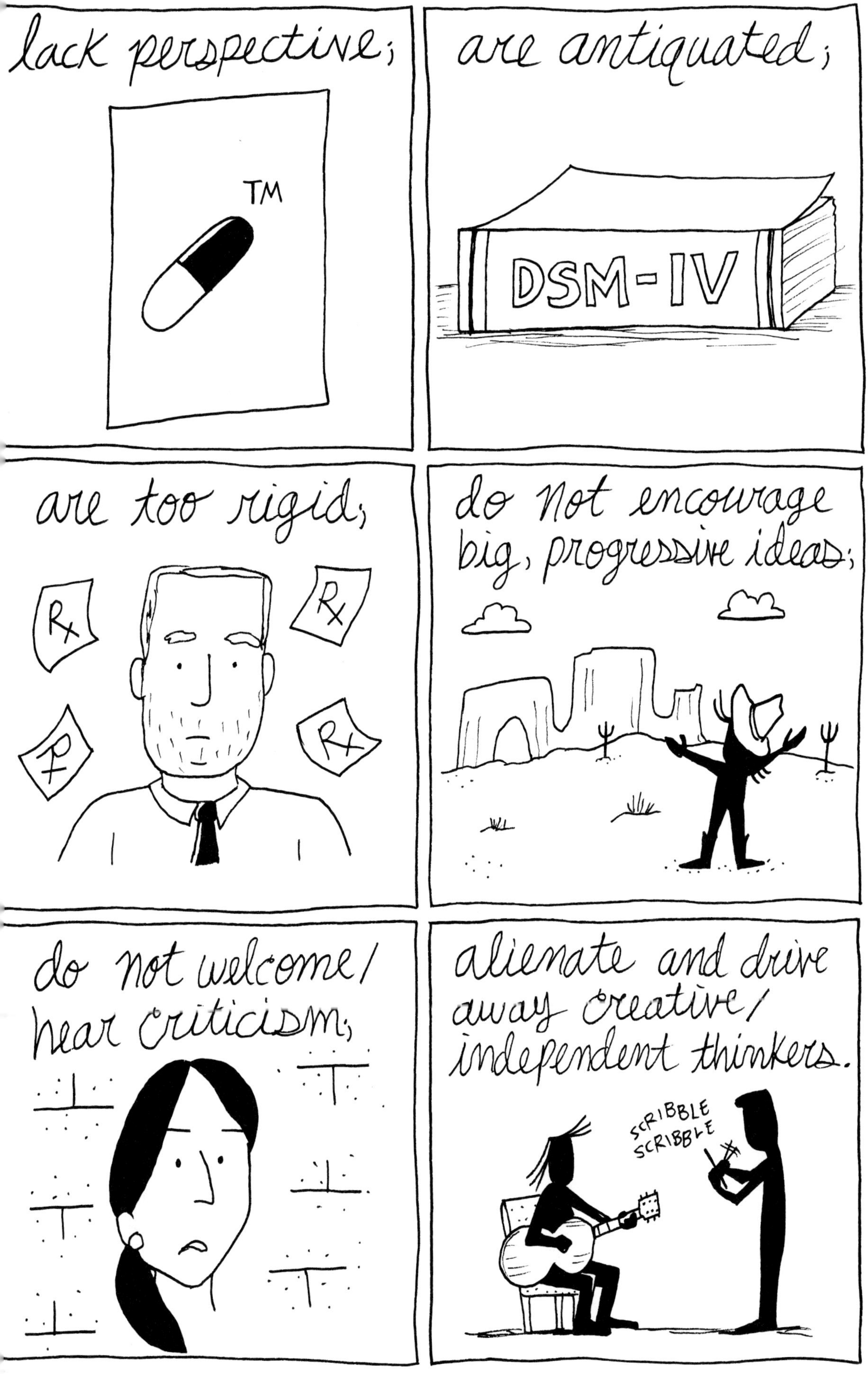
lack perspective;
TM
are antiquated;
DSM-IV
are too rigid;
Rx
Rx
Rx
Rx
do not encourage big, progressive ideas;
do not welcome/hear criticism;
alienate and drive away creative/independent thinkers.
SCRIBBLE SCRIBBLE

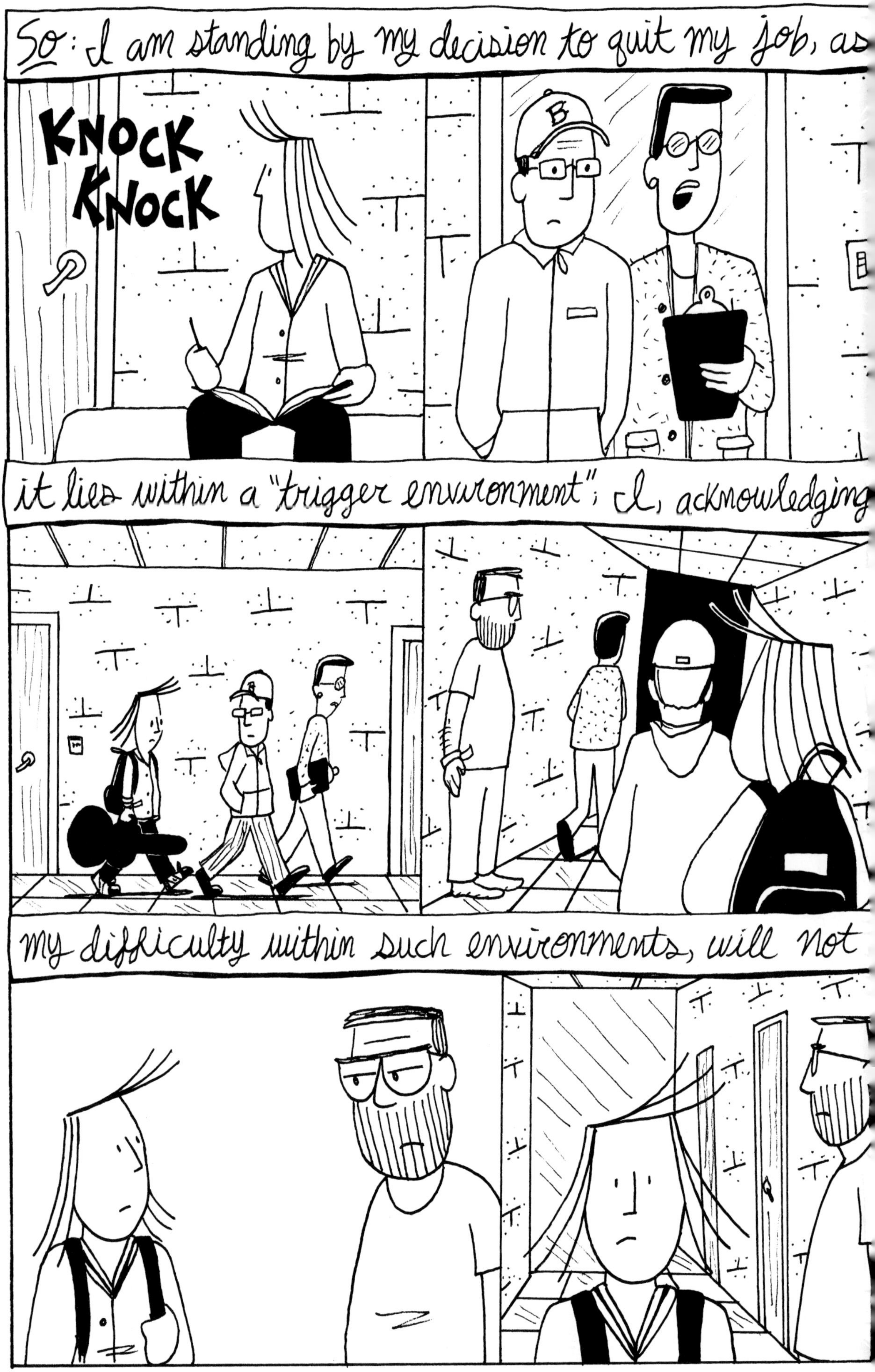
So: I am standing by my decision to quit my job, as
KNOCK KNOCK
it lies within a "trigger environment"; I, acknowledging
my difficulty within such environments, will not

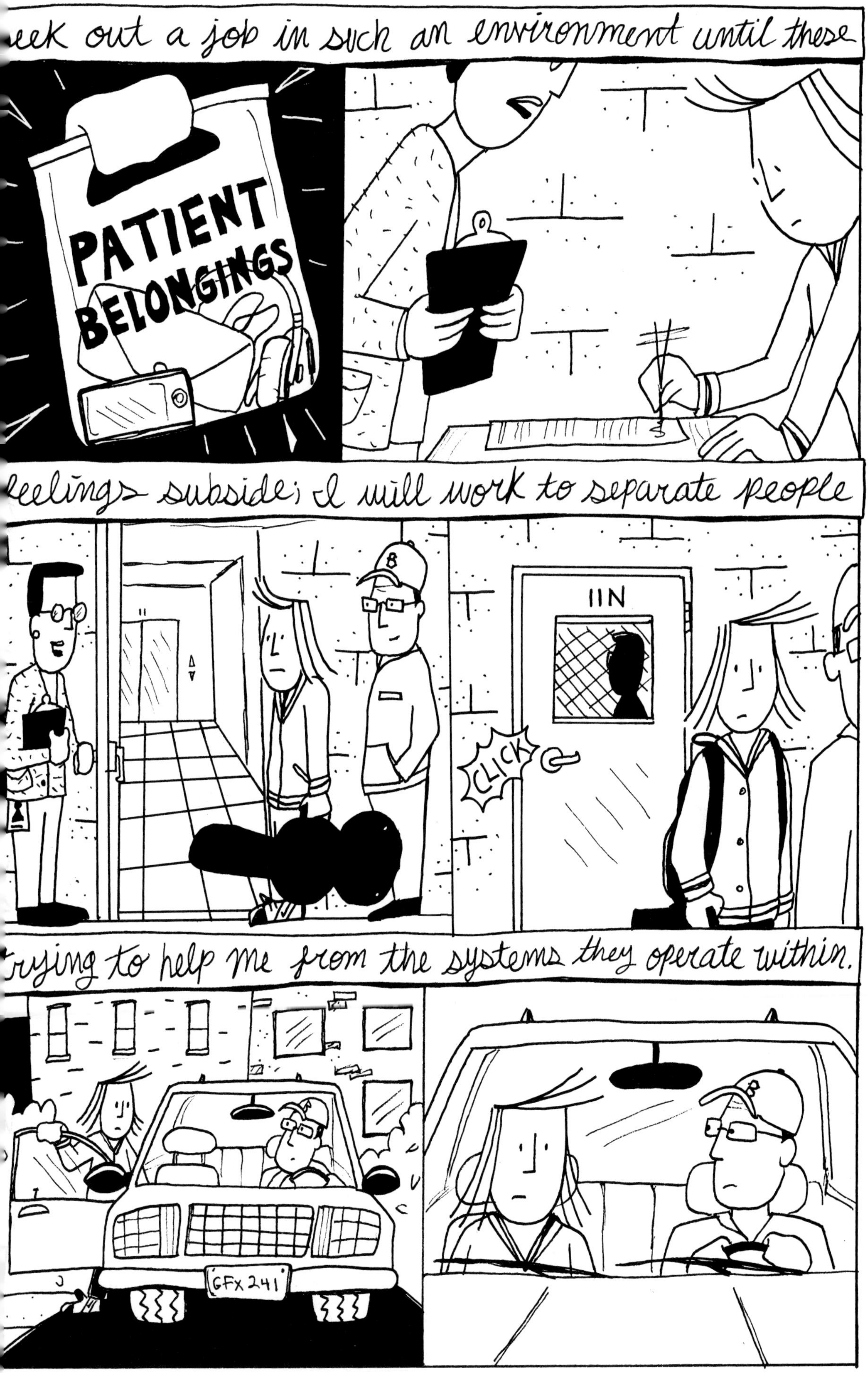
eek out a job in such an environment until these
PATIENT BELONGINGS
feelings subside; I will work to separate people
IIN
CLICK
trying to help me from the systems they operate within.
GFX 241

I will stop thinking of the world in these terms.

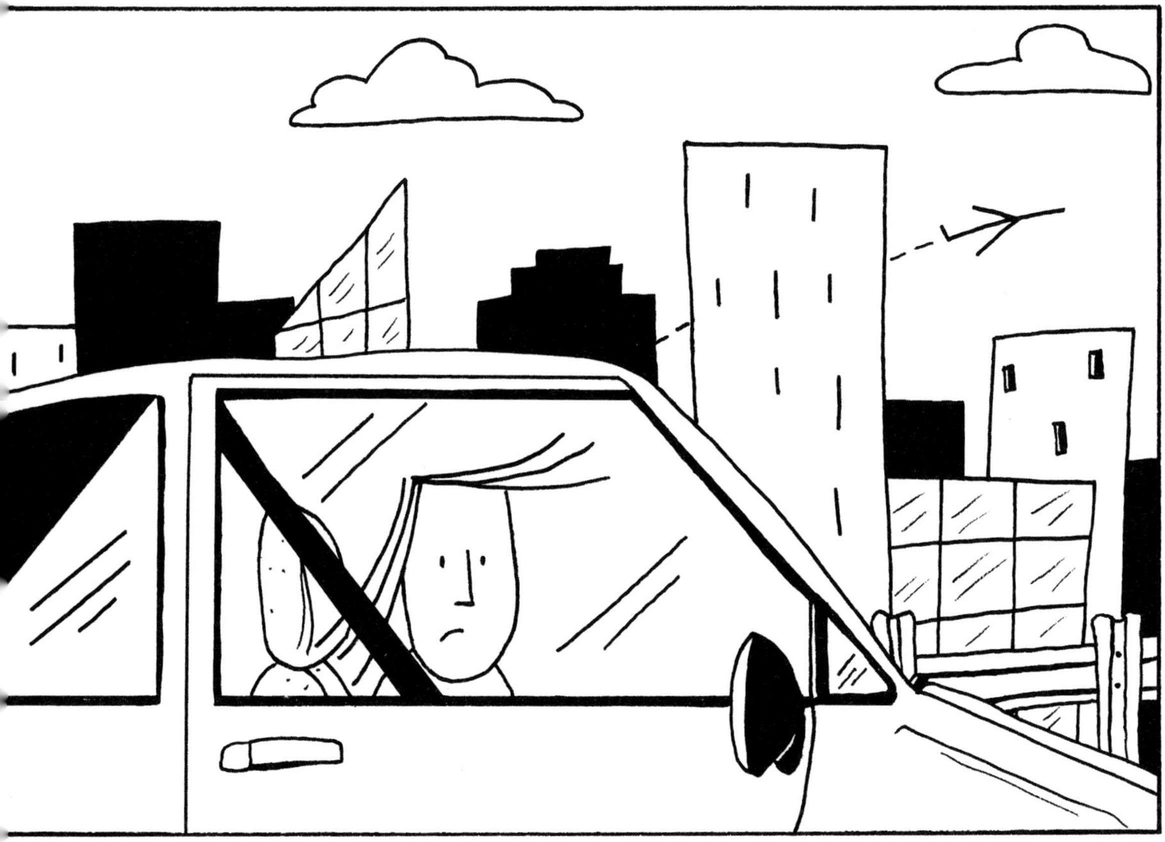

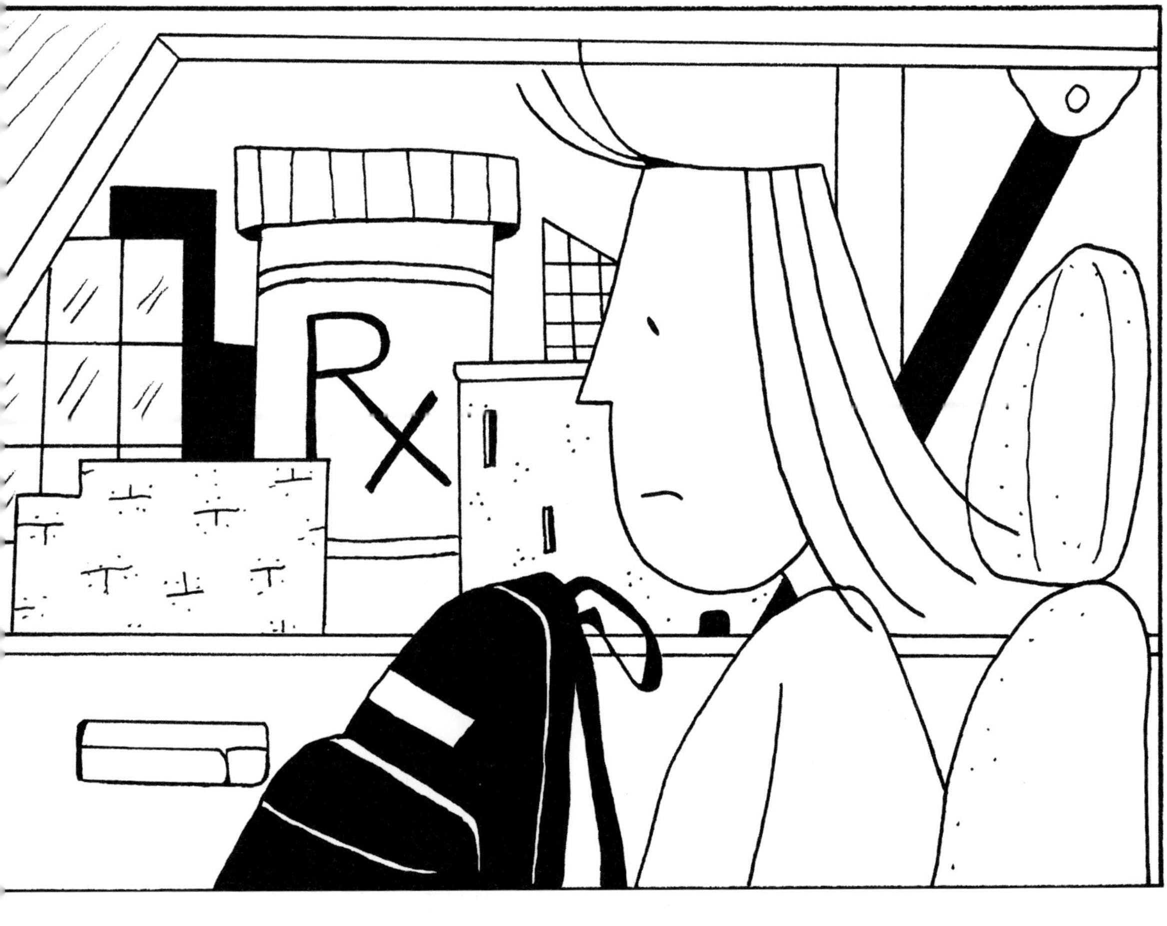
Rx

Wellness.

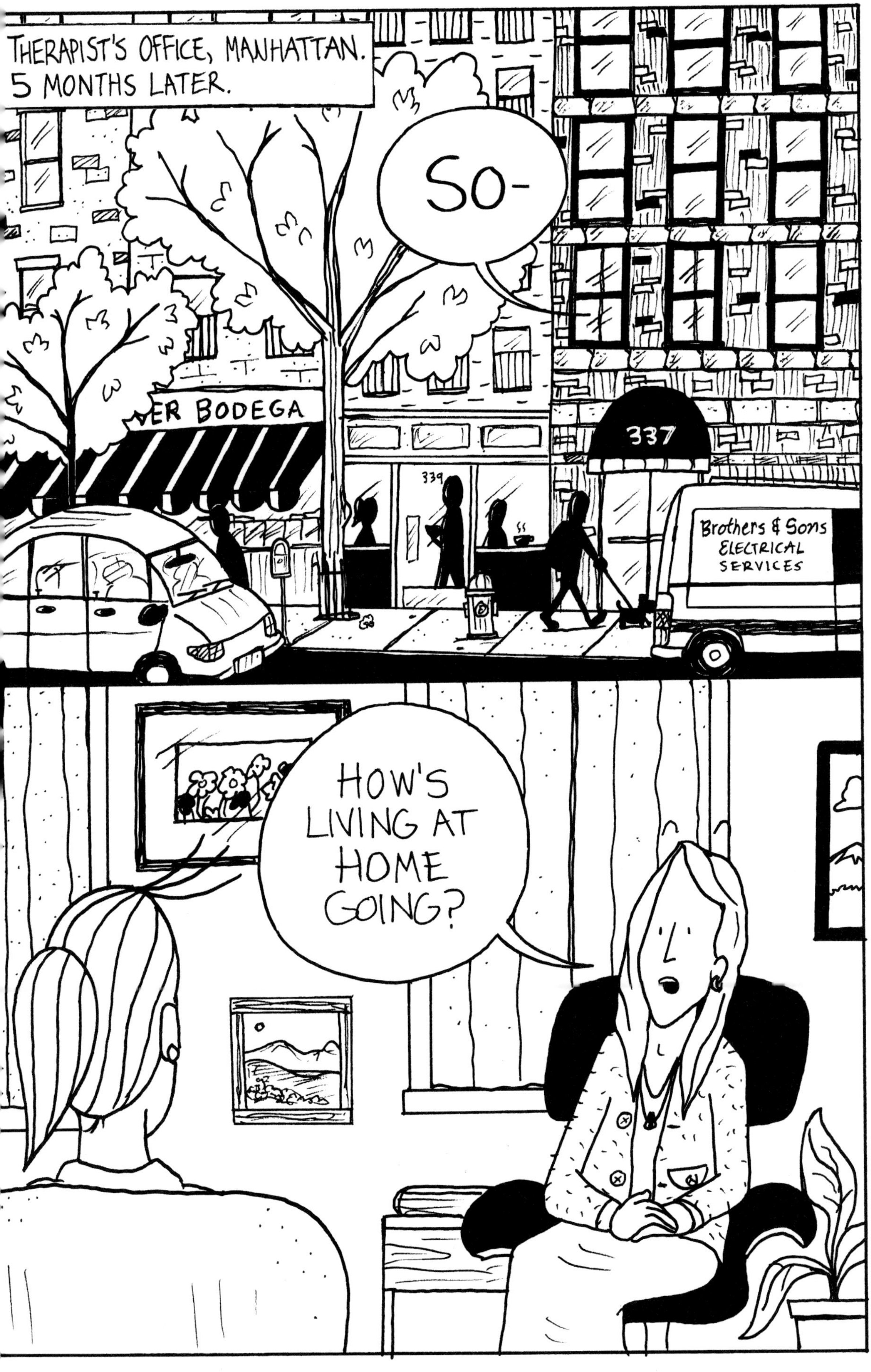
THERAPIST'S OFFICE, MANHATTAN. 5 MONTHS LATER.
SO-
BODEGA
337
339
Brothers & Sons ELECTRICAL SERVICES
HOW'S LIVING AT HOME GOING?

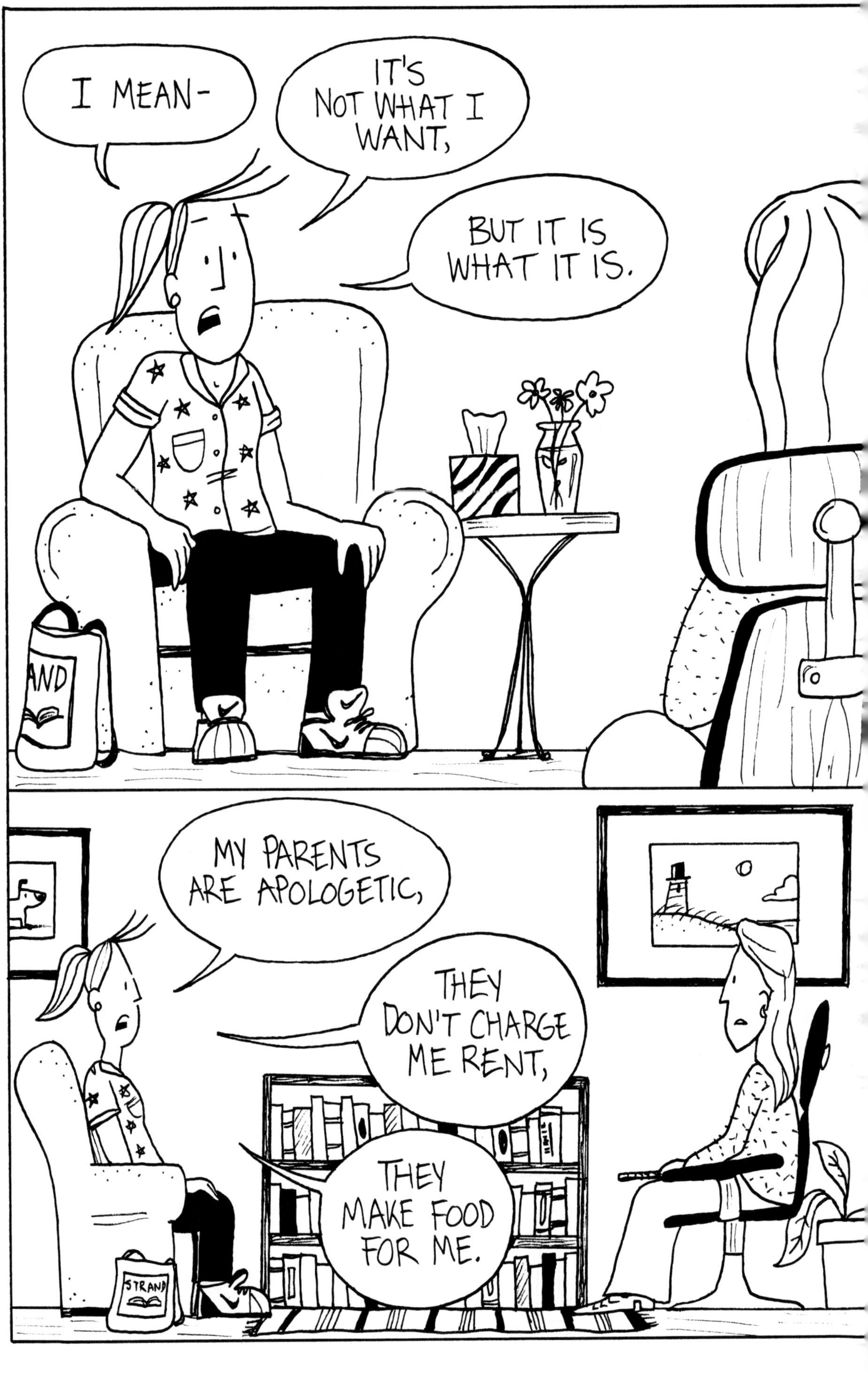
I MEAN-
IT'S NOT WHAT I WANT,
BUT IT IS WHAT IT IS.
MY PARENTS ARE APOLOGETIC,
THEY DON'T CHARGE ME RENT,
THEY MAKE FOOD FOR ME.
STRAND

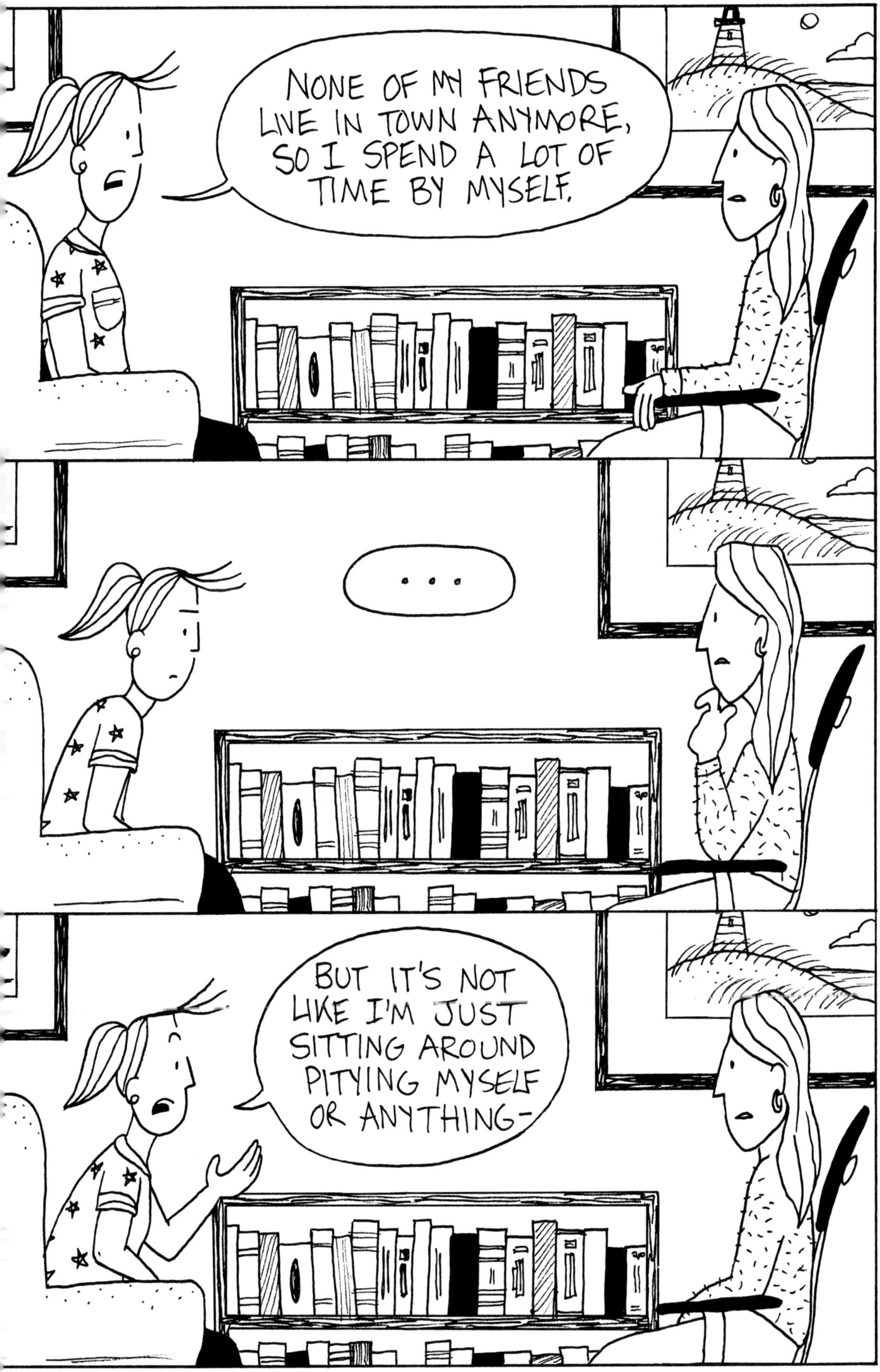
NONE OF MY FRIENDS LIVE IN TOWN ANYMORE, SO I SPEND A LOT OF TIME BY MYSELF.
. . .
BUT IT'S NOT LIKE I'M JUST SITTING AROUND PITYING MYSELF OR ANYTHING-

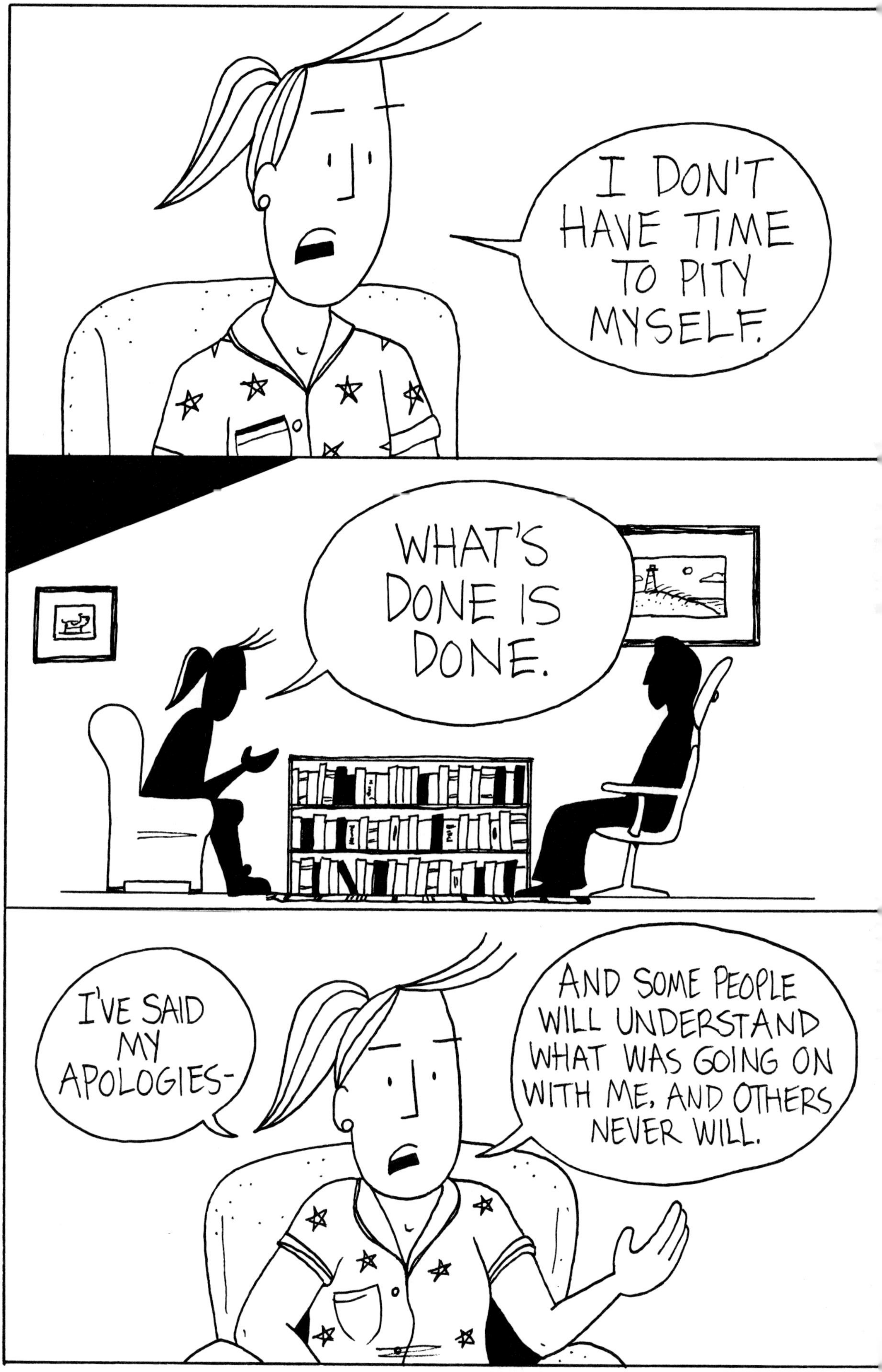
I DON'T HAVE TIME TO PITY MYSELF.
WHAT'S DONE IS DONE.
I'VE SAID MY APOLOGIES-
AND SOME PEOPLE WILL UNDERSTAND WHAT WAS GOING ON WITH ME, AND OTHERS NEVER WILL.

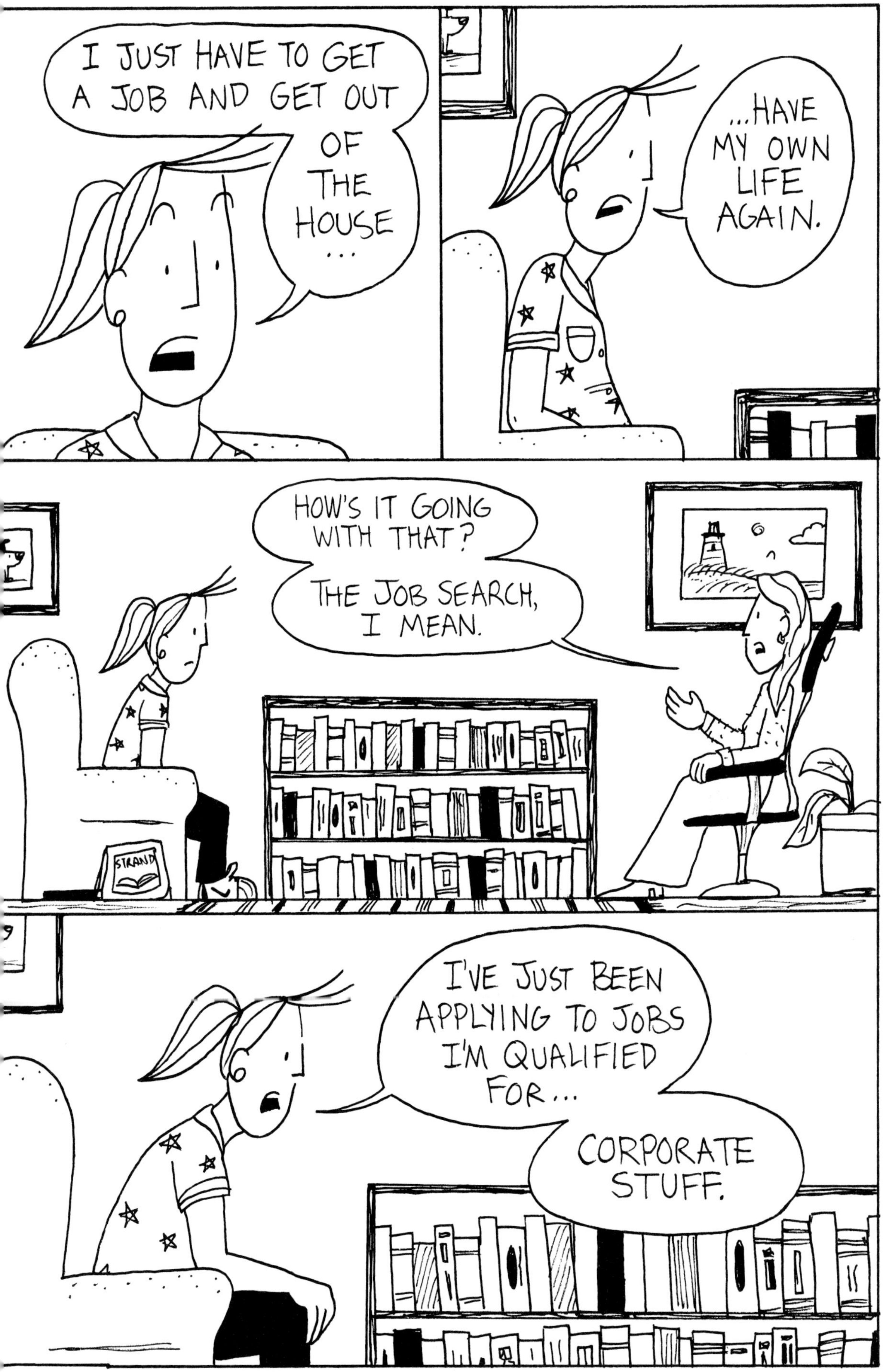
I JUST HAVE TO GET A JOB AND GET OUT
OF THE HOUSE...
...HAVE MY OWN LIFE AGAIN.
HOW'S IT GOING WITH THAT?
THE JOB SEARCH, I MEAN.
STRAND
I'VE JUST BEEN APPLYING TO JOBS I'M QUALIFIED FOR...
CORPORATE STUFF.

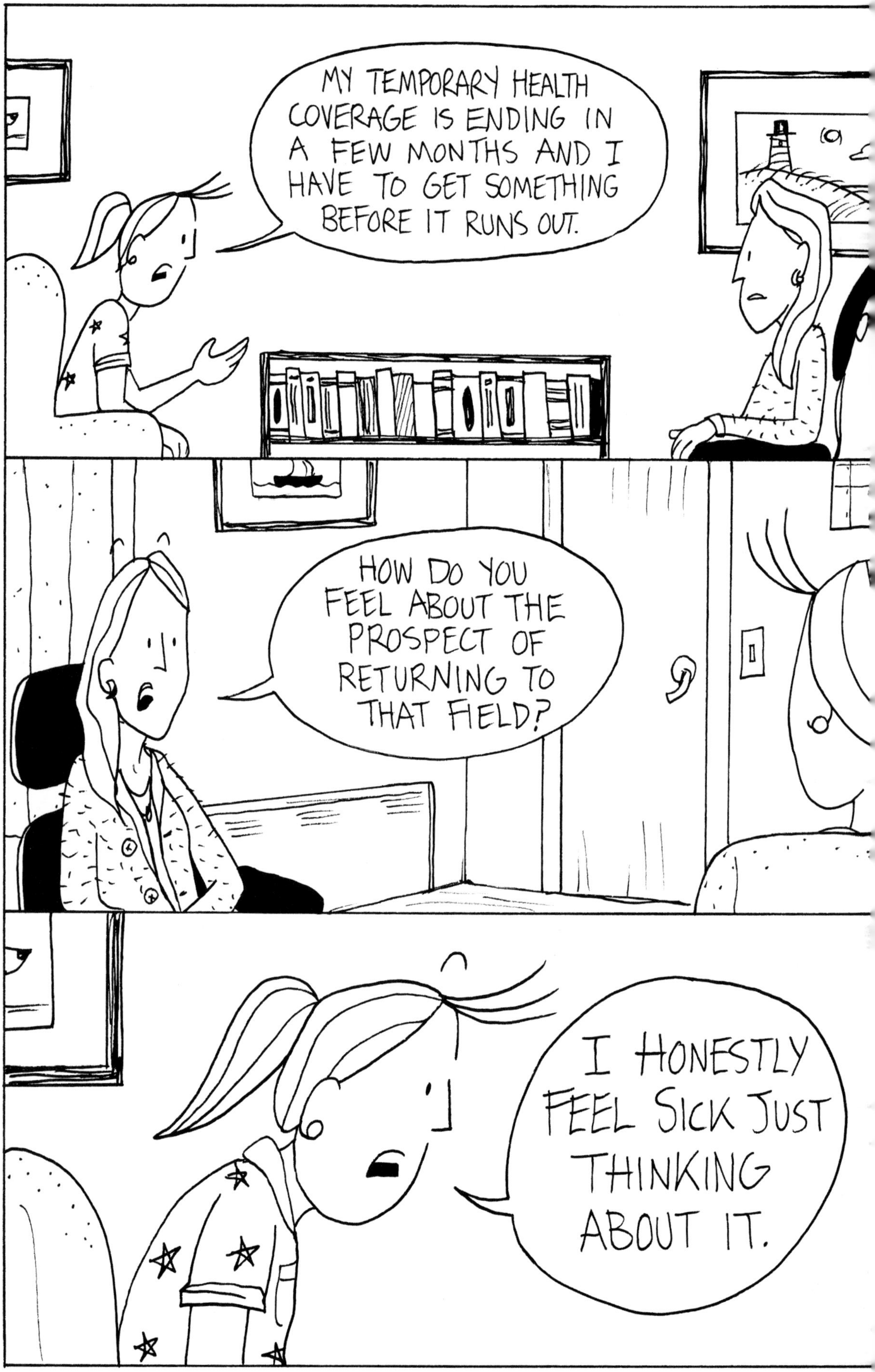
MY TEMPORARY HEALTH COVERAGE IS ENDING IN A FEW MONTHS AND I HAVE TO GET SOMETHING BEFORE IT RUNS OUT.
HOW DO YOU FEEL ABOUT THE PROSPECT OF RETURNING TO THAT FIELD?
I HONESTLY FEEL SICK JUST THINKING ABOUT IT.

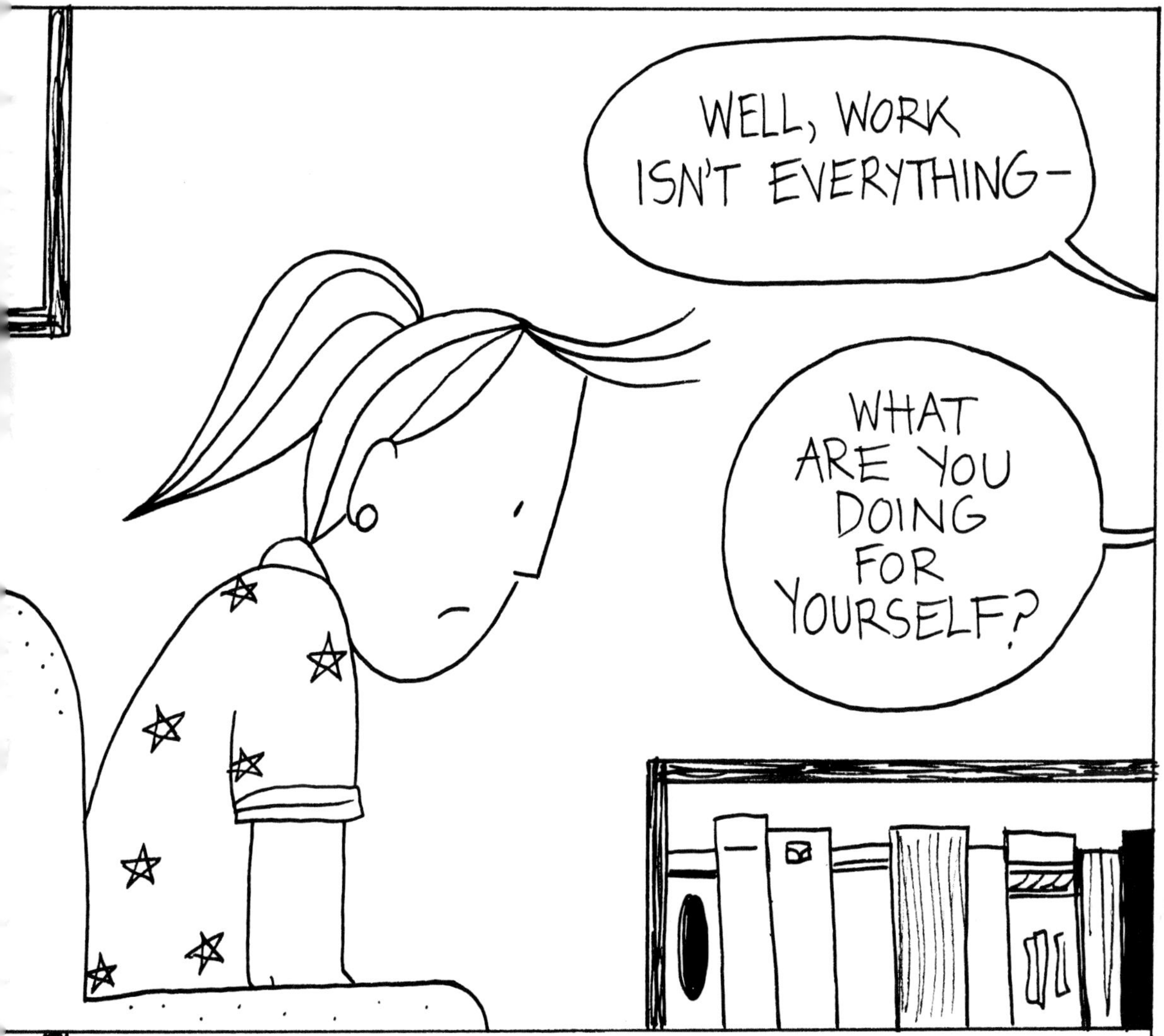
WELL, WORK ISN'T EVERYTHING-
WHAT ARE YOU DOING FOR YOURSELF?

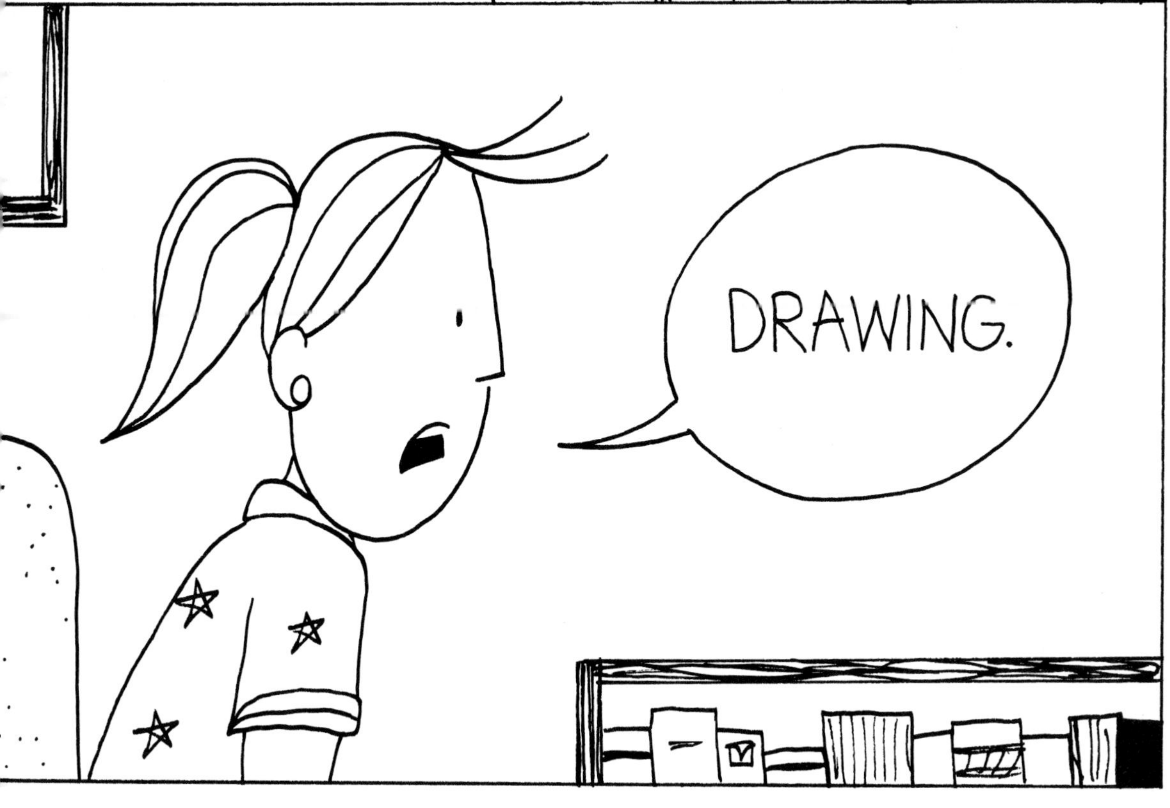
DRAWING.

THE MINUTE I WAS COMMITTED, I KNEW I WOULD WRITE THIS BOOK.

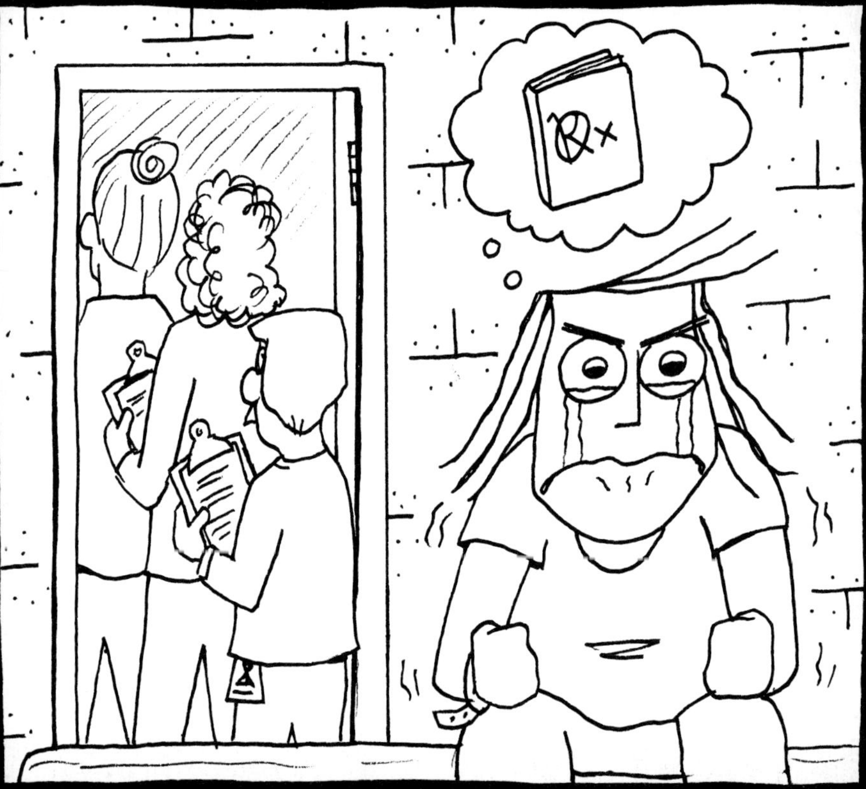

AND IT STARTED THERE, IN A JOURNAL, IN THE COMMON ROOM.

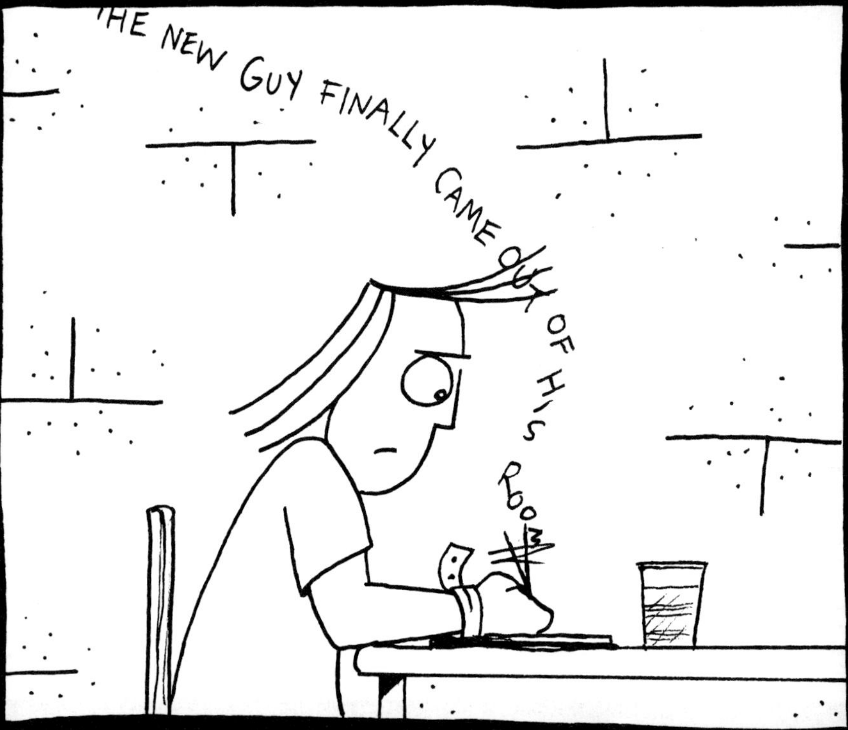
THE NEW GUY FINALLY CAME OUT OF HIS ROOM

I RETURNED TO THE CORPORATE WORLD AFTER 8 MONTHS OF LIVING WITH MY PARENTS, AFTER FAILING TO FIND A CREATIVE JOB OR HEALTH INSURANCE IN ANOTHER CAPACITY.

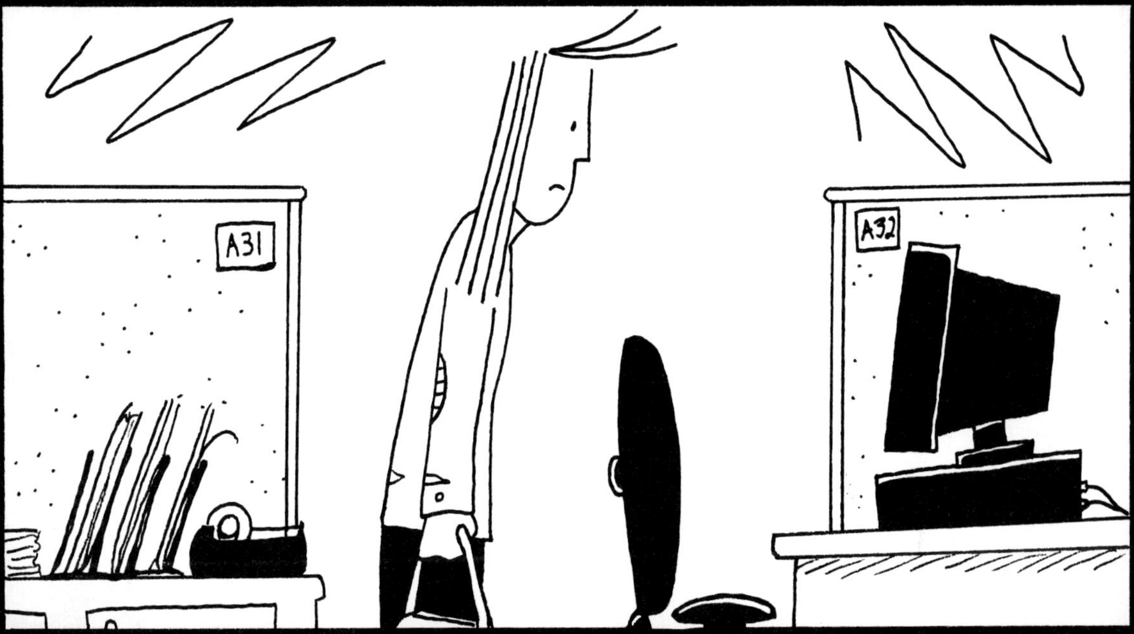
A31
A32

I EXPERIENCED THE SAME FRUSTRATIONS- I FELT LIKE A FAILURE TO MYSELF.

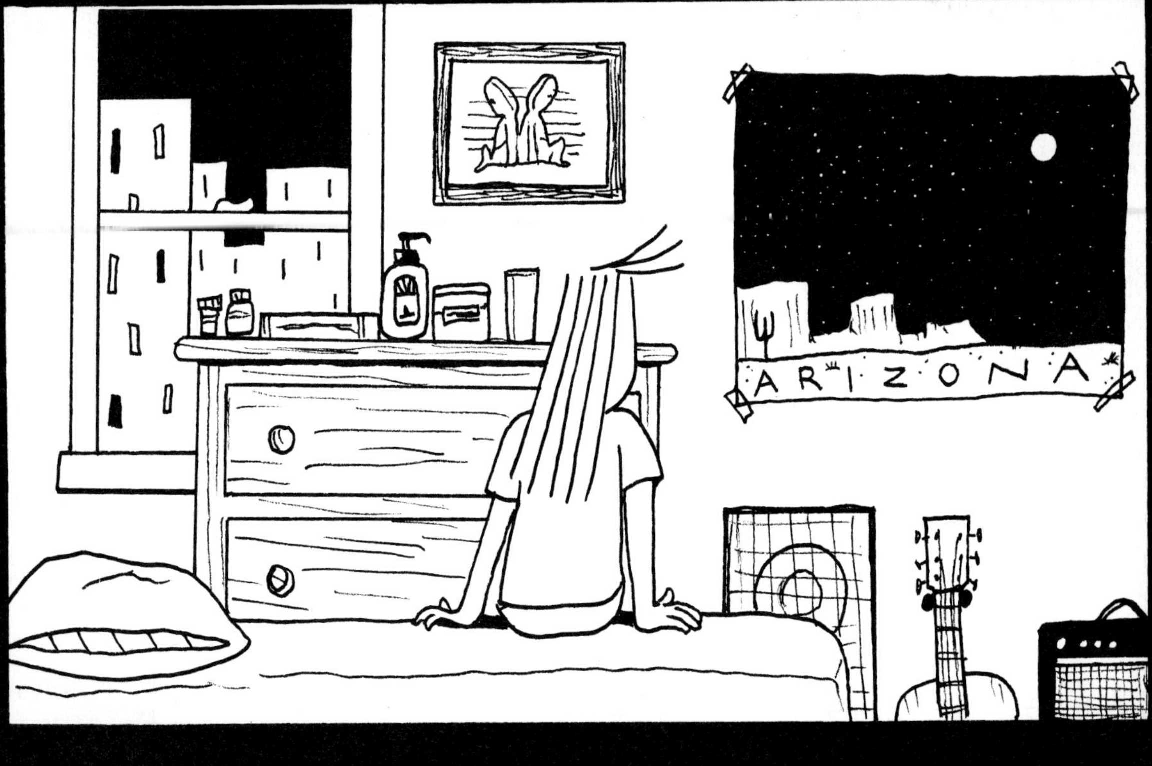
ARIZONA

BUT THIS STORY, AND MY INTENTIONS FOR IT, NEVER LEFT ME.

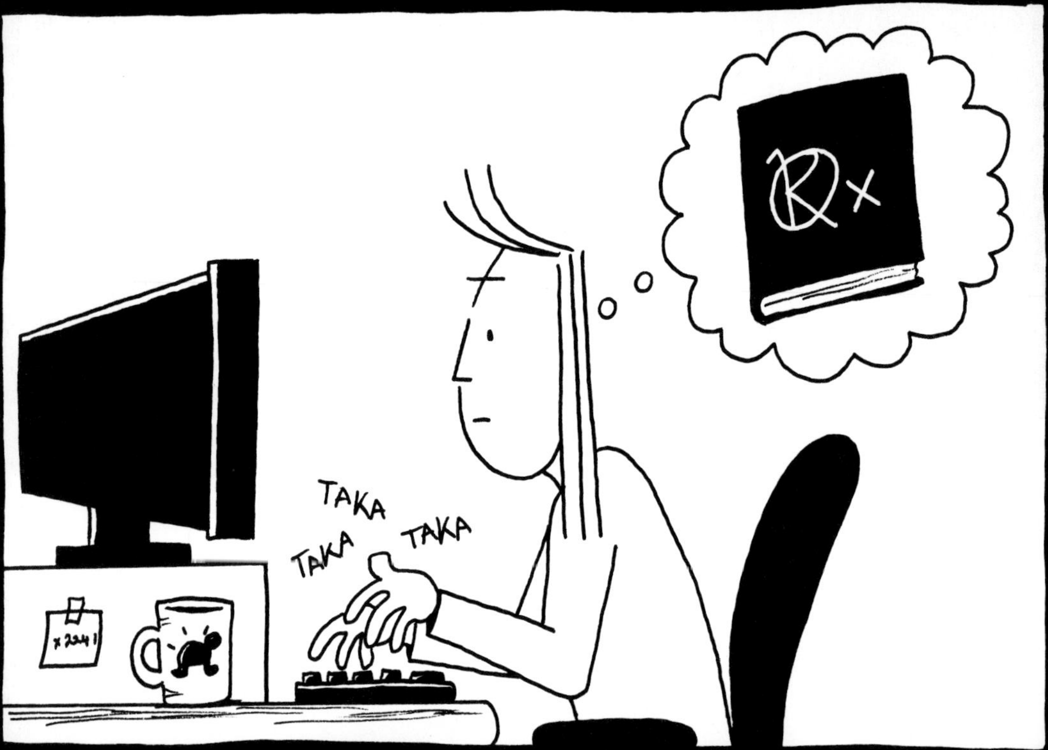
Rx
TAKA
TAKA
TAKA

THE PROJECT BECAME MY REVENGE, MY HEALING, MY IMPERATIVE.

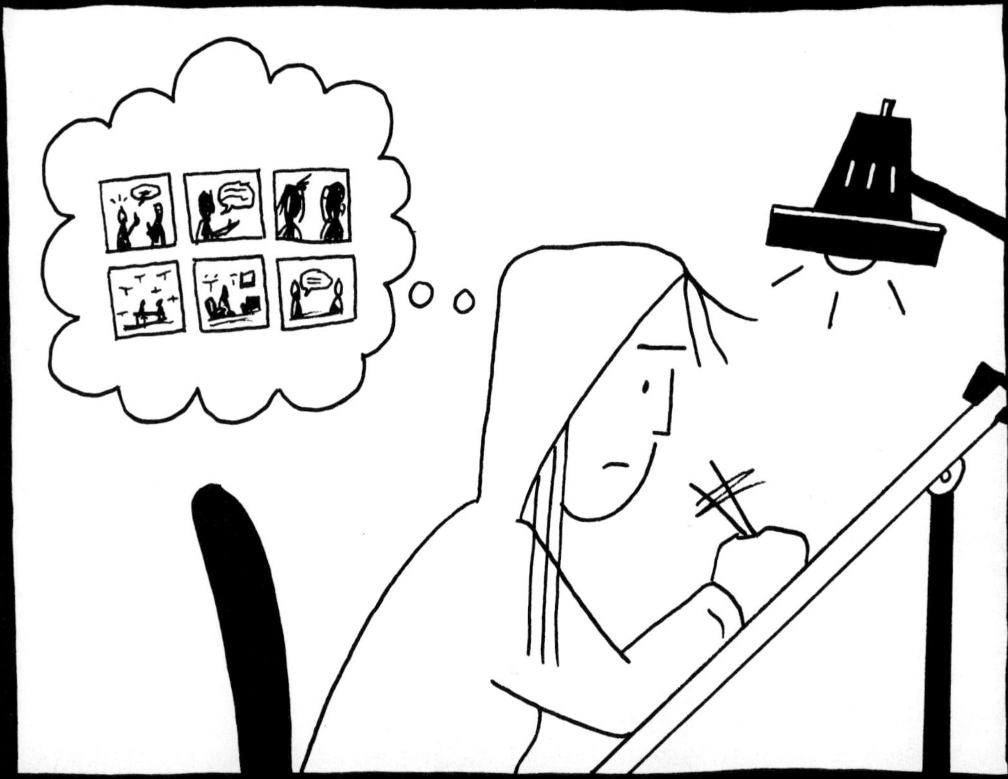

IF ONLY I HAD KNOWN,
DURING MY DARKEST DAYS IN THE WARD,

...THAT THE HOSPITALIZATION WOULD LEAD ME
TO EXACTLY THE LIFE I FELT SO VICIOUSLY DENIED.

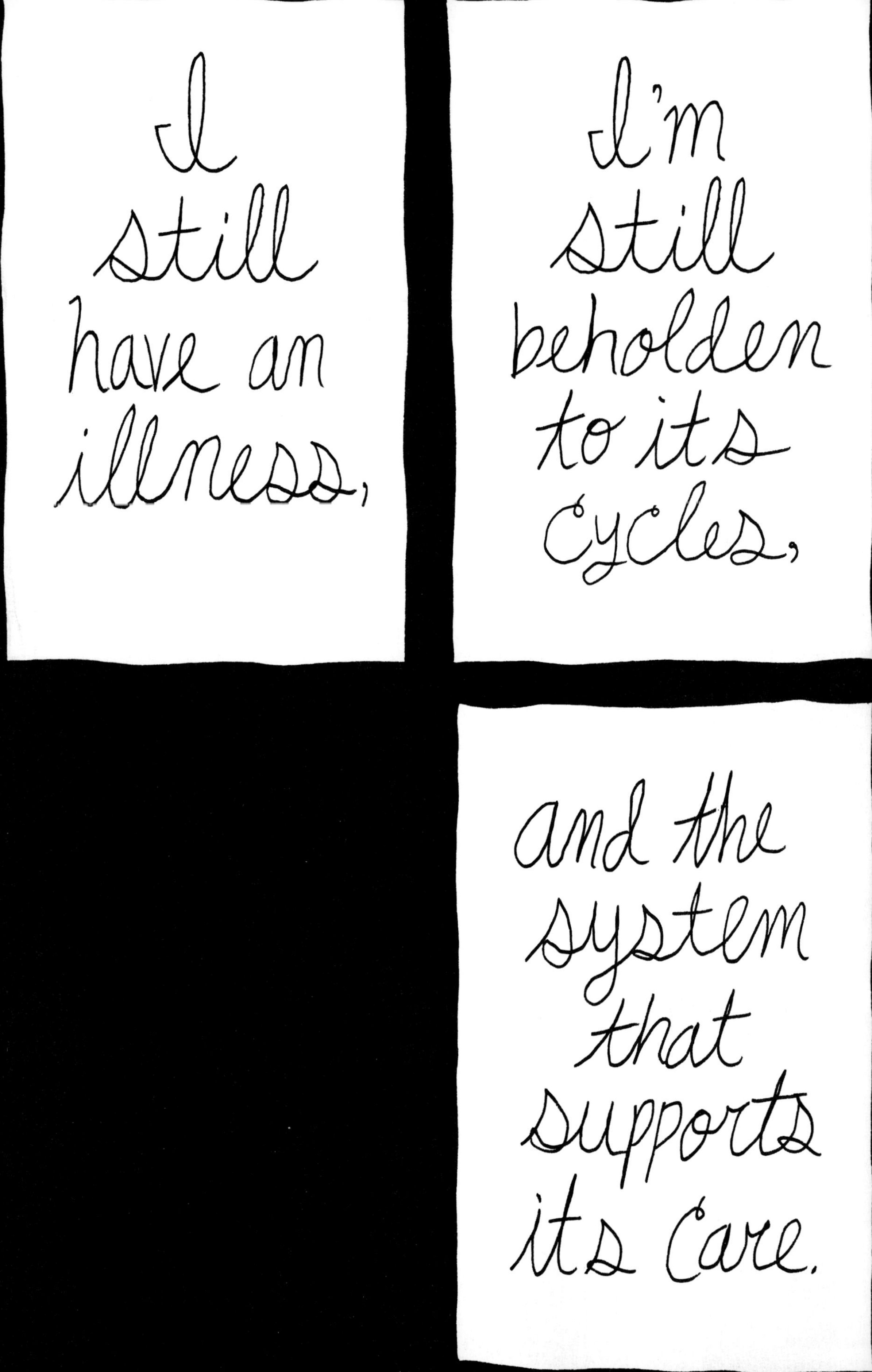
I still have an illness,
I'm still beholden to its cycles,
and the system that supports its care.

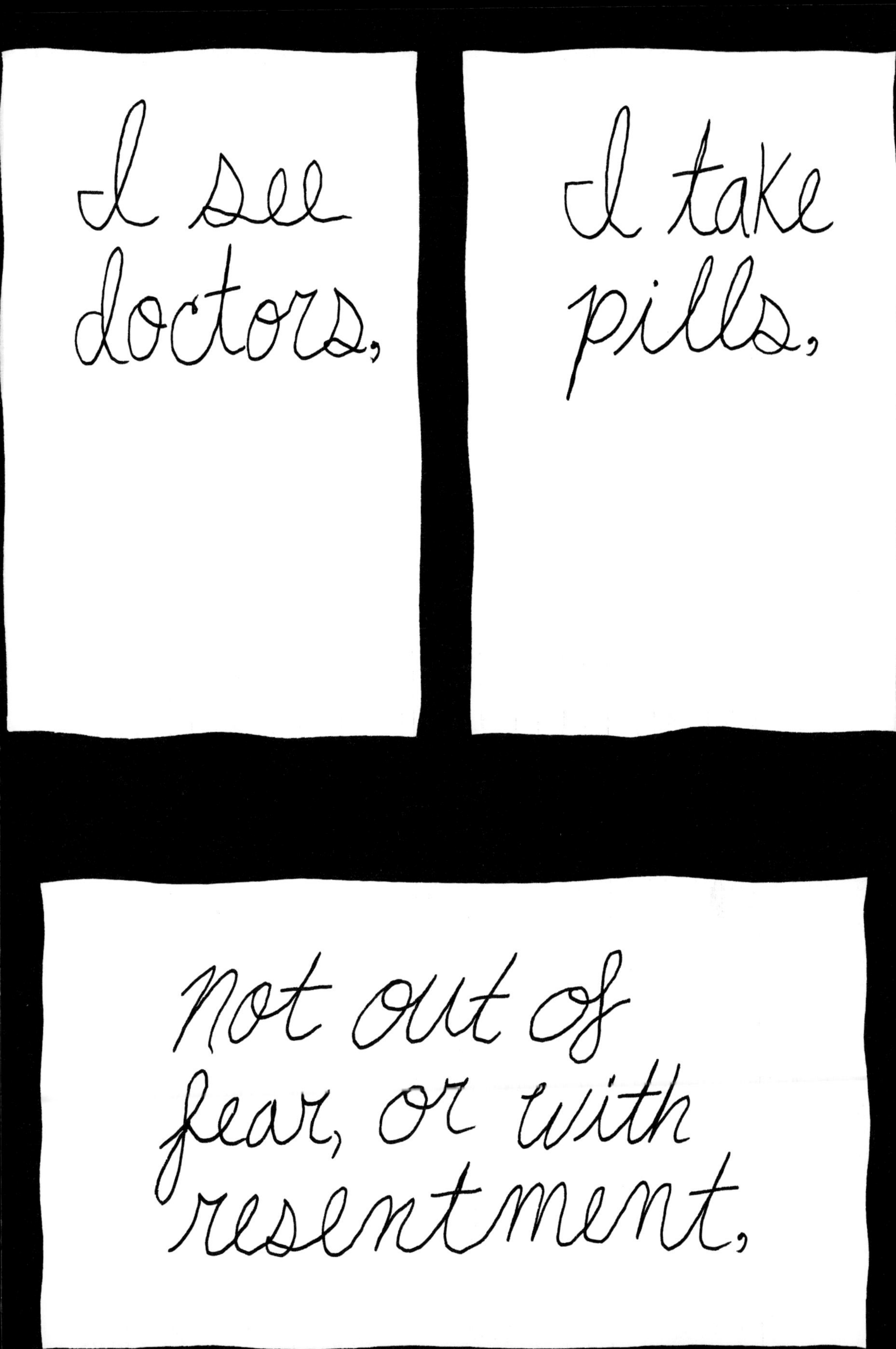
I see doctors,
I take pills,
not out of fear, or with resentment,

but out of
respect for myself
and all that I've
accomplished.

I walk the line
as confidently
as possible.

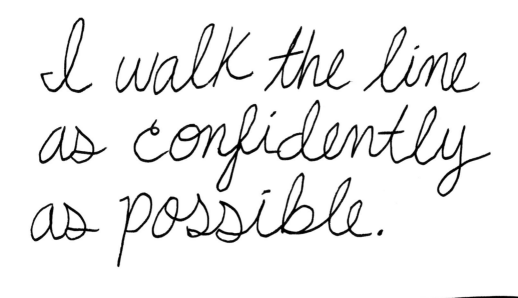

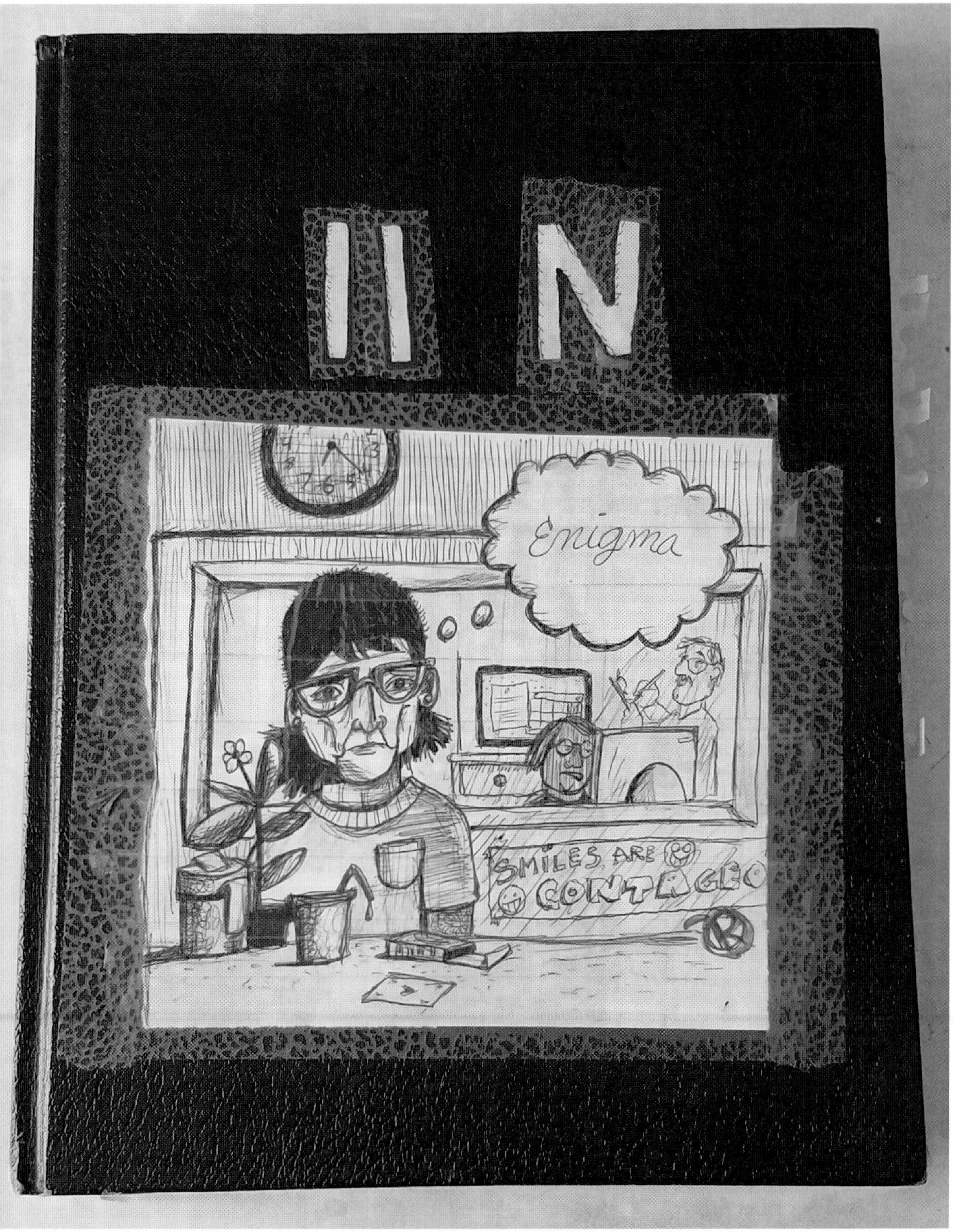

IIN
Enigma
SMILES ARE
CONTAGEO

THIS BOOK, 2011.

ACKNOWLEDGMENTS.

IT TAKES A VILLAGE TO WRITE A BOOK ABOUT YOURSELF, AND I HAVE BEEN SURROUNDED BY LOVING SUPPORT FOR THIS PROJECT DURING ALL PHASES OF ITS CREATION.

THANK YOU TO MY FAMILY — KAREN, BILL, AND MOLLY LINDSAY — FOR NEVER QUESTIONING MY NEED TO TELL THIS STORY, OR THE CHANGES I MADE IN MY LIFE TO PURSUE IT.

THANK YOU TO DR. KAY REDFIELD JAMISON FOR YOUR WORK ON BIPOLAR DISORDER. YOUR COMPASSIONATE EXAMINATION AND PORTRAYAL OF MANIC-DEPRESSIVE ILLNESS, IN PARTICULAR YOUR OWN EXPERIENCE, PROFOUNDLY IMPACTED MY UNDERSTANDING OF MYSELF AND THIS DISEASE, AND RESTORED FAITH IN MY CREATIVE AND INTELLECTUAL POTENTIAL AS SOMEONE DEEMED CLINICALLY INSANE.

I CANNOT EXPRESS MY GRATITUDE TO ALISON BECHDEL FOR HER WISDOM AND ENCOURAGEMENT FROM THE FIRST DRAFT TO THE FINAL. YOUR BELIEF IN ME HAS MEANT SO MUCH.

THANK YOU TO MY AGENT, ROSS HARRIS, AND EDITOR, MADDIE CALDWELL, FOR YOUR COMMITMENT TO MAKING THIS BOOK HAPPEN. WE DID IT!

THANK YOU TO STEPHANIE ZUPPO FOR THE CLUTCH COMPUTER ASSISTANCE AT THE ELEVENTH HOUR.

AND THANK YOU TO ALL THE FRIENDS, FAMILY, AND NEAR STRANGERS THAT HAVE LENT AN EAR OR AN EYE TO Rx — YOU ARE ALL A PART OF THIS.

-R

Monika Rivard

Rachel Lindsay is a Burlington, Vermont-based cartoonist. She is the creator of the comic strip *Rachel Lives Here Now* (2013-present), which appears weekly in *Seven Days*. She is a graduate of Columbia University. This is her first book.

WWW. RachelLivesHereNow.com

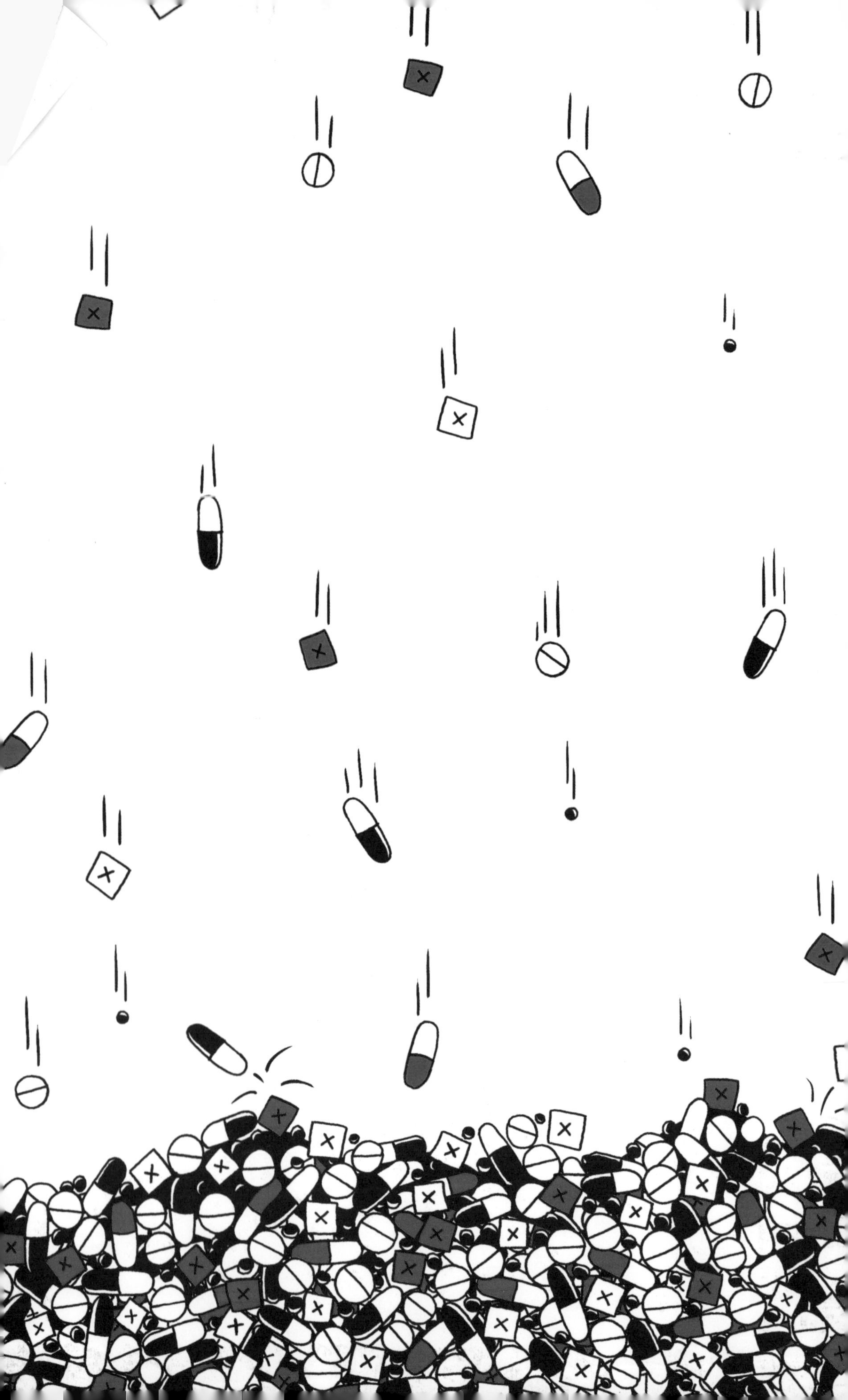